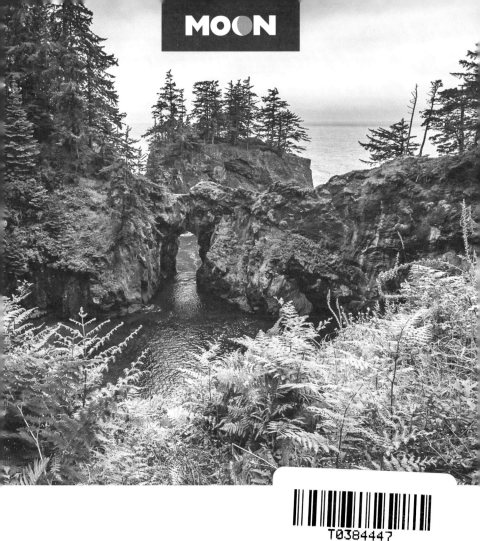

Coastal Oregon

MATT WASTRADOWSKI

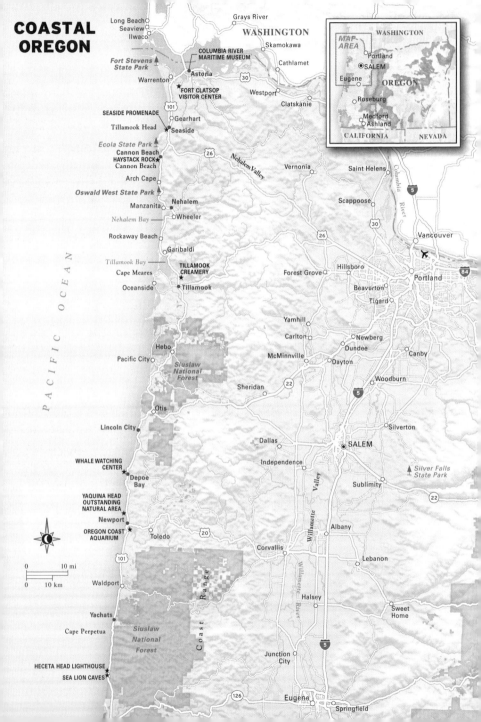

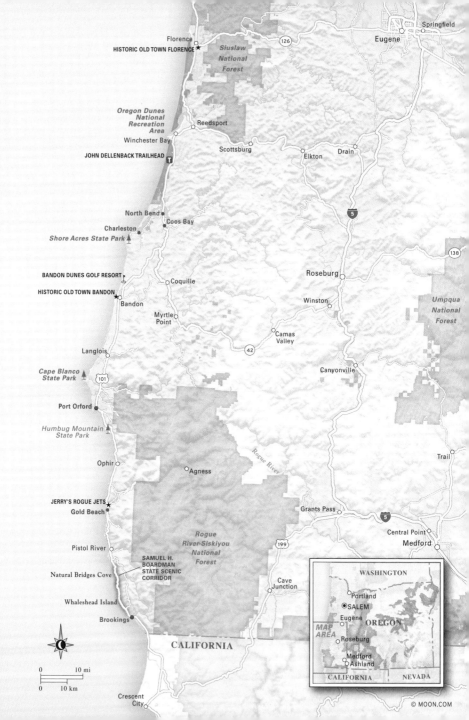

Contents

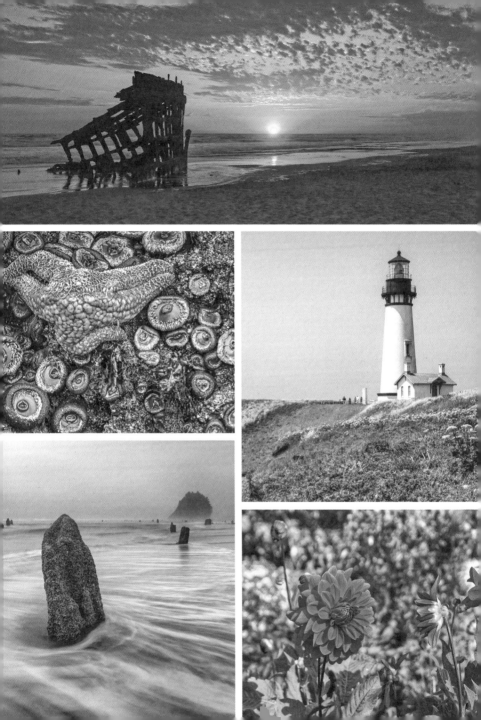

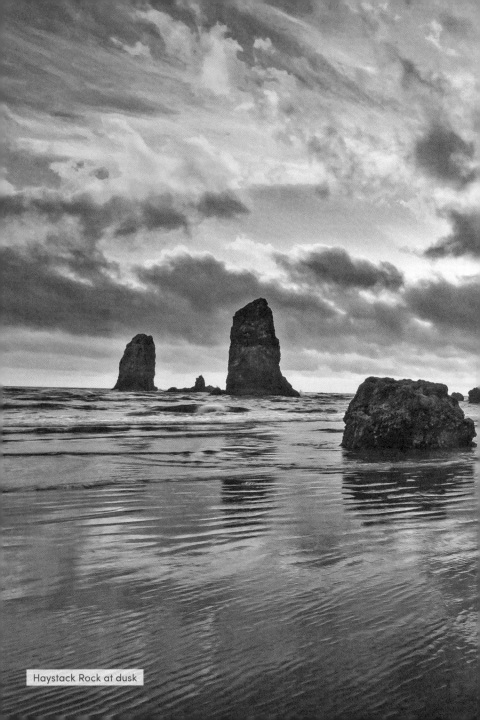

Haystack Rock at dusk

WELCOME TO

Coastal Oregon

To visit the Oregon Coast is to dance with Mother Nature, whose influence is felt along every inch of the state's 363-mile (584-km) coastline.

Here the craggy coast has been shaped by millions of years of volcanic activity—and eroded by centuries of punishing storms. Tidepools in the shallow recesses of that rocky shoreline offer an ephemeral glimpse at starfish, sea anemones, and other underwater creatures—at least until the tide rolls in and the cycle begins anew. And at countless eateries, from dim dive bars to regal restaurants, food menus are built with whatever's fresh that day—and beer taps pour award-winning brews crafted with ingredients you'll pass on the highway.

These are all marvels molded by Mother Nature—and memories you can make all year long.

Those who weather the Oregon Coast's notorious winter storms bask in cozy vibes at waterfront inns and spy some of the 25,000 gray whales that pass by on their annual migration. Come spring, muddy trails take intrepid hikers through moody forests of Sitka spruce—and onto wide-open viewpoints atop windswept bluffs. By summer, crashing waves drown out the chatter of children building sandcastles at the foot of Haystack Rock, while lines form for scoops of ice cream at the Tillamook Creamery. Fall, meanwhile, is the perfect time for a quiet road trip through the rugged Samuel H. Boardman State Scenic Corridor—perhaps the most scenic stretch of the Oregon Coast.

No matter the month, your time on the Oregon Coast will undoubtedly be informed by the world around you. And the dynamic nature of that experience means you won't just enjoy all-new adventures from season to season; you may enjoy new views, brews, dishes, and memories from day to day.

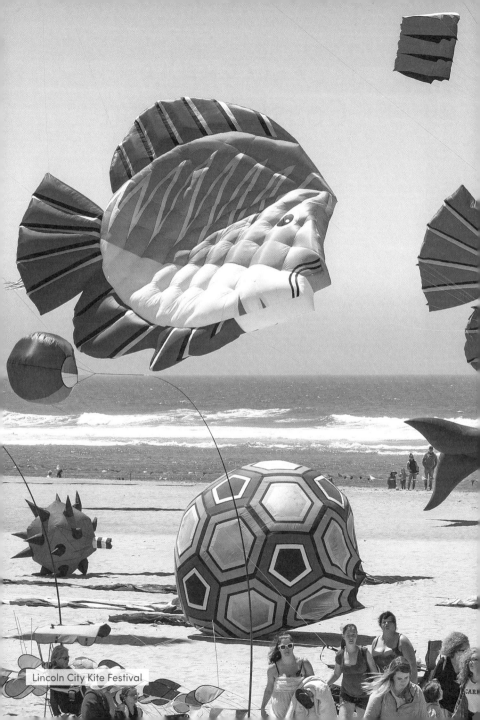

Lincoln City Kite Festival

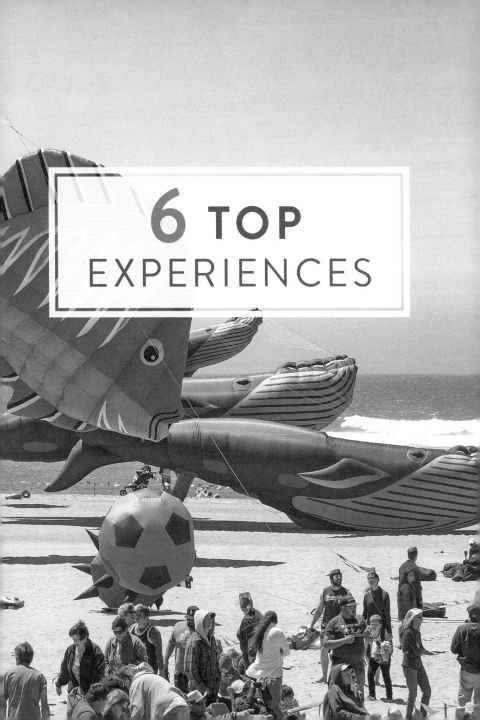

6 TOP EXPERIENCES

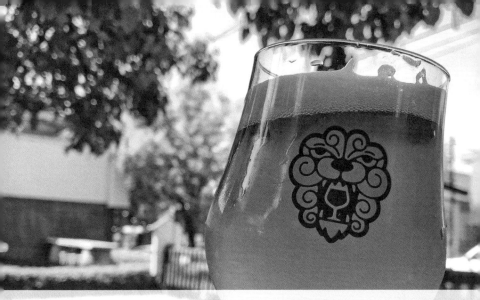

1 Sampling award-winning **craft brews:** Some of Oregon's biggest and best breweries produce renowned IPAs, lagers, and more in Portland (pages 44, 45, 47, and 48).

2 Catching a sunset at **Haystack Rock:** The iconic crag, towering over the surf in Cannon Beach, symbolizes the rugged nature and endless beauty of the Oregon Coast (page 91).

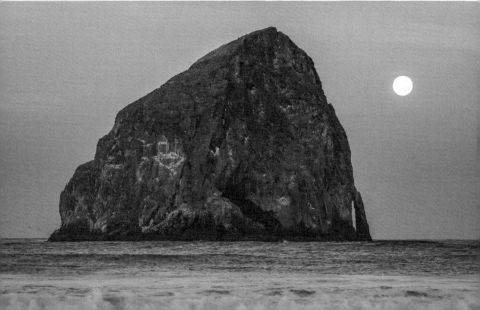

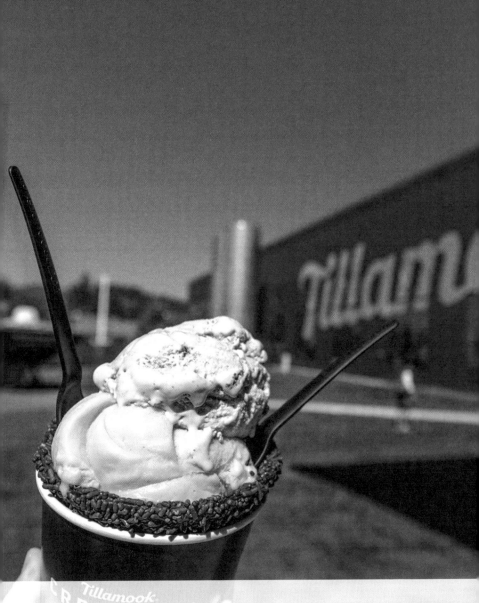

3 Eating your way through the **Tillamook Creamery:** The iconic creamery offers interpretive exhibits, self-guided tours, and a spacious café with grilled cheese sandwiches, macaroni and cheese, fried curds, and nearly two dozen flavors of ice cream (page 103).

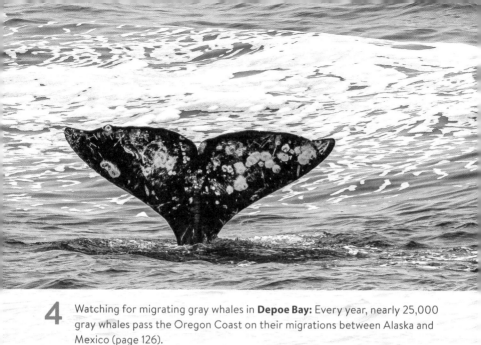

4 Watching for migrating gray whales in **Depoe Bay:** Every year, nearly 25,000 gray whales pass the Oregon Coast on their migrations between Alaska and Mexico (page 126).

5 Traversing the **Oregon Dunes:** An otherworldly attraction that runs roughly 40 miles (64 km) along a bustling stretch of the coast, perfect for camping, off-highway vehicle riding, hiking, paddling, and other fun adventures (page 146).

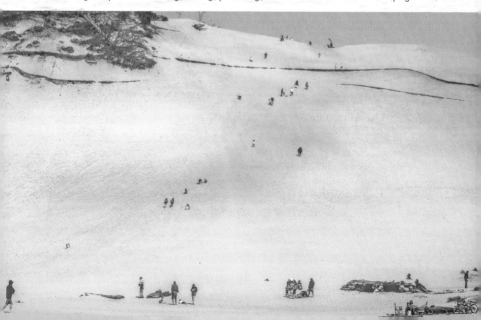

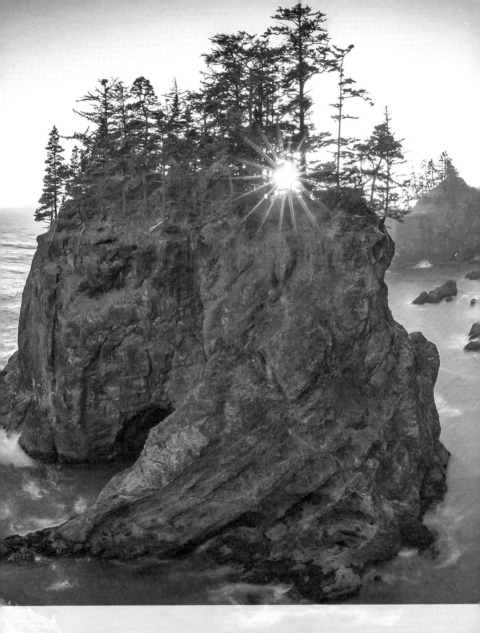

6 Driving the **Samuel H. Boardman State Scenic Corridor:** The most scenic stretch of the Oregon Coast passes myriad waysides and viewpoints of headlands, sea stacks, rock formations, gurgling creeks, craggy bluffs, and more (page 197).

Planning Your Trip

WHERE TO GO

Portland

Natural wonder and urban charms collide in **Portland,** home to myriad friendly yet chic neighborhoods and a perfect gateway to the Oregon Coast. Get your nature fix in the wooded hillsides of **Forest Park** or the sprawling **Washington Park**—and follow it all up on the patio at some of the city's beloved craft breweries, a renowned restaurant, or one of the city's many food cart pods along the likes of **Mississippi Avenue** or **Hawthorne Boulevard.**

North Coast

Headlands and sea stacks are frequent features along Oregon's north coast, with the citadel-like **Haystack Rock,** the sandy **Cape Kiwanda,** and others drawing visitors in droves. In between, a mishmash of communities offer disparate beach experiences. **Astoria** sits just inland from where the Columbia River flows into the Pacific Ocean and boasts a strong fishing heritage, one that can be enjoyed today

by sampling the city's fresh seafood, while **Seaside, Cannon Beach,** and **Pacific City** welcome families eager to snack on saltwater taffy and spend sunny days in the sand.

Central Coast

All manner of outdoor beauty dots the landscapes between bustling **Lincoln City** in the north and the sleepier fishing community of **Winchester Bay** in the south. Go tidepooling or whale-watching at rocky capes and windswept bluffs, several of which are home to historic lighthouses—or frolic in the **Oregon Dunes,** among the longest stretches of coastal dunes in the world. **Newport** hosts the popular **Oregon Coast Aquarium** and other family attractions, while **Yachats** offers a quiet getaway at the base of **Cape Perpetua.**

South Coast

Oregon's sleepy south coast stretches between **Coos Bay** and the California border—but offers plenty of natural beauty for those who make the trek. Explore sea stacks, reefs, and incredible wildlife-watching from along the **Cape Arago Beach Loop,** stroll the artsy community of **Bandon** (noted for its **Historic Old Town neighborhood**), take a jet boat ride up the **Rogue River,** or enjoy scenic hiking trails around **Gold Beach** and **Brookings-Harbor.** Along the way, make time for the many roadside pullouts along the **Samuel H. Boardman State Scenic Corridor**—perhaps the most beautiful stretch anywhere on the Oregon Coast.

Columbia River waterfront in Astoria

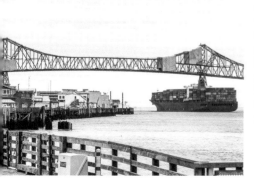

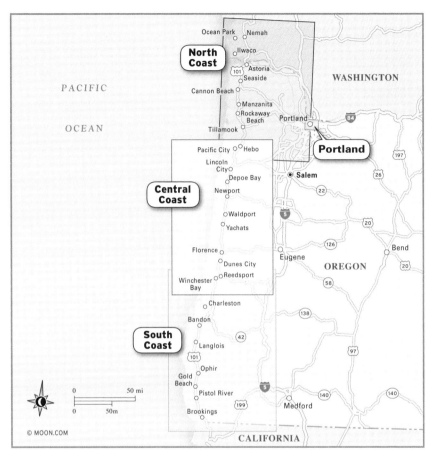

WHEN TO GO

Summer

A summer visit typically means **sunshine** across the state. Early-morning cloud cover typically gives way to clear skies every afternoon on the Oregon Coast.

Climate change is having an impact on Oregon summers, leading to warmer temperatures and an unpredictable **wildfire season** that can start as early as July and last into late September. Certain destinations may be closed, and outdoor activities may not be recommended if air quality is

unhealthy; download the OregonAir or AirNow mobile apps to check real-time air quality around the region.

Autumn

Surprisingly, autumn just might be the best time to visit Oregon. The stretch between mid-September and mid-October typically brings cooler temperatures, dramatic **fall foliage,** and the height of **harvest season** for the state's farmers. By mid-October, the season's **first rains** have

arrived on the Oregon Coast and in Portland; even so, Oregon is better known for rain showers and overcast skies than a steady, hours-long drumbeat of rain.

Winter

Snow is rare, though rain showers are frequent and near-freezing temperatures aren't unheard of. Unsurprisingly, **storm-watching** is a popular pastime on the Oregon Coast. In December-January, nearly 25,000 gray whales pass the Oregon Coast on their annual migration to Mexico—so whale-watching is a popular winter activity throughout the coast.

Spring

Spring can be an unpredictable yet rewarding time to visit Oregon. It's not uncommon for afternoon sun breaks to follow early-morning **rain showers**—only for the gray skies to return by dinnertime; assume you'll encounter rain and plan accordingly. March-June is a great time to see the thousands of gray whales that migrate to Alaska for the summer, with several charters offering whale-watching tours as the weather warms up.

KNOW BEFORE YOU GO

Transportation

Most travelers flying to Oregon will arrive at **Portland International Airport** (PDX, 7000 NE Airport Way; 503/460-4234; flypdx.com)—but other major airports around Oregon include **Eugene Airport** (EUG, 28801 Douglas Dr.; 541/682-5430; eugene-or.gov), just northwest of its namesake city in the Willamette Valley, and **Rogue Valley International-Medford Airport** (MFR, 1000 Terminal Loop Parkway; 541/776-7222; jacksoncountyor.org) in southern Oregon.

Portland visitors can get around without a car—a point of local pride. The city is well-served by the **Biketown** (biketownpdx.com; $1 to unlock, $0.20 per minute) bike-share program and **TriMet** (503/238-7433; trimet.org; 2.5-hour ticket $2.50, day pass $5), the latter of which operates the city's public transit. A few bus lines connect Portland and Willamette Valley communities (such as Corvallis and Eugene) to the Oregon Coast; that said, a vehicle is almost required for visiting more rural communities along the coast—and for enjoying most of the region's heralded outdoor destinations.

What to Bring

Pack your favorite pieces of **outdoor gear,** depending on the adventures you have in mind, and **sunscreen** with an SPF of at least 30. If you're visiting in any season other than summer, be prepared for precipitation. You could bring an umbrella certainly, but this will undoubtedly mark you as a tourist; outerwear with a **hood or a hat** is typically preferable. At the least it's a good idea to pack a **water-resistant jacket,** though a **waterproof jacket and pants** could come in handy if you're planning on extended outdoor time fall-spring. **Layers** are also key in any season, as temperatures can vary over the course of the day; standards include a base layer (like a T-shirt or moisture-wicking shirt), middle layer (like a fleece pullover to retain body heat and protect from the cold), and an outer layer (such as a heavier shirt or jacket that shields you from wind and rain). For the most part, outdoor and casual clothing is appropriate almost everywhere in the state (not just on trails), including in most breweries, wineries, and restaurants. Be sure to also pack an **extra bag** for all the local wines, beers, handcrafted goods, and other products you'll want to bring back home.

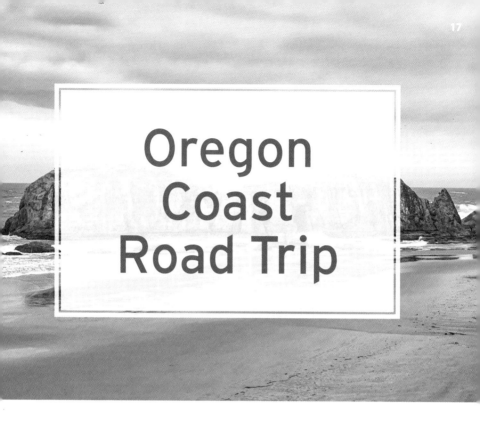

Oregon Coast Road Trip

Fresh seafood, family fun, and outdoor sights are all hallmarks of the Oregon Coast—and a week is a good amount of time to dive into all the coast has to offer (and even enjoy a scenic sunset along the way). The best time to visit is **July-September,** when shops and eateries are open extended hours, outfitters are typically staffed up, and foggy mornings give way to long, sunny afternoons.

Day 1
Portland and Astoria
95 MILES (153 KM)/2 HOURS

From Portland, make the two-hour drive northwest via **US-26** and **US-101** to **Astoria**—not technically on the Oregon Coast, but just inland from the mouth of the Columbia River, where it flows into the Pacific Ocean. Get your bearings from atop the **Astoria Column,** which affords 360-degree views of the Columbia River, surrounding waterways, and the city below.

For a trip back in time, brush up on Lewis and Clark's famous journey at **Fort Clatsop,** or learn about the region's historic fishing industry at the **Columbia River Maritime Museum.** Grab fried tuna out of a converted fishing boat for lunch at **Bowpicker Fish & Chips,** and walk it off with a stroll along the **Astoria Riverwalk.** Hop back in your car for a quick trip out to **Fort Stevens State Park,** where you can walk up to the half-submerged shipwreck of the *Peter*

Iredale, explore old military installations, and enjoy scenic beach views.

Return to Astoria, check into your hotel (**Norblad Hotel** if you're on a budget, **Bowline Hotel** if you're not), and head out for a night on the town. **Fort George Brewery & Public House** serves outstanding pub grub and creative pizzas alongside a wide-ranging mix of beers; **Bridge & Tunnel Bottleshop & Taproom,** meanwhile, is noted for pouring a curated selection of ales and lagers from throughout the Pacific Northwest.

Day 2
Astoria to Cannon Beach
26 MILES (42 KM)/45 MINUTES

Ease into the day with fresh-baked pastries, piping-hot coffee, barking sea lions, and wide-open Columbia River views at **Coffee Girl** at the end of Pier 39. Head west on **US-30** and continue following the road as it joins **US-101**—which you'll eventually follow for nearly 350 miles (565 km) en route to the Oregon-California border. As the highway heads south from Astoria, you'll encounter few ocean views before arriving in the resort town of **Seaside.**

Once in town, stroll the **Broadway Corridor,** lined on both sides by souvenir shops, home-grown restaurants, and family attractions. Head to Broadway's westernmost point, where it joins the **Seaside Promenade** mere steps from the Pacific Ocean. Head north or south on the wide, flat, paved path—or follow one of the many access points to the beach. Grab lunch at the **Osprey Café,** noted for its international inspiration, and continue south toward the day's destination: **Cannon Beach.** There you'll enjoy sweeping coastline views from **Ecola State Park,** sip a house-made beer at **Public Coast Brewing Co.,** peruse the community's celebrated galleries, and gaze at the scenic **Haystack Rock** just offshore.

Check into the regal **Stephanie Inn.** Enjoy dinner in the hotel's celebrated dining room, or nosh on fresh fare at **Ecola Seafood Restaurant and Market.** If the weather cooperates, cap your night with a beach campfire at **Tolovana Beach State Recreation Site** while the sun sets behind **Haystack Rock.**

beach views from Ecola State Park

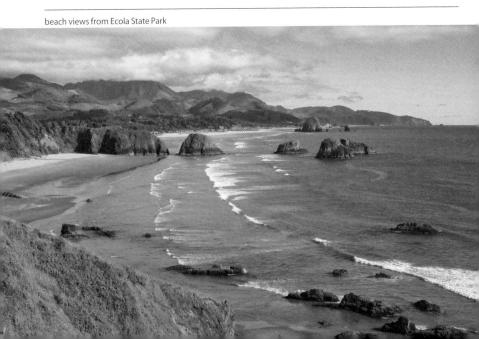

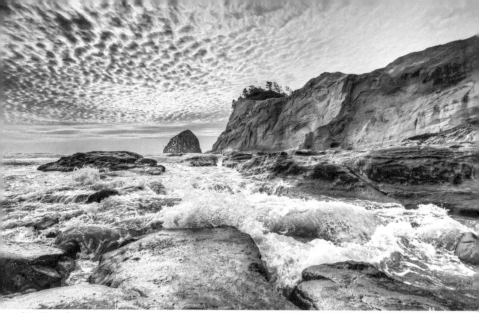

Cape Kiwanda

Day 3
Cannon Beach to Pacific City
65 MILES (105 KM)/1.5 HOURS

Enjoy a light breakfast before continuing south. Just outside of town, hike through a coastal rainforest to **Cape Falcon** in **Oswald West State Park,** where you might spot migrating gray whales from a wide-open bluff. On your way back to your vehicle, make the detour to **Short Sand Beach** for a little relaxation. Treat yourself to lunch at **Rockaway Pronto Pup,** where the corn dog-like treat was allegedly invented, or to fresh seafood on the docks at **The Fish Peddler at Pacific Oyster.**

Farther south, **Tillamook Creamery** beckons with self-guided tours of its regionally famous creamery and a food court dishing nearly two dozen flavors of ice cream. Before heading south, take a detour along **OR-31** to **Cape Meares State Scenic Viewpoint,** home to the shortest lighthouse on the Oregon Coast and the so-called Octopus Tree—a centuries-old Sitka spruce noted for several limbs growing upward from its base. Head back to **US-101** and continue south

toward **Pacific City.** Check into your hotel at the **Inn at Cape Kiwanda,** drop your bags off, and cross the street, where the Pacific Ocean awaits; if your tired legs allow, hike to the sandy summit of **Cape Kiwanda**—and laugh uproariously as you run or roll down. Across the parking lot, nosh on locally sourced pub grub and award-winning beers at **Pelican Brewing Company.** Back at your room, enjoy the sunset beyond **Haystack Rock.**

Day 4
Pacific City to Newport
47 MILES (76 KM)/1 HOUR

Don't let the marginal drive time fool you: There's plenty to see and experience along **US-101** today. Start with a hearty breakfast at **Grateful Bread Bakery** before returning to the highway and continuing south. Before long, you'll come to **Lincoln City.** Walk the beaches in town, looking for glass floats as part of the city's **Finders Keepers** promotion, or try glassblowing yourself with a talented artist at **Lincoln City Glass Center.** Have a relaxing lunch at **Blackfish**

Café, celebrated for fresh, locally sourced seafood dishes.

As you continue south, watch for migrating gray whales and other sea life at the **Whale Watching Center** in **Depoe Bay;** another few minutes on, walk into a collapsed sea cave (if it's low tide) at **Devils Punchbowl State Natural Area.** Soon after, you'll arrive in **Newport.** Just beyond the northern edge of town, enjoy wide-open Pacific Ocean views, go tidepooling, and stand at the base of the tallest lighthouse on the Oregon Coast at **Yaquina Head Outstanding Natural Area.** From there, check out the **Oregon Coast Aquarium** for an up-close look at regional marine life. Check into your room at **Hallmark Resort Newport,** savor the oceanfront views, and head out for a walk along **Newport's Historic Bayfront.** Enjoy dinner at the renowned **Local Ocean Seafoods,** and grab a nightcap at **Rogue Ales & Spirits** nearby.

Day 5
Newport to Bandon
122 MILES (196 KM)/2.5 HOURS

Start your day with breakfast before heading south, through **Yachats,** on the way to **Cape Perpetua Scenic Area.** There's a full day's worth of fun to be had at Cape Perpetua—but hit the highlights along the paved **Captain Cook Trail,** where you'll see the headland's most notable natural features, such as the rocky **Cook's Chasm; Spouting Horn,** a partially collapsed sea cave; and **Thor's Well,** a circular sinkhole in the rocky shoreline. Briefly retrace your steps north, back to Yachats, and grab fresh fish-and-chips at **Luna Sea Fish House and Village Fishmonger;** if time allows, wash it down with a flight of creative beers at nearby **Yachats Brewing + Farmstore.**

Continue south to **Heceta Head Lighthouse State Scenic Viewpoint** for up-close views of the namesake lighthouse and sweeping vistas of the Pacific Ocean; a few minutes south, the **Sea Lion Caves** is home to hundreds of barking Steller sea lions. Soon, you'll come to the city of **Florence** at the northern edge of the

Oregon Dunes National Scenic Area; gaze upon the ever-shifting sands at the **Oregon Dunes Overlook and Day-Use Area,** or hike out onto the dunes along the **John Dellenback Trail.** As you continue south, leave US-101 in the community of **North Bend** for a side trip along the **Cape Arago Beach Loop,** where three state parks and overlooks offer sweeping vistas, excellent wildlife-watching, and (in winter) renowned storm-watching opportunities. Return to US-101 and continue south to the city of **Bandon;** check into the **b.side Motel & RV,** home for the night, and grab fresh seafood dinner at **Tony's Crab Shack.**

Day 6
Bandon to Brookings-Harbor
83 MILES (134 KM)/1.5 HOURS

Bandon deserves to be more than a stopover on the way to your next stop—so rise and shine with biscuits at **The Rolling Pin Bake & Brew,** and enjoy a stroll around **Historic Old Town Bandon;** highlights include the thought-provoking **Washed Ashore Gallery** and local delicacies at **Cranberry Sweets & More.** Away from the working waterfront, **Face Rock Creamery** produces a variety of creative cheeses, and **Bandon Rain** crafts hard ciders from local ingredients. Nearby, **Face Rock State Scenic Viewpoint** offers dramatic Pacific Ocean vistas and wildlife-watching opportunities. As you head south, stop into **The Crazy Norwegian's Fish & Chips** for lunch (assuming you haven't tired of seafood yet), and admire the sea-stack views at **Battle Rock Wayside Park** in the community of **Port Orford.**

As you continue south through **Gold Beach,** sample some of the Oregon Coast's best brews at the cozy **Arch Rock Brewing Company.** Soon after, you'll enter the 12-mile-long (19-km) **Samuel H. Boardman State Scenic Corridor,** where a dozen or so pull-outs, viewpoints, and hiking trails showcase dramatic vistas of sea stacks, craggy rock formations, and other natural wonders—one of the most scenic stretches anywhere on the Oregon Coast. You'll soon arrive in

Best Beaches and Sunset Views

Oregon's beaches are technically considered public highways—which means they're protected from development and open to all. Naturally, all that access means plenty of epic sunset spots, a few of which we've listed here. (Pro tip: Due to seasonal weather patterns, the sun often sets behind a bank of clouds on the horizon all summer long; as such, the best, clearest sunsets typically occur on clear days in winter and spring.)

- **Fort Stevens State Park:** Watch the sun as it sets beyond the partially submerged shipwreck of the *Peter Iredale* (page 84).

- **Cannon Beach:** Enjoy wide-open views of Haystack Rock—and dramatic, starry night skies once the sun disappears (page 91).

- **Cape Kiwanda:** Right in the heart of Pacific City, bask in the glow near the base of *another* citadel-shaped Haystack Rock (page 109).

- **Yaquina Head Outstanding Natural Area:** Sit atop the windswept bluff, where expansive views await up and down the coastline (page 133).

- **Samuel H. Boardman State Scenic Corridor:** Myriad viewpoints line the highway along what might be the most scenic stretch of the entire Oregon Coast—with several that look down on sun-kissed sea stacks in the surf (page 197).

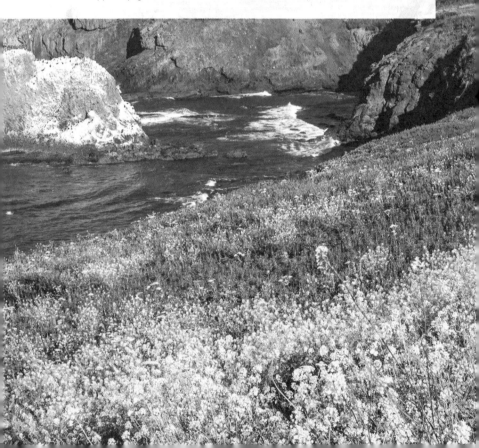

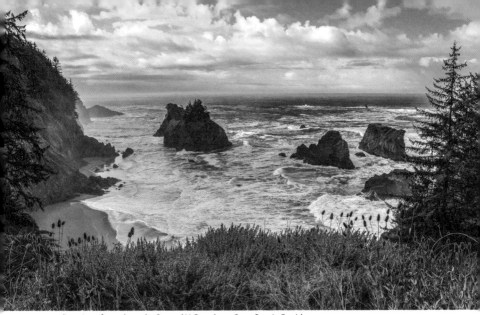
coastline views from along the Samuel H. Boardman State Scenic Corridor

Brookings-Harbor near the Oregon-California border; check into your room at **Beachfront Inn,** sample creative pub grub at **Oxenfrē Public House,** and wind down with a variety of locally sourced ales and lagers at **Chetco Brewing.**

Day 7
Return to Portland
330 MILES (531 KM)/6 HOURS

A handful of highways cross the Oregon Coast Range, linking the Oregon Coast with the I-5 corridor and offering an easy return trip to Portland. You can't go wrong with any of them, but retracing your route north and eventually heading east at **Reedsport** shows off some of what you missed on the way south. So start your final day along the Oregon Coast with breakfast at a local café or bakery, then head north on **US-101.** At the north end of Brookings, gaze upon an especially rugged stretch of coastline from **Harris Beach State Park;** as you continue north, the **Cape Sebastian State Scenic Corridor** offers dramatic views from high above the coastline. Savor even more coast views from **Cape Blanco State Park;** the westernmost point in Oregon is also home to the **Cape Blanco Lighthouse,** which dates back to 1870.

As you arrive in Coos Bay, take a short walk along the **Coos Bay Boardwalk,** which affords excellent wildlife opportunities and interpretive panels along the city's working waterfront; follow it up with one last seafood dish at **The Boat Fish & Chips** (housed, yes, in a landlocked houseboat) and a self-guided tour of **Coos Art Museum,** home to a gallery that pays tribute to long-distance runner and local legend Steve Prefontaine. As you continue north, turn east onto OR-38 toward I-5 and Portland; if time allows, stop at **Dean Creek Elk Viewing Area** along the highway, where a resident herd of up to 100 Roosevelt elk linger all year long.

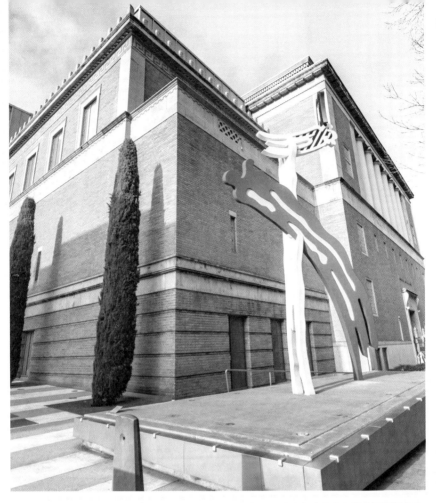

Oregon's Indigenous History

Since time immemorial, indigenous people have fished, foraged, hunted, traded, and lived on land known today as Oregon. That rich history is on display at museums throughout the state, some owned and operated by regional tribes. If you'd like to dig into Oregon's indigenous history, these museums offer excellent opportunities for doing so:

- **Portland Art Museum:** Enjoy a collection of more than 3,500 objects and pieces from roughly 200 cultural groups across North America (page 27).

- **Chachalu Museum and Cultural Center (Central Coast):** Explore the past and present of the Confederated Tribes of Grand Ronde through cultural artifacts, interpretive panels, and more (page 118).

- **Coos History Museum (South Coast):** View baskets, tools, and more from the Coquille and Confederated Tribes of Coos, Lower Umpqua and Siuslaw Indians (page 169).

Above: Portland Art Museum

Portland

Oregon's largest city is famously playful and progressive, welcoming dreamers, creatives, and makers who infuse the community with a sense of whimsy yet don't take themselves so seriously that they forget that life demands to be enjoyed—at a leisurely pace, preferably with an IPA in hand.

Indeed, in Portland, you might look up from your craft beer while sitting at one of the city's 70 breweries and catch 10,000 naked cyclists barreling down the boulevard, browse the biggest bookstore in the world, eat locally sourced meals from food carts and doughnuts adorned with your favorite childhood cereal, stroll hip neighborhood streets amid a sea of leafy residences, literally smell the roses at beloved gardens, and forget you're in city limits while hiking amid the ferns and Douglas fir trees of Forest Park.

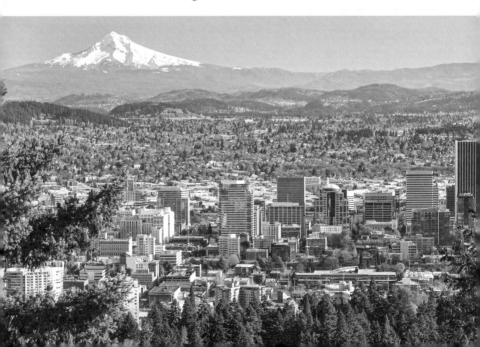

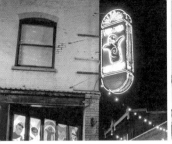
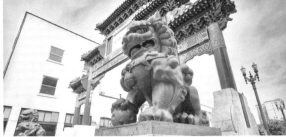

Highlights

Look for ★ to find recommended sights, activities, dining, and lodging.

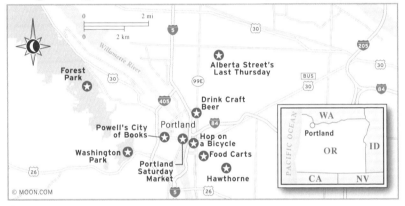

★ **Browse the biggest bookstore in the world:** Taking up a full city block, **Powell's City of Books** is said to house more than a million new and used titles (page 32).

★ **Enjoy the attractions of Washington Park:** Portland's signature green space is home to some of the city's best-loved cultural institutions, including the International Rose Test Garden, Portland Japanese Garden, and Oregon Zoo (page 32).

★ **Stroll around hip Hawthorne:** This neighborhood oozes hipster cool with its vintage boutiques, bustling bars, and popular restaurants (page 36).

★ **Get festive at Alberta Street's Last Thursday:** This year-round arts celebration turns into a summertime street fair, with live musicians, performance artists, and local vendors (page 37).

★ **Hike in Forest Park:** Miles of trails crisscross one of the nation's largest urban parks; you'll forget you're in city limits (page 41).

★ **Hop on a bicycle:** Going for a ride in this city renowned for its bike culture is pure pleasure (page 41).

★ **Drink craft beer:** No trip to Portland—it's nicknamed "Beervana," after all—is complete without enjoying some of its many brewpubs (pages 44, 45, 47, and 48).

★ **Find the perfect souvenir:** The open-air **Portland Saturday Market** is among the largest arts-and-crafts fairs in the country, amid a lively atmosphere along the banks of the Willamette River (page 53).

★ **Take a bite out of Portland's food cart scene:** Some of the city's most popular cuisine is dished at food carts, which serve as community gathering spaces and incubators for up-and-coming chefs (pages 56 and 60).

This combination of distinctive urban delights and natural beauty—the downtown core is backed by hills, the Willamette River flows through town, and on a clear day, you can see Mount Hood, Oregon's tallest peak—is what draws people here. Come and play.

ORIENTATION

Finding your way around Portland is easy if you understand what locals call the **"five quadrants"** (it doesn't make sense to us, either, but that's part of the city's charm): **Southwest, Southeast, Northwest, Northeast,** and **North Portland.** North and south are separated by **Burnside Street,** while the east-west dividing line is the **Willamette River.** Address prefixes indicate quadrants.

Other than in downtown, which is in the Southwest quadrant, Portland is mostly laid out on a grid system, with avenues running north-south and streets running east-west. In NW Portland, streets progress in alphabetical order as they head north from Burnside (i.e., Couch, Davis, Everett). Avenues are numbered heading west and, more sporadically, east from the Willamette River.

While the westside is home to downtown and many of the city's bigger attractions, the eastside is where you'll find more of Portland's famous quirk and creativity, in neighborhood corridors typically populated by local businesses, as well as one-offs and pockets of cool in between.

PLANNING YOUR TIME

Portland isn't a town of huge attractions that need to be checked off a list; its primary draws tend to be more experiential. Give yourself at least **2-3 days** to soak up its vibe. While you can certainly zip around town trying to see it all, the city is best explored at a laid-back pace. Portland is defined by its myriad neighborhoods, each with its own charm and character, and choosing a few to explore in-depth will yield a more memorable experience than trying to crisscross the city to fit everything in. Leaving a bit more breathing room in your itinerary will also allow you to enjoy that great live show happening just down the street later that night that a bartender clues you into, the exciting new release at a neighboring brewery that someone mentions, or the food cart your restaurant server recommends you check out. Slowing down and hanging out also reveals glimmers of the "Keep Portland Weird" mantra so common on bumper stickers around town; you never know when you'll spot a cyclist riding a custom tall bike down the street or walk by a tiny toy horse tied to a historic horse ring on a sidewalk, an ode to a time when horses and horse-drawn vehicles shuttled Portlanders around the city.

Outside of summer, when just a few token rain showers remind you that, yes, you're still in the Pacific Northwest, travelers can expect the frequent **precipitation** for which Portland is famous. Take this into consideration, but don't let it deter you; locals don't usually let the rain—as it's typically the drizzly rather than drenching variety—stop them, and neither should you (though you'll want to pack accordingly). Note that using an umbrella will mark you as a tourist; for locals, hats and hoods typically suffice.

Previous: Mount Hood rising above the Portland skyline; Voodoo Doughnut; Chinatown Gateway.

Sights

DOWNTOWN AND THE PEARL DISTRICT
Downtown

Located in the **Southwest quadrant,** Portland's downtown is bordered by Burnside Street to the north, the Willamette River to the east, and I-405 to the south and west. While you're walking around, keep an eye out for **Benson Bubblers,** roughly 50 historic drinking fountains that trace their roots to the early 1900s, when local philanthropist Simon Benson donated $10,000 to purchase and install them; these typically flow 5:30am-11:30pm daily, and the water isn't just safe to drink—it's downright delicious.

Pioneer Courthouse Square

Pioneer Courthouse Square (701 SW 6th Ave.; 503/223-1613; thesquarepdx.org; free) is nicknamed "Portland's living room," and the moniker is apt. The brick-lined public plaza occupies a full city block and is almost always buzzing with activity; busking musicians, political activists, and local nonprofits routinely make the square their base of operations. People-watch from the steps ringing the plaza and grab breakfast or lunch at the **Carts on the Square** (thesquarepdx.org) food cart pod.

Portland Art Museum

The **Portland Art Museum** (1219 SW Park Ave.; 503/226-2811; portlandartmuseum.org; 10am-5pm Wed.-Sun.; $25 adults, $22 seniors over 61 and college students, free for children 17 and under) was founded in 1892, making it the oldest art museum in the Pacific Northwest. The museum fills two buildings and four floors with an ever-changing lineup of works from around the world, some from its permanent collection and others via traveling exhibits (which sometimes require an additional admission fee). The Arlene and Harold Schnitzer Center for Northwest Art exclusively spotlights artists from the Pacific Northwest, with works dating back to the 19th century. Also of note is the museum's collection of Native American artworks, which comprises 3,500 objects including masks, baskets, and sculptures by artists representing roughly 200 cultural groups from throughout North America. Some pieces date back centuries, while others are by contemporary artists such as Lillian Pitt, who was born and raised on the Warm Springs Reservation in Central Oregon. Give yourself 2-4 hours to explore.

Oregon Historical Society Museum

Learn about Oregon's past—the good, the bad, and the ugly—at the three-story **Oregon Historical Society Museum** (1200 SW Park Ave.; 503/222-1741; ohs.org; 10am-5pm Mon.-Sat., noon-5pm Sun.; $10 adults, $8 students, teachers, and seniors 60 and over, $5 ages 6-18, free for children 5 and under and residents of Multnomah County). Its permanent Experience Oregon exhibit takes up a full floor and offers an excellent, well-rounded introduction to the people, places, and events that have shaped Oregon, with deep dives into its Native American cultures and the state's racist beginnings. Rotating exhibits touch on a wide range of movements and moments in Oregon's history, for example the rise of craft beer and The Beatles' performance in Portland. Another highlight is the "Portland Penny"—which was used in an 1845 coin toss to name the burgeoning city either Portland or Boston. Budget 2-4 hours for a visit.

Old Town and Chinatown

When Portland grew into an honest-to-goodness city in the late 1800s, its original downtown core was located on the site of the city's present-day **Old Town Chinatown** (roughly between NW Broadway, the Willamette River, and W. Burnside St.)—making it the city's oldest neighborhood.

Portland

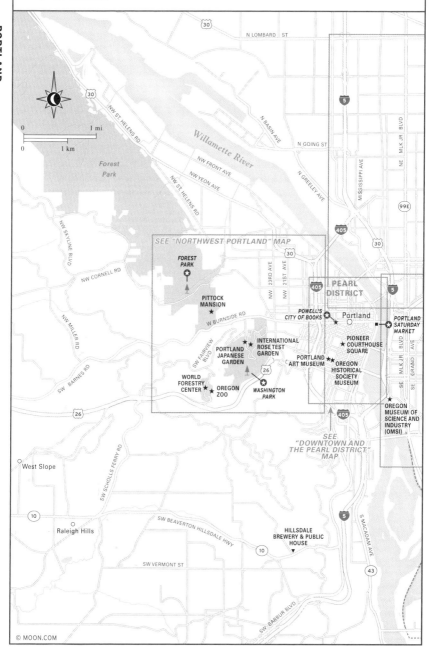

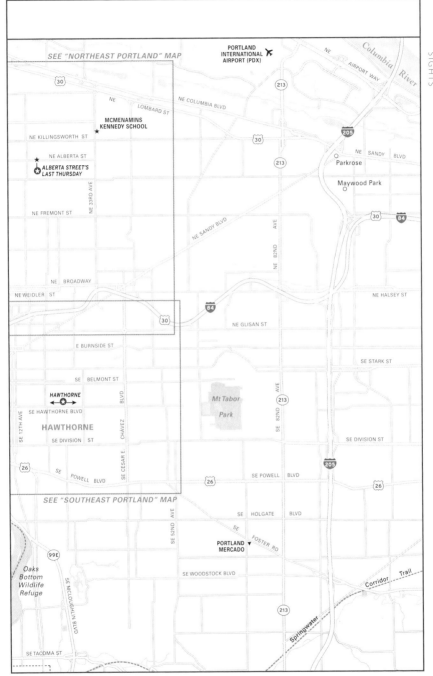

SEE "NORTHEAST PORTLAND" MAP

PORTLAND
INTERNATIONAL
AIRPORT (PDX)

Columbia River

NE AIRPORT WAY

NE

30

NE LOMBARD ST

NE COLUMBIA BLVD

213

205

MCMENAMINS
KENNEDY SCHOOL

NE KILLINGSWORTH ST

30

NE SANDY BLVD

NE ALBERTA ST

213

Parkrose

ALBERTA STREET'S
LAST THURSDAY

Maywood Park

NE 33RD AVE

NE FREMONT ST

NE SANDY BLVD

NE 82ND AVE

30

84

NE BROADWAY

NE WEIDLER ST

NE HALSEY ST

84

30

NE GLISAN ST

E BURNSIDE ST

SE STARK ST

SE BELMONT ST

SE 82ND AVE

HAWTHORNE

SE BLVD

*Mt Tabor
Park*

213

SE HAWTHORNE BLVD

HAWTHORNE

SE CESAR E. CHAVEZ BLVD

SE DIVISION ST

SE 12TH AVE

SE DIVISION ST

26

205

SE POWELL BLVD

SE POWELL BLVD

26

26

SEE "SOUTHEAST PORTLAND" MAP

SE 52ND AVE

SE HOLGATE BLVD

SE

FOSTER RD

PORTLAND
MERCADO

99E

SE WOODSTOCK BLVD

Corridor Trail

*Oaks
Bottom
Wildlife
Refuge*

SE MCLOUGHLIN BLVD

213

Springwater

SE TACOMA ST

Almost since its inception, it has been a destination for immigrants. In the late 1880s and 1890s, Portland had the second-largest Chinatown in the country, second only to San Francisco—until the U.S. Congress passed the Chinese Exclusion Act of 1882, dramatically reducing the number of Chinese immigrants moving to the city.

A new wave of immigration to the area, by Japanese people, led to the neighborhood's transformation into Japantown by the early 1900s. Then, in 1942 after the bombing of Pearl Harbor in World War II, President Roosevelt issued Executive Order 9066, authorizing the internment of Japanese Americans; many Japantown residents were forced to give up their homes and businesses and sent to camps, decimating the thriving community. A new generation of Chinese businessowners moved into the neighborhood in the decades after World War II.

Today, the neighborhood preserves this history in two notable museums, and visitors are welcomed by the arched **Chinatown Gateway** (W. Burnside St. and NW 4th Ave.).

Lan Su Chinese Garden

The gorgeous **Lan Su Chinese Garden** (239 NW Everett St.; 503/228-8131; lansugarden. org; 10am-4pm daily; $12.95 adults, $11.95 seniors 62 and over, $9.95 children 6-18 and college students, free for children under 6) is the end result of a collaboration between Portland and Suzhou, its sister city in the Chinese province of Jiangsu—which is famous for its Ming dynasty gardens. Lan Su features beautiful botanical gardens, peaceful walkways, koi ponds, ornate pavilions, and an on-site tea house. Taken together, it feels like a tranquil escape from the hustle and bustle of the city that surrounds it.

Portland Chinatown Museum

Portland Chinatown Museum (127 NW 3rd Ave.; 503/224-0008; portlandchinatown-museum.org; 11am-3pm Fri.-Sun.; $8 adults, $6 seniors, $5 students, free for children under 13) educates visitors on the neighborhood's past, with stories of Chinese immigrant experiences told through oral histories and artifacts, as well as showcases works by contemporary Asian American artists.

Japanese American Museum of Oregon

Exhibits at the **Japanese American Museum of Oregon** (411 NW Flanders St.; 503/224-1458; jamo.org; 11am-3pm Fri.-Sun.; $8 adults, $6 seniors, $5 students, free for children under 12) cover Japanese immigration, the evolution of the Portland neighborhood that was for a time Japantown, the horrific impacts of World War II on the local Japanese community, and life for Japanese Americans in Oregon today.

Pearl District

In the 1890s, the neighborhood that would become the **Pearl District** (bordered by NW Broadway, W. Burnside St., I-405, and the Willamette River) was little more than a collection of railyards and warehouses built to support the city's shipping industry. In the mid-1980s, artists began occupying the downtrodden neighborhood and opening galleries. Today, "the Pearl," as it's most commonly known around town, feels thoroughly upscale, home to celebrated Powell's and chockablock with sleek venues, though signs of the neighborhood's industrial past abound, with art galleries, local and national shops, and restaurants in repurposed brick warehouses and disused rail lines visible on neighborhood streets.

First Thursday

The Pearl's art galleries open new shows each month on **First Thursday** (5pm-10pm first Thurs. of the month), when a handful of galleries remain open well into the evening and host receptions, typically accompanied by wine and snacks, that showcase the latest works from local, regional, and national artists. The Portland Art Dealers Association (padaoregon.org) rounds up participating galleries and provides a downloadable map. When the weather warms up, the celebration

Downtown and the Pearl District

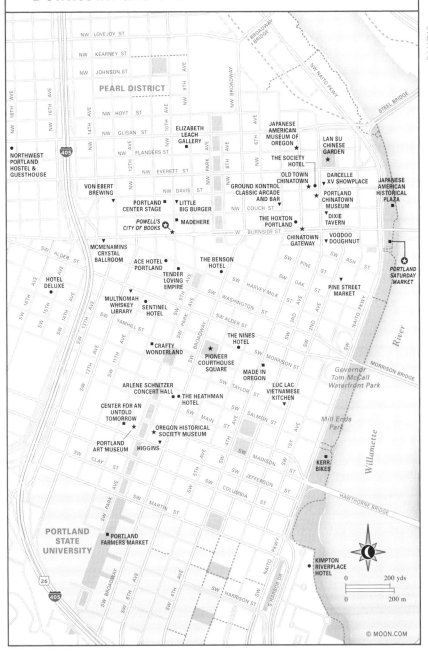

© MOON.COM

heads outside for the **First Thursday Street Gallery** (urbanartnetwork.org; 5pm-10pm first Thurs. of the month Apr.-Oct.), where a four-block stretch of NW 13th Avenue is closed to vehicles and thousands of people fill the streets to scope out paintings, sculptures, and other works by local artists.

★ Powell's City of Books

Powell's City of Books (1005 W. Burnside St.; 503/228-4651; powells.com; 10am-9pm daily) is an institution in Portland. The mammoth bookstore occupies an entire city block and claims to be the largest new and used bookstore in the world, with four floors hosting more than one million books. You could spend all day browsing the shelves, which nearly stretch to the ceiling in each of the bookstore's 10 rooms, and still only scratch the surface of Powell's eye-popping offerings across every genre imaginable. A dizzying number of displays scattered across the store showcase regional titles, staff recommendations, bestsellers, and books grouped by theme (such as commonly banned books or tomes on current events).

Round out your experience with an author event, commonly arranged as conversations between similar writers, or while away a rainy afternoon at the on-site coffeeshop. Expect a store packed with fellow bookworms on weekends; visit on weeknights to enjoy a quieter outing, and pick up a store map near each entrance. A much smaller satellite store can also be found on Hawthorne.

★ WASHINGTON PARK

Washington Park (503/823-5379; portland. gov; 5am-10pm daily; free) is just west of downtown and has been a point of civic pride since the 1880s, when the park's first keeper—drawing on the grandeur of his native Europe—oversaw the construction of winding roads, planting of manicured gardens, and creation of what would become the Oregon Zoo. Measuring 410 forested acres, the city's signature green space is threaded with walking paths and dotted with playgrounds and

picnic areas. It's also home to many of the city's best-loved attractions.

Parking is $2 per hour ($8 max per day) and extremely limited, especially 9am-3pm on spring-summer weekends. It's possible to walk to the park from downtown—it's just over a mile up about a 260-foot incline from Pioneer Courthouse Square to Washington Park's eastern edge. Mass transit options include **TriMet bus 63,** which stops at some of the park's main attractions, and the **MAX Light Rail Blue** and **Red Lines** (fun fact: they actually stop in a tunnel under the park that's 260 feet belowground—making it the deepest transit station in North America). From the Washington Park MAX Light Rail Station's upper level, you can catch the wheelchair-accessible **Washington Park Free Shuttle** (9:30am-7pm daily Apr.-Sept., 9:30am-4pm daily Oct.-Mar.; free), which provides year-round service to the park's attractions.

For more information, visit explorewashingtonpark.org, which also includes real-time capacity updates at Washington Park's various parking areas.

International Rose Test Garden

Portland is nicknamed the "City of Roses," and it's easy to see why after a stroll around the **International Rose Test Garden** (400 SW Kingston Ave.; 503/823-3636; portland. gov; 5am-10pm daily; free). Late May-October, more than 10,000 rose bushes—representing more than 610 varieties—make the park pop with vibrant hues of red, pink, orange, and white. Ostensibly, the rose garden is a testing ground for new varieties (as it has been since World War I, when Europeans feared the flower might be bombed into extinction—and sent roses to Portland for safekeeping), and 10-20 new varieties are still planted each year.

Portland Japanese Garden

No less than Nobuo Matsunaga, the former ambassador of Japan to the United States,

1: Powell's City of Books **2:** colorful maple tree in the Portland Japanese Garden at Washington Park **3:** Pittock Mansion **4:** elephants at the Oregon Zoo

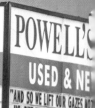

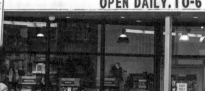

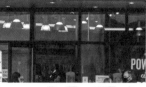

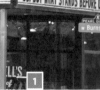

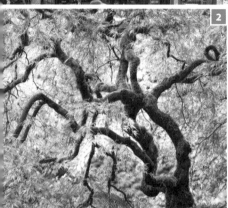

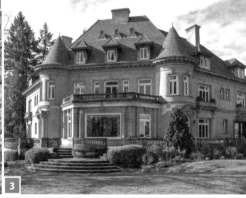

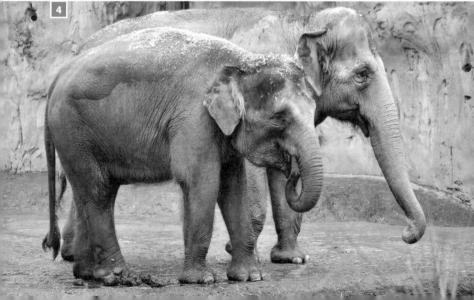

called the **Portland Japanese Garden** (611 SW Kingston Ave.; 503/223-1321; japanesegarden.org; 10am-5:30pm Wed.-Mon.; $18.95 adults, $16.25 seniors 65 and over, $15.25 students, $13.50 children 6-17, free for children under 6) "the most beautiful and authentic Japanese garden in the world outside of Japan." That's high praise, and the urban oasis earns the acclaim with eight garden spaces (each reflecting various aspects of Japanese garden history and design, such as one designed as a strolling pond garden), a tea house, bubbling streams, and views of Mount Hood. The garden is a year-round treat but is especially captivating during fall's colorful foliage displays and spring during cherry blossom season.

Oregon Zoo

Dating to 1888, the **Oregon Zoo** (4001 SW Canyon Rd.; 503/226-1561; oregonzoo.org; 9:30am-5:30pm daily; $24 adults, $19 children 2-11, free for children under 2) has earned plaudits for its conservation efforts, attention to animal welfare, and thoughtfully crafted exhibits. The zoo hosts more than 2,500 birds, reptiles, amphibians, fish, invertebrates, and mammals, including Asian elephants and polar bears. Other on-site attractions include children's play areas, a carousel, and a six-minute train ride that heads into the surrounding forest. During the winter holiday season, **ZooLights** (late Nov.-early Jan.; $15-20 adults, $10-15 for children 3-11, free for children 2 and under) showcases displays of more than 1.5 million lights and also features a lighted train and carousel, hot drinks, and fare from local food carts.

Other Attractions

Another popular stop within the park is the family-friendly **World Forestry Center** (4033 SW Canyon Rd.; 503/228-1367; worldforestry.org; 11am-4pm Wed.-Sun.; $5 adults, free for children under 3), which looks at the many benefits of forests through interactive displays and hands-on exhibits. Also forest-focused is **Hoyt Arboretum** (4000 SW Fairview Blvd.;

hoytarboretum.org; visitor center 10am-4pm daily, grounds 5am-10pm daily; free), "a museum of living trees," which features 12 miles (19 km) of hiking trails that pass 2,300 species of trees and shrubs in the park. Stop by the visitor center to pick up a trail map.

NORTHWEST PORTLAND

Adjacent to downtown, NW Portland sits where the hustle and bustle of the city gradually gives way to laid-back, pedestrian-friendly boulevards and leafy parkland.

Pittock Mansion

Just north of Washington Park, **Pittock Mansion** (3229 NW Pittock Dr.; 503/823-3623; pittockmansion.org; 10am-5pm Wed.-Mon. and noon-5pm Tues. June-Labor Day, 10am-4pm Wed.-Mon. and noon-4pm Tues. Labor Day-May; $12 adults, $10 seniors 65 and over, $8 children 6-18, free for children under 6) was constructed by real estate magnate and newspaper publisher Henry Pittock in 1914 and today offers a glimpse into Portland's stately past. The picturesque French Renaissance-style home features 23 rooms and can be explored via self-guided tour or docent-led outing. Make time to enjoy the grounds surrounding the mansion, where you'll find a lavish rose garden (awash in color May-June) and impressive views of Portland's skyline—indeed, it's worth coming here just for the views even if you're not interested in the mansion (the grounds are free to wander).

Parking is $2 per hour ($8 max per day) 9:30am-8pm daily, and the lot can fill to capacity in summer and mid-November-December, when holiday displays make the mansion a popular seasonal attraction. Consider early-morning or weekday visits to avoid congestion.

NW 21st and 23rd Avenues

NW 21st Avenue and **NW 23rd Avenue** run through stately residential neighborhoods, and along each tree-lined thoroughfare, roughly from Burnside to NW Thurman Street, you'll find restaurants, coffee shops, and other venues, with distinctly different

Northwest Portland

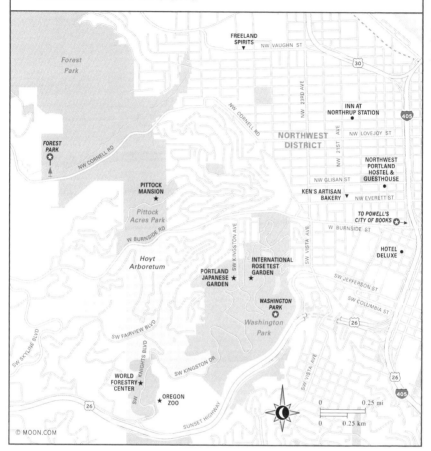

vibes. NW 21st Avenue is the more laid-back of the two, with down-home eateries, dive bars, and neighborhood cafés. Two blocks west, NW 23rd is a much hipper, contemporary strip, boasting outposts of some of Portland's most popular restaurants and an array of local and national retailers. It's pleasant to stroll up one street and down the other, stopping at whatever catches your fancy.

SOUTHEAST PORTLAND

SE Portland is perhaps the most "Portland" of the city's five quadrants, home to many eclectic neighborhoods—bustling business corridors amid large stretches of quiet residential neighborhoods—and best-loved restaurants and craft breweries.

Oregon Museum of Science and Industry

Situated along the Willamette River, the expansive **Oregon Museum of Science and Industry** (1945 SE Water Ave.; 503/797-4000; omsi.edu; 9:30am-5:30pm daily; $15 adults, $12 seniors over 62, $10.50 children 3-13, free for children under 3), known as OMSI,

Southeast Portland

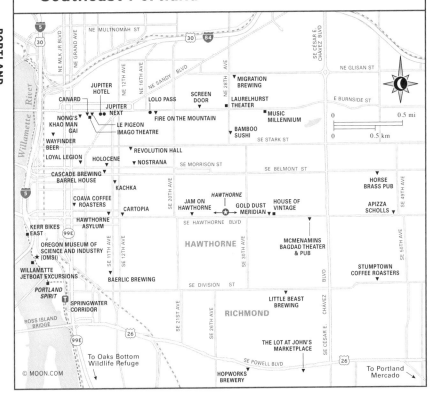

hosts thoughtful, well-designed educational attractions for kids of all ages, with interactive exhibits illuminating the natural sciences, physics, chemistry, and space. For additional fees, visitors can see traveling exhibits that cover topics like the history of the Marvel universe and the undersea explorations of filmmaker James Cameron (prices vary), tour the USS Blueback submarine ($8.50) docked next to the museum, watch hit films in the state-of-the-art Empirical Theater ($6-7.50), or catch a show at the planetarium ($7.50), which sometimes features laser light shows set to music by, for example, Pink Floyd and The Beatles. The museum also hosts popular events including **OMSI After Dark** (6pm-10pm last Wed. of the month; $25) for the over-21 crowd,

with themed nights and alcoholic beverages, and **OMSI Science Pub** (monthly; $5), featuring a guest speaker on special topics, with food and drink available.

★ Hawthorne

Everything that makes Portland, well, Portland is distilled to its most charming essence along the 2.2-mile (3.5-km) stretch of **Hawthorne Boulevard,** roughly between SE 9th Avenue and SE 50th Avenue. Attracting locals and visitors alike, the hodgepodge neighborhood features locally owned businesses in low-rise buildings and the occasional converted house. One of Portland's oldest—and still going strong—food cart pods, Cartopia, is here, along with

vintage boutiques, popular eateries, and bustling bars, where hipsters and hippies come together over tallboys. The atmosphere is typically laid-back, even as sidewalks swell with outdoor diners and coffee drinkers, playful buskers, and curious shoppers on weekend afternoons.

Six blocks north, the parallel **SE Belmont Street** thoroughfare, between SE 20th and 35th Avenues, is something of a little sister to Hawthorne, with similar draws—lively cafés, pubs, and shops—on a quieter, tree-lined street.

Division

If Hawthorne reflects Portland's quirky past, then **Division Street,** about 10 blocks south and running parallel, showcases its changing present, with mixed-use apartments and condos lining the street and hosting ground-level businesses, including some of the city's signature restaurants and respected breweries. Most of the most popular spots are between SE 11th Avenue and César E. Chávez Boulevard/SE 39th Avenue.

Two blocks south and parallel to Division is the quainter enclave of **Clinton Street** (centered around SE Clinton St. and SE 26th Ave.), which also has eateries, coffee shops, and bars in the heart of a friendly, leafy neighborhood.

NORTHEAST PORTLAND

Like SE Portland, NE Portland is characterized by quiet neighborhoods punctuated by lively business corridors lined with restaurants, brewpubs, boutiques, and other home-grown businesses.

Alberta

Even as it's grown and gentrified in recent years, **Alberta Street** between NE 10th and NE 31st, also known as the **Alberta Arts District,** remains the kind of neighborhood where clapboard storefronts and historic brick buildings still host quiet coffee shops and old-school dive bars—in the shadow of new condos and just-opened outposts of citywide chains. Popular with young professionals, the Alberta Arts District earns its moniker by hosting a number of art galleries (many of which emphasize local and BIPOC artists), showcasing dozens of colorful murals on benches and buildings, and displaying sculptures, mosaics, and other forms of public art. Look for Alberta's **Black Heritage Markers** (sidewalks between NE 11th and NE 24th; albertamainst.org). For decades, NE and North Portland had the highest percentage of Black homeowners in the city and was home to jazz clubs graced by the likes of Duke Ellington and John Coltrane, until the community was splintered by the construction of Interstate 5 and increasingly gentrified. These public art pieces document the history of the neighborhood and pay tribute to Black Portlanders. An excellent resource for the neighborhood—with links to galleries, downloadable maps of public art, and news on the latest community projects—is **Alberta Art Works** (albertaartworks.org).

★ Last Thursday

To best experience the Alberta neighborhood, time your visit for **Last Thursday** (6pm-9pm last Thurs. of the month; lastthursdayalberta. org); the blocks-long event celebrates the street's art galleries, which open new shows on these nights, accompanied by wine, snacks, and occasional discussions with featured artists. The event also features live music, arts and crafts vendors, and food specials. Last Thursday runs year-round but really gets lively in summer (June-Aug.), when a 15-block stretch of Alberta Street closes to vehicular traffic, and street performers—like acrobat troupes, energetic buskers, stand-up comedians, and fire dancers—create a carnival-like atmosphere.

McMenamins Kennedy School

McMenamins Kennedy School (5736 NE 33rd Ave.; 503/249-3983; mcmenamins. com) is a former schoolhouse dating to 1915 that's been charmingly renovated by the regional McMenamins chain into a hotel. Even

Northeast Portland

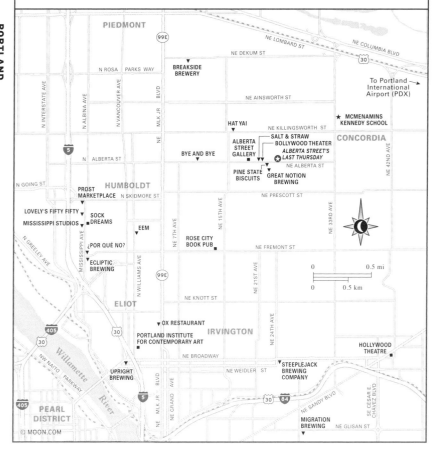

PIEDMONT

99E

NE LOMBARD ST

NE COLUMBIA BLVD

NE DEKUM ST

30

N ROSA PARKS WAY

▼ BREAKSIDE
BREWERY

NE AINSWORTH ST

N INTERSTATE AVE

N ALBINA AVE

N VANCOUVER AVE

NE MLK JR BLVD

To Portland →
International
Airport (PDX)

HAT YAI
▼

NE KILLINGSWORTH ST

★ MCMENAMINS
KENNEDY SCHOOL

5

N ALBERTA ST

BYE AND BYE
▼

ALBERTA
STREET
GALLERY

SALT & STRAW
BOLLYWOOD THEATER
ALBERTA STREET'S
⊕ *LAST THURSDAY*

CONCORDIA

NE 42ND AVE

NE ALBERTA ST

PINE STATE
BISCUITS

GREAT NOTION
BREWING

N GOING ST

PROST
MARKETPLACE N SKIDMORE ST

HUMBOLDT

NE PRESCOTT ST

NE 33RD AVE

LOVELY'S FIFTY FIFTY ▼

MISSISSIPPI STUDIOS ■ SOCK
                      ■ DREAMS

EEM
▼

NE 15TH AVE

NE FREMONT ST

N GREELEY AVE

MISSISSIPPI AVE

¿POR QUÉ NO?
▼

ECLIPTIC
BREWING

N WILLIAMS AVE

N 7TH AVE

ROSE CITY
BOOK PUB
■

NE 21ST AVE

0   0.5 mi

0   0.5 km

99E

NE KNOTT ST

ELIOT

NE 24TH AVE

405

30

OX RESTAURANT
▼

PORTLAND INSTITUTE
FOR CONTEMPORARY ART

IRVINGTON

HOLLYWOOD
THEATRE
■

30

NW NAITO PARKWAY

NE BROADWAY

NE WEIDLER ST

▼ STEEPLEJACK
BREWING
COMPANY

SE CESAR E
CHAVEZ BLVD

UPRIGHT
BREWING
▼

NE MLK JR BLVD

NE GRAND AVE

5

30

84

NE SANDY BLVD

405

PEARL
DISTRICT

Willamette River

MIGRATION
BREWING   NE GLISAN ST
▼

© MOON.COM

if you're not staying here, you can come to eat at the restaurant, which offers pub fare in the onetime cafeteria; drink at four bars pouring McMenamins' own beer, cider, wine, and spirits; catch a movie in a theater outfitted with plush couches and cozy chairs ($5 adults, $3 children 3-12, free for children under 3); or unwind in a saltwater soaking pool ($8 adults, $4 children 3-11, free for children under 3 and hotel guests; reservations required for non-hotel guests; bring your own towel). It's possible to spend the day simply hopping between venues and lounging on the grounds,

and you'll be hanging out with locals as well as out-of-towners.

NORTH PORTLAND

Portland's "fifth quadrant" occupies a wide swath of land, home to tree-lined neighborhoods and industrial businesses, but what draws most visitors here is one of the city's trendiest neighborhoods.

Mississippi

"Old Portland" and "New Portland" come together along **Mississippi Avenue** (between

The McMenamins Empire, Explained

Brothers Mike and Brian McMenamin opened their first brewpub—and the state's first since Prohibition—in Portland in 1983, helping launch a craft-beer revolution in the Pacific Northwest that's still going strong today. Today, **McMenamins** (mcmenamins.com) comprises more than 50 pubs, hotels, and concert venues throughout the Pacific Northwest, many of which are historical properties that have been refurbished in a characteristic whimsical style and often include entertainment like movie theaters, soaking pools, and colorful bars serving McMenamins' own beer, spirits, wine, and cider. The public is welcome to enjoy the properties' amenities even if they're not overnight guests at the hotels, and locals as well as visitors hang out at these venues. Avid fans can purchase a **McMenamins Passport** ($35) and collect stamps at any McMenamins venue to earn prizes like free Cajun tots (a staple of the chain's food menu), burgers, and souvenirs including pint glasses. Around Portland, the **Kennedy School** is a draw, but it's far from the only destination-worthy McMenamins venue in Oregon. Here are a few favorites:

· **Crystal Ballroom,** Portland: This live music venue occupies a former ballroom, and you won't be able to stop dancing on its signature springy floors (page 44).

· **Bagdad Theater & Pub,** Portland: Since 1927, this regal theater has been showing movies in an auditorium framed by towering arches, wrought-iron fixtures, and other artistic flourishes (page 50).

· **Hillsdale Brewery & Public House,** Portland (1505 SW Sunset Blvd.; 503/246-3938; 11am-10pm Sun.-Thurs., 11am-11pm Fri.-Sat.): Visit Oregon's first official brewpub since Prohibition, where several of the chain's best beers were born. Eccentric artwork, hanging plants, and a few neon lights create a fun, laid-back atmosphere.

· **Edgefield,** Troutdale (2126 SW Halsey St.; 503/669-8610; hours vary by venue): Built in 1911, this former farm at the western edge of the Columbia River Gorge is now home to a sprawling hotel that serves as a kind of amusement park for adults with its several restaurants and bars, soaking pool, golf course, movie theater, spa, winery, distillery, and brewery. Edgefield is also a popular outdoor summertime concert venue that's hosted the likes of Lizzo, Robert Plant, and Willie Nelson.

N. Skidmore St. and N. Cook St.) like nowhere else in the city. Within the walkable North Portland neighborhood, you'll find a music venue housed in a converted Baptist church, restaurants and bars occupying vintage homes, and a coffee shop residing within a long-closed drug store. Newly constructed condos are wedged between century-old homes and overhauled storefronts. Most businesses along the corridor are locally owned and frequented by young professionals and young families alike. And many of the fixtures in the veteran establishments—including windows, doors, and tiling—comes from a neighborhood warehouse that sells reclaimed building materials, usually from shuttered businesses and remodeled homes in the area.

A dozen or so blocks east and directly parallel to Mississippi, **Williams Avenue,** which separates North Portland from NE Portland, also offers a mix of eateries, brewpubs, and indie shops in a changing neighborhood. Here new condos seem to vastly outnumber the kinds of stately homes found along Mississippi Avenue. Nevertheless, elements of the classic Portland experience—hidden bar patios, sidewalk dining, and designated bike lanes—remain in the growing district.

Recreation

PARKS
Governor Tom McCall Waterfront Park

If Pioneer Courthouse Square is Portland's living room, **Governor Tom McCall Waterfront Park** (Naito Pkwy. between NW Glisan St. and SW Harrison St.; 503/823-5379; portland.gov; 5am-midnight daily; free) is the city's backyard. The 1.5-mile-long (2.4-km) strip of land, named for the environmentally conscious Oregon governor, is set along the Willamette River on the city's westside. A walking-biking path follows the river, flanked by grassy space for lounging. The Portland Saturday Market takes place in the park, and numerous festivals are held on the grounds each summer. If you're visiting March-April, be sure to head to the **Japanese American Historical Plaza** (Naito Pkwy. And NW Couch St.)—dedicated to the memories of those who were forcibly sent to internment camps during World War II—where you may be lucky enough to catch the plaza's 100 cherry trees blossoming in spring.

Mill Ends Park

"Keep Portland Weird" has been a citywide mantra for decades—so it's only fitting that one of the city's claims to fame is what might be the world's smallest park: **Mill Ends Park** (SW Naito Pkwy. and SW Taylor St.; 503/823-5379; portland.gov; free). Consisting of a solitary tree, the park measures just two feet across—roughly the size of a footstep—and sits on a median strip in a busy intersection. You won't spend much time here, but Mill Ends makes for an adorable, only-in-Portland diversion. Seasonal displays add to the charm.

Mt. Tabor

Enjoy a hike, take in skyline views, or unwind with a picnic at **Mt. Tabor Park** (SE 60th Ave. and Salmon St.; 503/823-5379; portland.gov; 5am-midnight daily; free), which sits inside an

Mill Ends Park in Portland

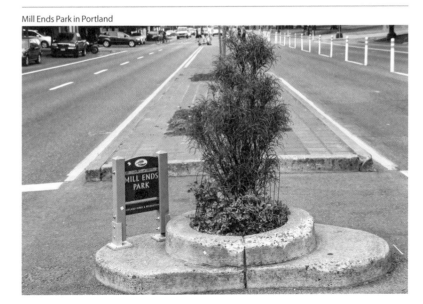

extinct volcano. The park was designed with gently curving roads and a network of walking trails, as well as gardens, picnic areas, a playground, horseshoe pits, and basketball courts. The sunset views from here, looking out over the city skyline and the Tualatin Mountains, are among the best in Portland. A visit here pairs nicely with a day strolling Hawthorne—which dead-ends right into the park.

41

HIKING
★ Forest Park

Located on the northwest edge of Portland, **Forest Park** (503/823-5379; portland.gov; 5am-10pm daily; free) is one of the largest forested natural areas within city limits in the United States. At about 5,200 acres (2,100 ha), the park provides refuge for hundreds of species of native plants and animals—such as towering Douglas fir and colorful bigleaf maple trees, as well as finches, woodpeckers, and black-tail deer. It boasts more than 80 miles (125 km) of trails popular with hikers and offers more than 40 access points. Hiking in this heavily wooded, hilly park, especially its farther-flung northern parts, it's easy to feel far from the urban world—making it feel even more remarkable that you're still in city limits. Learn more about the park's myriad trails from the **Oregon Hikers Field Guide** (oregonhikers.org) or the **Forest Park Conservancy** (forestparkconservancy.org).

Winding through it all is the **Wildwood Trail,** snaking some 30 miles (50 km) through the park. The **Lower Macleay Trail to Pittock Mansion** connects to the Wildwood Trail and is great for a quick introduction to Forest Park.

Lower Macleay Trail to Pittock Mansion
Distance: *6.4 miles (10.3 km) round-trip*
Duration: *3 hours*
Elevation Gain: *1,010 feet (300 m)*
Effort: *Easy/moderate*
Passes/Fees: *None*

Trailhead: *Lower Macleay Park, west end of NW Upshur St.*

From Lower Macleay Park, start off on the **Lower Macleay Trail,** which soon follows the bubbling **Balch Creek** through a wooded canyon. The first 0.25 mile (0.4 km) is paved and wheelchair accessible. At mile 1 (1.6 km), you'll come upon the graffiti-covered **Stone House,** more commonly known as the "Witch's Castle"; built in the 1930s, it was originally a restroom. From here, continue on the **Wildwood Trail** as it ascends out of the canyon, crosses Northwest Cornell Road, and climbs a hillside covered in maple and Douglas fir. You'll encounter numerous intersections, but continue following signage for the Wildwood Trail, which ends at the parking area for **Pittock Mansion.** There's an admission fee to enter the mansion, now a historical museum, but it's free to wander the grounds; head to the property's easternmost point for one of the best views of Portland's skyline and the surrounding mountains. On your way back, consider turning left onto the **Upper Macleay Trail** after 0.75 mile (1.2 km). While it doesn't present a dramatically different view of the urban forest, it's a nice change of pace. The trail reconnects with the **Wildwood Trail** again just before you cross Northwest Cornell Road in another 0.5 mile (0.8 km).

★ BICYCLING

Bicycling is big in Portland: It has more than 400 miles (650 km) of neighborhood greenways, bike lanes, and dedicated paths, and more than 6 percent of the city's residents commute by bike, the highest percentage of any large U.S. city.

This bike-friendly culture makes it a great place for a ride. Cruising along Portland's paved and flat Willamette River waterfront is a pleasant and easy option. A ride along the **Governor Tom McCall Waterfront Park** is popular, or for a less-crowded path, head across the river for the **Springwater Corridor Trail** (portland.gov), which begins just south of the Oregon Museum of Science and Industry on the waterfront at

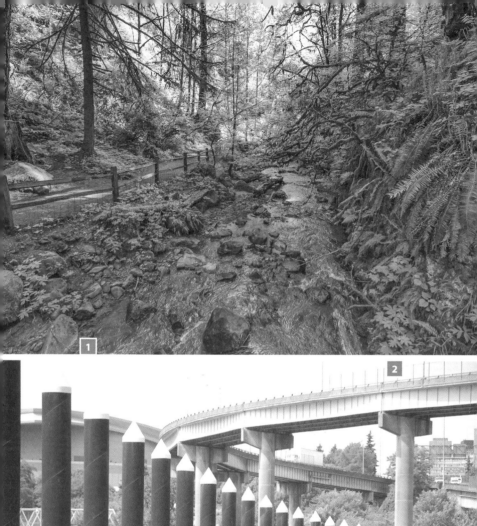

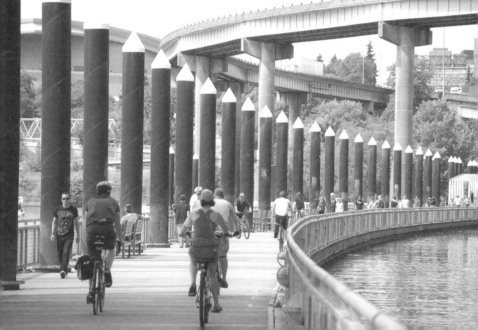

SE Ivon Street. The multiuse path runs 21 miles/34 km (one-way) through forests, wetlands, residential neighborhoods, parks, and other ecosystems to the small town of Boring (yes, that's its real name), while offering a quiet cycling experience in the heart of the city. Since it's an out-and back greenway, just turn around whenever you'd like. A few spots that make good destinations include **Oaks Bottom Wildlife Refuge** (at mile 2.6 along the Springwater Corridor Trail; portland.gov; 5am-midnight daily; free), which provides important habitat for salmon and more than 175 bird species; the quaint **Sellwood neighborhood** (at mile 3 along the Springwater Corridor Trail), which has a cluster of businesses just off the trail, primarily along SE 13th Avenue; and **Cartlandia** (at mile 9 along the Springwater Corridor Trail; cartlandia.com; hours and prices vary by cart), a pod with some 30 food carts and covered outdoor seating.

Cyclists looking for hillier terrain amid a more natural setting can find roughly 30 miles (50 km) of roads in **Forest Park** that are open to bikers. The 11.2-mile (18-km) **Leif Erickson Drive** (trailheads along NW Thurman St. and NW Germantown Rd.) is a popular choice.

To really get a sense of Portland's love affair with bicycling, keep an eye out for two-wheeled events around town, including **Pedalpalooza,** comprising weeks of themed rides all across the city—including the **World Naked Bike Ride**—**Portland Sunday Parkways** (portland.gov; summer), which closes off neighborhood streets to cars a few times each year, and **Bridge Pedal,** which allows cyclists the opportunity to cross many of Portland's bridges (see Festivals and Events for more details).

For rentals, locally owned **Kerr Bikes** (westside 1020 SW Naito Pkwy.; 503/808-9955; eastside 1945 SE Water Ave., Bldg. B; 503/802-5271; albertinakerr.org; hours vary Mar.-Oct., by appointment Nov.-Feb.; per hour $10-36, half day $25-90, full day $35-200) has convenient locations on both sides of the river. It offers a wide variety of options, including a healthy selection of kid-friendly and adaptive rides for cyclists of all abilities. Funds raised from rentals go toward a local nonprofit that supports adults with developmental disabilities and mental health challenges.

More information, including suggested routes and maps, are available via the **City of Portland** (portland.gov) and **BikePortland** (bikeportland.org).

SIGHTSEEING TOURS AND CRUISES

If you want to see Portland from the water, take a boat tour with *Portland Spirit* (110 SE Caruthers St.; 503/224-3900; portlandspirit.com), which travels south along the Willamette River and offers views of the city skyline, surrounding parks, and Mount Hood rising above it all. Cruises include the 2.5-hour **Downtown Dinner Cruise** ($96 adults, $48 children under 13), 2-hour **Downtown Portland Brunch Cruise** ($72 adults, $36 children 1-12, $10 for children under 1), and 2-hour **Downtown Portland Lunch Cruise** ($64 adults, $32 children 1-12, $10 for children under 1). Each outing includes locally sourced meals, live music, and the captain's narration. If you just want to go for a boat ride sans meal, there's the **Portland Sightseeing Cruise** ($40-50 adults, $25 children).

For a far more thrilling way to see Portland, try **Willamette Jetboat Excursions** (1945 SE Water Ave.; 503/231-1532; willamettejet.com; May-Sept.; $23-65). The local outfitter offers Willamette River tours that last 30 minutes-3 hours and showcase sights such as Portland's bridges and Willamette Falls, the second-largest waterfall by volume in the United States. It's not uncommon to spy bald eagles perched in the trees along the riverbanks or see osprey soaring overhead.

1: a hiking trail along Balch Creek in Forest Park
2: cyclists along the Willamette River

Beer and Nightlife

DOWNTOWN AND THE PEARL DISTRICT

Old Town Chinatown is known for its nightlife, home to the city's **Entertainment District** (bordered by W. Burnside St. and NW Everett St., NW 2nd Ave. and NW 4th Ave.), a collection of nightclubs and woo-girl bars specializing in strong drinks and pulsating DJ sets. On Friday and Saturday nights, a few blocks in the heart of the neighborhood are closed to vehicles. The two-story **Dixie Tavern** (32 NW 3rd Ave.; 503/234-9431; dixiepdx.com; 6pm-2:30am Wed.-Sun.) is known for themed parties and servers who dance on the bar.

★ TOP EXPERIENCE

★ Brewpubs

The tap list at ★ **Von Ebert Brewing** (131 NW 13th Ave.; 503/820-7721; vonebertbrewing.com; 11:30am-10pm Mon.-Sat., 11:30am-9pm Sun.) is always sprawling and well worth sampling—but, of note, the brewery slings some of Portland's best-loved lagers and IPAs (including the pine-tinged, award-winning Volatile Substance) inside this massive pub with plenty of natural light. Outdoor seating is also available. The brewery also has three outposts elsewhere in the Portland area.

Bars

Long before barcades were in vogue, **Ground Kontrol Classic Arcade and Bar** (115 NW 5th Ave.; 503/796-9364; groundkontrol.com; noon-midnight daily) perfected the retro night out with classic video games ($0.25-1.00 per game), craft cocktails, and a calendar stuffed with fun events. The two-story arcade has more than 100 games featuring all your favorite childhood titles plus a stellar pinball selection, basic bar food dished alongside crushable beers, and regular live performances from DJs to stand-up comedians. On

the last Wednesday every month, you can enjoy free play after paying the $10 cover. Ground Kontrol is open to all ages until 5pm and then adults over 21 only after 5pm.

As the name implies, whiskey takes center stage at the dimly lit **Multnomah Whisk(e)y Library** (1124 SW Alder St.; 503/954-1381; mwlpdx.com; 4pm-11:15pm Tues.-Thurs., 4pm-12:15am Fri.-Sat., 4pm-10:15pm Sun.). More than 2,000 whiskeys from dozens of countries are available, with dive-bar standbys offered alongside spirits from centuries-old distilleries. The bar is technically a members-only affair—but would-be imbibers can visit the website to purchase a one-day "Hall Pass" for $25 up to two weeks in advance; the reservation, available Sunday-Thursday, is good for two hours.

LGBTQ

Since 1967, **Darcelle XV Showplace** (208 NW 3rd Ave.; 503/957-6723; darcellexv.com; cover $5-25) has offered boisterous Vegas-style cabaret and female impersonation revues in the heart of Portland's Old Town Chinatown neighborhood. Sunday drag brunches are always popular, as are weekend shows featuring the club's top performers.

Live Music

At the western edge of downtown, the historic **McMenamins Crystal Ballroom** (1332 W. Burnside St.; 503/225-0047; crystalballroompdx.com) carries on a live-entertainment tradition that dates to 1914 when the venue opened as—yes—a ballroom. It's famed for its springy wooden floors, which you can feel bouncing beneath your feet among excited concertgoers grooving to the acts such as Modest Mouse, Santigold, and the Flaming Lips, or at the occasional themed dance party, like a '90s night featuring the music of Nirvana, TLC, and the Spice Girls.

NORTHWEST PORTLAND

Distilleries

Woman-owned and -operated distillery **Freeland Spirits** (2671 NW Vaughn St.; 971/279-5692; freelandspirits.com; noon-6pm daily) prides itself on sourcing ingredients from Pacific Northwest producers—and has brought that sense of farm-to-bottle freshness to a wide-ranging lineup that includes a well-rounded gin, a flavorful bourbon, and classic cocktails. A warm aesthetic pervades the bar, thanks to plenty of greenery, tons of natural light, windows that peer into the distillery, and high ceilings. Some outdoor seating is available, even in winter.

SOUTHEAST PORTLAND

TOP EXPERIENCE

★ Brewpubs

★ **Wayfinder Beer** (304 SE 2nd Ave.; 503/718-2337; wayfinder.beer; noon-10pm daily) draws on Old World influences for its excellent lineup of refreshing lagers—including Italian- and Czech-style pilsners, and a Bavarian-inspired helles. Cider, wine, and cocktails are also available. The food menu, highlighting upscale takes on international classics (banh mi, schnitzel, fish-and-chips), is likewise worth perusing. When the weather cooperates, Wayfinder's spacious patio—on an elevated deck that's heated in winter—is always bustling.

Baerlic Brewing (2239 SE 11th Ave.; 503/477-9418; baerlicbrewing.com; 11am-10pm daily)—whose name is pronounced "bear-lick"—has earned acclaim for its refreshing, flavorful takes on classic styles, from its Dad Beer lager to a fruity Punk Rock Time IPA. This flagship brewpub is thankfully bereft of televisions, video games, and other distractions, and a lush beer garden offers outdoor sipping on sunny days. All ages are welcome until 9pm.

In a craft beer scene headlined by hop-heavy IPAs, **Little Beast Brewing** (pictured page 10; 3412 SE Division St.; 503/208-2723; littlebeastbrewing.com; noon-9pm Sun.-Thurs., noon-10pm Fri.-Sat.) stands out for its inventive lineup of mixed-culture beers, noted for their tart, fruity, and sour notes; Little Beast does them better than just about anyone in town. Dialed-in IPAs, lagers, and other common styles are also on tap—and all taste better on the brewery's outdoor beer garden, a fun summertime destination. Located inside the brewery is the **Lawless BBQ** kitchen, so you can order some Kansas City-style barbecue to accompany your beer.

The long-running **Hopworks Brewery** (2944 SE Powell Blvd.; 503/232-4677; hopworksbeer.com; 11:30am-9pm Sun.-Thurs., 11:30am-10pm Fri.-Sat.) stands out in Portland's crowded scene with palate-pleasing organic beers across a wide range of styles. The family-friendly brewpub's food menu leans heavily on locally sourced fare and organic ingredients, and outdoor seating is available. Cocktails, house-made hard seltzer, cider, and wine are also available.

For some of the Pacific Northwest's best sour ales, look no further than **Cascade Brewing Barrel House** (939 SE Belmont St.; 503/265-8603; cascadebrewingbarrelhouse.com; 4pm-10pm Wed.-Thurs., noon-10pm Fri.-Sat., noon-8pm Sun.). It crafts beloved sours aged in French oak barrels and Pacific Northwest wine barrels—each imbuing the resulting beer with just the right amount of acidity, tartness, and fruitiness. Cider and wine are also available. A covered patio offers outdoor seating.

Bars

Oregon's craft brewing scene is put on loving display at **Loyal Legion** (710 SE 6th Ave.; 503/235-8272; loyallegionpdx.com; 3pm-midnight Mon.-Thurs., noon-2am Fri.-Sat., noon-midnight Sun.), which boasts up to 99 Beaver State-brewed beers on tap at any given time. Seemingly every possible style is typically available. Wine, cider, and cocktails are also available, and the food menu includes burgers, sausages, and salads crafted with locally sourced ingredients.

Oregon's Craft Beer Culture, Past and Present

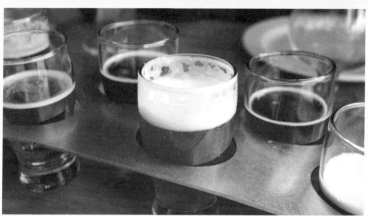

flight of Oregon craft beer

Brewers have been plying their trade in Oregon since the 1850s, but it wasn't until the 1980s that the state's craft beer craze started up in Portland, when a few craft breweries in the area launched and began toting their kegs to bars around town—and then Governor Vic Atiyeh in 1985 signed what became known as the Brewpub Bill, allowing breweries to sell their own suds at on-site pubs. That same year, brothers Mike and Brian McMenamin opened Oregon's first brewpub, **Hillsdale Brewery & Public House,** in Portland, and a revolution was born.

Nearly 40 years after brewpubs became legal in Oregon, the state is home to more than 300 craft breweries, and Portland alone has more than 70 breweries. Oregon even has an official state microbe: Saccharomyces cerevisiae, better known as brewer's yeast. Craft beer is embedded in the state's and, especially, the city's culture. Nicknamed "Beervana," Portland hosts numerous beer festivals every year, such as the SheBrew Brewfest, the Baker's Dozen Coffee Beer & Doughnut Fest, and the Nano Beer Fest. A popular statewide event in February is **Zwickelmania,** which takes place in breweries across Portland over one weekend and the rest of the state over another, with tours, tastings, and more. It's also possible to enjoy award-winning ales and lagers while engaged in almost any given activity in Portland, whether you're going to the movies or a bookstore, getting a haircut, or folding your clothes at a laundromat.

Throughout this book, look for our ★ **top brewpub picks.**

Horse Brass Pub (4534 SE Belmont St.; 503/232-2202; horsebrass.com; noon-midnight Sun.-Wed., noon-1am Thurs.-Sat.) opened in 1976 and has since been recognized, time and again, as one of the best bars in the country. The dimly lit, English-style bar boasts one of the city's stronger beer selections—roughly 60 taps pour a mix of new offerings from up-and-coming breweries alongside rare, one-off releases from some of the country's biggest producers—and traditional pub grub (fish-and-chips are the standout here) is served. Cider, wine, and cocktails are also available. All ages are welcome until 5pm.

Of all the bars along Hawthorne, **Gold Dust Meridian** (3267 SE Hawthorne Blvd.; 503/239-1143; 2pm-2:30am daily) stands out for doing a little of everything—and doing it well. Craft cocktails are creative

and well-balanced, the food menu (featuring deviled eggs and a rich macaroni and cheese dish topped with potato chips) is a step above typical bar fare, and happy hour (2pm-8pm daily) is generous. Half-circle booths invite lingering, and midcentury wall paneling creates a fun retro vibe. Outdoor seating butts up against the always-bustling boulevard—and is typically packed.

Live Music

Class is always in session at **Revolution Hall** (1300 SE Stark St.; 971/808-5094; revolutionhall.com), an inventive venue housed in a historic high school. Shows are staged in an updated 850-seat auditorium. Performers in recent years have included acclaimed musicians (from rock band Japandroids to Princess—a Prince cover band led by actress Maya Rudolph), stand-up comedians (like Portland's own Ian Karmel), and authors (such as Zadie Smith). Almost as fun as the shows is Revolution Hall's **rooftop bar** (Apr.-Oct.), open to attendees, which boasts 360-degree views of the city.

Clubs

Artsy **Holocene** (1001 SE Morrison St.; 503/239-7639; holocene.org) is an undeniably Portland nightlife destination. The two-story nightclub (capacity 300) is housed in a former auto parts warehouse and features a calendar full of events like LGBTQ- and BIPOC-friendly dance parties, podcast recordings, and live performances by Portland musicians as well as touring acts such as Norwegian DJ Prins Thomas, one of the many techno and electronic musicians to perform at Holocene over the years.

NORTHEAST PORTLAND

TOP EXPERIENCE

★ **Brewpubs**

North of Alberta Street, ★ **Breakside Brewery** (820 NE Dekum St.; 503/719-6475; breakside.com; noon-9pm Sun.-Thurs.,

noon-10pm Fri.-Sat.) does everything well—but its hoppy beers are the undeniable stars of the show. Its flagship IPA boasts well-rounded notes of pine and citrus, while the hazy What Rough Beast blends hop-forward characteristics of Pacific Northwest IPAs with tropical notes common among New England IPAs. One-offs, small-batch beers, and seasonal releases (including a delightfully tart passion-fruit sour ale) likewise reward adventurous imbibers. The brewery also offers cider, wine, and cocktails, as well as a decadent macaroni and cheese dish and heaping plates of nachos. It has four other outposts around the Portland metro area, but covered outdoor seating and a relaxed neighborhood vibe make this one a particularly fun location.

When it opened in 2016, **Great Notion Brewing** (2204 NE Alberta St., Ste. 101; 503/548-4491; greatnotion.com; noon-9pm Sun.-Thurs., noon-10pm Fri.-Sat.) made an instant splash with its audacious mix of hazy IPAs and food-inspired ales such as Double Stack, an imperial stout fermented with maple syrup and aged on whole-bean coffee. In the years since, Great Notion has grown wildly (including opening two more brewpubs in the metro area), buoyed by excellent IPAs, decadent pastry stouts, and flavorful sour ales. Cider, wine, and hard seltzer are also available.

Steeplejack Brewing Company (2400 NE Broadway; 503/206-8880; steeplejackbeer. com; 9am-10pm daily) crafts a well-rounded tap list of creative ales and lagers—and its setting is as awe-inspiring as the beer: The brewery is housed inside a former church that dates to the early 1900s, and visitors can enjoy Belgian-inspired beers, Mexican lagers, and a wide range of creative offerings in the high-ceilinged nave with artful stained glass on seemingly all sides. Cocktails, wine, and cider are also served. A few smaller side rooms offer more intimate settings if you'd prefer something quieter than the main hall. Some outdoor seating is available.

Whether you're a hardcore craft beer geek or are dipping your toes into the

microbrewery waters, **Migration Brewing** (2828 NE Glisan St.; 503/206-5221; migrationbrewing.com; 11:30am-10pm Sun.-Thurs., 11:30am-11pm Fri.-Sat.) offers the best of both worlds: Its flagship beers are all approachable, exemplary takes, while one-offs showcase the brewery's creativity. This is Migration's flagship pub, which boasts a spacious patio, but the brewery also operates three other pubs in the Portland area.

Bars

There's a lot to love about **Bye and Bye** (1011 NE Alberta St.; 503/281-0537; thebyeandbye.com; noon-midnight Mon.-Thurs., noon-2:30am Fri., 10am-2:30am Sat., 10am-midnight Sun.), a neighborhood watering hole in the heart of the Alberta Arts District. Garage doors let in plenty of natural light, craft cocktails are always well-made, and the inventive, vegan-friendly pub food menu (featuring a veggie meatball sub sandwich, a rice bowl with barbecued tofu and brussels sprouts, and brunch dishes) will win over even the most ardent skeptics. Bye and Bye also has two patios with plenty of outdoor seating.

NORTH PORTLAND

TOP EXPERIENCE

★ **Brewpubs**

Just north of the Oregon Convention Center, ★ **Upright Brewing** (240 N. Broadway; 503/914-5130; uprightbrewing.com; 3pm-9pm Mon.-Fri., 11am-9pm Sat.-Sun.) made a name for itself with its Belgian-style farmhouse ales, but today the outstanding brewery also produces some of the city's most creative IPAs,

English-style ales, and barrel-aged beers. Unusual ingredients show up all over the tap list, such as in a gose made with lobster mushrooms or a stout crafted with regional oysters. Garage doors at the high-ceiling pub roll up when the weather's nice.

Space-themed **Ecliptic Brewing** (825 N. Cook St.; 503/265-8002; eclipticbrewing.com; noon-8pm Tues.-Thurs. and Sun., noon-10pm Fri.-Sat.) pours an extensive selection of well-balanced interpretations of classic styles. IPAs, porters, red ales, and lagers claim most of the space on the tap list, but the fruited beers are usually highlights. Ecliptic also serves cider, wine, and cocktails, as well as upscale dishes that lean heavily on appetizing, vegetarian-friendly fare, such as the slightly spicy roasted beet and cauliflower tagine. The pub sits at the base of the bustling Mississippi neighborhood, and its outdoor patio is a hotspot on sunny days.

Live Music

Mississippi Studios (3939 N. Mississippi Ave.; 503/288-3895; mississippistudios.com) is part-venue, part-recording studio, and a wide range of musicians and comedians on the come-up have recorded albums in the space over the years. Local indie performers as well as touring national acts routinely take to the stage in an intimate room (capacity 300) with excellent acoustics. Headliners at the former church have included regional folk band Blind Pilot and Portland-based soul legend Ural Thomas & the Pain. An attached bar—**Bar Bar**—hosts a bustling patio, slings popular burgers, and is a fun place in the Mississippi neighborhood to hang out, whether you're seeing a show or not.

The Arts

PERFORMING ARTS

The **Oregon Symphony** (503/228-1353; orsymphony.org) is the oldest orchestra west of the Mississippi River and routinely packs

the **Arlene Schnitzer Concert Hall** (1037 SW Broadway; 503/248-4335; portland5.com). The Grammy-nominated symphony performs with guest musicians, presents beloved works

by the world's best-known classical musicians, and showcases live scores from beloved movies, from Alfred Hitchcock's *Psycho* to *Star Wars: Return of the Jedi.*

Portland is home to a range of theater companies, and the largest of them is **Portland Center Stage** (128 NW 11th Ave.; 503/445-3700; pcs.org). PCS, as its informally known, fills its season with about 10 productions, featuring a mix of classic, contemporary, and world premiere productions such as *Rent, In the Heights,* and *Astoria,* based on the historical nonfiction book of the same name by writer and historian Peter Stark.

Imago Theatre (17 SE 8th Ave.; 503/231-9581; imagotheatre.com) is known for incorporating unusual influences—such as dance, puppetry, or vaudeville—into its shows, which includes original performances as well as the occasional classic production.

The **Portland Institute for Contemporary Art** (15 NE Hancock St.; 503/242-1419; pica.org) connects visitors with contemporary art through a full slate of cutting-edge offerings that include multimedia exhibits, dance and theatrical performances, and lectures. PICA is perhaps best known for its annual **Time-Based Art Festival** (citywide; pica.org; Sept.; prices vary), which brings artists from around the world to Portland for exhibitions, multimedia productions, live concerts, and other thought-provoking events.

ART GALLERIES
Pearl District

Long a home for creative types, Portland unsurprisingly hosts a number of art galleries, many of which can be found in the Pearl. One of the neighborhood's most celebrated spots is the **Elizabeth Leach Gallery** (417 NW 9th Ave.; 503/224-0521; elizabethleach.com; 10:30am-5:30pm Tues.-Sat.), which opened in 1981. One of the city's oldest galleries, it's earned a reputation for showcasing artists from around the world, as well as those based in the Pacific Northwest, working across a variety of media.

To best experience the neighborhood's galleries, come on a **First Thursday** (5pm-10pm first Thurs. of the month), when galleries stay open later and host receptions. The event gets especially lively during the warmer months, when a four-block stretch of NW 13th Avenue closes to vehicular traffic, and vendors showcase their paintings, sculptures, and other works outdoors amid buskers and other street performers.

Arlene Schnitzer Concert Hall and its famous marquee

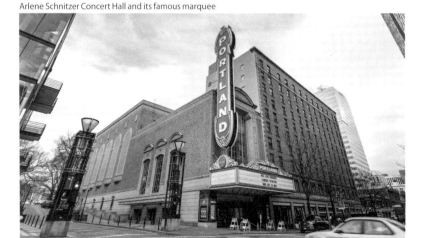

Alberta

The Alberta Arts District also has a number of galleries. A standout among them is **Alberta Street Gallery** (1829 NE Alberta St.; 503/954-3314; albertastreetgallery.com; 11am-7pm daily), which spotlights jewelry, paintings, photography, and more from 30 local artists at any given time. The gallery also hosts regular artist talks and classes and prices its works with an emphasis on affordability.

For a more whimsical affair than First Thursday, check out Alberta's **Last Thursday** (lastthursdayalberta.org; 6pm-9pm last Thurs. of the month), when the neighborhood's galleries hold reception parties and the neighborhood comes alive with live music. Summer is also the time to experience this event, when a 15-block stretch of Alberta Street closes to vehicles and celebrations spill into the street, with arts and crafts vendors selling their handcrafted paintings, drawings, and other works and street performers including acrobat troupes and fire dancers.

CINEMA

Portland is a city of film geeks, where neighborhood theaters outpace chain multiplexes and under-the-radar and cult films are shown seemingly every night.

The **Bagdad Theater & Pub** (3702 SE Hawthorne Blvd.; 503/236-9234; mcmenamins.com; $9-11 adults, $8 for seniors 60 and over and children 12 and under) opened in 1927 and, a century later, is as much of a draw as what's on the screen. The palatial auditorium is adorned with barreled arches, wrought-iron fixtures, and colorful mosaics. For all the Bagdad's old-school charm, though, its modern conveniences include a high-quality surround-sound system, upscale concessions (like slices of pizza and McMenamins beer), and first-run films.

The art deco-styled **Laurelhurst Theater** (2735 E. Burnside St.; 503/238-4088; laurelhursttheater.com; $9 adults, $6.50 seniors 64 and over and children 11 and under, $6 for all shows starting before 5:30pm) opened in 1923 and, a century later, has four auditoriums screening first-run films in a classic setting. Pizza, salads, and cookies complement the usual concession-stand fare, and a handful of locally crafted beers and wines are available to sip during the show. All shows starting after 8pm are 21 and over only; for all shows before 8pm, anyone 20 or younger must be accompanied by a parent or guardian.

With a lovingly restored neon sign, the **Hollywood Theatre** (4122 NE Sandy Blvd.; 503/493-1128; hollywoodtheatre.org; $10 adults, $8 students, seniors, and children) is a cinema palace in Portland. Its creative programming spans hit movies, classic films, festival-circuit darlings, and inventive series spotlighting everything from an annual month-long celebration of women in film to kung fu movies from the 1970s and 1980s from the programmer's own collection.

Cinema in its many forms is celebrated at the **Center for an Untold Tomorrow** (503/221-1156; pamcut.org), which hosts special screenings, themed series (spotlighting the films of Tilda Swinton or David Bowie, for example), and cutting-edge experiences (such as screenings paired with live musical performances). Film screenings take place at the Portland Art Museum's **Whitsell Auditorium** (1219 SW Park Ave.; $8-12). The center also hosts an outdoor film series each summer.

Festivals and Events

Portland knows how to party. In addition to regular free events—like Alberta's **Last Thursday** and the Pearl's **First Thursday,** which are centered around new shows at the neighborhoods' art galleries, and **Sunday Parkways,** when city streets shut down to cars and open to pedestrians and cyclists— the city is host to many beloved annual events.

Winter

In the early and mid-1900s, Portland was home to a thriving jazz scene that hosted some of the day's top musicians. Most of the city's popular clubs were razed to make way for construction of I-5, but Portland's connection to jazz lives on in myriad ways, chief among them the weeks-long **PDX Jazz Festival** (citywide; pdxjazz.org; Feb.; prices vary), which celebrates its namesake art form each winter with concerts, lectures, and other events that showcase local musicians as well as legendary artists.

Don't let the long winter nights get you down; embrace the darkness with the **Portland Winter Light Festival** (citywide; pdxwlf.com; Feb.; free). The annual festival showcases more than 100 art installations, performances, and workshops that incorporate the concept of light in one form or another. The light-up displays (many of them interactive), glowing art pieces, and fiery sculptures are magical after-dark experiences.

Every February **Zwickelmania** (citywide; oregoncraftbeer.org; Feb.; free) celebrates Oregon's craft beer scene with behind-the-scenes tours and tastings, food-and-beer pairings, new releases, and other fun events at breweries around town. Named for the valve mounted on a tank of beer, Zwickelmania takes place across two weekends: one starring Portland breweries and the other featuring breweries across the rest of Oregon. The event is mostly free, but pours of some just-released beers may cost up to $5.

Spring

The surest sign of spring's arrival is the **Portland Rose Festival** (citywide; rosefestival.org; May-June; prices vary) which, since 1907, has celebrated Portland with a variety of family events. The fun includes a carnival, multiple parades—including the **Grand Floral Parade,** featuring dozens of floats crafted with flowers—and Fleet Week, when visiting Navy ships dock on the Portland waterfront and offer tours.

One of Portland's many nicknames is "Beervana," so it's only fitting the city hosts a variety of outstanding beer festivals—many of which take place each winter and spring. Some of the city's creative events include the **Nano Beer Fest** (nanobeerfest.com; Jan.; $39-60), featuring beers from the region's smallest producers; the **SheBrew Brewfest** (shebrew.beer; Mar.; $30-60), which spotlights female-identified craft brewers and cider makers; and the **Baker's Dozen Coffee Beer & Doughnut Fest** (instagram.com/bakersdozenfest; Apr.; $30-60), which pairs a dozen doughnuts from local makers with a dozen beers featuring locally roasted coffee.

Summer

Portland's biking culture is the stuff of legend, and it's at its most playful during **Pedalpalooza** (citywide; pedalpalooza.org; June-Aug.; mostly free). Hundreds of bike-themed events and guided rides comprise the festival. Anyone can lead a ride, and most events are free and open to the public. Rides might revolve around enjoying breakfast on the city's famous bridges, pizzeria-hopping, or grooving to the music of Prince. The biggest of all Pedalpalooza rides, however, is the **World Naked Bike Ride** (pdxwnbr.org; Aug.; free)—when up to 10,000 bicyclists get as bare as they dare for a ride around the city; nominally, the ride is meant to highlight the vulnerability of cyclists, but many bike to

promote body positivity, protest our dependence on oil, or just because it's plain old fun. The route changes every year, and the ride is a huge event around town, akin to a lively parade, with people cheering and high-fiving riders en route. While the World Naked Bike Ride isn't a homegrown event—rides have been held in 20 countries around the world—Portland's is the world's largest.

Summer doesn't truly begin around town until the **Waterfront Blues Festival** (Governor Tom McCall Waterfront Park; waterfrontbluesfest.com; first weekend of July; one-day pass $35-40, four-day pass $105-230) kicks off along the Willamette River. The festival features four stages with live music, with a typically star-studded lineup that includes jazz, funk, soul, blues, and zydeco performers—capped off with a fireworks display on July 4.

Roughly a dozen bridges cross the Willamette River in Portland, hence the city's "Bridge City" nickname. **Providence Bridge Pedal and Stride** (begins and ends downtown; providence.org/lp/bridge-pedal; Aug.) offers cyclists the chance to cross up to nine of those bridges ($35-60), including some that

are closed to vehicular traffic for the event. Families can enjoy a free Kids Pedal with their little ones, and non-cyclists can take part in a walk ($25-35)—both of which cross two bridges.

Every summer, **Pickathon** (Pendarvis Farm, Happy Valley; pickathon.com; first weekend of Aug.; one-day pass $150-175 adults, four-day pass $350 adults, $175 teens 13-16, free for children 12 and younger) showcases a mix of musical styles from bluegrass to hip-hop in a magical forest setting on a farm just outside Portland city limits. Its intimate stages and scores of string lights lining trails in the woods make the festival feel like a fairy tale. Those with weekend passes can camp on-site. Roughly a dozen local food carts offer sustenance. Pickathon has also earned plaudits for its sustainable practices—a rarity for multiday music festivals; attendees purchase reusable pint cups and dishware (which make fun souvenirs) and take environmentally friendly transportation to and from the event.

Fall

Every September, the Portland Institute for Contemporary Art puts on its **Time-Based**

Portland Saturday Market

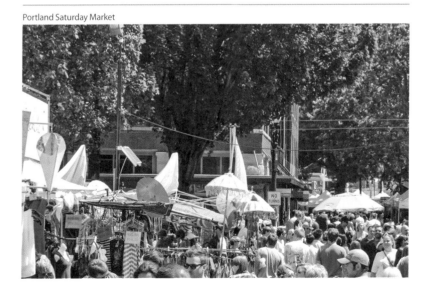

Art Festival (citywide; pica.org; Sept.; prices vary), which brings artists from around the world to Portland for exhibitions, multimedia productions, live concerts, and other thought-provoking events.

Portland is a literary city—and every autumn, the **Portland Book Festival** (South Park Blocks; literary-arts.org; Nov.; $15-25, free for children 17 and younger) brings together dozens of authors for discussions, pop-up readings, workshops, a book fair, and other fun events.

Shopping

The creative culture of Portland, along with a lack of sales tax, makes the city a fun place to shop. Locally produced goods are abundant and available at boutiques and markets around town.

DOWNTOWN AND THE PEARL DISTRICT

★ Portland Saturday Market

More than 150 local artisans sell their wares at the freewheeling **Portland Saturday Market** (2 SW Naito Pkwy.; 503/222-6072; portlandsaturdaymarket.com; 10am-5pm Sat. Mar.-Dec. 24), which has been going strong since 1974 and bills itself as the largest continually operating outdoor arts-and-crafts market in the United States. In addition to vendors selling paintings, wooden art, leather goods, and other crafts, a key part of the sprawling market's appeal is the vibrant atmosphere it creates each weekend at the edge of downtown. Set under the Burnside Bridge and in the shadow of some of Portland's oldest buildings, the market brings buskers and performing artists who enchant throngs of families, and open-air plazas along the Willamette River invite people-watching. The market's food court boasts nearly 20 chefs dishing cuisine from all over the world.

Arts and Crafts

Tender Loving Empire (412 SW 10th Ave.; 503/548-2925; tenderlovingempire.com; 11am-7pm daily) traffics in all things creative, with an eye toward community: The local chain sells locally made or designed home goods, jewelry, apparel, accessories, and works by hundreds of local artists. It also runs an in-house record label that's put out releases from a range of regional acts. An outpost is at the Portland International Airport.

In addition to running annual markets and mixers, **Crafty Wonderland** (808 SW 10th Ave.; 503/224-9097; craftywonderland.com; 11am-5pm Thurs.-Mon.) has a brick-and-mortar retail shop teeming with items made exclusively by Portland artists, with a varied selection that includes art prints, jewelry, apparel, books, and souvenirs. A second location is on NE Alberta.

Clothing and Accessories

Since 2014, **MadeHere** (40 NW 10th Ave.; 503/224-0122; madehereonline.com; 11am-6pm daily) has showcased the work of more than 200 makers, with an eye toward high-quality, upscale goods, and an emphasis on products by BIPOC creators. Apparel, jewelry, candles, apothecary items, and even Oregon-made pet food rounds out the selection.

Gifts

Since its first outpost opened in 1975, **Made in Oregon** (340 SW Morrison St., Ste. 1300; 503/241-3630; madeinoregon.com; 10am-6pm Mon.-Thurs., 10am-7pm Fri.-Sat., 11am-6pm Sun.) has earned acclaim for showcasing a wide range of products that are made, designed, or grown in the Beaver State. Decades on, the store's selection is limited only by what you can fit in your suitcase: gift baskets, wine, food items, kitchen accessories, Oregon-themed apparel—with many items from legendary Oregon brands, such as Tillamook

and Pendleton. This downtown location is in Pioneer Place Mall, but there's also one conveniently located at Portland International Airport.

SOUTHEAST PORTLAND
Clothing and Accessories

It's easy to get lost in the racks at **House of Vintage** (3315 SE Hawthorne Blvd.; 503/236-1991; houseofvintagenw.com; noon-7pm daily), where more than 60 vendors come together under one roof to sell retro clothing, pop culture collectibles, art, and other long-forgotten goods.

Record Stores

Far more than your run-of-the-mill record store, **Music Millennium** (3158 E. Burnside St.; 503/231-8926; musicmillennium.com; 10am-7pm Mon.-Sat., 11am-7pm Sun.) has been a Portland institution since opening in 1969. Today, the shop boasts one of the city's best selections of vinyl—from rare and out-of-print albums to the latest releases—along with tapes, CDs, and gift items. It routinely hosts in-store performances and other events.

NORTHEAST PORTLAND
Bookstores

Yes, there are bookstores in Portland besides Powell's. Part-bookstore, part-bar, **Rose City Book Pub** (1329 NE Fremont St.; 503/287-4801; rosecitybookpub.com; noon-midnight daily) is all fun. The shop is stuffed with new and used titles, which readers can flip through while nursing a regional beer or glass of wine. Seating is available indoors and out. The pub routinely hosts author events, live music, and trivia nights.

NORTH PORTLAND
Clothing and Accessories

Portland-based **Sock Dreams** (3962 N. Mississippi Ave.; 503/232-3330; sockdreams.com; noon-6pm Thurs.-Sun.) launched as an online-only venture in 2000 and today offers a selection of more than 1,500 styles. Browse the immense lineup at its brick-and-mortar shop, where you'll find trendy styles, fun patterns, and outlandish colors for folks of all ages and sizes. In addition to traditional socks, leggings, tights, and leg warmers are all accounted for here. A portion of profits from the sale of certain socks is donated to social justice-oriented nonprofits.

Food

Portland is at the forefront of **Pacific Northwest cuisine,** which focuses on sourcing ingredients locally—whether produce and mushrooms, beer and wine, or fish and meat—and incorporating them into creative takes on cuisines from around the world, from food carts to fine-dining establishments.

It's helpful to know that in addition to restaurants it's often possible to find a good meal in most bars around Portland. The Oregon Liquor and Cannabis Commission (OLCC) mandates that any establishment serving distilled spirits by the drink offer at least five of what regulators call "substantial food items" that are prepared on-site. And while some bars stick to the minimum and basic items like tater tots and fries, many deliver full menus and killer happy-hour deals on food as well as drink. Breweries aren't technically required to serve food, but many do in order to meet an OLCC family-friendly requirement; as such, many breweries welcome families.

DOWNTOWN AND THE PEARL DISTRICT
Pacific Northwest Cuisine

When it opened in 1994, ★ **Higgins** (1239 SW Broadway; 503/222-9070; higginsportland.com; 11:30am-9:30pm Wed.-Thurs., 11:30am-10:30pm Fri., 5pm-10:30pm Sat.,

Portland's Acclaimed Chains

Portland's vibrant culinary scene includes a few home-grown restaurants that now boast multiple locations around town, throughout the Pacific Northwest, and even across the country.

- **Pine State Biscuits** (pinestatebiscuits.com): The fluffy yet filling biscuits are of course the star at this Southern-inspired spot, and best enjoyed via gravy-laden biscuit sandwiches. There are four locations in Portland, including outposts on NW 23rd Avenue, Division, and Alberta.

- **Little Big Burger** (littlebigburger.com): This fast-casual burger joint sources its beef from a local rancher, tosses its fries in white truffle oil, and makes its own ketchup and fry sauce. It has nearly 10 locations around the city, including in the Pearl District, NW 23rd Avenue, Division, Alberta, and Mississippi.

- **Bamboo Sushi** (bamboosushi.com): In 2008, Bamboo Sushi was named the world's first sustainable sushi restaurant, and today the popular eatery has grown to four locations in Portland, with one downtown as well as on NW 23rd Avenue and Alberta. The original is on SE 28th Avenue, nestled along a small corridor of other eateries and bars.

- **Salt & Straw** (saltandstraw.com): Creative ice cream flavors abound at this celebrated chain; here, you can enjoy scoops crafted with, for example, lavender petals or Oregon olive oil. Three locations are in the city (NW 23rd Avenue, Division, and Alberta), each notorious for long lines. Tip: If you're just purchasing a pint to go, you can skip the line and head straight for the register.

- **Stumptown Coffee** (stumptowncoffee.com): Portland is synonymous with good coffee, and it all started with Stumptown. The chain is no longer locally owned, but it still pours a quality cup. Stumptown cafés are in downtown and SE Portland, as well as at Portland International Airport.

- **Coava Coffee Roasters** (coavacoffee.com): The newer cool coffee kid in town is locally owned Coava, which offers a single-origin menu that changes seasonally, makes its syrups in-house, and uses small-batch chocolate in its thoughtfully crafted mochas. It has three locations in SE Portland, including Hawthorne.

5pm-9:30pm Sun.; $26-47) was at the forefront of the farm-to-table dining revolution that would sweep through Portland in the ensuing years. Today, the fine-dining restaurant is no less a pioneer, serving risotto, pasture-raised meats, sustainably caught seafood, and other regional cuisine using local ingredients.

Vietnamese

Load up on Vietnamese favorites at **Luc Lac Vietnamese Kitchen** (835 SW 2nd Ave.; 503/222-0047; luclackitchen.com; 11am-2:30pm and 4pm-11pm daily; $10-21), a stylish counter-service eatery in the heart of downtown. You can't go wrong with the pho, served with house-made rice noodles and a beef broth made with five spices (a secret family recipe), but the restaurant's vermicelli

bowls, banh mi, and curries are also excellent. A selection of creative cocktails rounds out the menu.

Food Halls

Local vendors have come together to serve a wide range of cuisines and local libations at the **Pine Street Market** (126 SW 2nd Ave.; pinestreetpdx.com; 11am-8pm Wed.-Sun.; prices and hours vary by vendor), a massive food hall housed in a building that dates to 1886. Fill up on the likes of burgers, Chinese dumplings, and Latin American cuisine, and wash it all down at the **Pine Street Taproom** (11am-8pm Wed.-Sun.), an on-site bar slinging flavorful cocktails along with a dozen beers, seltzers, and ciders from local producers.

Doughnuts

You can't write about Portland's culinary offerings without a nod to **Voodoo Doughnut** (22 SW 3rd Ave.; 503/241-4704; voodoodoughnut.com; 5am-3am Sat.-Thurs., 8am-3am Fri.; $1-5), which launched in 2000 and earned worldwide notoriety for its doughnuts topped with ingredients like Oreo cookies, Cap'n Crunch cereal, and M&Ms. Voodoo's signature doughnut is the slightly salty, slightly sweet bacon maple bar. Its flagship location is here in downtown, where lines are common, but you can also head across the river for its less crowded **eastside outpost** (1501 NE Davis St.; 503/235-2666), which is open 24 hours daily.

Farmers Markets

Portland Farmers Market at PSU (along SW Park Ave. between SW College and Mill Sts.; 503/241-0032; portlandfarmersmarket.org; 8:30am-2pm Sat. Apr.-Oct., 9am-2pm Sat. Nov.-Mar.) started in 1992, when the idea of fresh, locally sourced produce was just gaining traction among conscious Portlanders. There are satellite markets around the city, but the longest-running and biggest is this weekly market at Portland State University, where up to 130 vendors take up four tree-lined city blocks year-round. Vendors sell produce, coffee, cheese, and baked goods, as well as hot food items (such as tamales and breakfast burritos). Joining the fun are buskers who bring a relaxed, upbeat vibe to the proceedings.

NORTHWEST PORTLAND

Bakeries and Cafés

Portlanders love their Sunday-morning baked goods, and **Ken's Artisan Bakery** (338 NW 21st Ave.; 503/248-2202; kensartisan.com; 8am-3pm daily; $4-12) has been a local institution since opening in 2001. The vaunted bakery's menu includes a range of breads, croissants, cookies, pastries, and sandwiches crafted with touches of creativity. The decadent Oregon croissant is stuffed with local berries and topped with pearl sugar.

SOUTHEAST PORTLAND
★ Food Carts

One of the city's oldest and best-known pods is ★ **Cartopia** (1207 SE Hawthorne Blvd.; cartopiafoodcarts.com), which is still going strong. It's home to eight food carts as well as a heated tent and three fire pits. Long-standing highlights include decadent Belgian-style fries, and particularly the poutine, from **Potato Champion** (503/477-7265; potatochampion.com; 11am-10pm Sun.-Thurs., 11am-11pm Fri.-Sat.; $8-13) and tots doused in fish sauce as well as two dozen beers on tap at **Bottle Rocket** (971/279-4663; bottlerocketburgers.com; 11am-1am daily; $6-11).

Two blocks away is a newer addition to Portland's food cart scene, the **Hawthorne Asylum** (1080 SE Madison St.). The pod hosts more than 20 food carts, including a bar cart with beer and wine, on an expansive and partially covered patio.

The Lot at John's Marketplace (3582 SE Powell Blvd.) is host to a handful of carts dishing fun fare. Craft beer lovers will appreciate **John's Marketplace** (3560 SE Powell Blvd.; 503/206-5273; johnsmarketplace.com; 11am-9pm daily), one of Portland's most beloved bottle shops. John's pours craft beer and cider on tap for those dining al fresco at the pod, which boasts plenty of covered seating.

For some of the city's best Latin American food, stop into **Portland Mercado** (7238 SE Foster Rd.; portlandmercado.org), where nine carts (along with a handful of indoor businesses) serve up fare from Mexico, Costa Rica, Cuba, Colombia, and Argentina. Fresh produce, smoothies, and local craft beers are also available.

Southern

★ **Screen Door** (2337 E. Burnside St.; 503/542-0880; screendoorrestaurant.com; 9am-2pm and 5pm-9pm daily; $14-27) has long been the standard-bearer of the Portland brunch experience—typified by hour-long waits on weekend mornings and a Southern-inspired menu that stars a towering stack

Food Carts in Portland

Food carts have been a Portland fixture for decades, but it wasn't until the Great Recession of 2007-2009 that the city's food-cart culture became a culinary phenomenon. Several factors collided to make it possible: Empty plots of land went undeveloped during the economic downturn, a generation of un- and underemployed creatives decided to pursue their dreams, and a low barrier of entry (in the form of cheap permits and fees) made mobile eateries affordable and easy to get off the ground.

Today, more than 500 food carts dot the city, dishing cuisine from around the world. And while a fair number of food carts move from point to point, what sets Portland's scene apart from others is that the majority remain planted in one location, typically in a pod with other carts. While some pods may be little more than a few carts and picnic tables, others have evolved into street-food dining destinations, with festive atmospheres including string lights, fire pits, covered seating, and on-site bars.

Developers in recent years have reclaimed many of the once-fallow parking lots that became fertile pod spaces, forcing some of the city's best-loved carts to find another home, open brick-and-mortar establishments, or close altogether, but surviving pods have become institutions and new pods continue to establish themselves.

We couldn't begin to list every last pod in the city, but we've included some favorites in this Food section.

If you're overwhelmed by the choices at any given pod, it's fun to turn a visit into a progressive feast, with small orders placed at multiple carts so you can sample widely.

of chicken and waffles, perfectly crisp praline bacon, and creative scrambles. These days, Screen Door's dinner dishes—a mix of comfort-food favorites and barbecue classics—are likewise earning raves. Reservations are recommended. A second, slightly less busy location is in the Pearl District.

Italian and Pizza

Classic, high-end Italian fare takes center stage at **Nostrana** (1401 SE Morrison St., Ste. 101; 503/234-2427; nostrana.com; 5pm-9pm Tues.-Thurs., 5pm-10pm Fri.-Sat.; $20-36), which features an ever-changing lineup of decadent pastas using locally sourced ingredients. Nostrana's thin-crust pizza is served unsliced, which you'll cut with a pair of scissors (provided). An excellent wine list spotlights Old World selections alongside regional favorites.

There's plenty of debate about the best pizza in Portland, but **Apizza Scholls** (4741 SE Hawthorne Blvd.; 503/233-1286; apizza-scholls.com; 4pm-7:45pm daily; $19-31) is always in the conversation. The purveyor

of neo-Neapolitan pies is known for its perfectly charred crusts, freshly sliced cheese, and a three-topping limit for balanced flavor profiles.

French

Canard (734 E. Burnside St.; 971/279-2356; canardpdx.com; 4pm-10pm Tues.-Sun.; $11-31), from acclaimed Portland chef Gabriel Rucker, artfully blends American comfort food with French elegance. The Steam Burger, for example, is an inspired take on White Castle's sliders, topped with pickles, onion, mustard, and gooey American cheese, while the Duck Stack features pancakes drizzled with duck gravy and topped with onions and a fried duck egg.

Right next door, Rucker's **Le Pigeon** (738 E. Burnside St.; 503/546-8796; lepigeon.com; 5pm-10pm Tues.-Sat.; $125) has been dazzling with French-inspired cuisine since 2006. Diners today eat their way through a five-course prix fixe meal (with a separate menu for vegetarians) that leans heavily on fresh, locally sourced ingredients. Dishes may include

seared foie gras, for instance, or a fresh summer risotto made with creamed corn, pickled cucumbers, queso fresco, and truffles. An excellent wine selection, featuring pours from all over the world, is a bonus. Reservations are required, and a 20 percent gratuity is automatically added to each bill.

Eastern European

Nationally acclaimed ★ **Kachka** (960 SE 11th Ave.; 503/235-0059; kachkapdx.com; 4pm-9pm Sun.-Tues. and Thurs., 4pm-10pm Fri.-Sat.; $11-32) dishes up some of the city's best cuisine from the former Soviet Union and eastern Europe, including dumplings, pickled fish, and borsch, lovingly prepared with local ingredients. Wash it all down with house-made infused vodkas.

Thai

Nong's Khao Man Gai (609 SE Ankeny St., Ste. C; 503/740-2907; khaomangai.com; 10am-8pm daily; $10-19) started life as a food cart and quickly became a local favorite, graduating to this colorful and casual brick-and-mortar eatery. It's run by titular James Beard-nominated chef Nong Poonsukwattana, who hails from Thailand. The star of her limited menu is, no surprise, khao man gai, a poached chicken and rice dish served alongside a house-made sauce bursting with ginger, garlic, and chili. A second downtown location serves the lunch crowd on weekdays.

Wings

Since 2005, the Grateful Dead-themed **Fire on the Mountain** (1708 E. Burnside St.; 503/230-9464; portlandwings.com; 11am-10pm Sun.-Thurs., 11am-11pm Fri.-Sat.; $13-17) has been showing Portland that the humble chicken wing can be more than a sports-bar afterthought. The chicken is sustainably sourced, and the lineup of 12 creative sauces are blended in-house daily; the bourbon-chipotle sauce, in particular, is recommended. Fire on the Mountain brews its own beer and hosts two other outposts around town—one in Northeast Portland and the other in North Portland.

Breakfast and Brunch

For more than 20 years, **Jam on Hawthorne** (2239 SE Hawthorne Blvd.; 503/234-4790; jamonhawthorne.com; 8am-2pm daily; $12-16) has earned citywide praise for a vegan- and veggie-friendly brunch menu, creative mimosas, and (of course) homemade jams that you can buy by the jar ($8). Scrambles and hearty entrées incorporate atypical ingredients—like huevos rancheros with smoked tempeh chorizo. Waits can reach an hour or more on weekends but are worth it. Outdoor seating is available when weather permits.

NORTHEAST PORTLAND
Thai

A few blocks north of Alberta, **Hat Yai** (1605 NE Killingsworth St.; 503/764-9701; hatyaipdx.com; 11:30am-9pm Sun.-Thurs., 11:30am-10pm Fri.-Sat.; $8-17) draws inspiration from southern Thailand—specifically, the city of Hat Yai on the Malay Peninsula. The casual eatery's menu focuses on regional street-food dishes, including perfectly crisp fried chicken, flavorful curries, and roti (a light, pan-fried bread). Some outdoor seating is available, and Hat Yai also has a second location on SE Belmont.

Indian

Bollywood Theater (2039 NE Alberta St.; 971/200-4711; bollywoodtheaterpdx.com; 4pm-9pm Thurs.-Sun.; $4-19) is a hip and high-ceilinged Indian eatery specializing in small plates of street food. Kati rolls, house-made paneer, vada pav (a potato dumpling dipped in chickpea batter and fried), and grilled tikka bowls are some of its most popular dishes. Photos, figurines, and other bric-a-brac adorns the walls, and old-school Bollywood films are occasionally shown in

1: steamed burgers at Canard 2: food carts in Portland 3: Matt's BBQ at Prost Marketplace

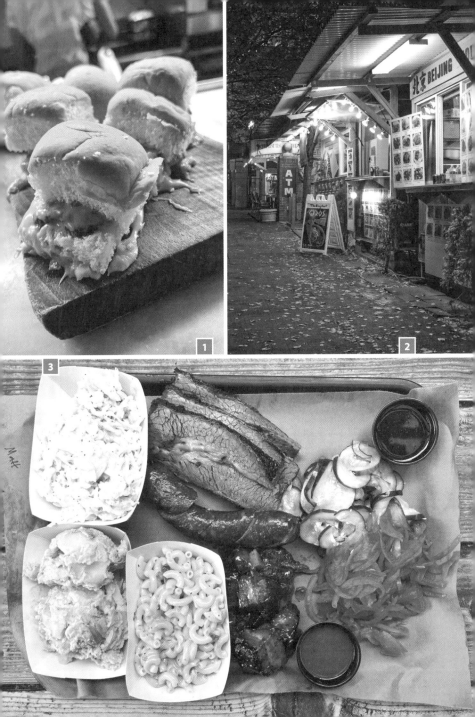

the dining room. A second outpost is on SE Division Street.

Argentinian

Ox Restaurant (2225 NE Martin Luther King Jr. Blvd.; 503/284-3366; oxpdx.com; 5pm-10pm Wed.-Sun.; $20-83) uses its mammoth wood-fired grill to prepare steaks, halibut, even spaghetti squash in Argentinian style. In addition to the meat-forward main dishes, Ox offers a salad menu teeming with locally sourced ingredients, creative appetizers, and a curated selection of wines from around the world.

NORTH PORTLAND
★ Food Carts

Prost Marketplace (4233 N. Mississippi Ave.) has grown over the years into a boozy Shangri-La at the north end of the Mississippi corridor; the pod shares space with German beer bar **Prost!** (4237 N. Mississippi Ave.; 503/954-2674; 11am-2:30am daily) and locally crafted beers and creative cocktails are available at the **Bloodbuzz** cart (no phone; bloodbuzzpdx.com; 8am-10pm daily). The handful of food carts include local stalwarts: **Matt's BBQ** (503/504-0870; 11:30am-8pm Sun.-Thurs., 11am-9pm Fri.-Sat. or until sold out; $10-15) dishes some of the city's best barbecue, **Fried Egg I'm in Love** (503/8690-5915; friedegglove.com; 8am-2pm; $4-11) serves filling breakfast sandwiches, and **Burger Stevens** (503/801-8017; burgerstevens.com; noon-7pm Mon., 11am-7pm Fri.-Sun.; $8-12) offers drool-worthy smash burgers. Covered and heated seating is available.

Pizza

Lovely's Fifty Fifty (4039 N. Mississippi Ave., Ste. 101; 503/281-4060; lovelys5050.com; 5pm-10pm daily; pizzas $15-29, ice cream $6-13) takes two classic dishes associated with childhood—pizza and ice cream—and imbues each with an elevated sense of care and craft. The wood-fired pizzas are topped with organic ingredients sourced exclusively from Oregon farms (pies topped with fresh heirloom tomatoes are a late-summer treat), while inventive ice cream flavors (such as cantaloupe and blackberry buttermilk) rotate seasonally. A small patio overlooks the perpetually busy Mississippi Avenue.

Thai

Eem (3808 N. Williams Ave., Ste. 127; 971/295-1645; eempdx.com; 11am-3pm and 4:30-9pm daily; $7-18) pairs its creative Thai dishes with an inventive cocktail menu. The menu is small but silly with highlights: fried rice with locally smoked brisket, savory curries with burnt ends and seasonal veggies, and some of the city's best sweet-and-sour fried chicken. Potted and hanging plants fill the interior, where massive windows let in plenty of natural light. Some outdoor seating is also available.

Mexican

¿Por Qué No? (3524 N. Mississippi Ave.; 503/467-4149; porquenotacos.com; 11am-10pm Mon.-Sat., 11am-9:30pm Sun.; $5-16) is Portland's busiest taqueria, thanks to a lineup of creative tacos crafted with organic, locally sourced ingredients and an interior and patio space decorated with bright floral tablecloths, string lights, and papel picado (Mexican-style decorative paper). Tamales, bowls, and a rotating cast of house-made agua frescas round out the menu. Another location is on SE Hawthorne Boulevard. Both restaurants offer outdoor seating and are typically jam-packed—so aim for an early lunch or happy hour to miss the longest lines.

Accommodations

Portland hosts a wide range of lodgings, from laid-back neighborhood hostels to upscale hotels in the heart of downtown. In addition to what's listed here, all the major chains can be found around town, as can vacation rentals.

DOWNTOWN AND THE PEARL DISTRICT
$150-250

Just a few blocks from downtown proper, **Hotel deLuxe** (729 SW 15th Ave.; 503/219-2094; provenancehotels.com/hotel-deluxe-portland; $210-366) boasts an elegant art deco aesthetic, retro-inspired room decor, mini bars stocked with selections from local producers, an old-school eatery, and a 1950s-inspired cocktail lounge. Other welcome touches include electric-vehicle charging stations and free bike rentals.

Housed in a building that dates to 1881, **The Society Hotel** (203 NW 3rd Ave.; 503/445-0444; thesocietyhotel.com; hostel beds $57, private rooms $100-300) offers a stylish mix of 62 private and hostel-style bunk rooms not far from downtown. Budget-friendly, minimalist rooms are clean but snug; only suites come with private bathrooms. A café and bar serve hungry guests on the 1st floor, and artifacts from the building's long history dot its walls. This is the place to be if you want to party in the city—you're smack in the middle of Portland's Entertainment District, full of nightclubs—but not if you want a good night's sleep. Note that this hotel is located in Portland's Old Town Chinatown neighborhood, where many of the city's social services are based, and you may encounter unhoused individuals and people struggling with addiction.

The **Hoxton Portland** (15 NW 4th Ave.; 503/770-0500; thehoxton.com/portland; $206-302) is a hip hotel that feels a bit like a

The Society Hotel

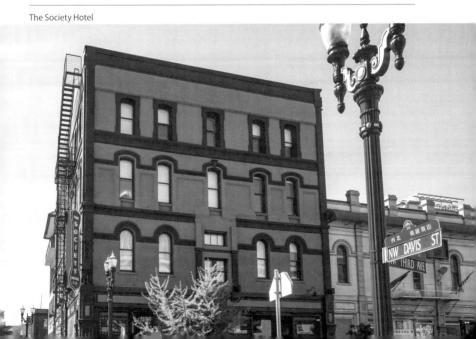

time machine: The exposed brick and original timber beams hearken back to the building's earliest days as a ramshackle lodging in the early 1900s, while its 119 rooms feature modernist touches, such as brass-accented lighting, that feel straight out of the 1960s. Rooms range from "Shoebox" and "Snug" to "Cosy" and "Roomy." Three restaurants and lounges are on-site, including **Tope,** a rooftop restaurant and bar with excellent skyline views.

Over $250

★ **The Nines Hotel** (525 SW Morrison St.; 503/222-9996; thenines.com; $321-939) may be located in a downtown building that dates to 1909, but it oozes modern, sophisticated charm. Rooms sport bright colors and vintage design patterns, plush bedding, and artwork by local college students—just some of the more than 400 works dotting the hotel at large. The Nines' atrium lets in plenty of natural light, inviting guests to unwind in cushy common seating areas. Amenities include a fitness center; **Urban Farmer,** an on-site restaurant; and **Departure,** a rooftop bar boasting views of the downtown skyline.

★ **Ace Hotel Portland** (1022 SW Harvey Milk St.; 503/228-2277; acehotel.com; $239-399) exudes a laid-back brand of vintage hipness that fits in nicely with Portland's kind of cool. Rooms range from basic, no-frills lodgings with shared bathrooms to larger, studio-like spaces with couches and desks, generally decorated with charming artwork, exposed brick walls, large windows, and (in some rooms) record players with vinyl.

Since 1927, ★ **The Heathman Hotel** (1001 SW Broadway; 503/241-4100; provenancehotels.com/the-heathman-hotel; $235-609) has been synonymous with luxury in downtown Portland. The 10-story hotel offers 150 pet-friendly rooms with plush bedding, flat-screen televisions, and in-room French press coffeemakers. Some rooms have views of the surrounding downtown scenery. An outstanding art collection is on view around the property and there's an on-site fitness center

and a library that boasts more than 2,700 titles signed by their authors.

Sentinel Hotel (614 SW 11th Ave.; 503/224-3400; provenancehotels.com/sentinel-hotel; $287-560) has been welcoming guests in some form or other since 1909 and today offers a luxurious stay, with leather and tweed furniture, in-room Bluetooth stereos, and pillowtop mattresses. Other offerings include free loaner bikes, health-and-wellness perks, and a trio of on-site lounges and eateries, including the old-school **Jake's Grill,** which serves steaks and seafood.

Even with the Willamette River running through town, waterfront lodging is a rarity in Portland. But **Kimpton RiverPlace Hotel** (1510 S. Harbor Way; 503/228-3233; riverplacehotel.com; $368-436) fills that void admirably. Situated steps from the river, it offers an elegant stay near downtown. Amenities include nightly wine receptions, yoga mats in every room, a kid-friendly DVD loaner library, two Tesla charging stations, and an on-site restaurant serving seafood.

Open since 1913, **The Benson Hotel** (309 SW Broadway; 503/228-2000; bensonhotel.com; $210-682), with its Italian marble floors and Austrian chandeliers, has attracted well-heeled visitors from around the world, including several celebrities and U.S. presidents. Today, The Benson retains an air of old-school elegance with 287 rooms, a well-appointed fitness center, meeting spaces for business travelers, and overnight shoeshine service.

NORTHWEST PORTLAND
Under $150

Northwest Portland Hostel & Guesthouse (479 NW 18th Ave.; 503/241-2783; nwportlandhostel.com; hostel beds $44-46, private rooms $99-149) is housed in the heart of a residential neighborhood not far from downtown and offers an excellent stay for budget-minded travelers. Private rooms are spartan, and hostel-style bunk rooms (which have up to eight beds per room) are appropriately cozy, but live music, game nights, walking tours, common areas, two kitchens,

and an on-site café add to a convivial scene. All rooms have shared restrooms.

Over $250

The stylishly retro, locally owned-and-operated **Inn at Northrup Station** (2025 NW Northrup St.; 503/224-0543; northrupstation.com; $232-294) has rooms that feel more like studio apartments, thanks to kitchens or kitchenettes in each room, private patios and balconies, and colorful decor around the property. A rooftop terrace invites lounging on sunny afternoons. The inn's location in close proximity to bustling NW 21st and 23rd Avenues and situated along the Portland Streetcar line makes you feel close to the action.

SOUTHEAST PORTLAND
Under $150

The chic **Lolo Pass** (1616 E. Burnside St.; 503/908-3074; lolopass.com; hostel beds $43-47, private rooms $163) caters to active travelers who spend most of their days on the go. So private rooms are stylish but compact, offering little more than a bed and private bathroom, and hostel-style bunk rooms feature up to eight beds. All rooms include fresh towels and linens, blackout shades, and works by local artists. A **rooftop bar** teems with travelers and locals alike on sunny days, and a 1st-floor café serves an excellent cup of coffee.

Over $250

Locally owned-and-operated **Jupiter Hotel** (900 E. Burnside St.; 503/230-9200; jupiterhotel.com; $161-323) hosts rooms on the vibrant East Burnside corridor just across the river from downtown. It's a two-story, old-school motor court-style lodging that's been updated with local artwork, flat-screen TVs, sleek furnishings, and chalkboard doors in case you'd like to get creative. Across the street, sister property ★ **Jupiter NEXT** (900 E. Burnside St.; 503/230-9200; jupiterhotel.com; $261-403), a newer addition that opened in 2018, is a modern six-story boutique hotel that's decked out in similarly stylish decor but in addition offers sweeping city views via oversized windows, 60-inch televisions, and a 5th-floor (guests-only) patio overlooking downtown. On the hotel's first floor, **Hey Love** is known as much for the bevy of plants adorning its interior as its tropical drink selection and stellar brunch.

NORTHEAST PORTLAND
Over $250

A former schoolhouse dating to 1915, **McMenamins Kennedy School** (5736 NE 33rd Ave.; 503/249-3983; mcmenamins.com; $260-286) has 57 guest rooms, some featuring original chalkboards. A stay here puts you farther from the city center, but you'll be just a 10-minute walk from the eastern end of the Alberta Arts District and you can enjoy the venue's many amenities, including a restaurant, four bars, a movie theater, and a delightful saltwater soaking pool (free for hotel guests).

Information and Services

VISITOR INFORMATION

Your best bet for brochures, maps, and in-person recommendations comes at the **Portland International Airport Welcome Center** (7000 NE Airport Way; 503/284-4620; traveloregon.com; 9am-10pm daily), housed on the airport's baggage claim level; in addition to Portland-area guides, you'll find resources for destinations across the state.

Travel Portland (travelportland.com) doesn't maintain a visitor center, but its helpful website offers a broad overview of the city, arts and entertainment listings, and recommendations for making the most of your time in town.

NEWS OUTLETS

The Oregonian (oregonlive.com) is the state's largest newspaper and covers breaking news, food and drink, and outdoor recreation in the Portland area.

Other noteworthy publications include **Willamette Week** (wweek.com), a free alt-weekly that you can pick up around town that also has a robust website, and the once alt-weekly now online-only **Portland Mercury** (portlandmercury.com), which offers excellent coverage of the city's arts and culture scene. Both are great for checking out happenings while you're in town.

Portland Monthly (pdxmonthly.com) produces quarterly magazines and maintains an oft-updated website.

Transportation

GETTING THERE

Air

Portland International Airport (PDX, 7000 NE Airport Way; 503/460-4234; fly-pdx.com) is located about 10 miles (16 km) northeast of downtown, about a 20-minute drive without traffic, and is served by 16 carriers.

Airport Transportation

MAX Light Rail Red Line (trimet.org; 2.5-hour ticket $2.50, day pass $5) provides easy access between the airport and downtown Portland. Trains run every 15 minutes 5am-1:45am, and tickets can be purchased via debit cards and credit cards from on-site ticket machines or with mobile wallets and contactless cards at digital fare readers.

Eight **car-rental companies** operate at or near the airport, as do several **taxi companies** and **rideshare services.**

Train

Amtrak (800/872-7245; amtrak.com) operates several routes that pass through Portland's **Union Station** (PDX, 800 NW 6th Ave.), which opened in 1896. Its **Cascades** route runs stops in Portland and runs north-south along the I-5 corridor between Vancouver, British Columbia, and Eugene, with stops in Seattle, among other cities. The **Empire Builder** route runs from Portland east to Chicago, with stops in Spokane, Minneapolis, and St. Paul. The **Coast Starlight** route runs north-south between Seattle and Los Angeles and stops in Portland.

Bus

Greyhound (800/231-2222; greyhound.com) has three bus stops in Portland: two in NW Portland, one in NE Portland. It provides transit to and from destinations including Salem, Eugene, Hood River, Pendleton, and Baker City. All tickets must be purchased on Greyhound's website in advance.

POINT Intercity Bus Service (888/846-4183; oregon-point.com) operates routes between Portland and the northern coast, and between Portland and Eugene.

Travelers can catch a ride with **FlixBus** (855/626-8585; flixbus.com), which provides direct routes to and from regional communities, including Salem, Corvallis, and Eugene. The budget-friendly carrier has earned acclaim for offering free Wi-Fi and power outlets at each seat. It has two stops in NW Portland.

Car

I-5 runs north-south through Portland and into neighboring states, connecting the city with Seattle, Los Angeles, and San Diego. **US-26** runs east-west through Portland, heading west toward Seaside and Cannon Beach on the Oregon Coast and east to Mount Hood before heading into Central and Eastern Oregon. **I-84** begins just east of Portland and continues to Eastern Oregon and on through

Boise, Idaho, before ending near Salt Lake City, Utah.

GETTING AROUND

Portland is highly walkable in general, especially downtown and the Northwest neighborhoods. Bridges connecting the central westside and eastside have sidewalks, making it easy to hop across the river. Neighborhoods tend to get farther flung on the eastside, when hopping on a bus can be helpful.

Public Transportation

Portland is well-served by public transit, all of it operated by **TriMet** (503/238-7433; tri-met.org; 2.5-hour ticket $2.50, day pass $5), which is equipped with bike racks as well as GPS technology so you can track arrivals in real time. Tickets are good for both buses and trains, so you can transfer between them. Public transit options are widespread and reliable, so a rental car may not be necessary if the city is your only destination. Even if you're continuing on, consider waiting to rent a car until you're ready to leave town so you don't need to deal with parking and related expenses. Hotels tend to charge $15-25 per day for parking lots or $25-50 per day if they have valet parking.

Buses are the most common way to get around town, with more than 80 routes crisscrossing Portland. Many routes begin running 4:30am-5am and continue until 1:30am or later, and the most popular routes run every 15 minutes or less. If you're riding 8pm-5am, you can ask the bus driver to stop anywhere along your route; just be sure to request your stop at least one or two blocks in advance. Tickets are available upon boarding. Useful routes for travelers include buses **2** (Division), **4** (Fessenden; stops along Mississippi), **8** (Jackson Park/NE 15; stops at Alberta), **14** (Hawthorne), and **15** (Belmont), which connect downtown to eastside destinations.

MAX light-rail trains run through all five quadrants, connecting downtown to the city's suburbs. Tickets are available at ticket machines or digital fare readers, both of which are available at all MAX stops. There are five MAX lines; for travelers, the most useful are likely the **Red and Blue Lines;** the former connects to the airport, and both lines include stops at Washington Park and the Oregon Convention Center.

A quaint but not particularly efficient way to get around town is the **Portland Streetcar** (503/222-4200; portlandstreetcar.org; 2-hour pass $2, 2.5-hour ticket also valid on TriMet $2.50, day pass also valid on TriMet $5), with three lines that loop around central Portland, including one that runs through NW and SW, and two that connect downtown with inner SE and NE Portland. Unlike MAX, the streetcars share the road with auto traffic, delaying arrivals and departures.

Bike and Scooter

Biketown (biketownpdx.com; $1 to unlock, $0.20 per minute) is Portland's bike-share program. The fleet of 1,500 orange e-bikes are equipped with pedal-assist technology, and 180 stations cover the quadrants. Riders need to sign up for Biketown via the service's website or mobile app and unlock bikes via QR code. Bikes come with lights but not helmets, so rent one or bring your own.

Electric scooter-sharing companies operating in Portland include **Lime** (li.me; $1 to unlock, $0.15 per minute), **Bird** (bird.co; $1 to unlock, $0.15 per minute), **Razor** (razor.com; $1 to unlock, $0.15-0.39 per minute), and **Spin** (spin.pm; $1 to unlock, $0.15-0.40 per minute). Note that Oregon law requires riders to wear a helmet while operating e-scooters, and scooting isn't allowed on sidewalks.

Helmet rentals are available from local vendors such as **Cycle Portland** (117 NW 2nd Ave.; 844/739-2453; portlandbicycletours.com; $10 per day) near downtown.

Taxi and Ridesharing Services

A few taxi companies operate in Portland, the most popular of which is the locally owned **Radio Cab** (503/227-1212; radiocab.net); passengers can get price estimates, book, and track their taxi's arrival through the

company's mobile app. No matter the company, taxis may take 30 minutes or longer to arrive when bars begin to close, typically midnight-2:30am.

Ridesharing companies **Lyft** (lyft.com) and **Uber** (uber.com) operate in Portland as well.

Car

Other than in downtown, where most streets are one-way, a grid system makes it easy to find your way around Portland. Note that I-5 and I-205 southbound slow to a crawl during the morning **rush hour** (7am-10am) and northbound during the afternoon rush hour (3pm-7pm). Traffic also slows considerably at interchanges with I-405, US-26, and I-84.

Expect to pay for **parking** (8am-7pm Mon.-Sat. and 1pm-7pm Sun. unless otherwise

noted) downtown, in NW Portland, and the city's inner SE and NE near the Willamette River. The farther you get from the city center, the more likely you are to encounter free street parking, typically with posted limits of 2-4 hours. Drivers can pay for parking via credit or debit card at pay stations or the **Parking Kitty mobile app** (parkingkitty.com), which buzzes with an audible "meow" when your session is about to expire and allows you to extend your time as allowed. If you find yourself downtown or in the Old Town Chinatown neighborhood, the city runs five **SmartPark garages** (portland.gov; $1.80-2 per hour) that are open 24/7, offer cheaper rates than privately owned lots, and accept validation stamps from certain businesses for limited free parking.

Biketown bikes

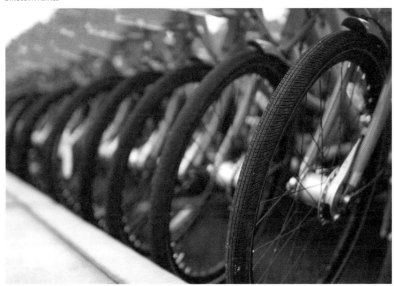

North Coast

Oregon's North Coast is a study in contrasts.
Just inland from the mouth of the Columbia River, the rainy, walkable
city of Astoria is a onetime fishing and logging community that has
seen its fortunes improve in recent years with the arrival of craft breweries and distilleries, must-visit museums, and a bootstraps culinary
scene where seafood is the star of the show; a bustling waterfront teems
with loudmouth sea lions and homegrown businesses taking over former cannery buildings. Farther south along the Oregon Coast, the likes
of Seaside, Cannon Beach, and Pacific City draw families in droves
with more conventional coastal attractions—windswept beaches, saltwater taffy, ice cream parlors, and perhaps the most-visited attraction
on the entire Oregon Coast: the famous Tillamook cheese factory.

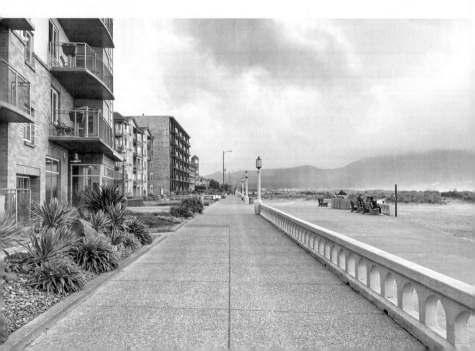

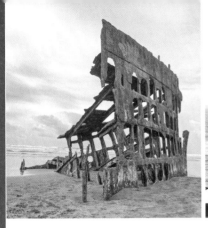
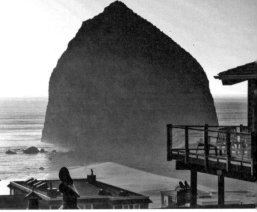

Highlights

Look for ★ to find recommended sights, activities, dining, and lodging.

★ **Visit the Columbia River Maritime Museum:** This popular museum tells the story of mariner life on the Columbia River through exhibits, interactive displays, and more (page 71).

★ **Step back in time at Fort Clatsop:** Walk through a replica of Lewis and Clark's 1805-1806 winter camp and learn about the duo's famous expedition (page 71).

★ **Walk up to a shipwreck at Fort Stevens State Park:** Walk right up to the half-submerged shipwreck of the *Peter Iredale* on the beach at one of the region's most popular parks (page 84).

★ **Stroll the Seaside Promenade:** The historic "Prom," as the locals call it, is a scenic (paved) walking path that borders the Pacific Ocean in the heart of Seaside (page 86).

★ **Gaze upon Haystack Rock:** The 235-foot (72-m) sea stack in Cannon Beach is among the most iconic sites on the Oregon Coast—and is home to tidepools and thousands of seabirds (page 91).

★ **Enjoy the sights of Oswald West State Park:** This park is among the most scenic—and popular—in Oregon, thanks to epic hiking trails and ideal surfing conditions (page 97).

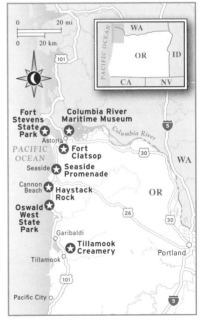

★ **Eat your way through the Tillamook Creamery:** See how the iconic creamery's cheese is made, learn about the region's renowned farming history and culture, and enjoy the company's delicacies—including ice cream and grilled cheese sandwiches (page 103).

What links the disparate cities is a close proximity to outdoor adventure—kayaking inlets and bays, hiking through coastal rainforests to windswept bluffs, watching for migrating gray whales just offshore, viewing massive sea stacks, and even surfing the Oregon Coast's frigid waters.

PLANNING YOUR TIME

Consider zeroing in on one or two specific towns or regions along the northern Oregon Coast when making plans; trying to cover too much ground risks long days of driving up and down US-101 while missing some of the area's best restaurants, sites, and outdoor opportunities. Any of the communities listed in this chapter can be explored in a **weekend;** if trying to see all the north Oregon Coast has to offer, consider spending **5-7 days.**

History buffs and craft beer geeks love **Astoria,** the oldest European settlement west of the Rocky Mountains—and home to a handful of beloved breweries (most boasting gorgeous Columbia River views); nearby **Fort Stevens State Park** can take a full day of exploration, so consider hitting one or two specific sites within the park if pressed for time. A mix of historic and hip lodgings make Astoria a fun getaway for couples and groups of friends; the town hosts a fun museum and is home to chattering sea lions, but better family destinations await nearby. If road-tripping the entire Oregon Coast, your trip south begins here.

Some 30 to 40 minutes south, you'll find a pair of beach communities—each appealing to different crowds. **Seaside** is a favorite weekend getaway destination for Portland families who love the arcade games, souvenir shops, and eateries along the **Broadway Corridor**—while **Cannon Beach** offers a more upscale experience with art galleries and fine dining; both afford easy beach access and close proximity to nearby outdoor opportunities.

Heading south, **Oswald West State Park** makes a popular day trip, with hiking trails and a lovely beach among its many charms. Next, you'll enter the **Nehalem Bay** area, home to **Manzanita, Wheeler,** and **Rockaway Beach,** about 20 to 30 minutes from Cannon Beach. Manzanita is the most popular of the three communities, thanks in part to a secluded vibe afforded by its location away from US-101.

At the southern edge of the north Oregon Coast sits **Tillamook Bay.** The inlet, along with the **Three Capes Scenic Loop,** shows off a mix of working fishing communities, sweeping headlands, small towns, and more. If you've ever wanted to shuck your own oysters or see migrating gray whales along the Oregon Coast, this is where to do it. **Pacific City,** meanwhile, hosts perhaps the most scenic brewery anywhere in Oregon, a handful of upscale inns, and easy access to outdoor recreation.

Previous: views from along the Seaside Promenade; the shipwreck of the *Peter Iredale*; Haystack Rock in Cannon Beach.

North Coast

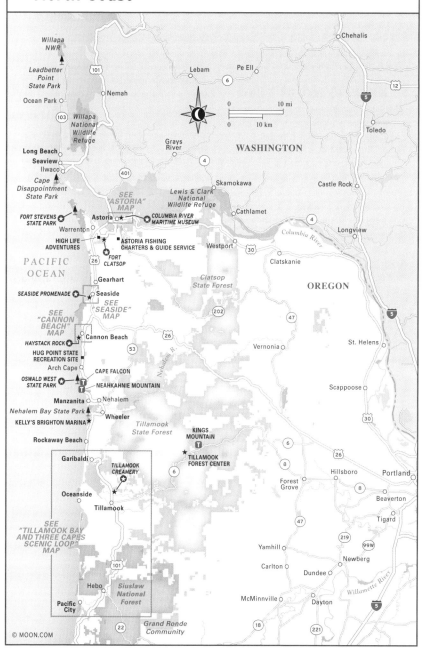

© MOON.COM

Astoria and Vicinity

Astoria sits near the mouth of the Columbia River at the far northwestern corner of Oregon—a trait that has defined the community since time immemorial.

European explorers first passed through while trying to find the mouth of the Columbia River—and tap into its potential as a hub for worldwide trade. That same impulse drove business magnate John Jacob Astor to establish a fur-trading post in Astoria; the first men from his party arrived in 1811, and today Astoria is the oldest U.S. settlement west of the Rocky Mountains.

The hilly community (pop. 10,000) developed in the early 1900s as a city of industry—most notably fishing. The last of the canneries that once lined the Columbia River are gone today, but echoes of the city's angling history remain in museums, repurposed processing plants, and a growing culinary scene. A sense of communal pride in the town's rebirth reverberates all over, especially through the popular refrain "We ain't quaint." In recent decades, Hollywood has taken a liking to Astoria—films such as *The Goonies* and *Kindergarten Cop* were filmed around town—and some of Oregon's biggest, best-known craft breweries have taken root in old auto dealerships and fish-processing plants.

Much of Astoria's appeal lies not just in the creativity displayed by chefs and brewers, but in its reputation as a working river town. Many of the buildings in the city's compact downtown core date back decades and exude a lived-in charm. Stroll the Astoria Riverwalk and you'll see anglers hauling in the day's catch, brewery workers shuttling kegs around the warehouse, and bar pilots heading out to help another ship cross the treacherous Columbia River bar. Stay up late and you'll get to know friendly locals in the town's darkened dive bars.

SIGHTS

★ Columbia River Maritime Museum

Astoria's past and present are inextricably linked to the Columbia River and Pacific Ocean at the city's doorstep—and there's no better place to learn about that tumultuous history than at the **Columbia River Maritime Museum** (1792 Marine Dr.; 503/325-2323; www.crmm.org; 9:30am-5pm daily; $16, $13 for seniors 65 and older, $5 for children 6-17, free for active-duty military members and children 5 and younger). A mix of permanent and rotating exhibits show off the history of fishing in and around Astoria (complete with replica boats and life-size fish displays), detail the treacherous terrain of the Columbia River bar (nicknamed the Graveyard of the Pacific), and honor local bar pilots who help guide ships through the mouth of the Columbia River. A 36-seat movie theater shows short, maritime-themed films in 3-D daily ($5).

★ Fort Clatsop

When Lewis and Clark's Corps of Discovery arrived at the Oregon Coast, not far from modern-day Astoria, in December 1805, the group erected a winter camp called **Fort Clatsop** (92343 Fort Clatsop Rd.; 503/861-2471; www.nps.gov; 9am-5pm daily Labor Day-mid-June, 9am-6pm daily mid-June-Labor Day; $10, free for children 15 and younger). The original encampment is long gone, but the site today is part of the larger Lewis and Clark National Historical Park, which spans the southern Washington Coast and the northern Oregon Coast.

A replica of that original encampment (constructed in 2006 and based on original sketches) invites visitors to experience what life must have been like for the explorers during an excruciatingly rainy winter; costumed

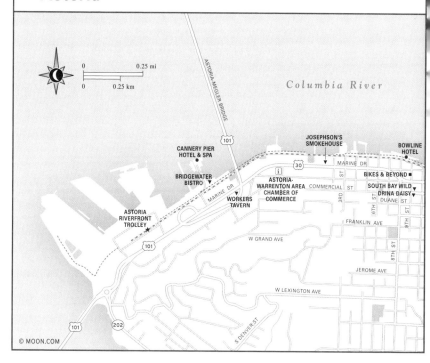

Astoria

Columbia River

rangers are occasionally on hand in summer to discuss the journey and the importance of Fort Clatsop. In addition to the replica camp, a visitor center hosts a bookstore and gift shop, and an exhibit hall details the Corps of Discovery's journey—as well as the role of York, an enslaved Black man who played an important part in the expedition. Two Lewis and Clark-related films play in an on-site movie theater, and several hiking trails crisscross the wooded area around the park. Restrooms and drinking water are available at the visitor center.

Astoria Column

Visiting the **Astoria Column** (1 Coxcomb Dr.; 503/325-2963; www.astoriacolumn.org; column open dawn-dusk daily, park open dawn-10pm daily, gift shop open 10am-5pm daily Oct.-Feb., 10am-6pm daily Mar.-Apr.,

9am-7pm daily May-Aug., 9am-6pm daily Sept.; $5 parking fee), and climbing its 164 winding steps, is a classic Astoria experience. Since 1926, the iconic column—painted with a European-centric mural that traces Astoria's history—has towered over the surrounding city while offering 360-degree views of the Columbia River, Pacific Ocean, nearby Youngs Bay, and nearby wilderness. A park at the column's base hosts a few picnic tables, restrooms, and a gift shop. If visiting December-May, keep an eye out for bald eagles in the treetops below.

Hanthorn Cannery Museum

Sitting at the end of Pier 39, **Hanthorn Cannery Museum** (100 39th St.; www.canneryworker.org; 9am-6pm daily; donations accepted) is housed in the oldest fish-processing plant anywhere on the Columbia

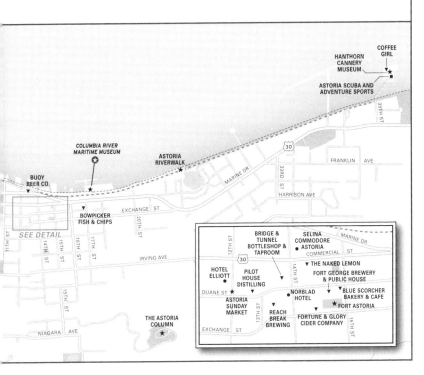

River. The ramshackle museum tells the story of the city's fishing and canning history through equipment displays, the occasional interpretive panel, news clips, and old documents from the cannery's heyday in the late 1800s and early 1900s. Funny enough, there was never an actual Hanthorn cannery, and the name was made up; this building was, for many years, home to the Bumble Bee seafood company. Organization is minimal, with few attempts to tell an overarching, chronological story—but the museum nevertheless offers an authentic look at an important part of Astoria's past. Even in summer, the museum can be chilly; bring a light jacket.

Astoria Sunday Market

Astoria is a community of makers, growers, and community-minded individuals—and nowhere is that clearer than at the **Astoria Sunday Market** (12th St., between Marine Dr. and Exchange St.; www.astoriasundaymarket.com; 10am-3pm Sun. early May-early Oct.). Every spring, summer, and fall, the market comes alive with farmers, food producers, and artists from all walks of life. Nowhere else on the Oregon Coast can you purchase handcrafted pasta, fresh herbs, handwoven baskets, and balloon art all in one place. Live music from local artists soundtracks the scene.

Astoria Riverwalk

Running 4.8 miles (7.7 km) along the Columbia River, the **Astoria Riverwalk** offers an enjoyable (and wheelchair-accessible) introduction to the city and its relationship with the river. The pathway, mostly paved with some sections of wooden boardwalk, runs from the mouth of Youngs Bay in the west to Tongue Point at the eastern edge of

Lewis and Clark National Historical Park

In all, five sites comprise the broader Lewis and Clark National Historical Park, which spans the southern Washington Coast and the northern Oregon Coast. Each of these sites explore some aspect of the Lewis and Clark Expedition, which lasted 1805-1806 and was authorized by President Thomas Jefferson to find an inland waterway to the Pacific Ocean. Meriweather Lewis and William Clark led the group, who camped near present-day Astoria (and the mouth of the Columbia River) from December 1805 to March 1806.

Today, the park's sites detail the journey, as well as the expedition's relationship with local Native American tribes, through interpretive panels and (at Fort Clatsop) a small museum. Here's a rundown of sites, along with what to know before visiting:

- **Sites:** In Washington, visitors can check out Dismal Nitch, where Lewis and Clark camped amid a brutal winter storm before seeing the Pacific Ocean. The park's four sites in Oregon include Fort Clatsop (home to a replica encampment and visitor center), Netul Landing (along the Lewis and Clark River), Middle Village and Station Camp (the site of a significant Chinook village), and the Lewis & Clark Salt Works (where members of the Lewis and Clark Expedition boiled water to produce salt) in Seaside.

- **Hiking trails:** Several miles of hiking trails cover the wooded areas just outside Astoria, following in the footsteps of the Lewis and Clark Expedition. The most famous of these is the 13-mile/21-km (round-trip) Fort to Sea Trail, which retraces the group's route between Fort Clatsop and the Pacific Ocean through muddy bogs and towering forests. Detailed information on hiking trails is available on the Lewis and Clark National Historical Park website (www.nps.gov).

- **Admission:** An admission fee (payable at the Fort Clatsop visitor center) is required at all Lewis and Clark National Historical Park sites. Admission is $10 per adult (valid for up to seven days) and free for children 15 and younger. Visitors can also purchase an Annual Oregon Coast Pacific Coast Passport for $35; the pass covers entry, parking, and day-use fees at all state and federal fee sites along the Oregon Coast.

town—all while offering river views throughout. Along the way, walkers, joggers, and cyclists pass Astoria's downtown core, some of the city's top destinations—including the **Bowline Hotel**—and, more often than not, the city's resident sea lions. Interpretive panels explain Astoria's industrial and cultural history. Access is plentiful from the downtown core; just walk toward the Columbia River, and you'll run into the path.

In summer, the **Astoria Riverfront Trolley** (www.old300.org; noon-6pm daily Memorial Day-Labor Day; $1-2) travels a central section of the Riverwalk; volunteer conductors discuss the city's history and offer tips for where to visit along the ride, which takes about one hour for a round-trip. Riders can wait for the trolley at nine stops—or flag the trolley down between stops by waving a $1 bill.

Fort Astoria

When John Jacob Astor sought to establish a fur-trading post in Astoria, his party set up camp and established **Fort Astoria** (15th & Exchange streets) in 1811—the first permanent U.S. settlement west of the Rocky Mountains. A British fur-trading company purchased the troubled post in 1813, and it was soon renamed Fort George; confusion about which country owned the fort reigned in the following years, but no matter: Fort George was abandoned in 1824. Today, a small park commemorates the early settlement with an interpretive panel, mural, and a reconstructed building. Note the green stripes painted on surrounding streets; these denote the fort's original boundaries.

RECREATION

Bicycling

Astoria occupies most of a thumb-shaped peninsula—bordered to the north by the Columbia River, and to the south by Youngs Bay—and is mostly hill. So if you're not up for a thigh-burning climb, the Astoria Riverwalk makes a fine ride for travelers on two wheels. The vast majority of the (mostly paved) path is protected from auto traffic, with countless opportunities to stop and enjoy the sights if you need to catch your breath.

If your hotel doesn't offer rentals, stop by **Bikes & Beyond** (125 9th St.; 503/325-2961; www.bikesandbeyond.com; 10am-6pm Mon.-Sat., 11am-5pm Sun.). The shop, a local mainstay since 1988, sits just a block from the Astoria Riverwalk and offers bike and e-bike rentals ($5 per hour, $20 per day)—as well as a wide range of repair and tune-up services.

Paddling

Given Astoria's close connection to the Columbia River, it's no surprise paddling is a popular pastime around town. Get on the river, not to mention the bays, inlets, and wetlands nearby, with a rental from **Astoria Scuba and Adventure Sports** (100 39th St.; 503/325-2502; 10am-6pm Tues.-Sat., 10am-4pm Sun.; www.astoriascuba.com). The outfitter offers sit-on-top kayaks ($25 for six hours, $50 for 24 hours), perfect for fishing and navigating the river's occasionally choppy waters, as well as stand-up paddleboards. Paddlers can drop into the water around Pier 39 from the shop or, provided they have transportation and the proper equipment, put in elsewhere around Astoria—such as at Coffenbury Lake at Fort Stevens State Park (page 84) or on the Lewis and Clark River at Lewis Netul Landing (page 74). Each rental includes paddles and a personal floatation device.

Fishing

Commercial fishing has been a historically important industry around Astoria—and remains so today. Each year, for instance, one million Chinook salmon pass Astoria on their migration up the Columbia River; other native species include coho salmon, sturgeon, and Dungeness crab.

Would-be anglers can join local charters, of which there are many. One popular guide is Jeff Keightley, who leads tours through **Astoria Fishing Charters and Guide Service** (503/436-2845; www.astoriafishing.com; $175-400). Keightley's tours cover all the usual suspects—salmon, sturgeon, steelhead, rockfish, and crab—with rods, reels, bait, tackle, and personal flotation devices included with each outing. Cleaning, vacuum sealing, and (when crabbing) cooking comes with each tour, as well.

Zip-Lining

Soar above the treetops with a tour through **High Life Adventures** (92111 High Life Rd., Warrenton; 503/861-9875; www.highlife-adventures.com; 10am-4pm Mon.-Tues. and Fri., 10am-5pm Sat.), based in a thick coastal forest just outside of Astoria. The standard, eight-line tour ($99, $69 for children 15 and younger) lasts about 2.5 hours, covers more than a mile of zip lines, and gets up to 75 feet off the ground while passing through a forest of fir, cutting across a large lake, and zipping over a few small ponds. High Life Adventures also offers on-site axe throwing ($40 for 30 minutes, $75 for one hour) if you prefer more ground-bound fun.

FESTIVALS AND EVENTS

Astoria is home to a wide range of annual events, many connecting with the city's history in one form or another.

Each year, the **Astoria Warrenton Crab, Seafood & Wine Festival** (www.astoriacrabfest.com; last weekend in April; $10-25 per day) celebrates the region's maritime industry with an event showcasing seafood, wine, and more from roughly 175 vendors.

Some of Astoria's earliest anglers were Scandinavian emigrants, and the **Astoria Scandinavian Midsummer Festival**

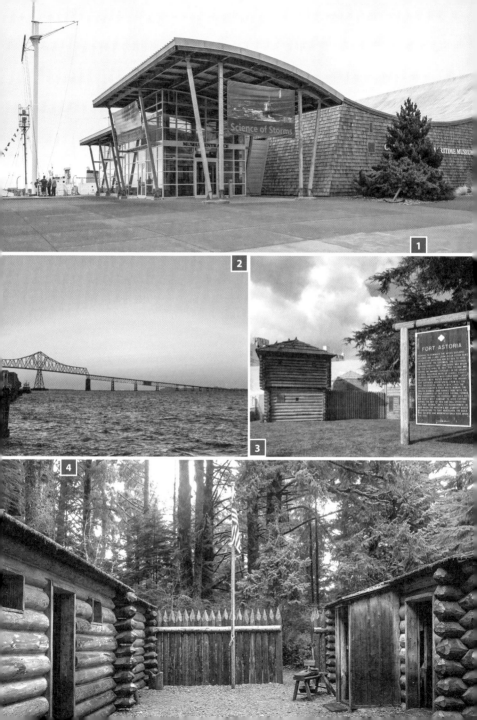

Oregon (www.astoriascanfest.com; June; $8, $3 for children 6-12, free for children 5 and younger) pays tribute to that history with a three-day festival with folk dancing, traditional food, live entertainment, and other fun events.

The annual **FisherPoets Gathering** (www.fisherpoets.org; last weekend in Feb.; $20) brings anglers and artists from around the world to Astoria each winter for a weekend packed with poetry readings, live music, film screenings, and other fishing-related events at venues all over town. Even if you're not an angler yourself, it's impossible not to be moved by poems, stories, and songs about far-off lands and life at sea.

BEER, WINE, AND NIGHTLIFE
Brewpubs and Cider Makers
The biggest brewery in town—and one of the most popular anywhere in Oregon—is ★ **Fort George Brewery & Public House** (1483 Duane St.; 503/325-7468; www.fortgeorgebrewery.com; noon-8pm Sun.-Thurs., noon-10pm Fri.-Sat.). The storied brewery sits on the site of the original Fort Astoria (later named Fort George); today, Fort George offers a beer-themed playground at three pubs across its campus, which takes up most of a city block. A small lounge invites visitors to sip fireside in one building, while pubs occupy two stories of another building—with a concrete courtyard offering outdoor imbibing in between. The brewery's IPAs and barrel-aged beers are highlights, but you can't go wrong with whatever you choose.

Since 2014, **Buoy Beer Co.** (1152 Marine Dr.; 503/325-4540; www.buoybeer.com; 11am-8pm Sat., noon-8pm Sun.-Fri.) has produced some of the best beer in Astoria, churning out dialed-in takes on a variety of classic styles; crisp, refreshing, flavorful lagers are among the brewery's many highlights. Buoy's food menu leans heavily on seafood; highlights

include fresh oysters from nearby Willapa Bay and an excellent rockfish-and-chips.

A relative newcomer to the Astoria craft beer scene, **Reach Break Brewing** (1343 Duane St., Ste. C; 503/468-0743; www.reachbreak.com; noon-8pm Sun.-Thurs., noon-9pm Fri.-Sat.) opened in early 2017 and has since earned acclaim for its ever-changing lineup of experimental offerings. Reach Break's Evolution IPA series features big, bold takes on double IPAs with new ingredients in every batch—not to mention a wide range of tart farmhouse ales, aged wild ales, and a few easy-drinking lagers. The brewery offers spacious outdoor seating, with on-site food carts dishing seafood, burgers, and more.

Astoria may be a beer town, but **Fortune & Glory Cider Company** (1450 Exchange St.; 971/704-2161; fgcider.com; 4pm-9pm Fri. and Mon., noon-9pm Sat., noon-6pm Sun.) has staked its claim as a purveyor of creative, refreshing ciders. Fortune & Glory's ciders use apples grown in the Pacific Northwest, along with beer yeasts that produce a slightly bitter, English-style beverage that foregoes the syrupy sweet flavors so common among ciders today. The cider maker's small-batch output means its tap list changes often; the only constant is that its ciders usually feature fascinating fruit combinations and inventive ingredients (such as botanicals and dried black tea).

Distilleries
The lone distillery in Astoria is **Pilot House Distilling** (1270 Duane St.; 503/741-3101; www.pilothousedistilling.com; noon-6pm Mon.-Sat., noon-4pm Sun.), which produces a lineup of easy-drinking whiskeys, canned cocktails, agave spirits, naturally infused vodkas, craft gins, artisan absinthe, and even coffee liqueur (using espresso beans from an Astoria-based coffee roaster). Pilot House routinely finds new, inventive ways to put a uniquely "Astoria" twist on its spirits; each batch of the distillery's "Come Hell or High Water" lineup of single malt whiskeys, for instance, is aged on various fishing vessels.

1: Columbia River Maritime Museum **2:** sunset from the Astoria Riverwalk **3:** Fort Astoria **4:** Fort Clatsop

Exploring the Long Beach Peninsula

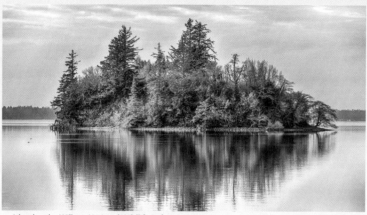

an island at the Willapa National Wildlife Refuge

Like many, you may be moved to drive across the dramatic, 4.1-mile/6.6-km **Astoria-Megler Bridge,** which connects Oregon to Washington and spans the Columbia River. And if you make the trip over to Washington, you should consider at least a day trip up the Long Beach Peninsula—long a regional destination popular with families and outdoor enthusiasts, buttressed on one side by the Pacific Ocean and on the other by Willapa Bay. Here's your guide to making the most of your time:

- **Cape Disappointment State Park:** The massive park (244 Robert Gray Dr., Ilwaco; 360/642-3078; www.parks.state.wa.us; 6:30am-dusk daily; $10 day-use fee) sits where the Pacific Ocean meets the Columbia River—hosting an interpretive center that explains the Lewis and Clark Expedition, disused bunkers and military batteries, easy beach access, two lighthouses, several miles of hiking trails, and a campground with more than 200 sites.

Bars

Every small town needs a community pub—and in Astoria that's **Bridge & Tunnel Bottleshop & Taproom** (1390 Duane St.; 360/244-5165; 11am-9pm Sun.-Thurs., 11am-10pm Fri.-Sat.). The pub's curated tap list shies away from beers brewed in Astoria, instead spotlighting nearly two dozen brews from throughout the United States (including some that are difficult, if not impossible, to track down anywhere else in Oregon); beer and cider from around the Pacific Northwest are available in a handful of well-stocked coolers, as well.

Astoria is likewise home to an eclectic lineup of dark dive bars that tend to attract fun-loving crowds from all walks of life. We could spend a whole chapter on Astoria's dive-bar culture, but the historic **Workers Tavern** (281 W. Marine Dr.; 503/338-7291; 9am-2am daily) is a notable standout. The laid-back bar has been slinging drinks for decades, is a popular local's haunt, and routinely hosts fun events (such as Meat Bingo, where players compete for slabs of store-bought meat). "Workers," as its informally known around town, also offers a back patio (with fire pits) beneath the Astoria-Megler Bridge and is perhaps best known for its Yucca—a vodka-based, lemon-flavored drink that you shake

- **Leadbetter Point State Park:** At the northern edge of the Long Beach Peninsula sits the park (northern end of WA-103; 360/642-3078; www.parks.state.wa.us; 6:30am-dusk daily; $10 day-use fee), which stretches from the Pacific Ocean (to the west) to Willapa Bay (to the east). The quiet park offers easy beach access, several hiking trails, and plentiful opportunities to spy native and migrating birds.

- **Willapa National Wildlife Refuge:** The quiet refuge (7112 67th Pl., Long Beach; 360/642-3860; www.fws.gov; dawn-dusk daily; free) was established in 1937 to protect migrating birds—and today encompasses a salt marsh, mudflats, old-growth forest, wetlands, and more. Pop into the refuge headquarters for more information on hiking, clamming, paddling, camping, and wildlife-watching in the waterways and forests just south of Willapa Bay (noted throughout the region for its tasty shellfish).

- **Local food and brews:** You'll find plenty of great food and locally crafted beer on the Long Beach Peninsula. The long-standing **Dylan's Cottage Bakery & Delicatessen** (118 Pacific Ave. S., Long Beach; 360/642-4441; www.cottagebakerylongbeach.com; 4am-5pm Wed.-Mon.; $2-10) is beloved for fresh-baked pastries, doughnuts, breads, and sandwiches; **The Depot Restaurant** (1208 38th Pl., Seaview; 360/642-7880; www.depotrestaurantdining.com; 4:30pm-8:30pm Fri.-Sat., 4:30pm-8pm Sun.-Thurs.; $29-48), housed in a converted train depot, specializes in Pacific Northwest fare crafted from locally sourced ingredients and fresh-caught fish; and **North Jetty Brewery** (4200 Pacific Way, Seaview; 360/642-4234; www.northjettybrew.com; noon-7pm Sun.-Tues., noon-9pm Wed.-Thurs., noon-10pm Fri.-Sat.) pours 16 house-made beers.

- **Overnight stays:** Several inns offer overnight accommodations on the Long Beach Peninsula. **Adrift Hotel** (409 Sid Snyder Dr., Long Beach; 360/642-2311; www.adrifthotel.com; $275-425) offers upcycled rooms alongside an on-site distillery and restaurant dishing locally inspired cuisine; **Boardwalk Cottages** (800 Ocean Beach Blvd. S., Long Beach; 360/642-2305; www.boardwalkcottages.com; $241-311) hosts 12 self-contained cottages a short walk from the beach; the historic **Shelburne Hotel** (4415 Pacific Way, Seaview; 360/642-2442; www.shelburnehotelwa.com; $209-309) is an elegant lodging and the longest continuously operating hotel in Washington; and **Salt Hotel** (147 Howerton Ave., Ilwaco; 360/642-7258; www.salt-hotel.com; $155-175) is a stylish inn boasting upcycled materials, an outdoor gathering space, and a 2nd-floor pub that overlooks Ilwaco's working harbor.

in a mason jar until the concoction turns into a boozy slushy. The tavern even hosts a pair of Airbnbs for overnight guests (www.airbnb.com; $116-176), one of which includes a pair of beds in frames crafted to resemble fishing boats.

FOOD
Seafood
Befitting its status as a historic fishing town, Astoria is practically swimming in fresh seafood; it's not uncommon to order a dish that was caught earlier that day. You'll find fresh fish, shrimp, and crab all over town, but these are a few favorite stops.

The family-owned-and-operated **South Bay Wild** (262 9th St.; 503/741-3000; www.southbaywild.com; 11:30am-8pm Wed.-Sat.; $16-21) opened in 2018—and quickly established itself as a premier purveyor of sustainably harvested seafood. The eatery comprises a sit-down restaurant (dishing seafood and chips, Native American-style fry bread topped with crab or shrimp, and even banh mi stuffed with oysters, grilled rockfish, or other fish) and a market selling fresh and smoked fish—much of it caught by one of South Bay Wild's co-owners.

The iconic ★ **Bowpicker Fish & Chips** (17th St. & Duane St.; 503/791-2942; www.

bowpicker.com; 11am-5pm Wed.-Sat. Mar.-Oct., 11am-3pm Wed.-Sat. Nov.-Feb.; $9-13, cash only) dishes its fried tuna out of a land-locked gillnet fishing boat, with a menu composed entirely of fish-and-chips. Visitors and locals alike line up all year long for the locally famous dish—crispy on the outside, flaky on the inside—with wait times occasionally topping an hour on bustling summer weekends. Note that Bowpicker closes due to heavy rains and howling winds; if the weather looks fierce, head online to see if the takeout spot is open that day.

Rising from the ashes of a beloved seafood restaurant that closed in 2017, **The Ship Out** (92351 Lewis and Clark Rd.; 503/468-0373; 11am-7pm Tues.-Sun.; $11-23) dishes some of the best fish-and-chips in town, with selections not commonly found at some of Astoria's more famous haunts. Standards like halibut and cod share space on the menu with the likes of fresh-caught steelhead and sturgeon, all beneath a lightly battered crust that puts the seafood front and center.

Bridgewater Bistro (20 Basin St., Ste. A; 503/325-6777; www.bridgewaterbistro.com; 11:30am-3pm and 4pm-8pm Mon., 11:30am-3pm and 4pm-8:30pm Tues.-Thurs., 11:30am-3pm and 4pm-9pm Fri.-Sat., 10:30am-3pm and 4pm-8:30pm Sun.; $12-36), housed in a historic cannery building, prides itself on serving upscale seafood fare crafted from locally sourced ingredients and fresh-caught fish. Highlights include oysters from nearby Willapa Bay, smoked salmon cheesecake, and wild-caught salmon; several chicken and steak dishes round out the menu, most of which is gluten-free. A small outdoor dining area (partially covered in fall, winter, and spring) affords dramatic views of the Columbia River and Astoria-Megler Bridge.

Eastern European

Drina Daisy (915 Commercial St.; 503/338-2912; www.drinadaisy.com; 4pm-8pm Wed.-Sun.; $18-25) specializes in Bosnian comfort food, dishing a menu unlike anywhere else in Astoria. Highlights include stuffed cabbage (available with beef or as a vegetarian dish) and a handful of pitas; unlike Mediterranean-style pocket breads, Drina Daisy's savory zeljanicas are filled with layers of filo dough, stuffed with a variety of fresh ingredients (including beef, spinach, and mozzarella cheese), and baked to order.

Bakeries and Cafés

For a fresh, filling start to your day, the worker-owned **Blue Scorcher Bakery & Café** (1493 Duane St.; 503/338-7473; www.bluescorcher.coop; 7am-3pm daily; $4-23) crafts a wide range of fresh-baked breads and pastries—along with quick-hit breakfast and lunch favorites (such as breakfast tacos and grilled cheese sandwiches). Ingredients are sourced locally whenever possible, with partner farms listed on a chalkboard in the airy café; several vegan dishes are available.

It's as much about the thoughtfully prepared food and piping-hot coffee as it is the views at **Coffee Girl** (100 39th St., Ste. 2; 503/325-6900; www.thecoffeegirl.com; 7am-4pm Mon.-Fri., 8am-4pm Sat.-Sun.; $2-11). Housed in an old cannery building at the end of a pier on the Columbia River, Coffee Girl serves up house-baked granola, scratch-made soup, toasty panini, and a variety of fresh pastries (crafted in-house); once you've ordered, cozy up next to the fireplace in the chic dining room—or, better yet, grab a table or bench outside, where unencumbered river views await.

What started as a pop-up bakery in 2016 has since transformed into one of Astoria's best-loved dessert destinations. **The Naked Lemon** (1423 Commercial St.; 503/741-3488; www.nakedlemonastoria.com; 9am-3pm Wed.-Sun.; $3-6), a Black-owned bakery, specializes in a creative assortment of handmade French macarons, as well as cupcakes, cookies, cakes, and other decadent desserts—all of it crafted and baked in-house.

Markets

Bring a taste of Astoria's famous seafood home with a little help from the

Bicycling the Oregon Coast

US-101 is one of the most scenic drives in all of Oregon—so it's no wonder the winding road is also enormously popular with cyclists, many of whom ride the entire length of the highway in Oregon each year.

Between Astoria and the California border, US-101 covers 370 miles/595 km (380 miles if cyclists explore the Three Capes Scenic Loop along the way) and boasts nearly 16,000 feet (5,000 m) of elevation change. Most riders take 6-8 days to travel the length of the coast, covering 50-65 miles (80-100 km) per day.

If you're interested in biking the Oregon Coast yourself, here are a few tips to get started:

- **Direction:** Most cyclists prefer riding north to south, which takes advantage of typical wind patterns and offers a nice tailwind. Riding north to south also offers easier access to turnouts and waysides—and offers the best views.

- **Getting to and from US-101:** If flying into Portland International Airport (PDX), you can take your bike on TriMet's MAX light rail line (which stops at the airport). Riders can then take The Point bus to Astoria (passengers can bring one bike, free of charge, if space allows) and begin their southbound ride there; the Oregon stretch of US-101 then ends at the California border. Getting back to Portland is a bit more difficult. Riders can take The Point bus between Brookings and the community of Cave Junction in the southern Oregon Cascades, at which point they can take a bus, provided by Josephine Community Transit, to the city of Grants Pass; there, riders can take The Point to Medford and fly home from the Rogue Valley International-Medford Airport—or catch a Greyhound bus north back to Portland.

- **Season:** Conditions are ideal between spring and early fall (May-early Oct.), with late August-early October being the best time to ride; otherwise, riders risk running into the downpours for which the Oregon Coast is so famous. And since several campgrounds offer hiker-biker spots, riders don't have to sweat reservations during the busy season (June-Aug.).

- **Maps:** The Oregon Department of Transportation (www.oregon.gov/odot/) provides an official Oregon Coast Bike Route Map that breaks down different segments of US-101 for cyclists—with elevation gain and loss charts, parks and amenities, tips for cycling across bridges and through tunnels, and more. Riders can also visit www.RideOregonRide.com for suggestions on where to ride, eat, and stay on their trips.

- **Caution:** Road shoulders can be quite small, and protected bike lanes are almost non-existent along US-101; keep an eye out for inattentive drivers whenever possible, especially through congested communities.

family-owned-and-operated **Josephson's Smokehouse** (106 Marine Dr.; 503/325-2190; www.josephsons.com; 11am-5pm daily). Since 1920, the market has sold smoked seafood (available hot or cold), a wide variety of canned seafood products (including albacore tuna, coho salmon, and rainbow trout), and flavorful salmon jerky.

ACCOMMODATIONS

Housed in a onetime seafood cannery and icehouse, the luxe **Bowline Hotel** (1 9th St.; 503/325-7546; www.bowlinehotel.com; $292-520) imbues each of its 40 rooms with a touch of Astoria's past and present. Exposed (original) beams dot the property, while rooms—some right on the river, others facing the Astoria Riverwalk—spotlight ceramics, blankets, coffee, tea, and more from local makers. Each room comes with a private balcony or patio; other amenities include an outdoor fire pit, an on-site cocktail bar and lounge, an electric vehicle charging station, and loaner bikes. The boutique hotel even offers earplugs in case the area's resident sea lions act up.

There may be no more iconic hotel in Astoria than the ★ **Cannery Pier Hotel & Spa** (10 Basin St.; 503/325-4996; www.cannerypierhotel.com; $509-1,299), built at the end of a pier on the Columbia River—and offering unbeatable views of the Astoria-Megler Bridge nearby. Housed on the site of a long-gone fish-packing company, the hotel puts luxury front and center with clawfoot tubs, jetted tubs, riverfront balconies, in-room fireplaces, and cozy bedding. Binoculars are provided to let guests monitor river traffic, and an on-site spa provides facials, massages, body treatments, and waxing.

Come for the easy downtown access, stay for the chic stylings of the locally owned **Norblad Hotel** (443 14th St.; 503/325-6989; www.norbladhotel.com; $109-300). The hotel (not wheelchair-accessible) sits in the heart of downtown and within an easy walk of most of the city's best-loved restaurants and attractions. Its cabins and suites (some with shared restrooms and showers) include pillow-top bedding and fast Wi-Fi; a loaner record player is available if you'd like to spin some vinyl in your room. Suites in the Astor Building (one block away) offer impressive views and high-end, vintage-inspired furnishings.

Also in downtown is the **Selina Commodore Astoria** (258 14th St.; 503/325-4787; www.selina.com; $229-356). The stylish (pet-friendly) hotel is adorned with colorful, vintage-inspired furniture, retro lighting, local artwork, and comfortable beds. Rooms generally run small, and some feature shared bathrooms. Friendly heads-up: The hotel sits along a main thoroughfare through town and is an older building—and offers earplugs to help counteract street noise and creaky hardwood floors.

Stepping into the 32-room **Hotel Elliott** (357 12th St.; 503/325-2222; www.hotelelliott.com; $279-359) feels a bit like stepping back in time. The hotel's Victorian design and ambiance is apparent in handcrafted bed linens and cabinetry and in-room fireplaces. A rooftop deck and garden affords 360-degree views of the city—from the Victorian homes dotting Astoria's hillsides to the rambling Columbia River.

INFORMATION AND SERVICES

The **Astoria-Warrenton Area Chamber of Commerce** (111 W. Marine Dr.; 503/325-6311; www.oldoregon.com; 9am-5pm Mon.-Fri., 10am-4pm Sat.-Sun.) is a good source for brochures, pamphlets, maps, recreation passes, and souvenirs. (The 1985 film *The Goonies* was filmed in and around Astoria, so you'll find plenty of movie-inspired merch, along with tips for visiting filming locations around town.)

GETTING THERE

Drivers coming from Portland have a few options for heading to Astoria, each with its own charms.

The most direct route is to take US-26 westbound out of downtown; when the road descends from the Oregon Coast Range and ends at the coast, follow US-101 north into town. The 95-mile (153-km) drive takes about 1 hour, 50 minutes.

Another popular route involves driving Interstate 5 northbound into Washington, crossing the state line at Longview, and taking US-30 westbound into town; the 99-mile (159-km) drive generally takes about 1 hour, 50 minutes—but can take longer if rush-hour traffic on I-5 slows to a crawl (as it so often does) 2pm-7pm on weekdays.

Drivers looking to enjoy a slower pace can simply take US-30 northwest out of Portland, mostly hugging the Columbia River the whole way; the 97-mile (156-km) drive usually takes about 2 hours.

The Point (888/846-4183; www.oregonpoint.com; $18 each way) runs twice-daily bus service between the Astoria Transit Center (900 Marine Dr.) and Union Station in downtown Portland (800 NW 6th Ave.); the bus also stops in nearby Warrenton,

---

1: Cannery Pier Hotel & Spa **2:** Bowpicker Fish & Chips **3:** Bridge & Tunnel Bottleshop & Taproom **4:** the shipwreck of the *Peter Iredale*

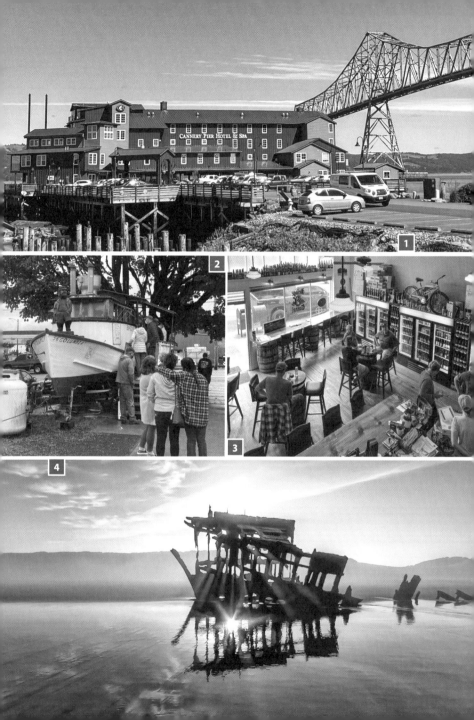

Gearhart, Seaside, and Cannon Beach along the way. **NW Connector** (503/861-7433; www.nworegontransit.org; $15) also offers thrice-daily bus service between the Astoria Transit Center and Portland's Union Station, with several stops in communities on US-30 along the way.

GETTING AROUND

Astoria is an extremely walkable city—unless you're hankering to hike up the city's steep hillsides.

Bus service around Astoria and to other communities on the north coast is available via **NW Connector** (503/861-7433; www.nworegontransit.org). If you'd rather drive, **Enterprise Rent-a-Car** (261 W. Marine Dr.; 503/325-6500; www.enterprise.com) offers rentals (Mon.-Fri.) at the western edge of town.

★ FORT STEVENS STATE PARK

Nestled at the mouth of the Columbia River, **Fort Stevens State Park** (100 Peter Iredale Rd., Hammond; 503/861-3170, ext. 21; www.stateparks.oregon.gov; sunrise-sunset daily; $5 day-use fee) occupies the site of a military installation that dates back to the Civil War,

when an earthen fort was constructed to protect the area. Later on, it served as the state's only coastal defense fort through World War I and World War II. The post was eventually abandoned and today is one of the state's most sprawling parks—complete with numerous historic sites, opportunities for outdoor recreation, a massive campground, and a popular disc golf course.

Sights

Far and away, the park's most famous (and most photographed) attraction is the **Peter Iredale** shipwreck. In 1906, the British sailing ship *Peter Iredale* ran aground near the mouth of the Columbia River, its wreckage instantly becoming a local curiosity. (Thankfully, no one died.) Today, visitors can walk right up to the remnants of the ship, which remain half-buried in the surf near the southern edge of the park. Head west through the campground, following signs for the shipwreck; a small, sandy parking area hosts restrooms and offers easy access to wreckage.

If driving to the shipwreck through Fort Stevens's campground entrance, it's worth a quick detour to one of two day-use sites centered around the quiet, freshwater

a military battery in the Historic Area at Fort Stevens State Park

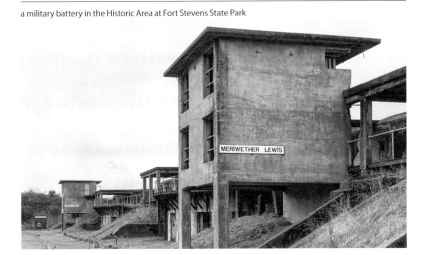

Coffenbury Lake, which is completely surrounded by a peaceful forest of fir, spruce, and pine. A flat, two-mile (3.2 km) hiking trail circles the lake, and paddlers with their own kayaks, canoes, or stand-up paddleboards can get on the water via docks and boat ramps at both day-use sites. Restrooms and picnic shelters are available at both day-use sites, not far from the lakeshore.

To the north is **Battery Russell,** constructed in 1904. When built, Battery Russell became the ninth such outpost at Fort Stevens. The concrete structure remains today and is open to visitors who want to climb its stairs and explore the eerie labyrinth. Access Battery Russell by following signs from the day-use entrance area in the heart of the park. Vault toilets are available at the parking area.

Farther north is the large **Historic Area,** centered around a visitor center and military museum (503/861-2000; www.visitftstevens. com; 10am-3pm Thurs.-Mon.) that offers a fine introduction to the park's history as a military outpost. From the main parking area, you can take a self-guided walking tour of several concrete batteries and encampments, as well as the site of a former Clatsop village. If exploring all 21 sites in the Historic Area, give yourself at least three hours. Restrooms are available near the visitor center.

And at the far northern edge of the park is the **South Jetty area** (sunrise-sunset daily), home to a pair of observation sites near the end of a spit that stretches into the Columbia River. From a pair of parking areas, you can climb into an observation tower or wildlife bunker and spy native and migrating birds, as well as deer and elk, in the surrounding woodlands and (on the east side of the spit) on the waters of Trestle Bay. Vault toilets are available at both observation areas.

Recreation

Newbies and veterans alike find plenty to love about the **Columbia Shores Disc Golf Course.** The course sports a mix of shorter and longer holes, generally shifting between wide-open meadows and more challenging holes in Sitka spruce forests; the 16th hole, in particular, measures just over 1,000 feet (300 m) long. Views range from the Columbia River to some of the military installation sites dotting the park. Cut yourself some slack when the region's famously furious winds knock your disc off course. And if you didn't bring your own discs, purchase a set at the park's visitor center and ranger station. Note that some holes are closed in winter—so be sure to follow and any all signage to avoid running afoul of park rules.

Accommodations

Fort Stevens hosts a sprawling, year-round **campground** (503/861-3170, ext. 21; www. stateparks.oregon.gov) that boasts 174 full-hookup sites, 36 of which are pull-through ($26-38); 302 electrical sites with water, 11 of which are pull-through ($24-35); six basic tent sites ($17-23); nine walk-in sites with parking nearby ($11); 15 yurts, 7 of which are pet-friendly and all of which offer power, heat, bunkbeds, and a futon couch ($43-64); and 11 deluxe cabins, 5 of which are pet-friendly and all of which include power, heat, private bathrooms with showers, and kitchenettes ($89-108). Eight cabins and 10 yurts are wheelchair accessible. Campground-wide amenities include flush toilets and hot showers; firewood is available to purchase and can be delivered directly to your site.

Fort Stevens is enormously popular—so book as soon as the reservation window opens (six months out) if planning a weekend visit in summer. Yurts and cabins are generally snapped up first, though you'll have an easier time finding those lodgings on off-season trips.

Getting There

From downtown Astoria, the 9.5-mile (15.3-km) drive to Fort Stevens State Park takes about 20 minutes via US-101, OR-104S, and NW Ridge Road. Plenty of signs point the way from US-101 and along the way to the park's many sites.

Seaside and Cannon Beach

Just 30 minutes south of Astoria via US-101 sit Seaside and Cannon Beach—and an Oregon Coast experience that couldn't be more different.

The Lewis and Clark Expedition arrived in the area in 1805, spending a rainy winter nearby (as if there's any other kind of winter on the Oregon Coast). Decades later, Seaside (pop. 7,200) rose to prominence as a coastal resort town in the 1870s—and has been the destination of choice for Portland families ever since, with a few craft breweries, locally sourced seafood, and easy access to paddling, hiking, wildlife-watching, and other outdoor recreation.

While Seaside boomed in the early 1900s as a popular destination for Portland-area families, Cannon Beach—just 8 miles (13 km) south—simmered as a less-traveled community at the base of Haystack Rock, a 235-foot (72-m) monolith just offshore. Away from the spotlight, the city (pop. 1,500) began to flourish as a haven for artists, creative chefs, and ambitious hoteliers. Today, the secret on Cannon Beach is most definitely out. Named for a cannon that washed ashore near the present-day community, Cannon Beach is one of the busiest towns on the northern Oregon Coast. Several art galleries dot the charming, walkable downtown, while the city's accessible stretch of shoreline is always teeming with activity on sunny summer weekends.

SEASIDE
Sights
★ Seaside Promenade

Ask anyone around town, and they'll say you haven't *really* seen Seaside until you've strolled at least some of the **Seaside Promenade,** known more commonly as "The Prom." The promenade is a flat, paved path running north-south at the western edge of downtown Seaside—and at the foot of the Pacific Ocean. Its northern terminus is at 12th Avenue, and its southern terminus is Avenue U; in between, you'll enjoy 1.5 miles (2.4 km) of steady beach views, easy access to Seaside's attractions, and close proximity to downtown. Numerous lodgings and cottages line the Prom, and the Tillamook Head rock formation looms over the horizon to the south. On a sunny summer day, you'll share the path with joggers, cyclists, and surrey riders.

Traffic is most congested at the Turnaround, a traffic circle roughly halfway through the Prom, at the western edge of Broadway (the main east-west thoroughfare through downtown). A bronze statue of Lewis and Clark sits in the center of the traffic circle, celebrating the end of the duo's cross-continent journey; they continued on farther south, trading with the local Clatsop people, but no matter. Here a few steps descend to the beach, where visitors can use the restroom, play on a swing set, or amble along the shore.

Broadway Corridor

Seaside is perhaps the most popular family destination on the northern Oregon Coast, and the community's bustling **Broadway Corridor** (Broadway St., between US-101 and the Seaside Promenade) is easily the most popular family destination in Seaside. Between US-101 and the Pacific Ocean, the east-west corridor is lined with souvenir shops selling saltwater taffy and kitschy trinkets, as well as family-friendly restaurants and the city's only two breweries. You'll also find **Funland Arcade** (201 Broadway St.; 503/738-7361; www.funlandseaside.com; 9am-10pm Sun.-Thurs. and 9am-11pm Fri.-Sat. Labor Day-mid-June, 9am-midnight daily mid-June-Labor Day), home to dozens of flashy arcade machines and the old-timey Fascination game (1pm-10pm Fri. and 11am-11pm Sat.-Sun. Labor Day-mid-June, 11am-midnight daily mid-June-Labor Day), a captivating cross between Skee-Ball and bingo.

Seaside

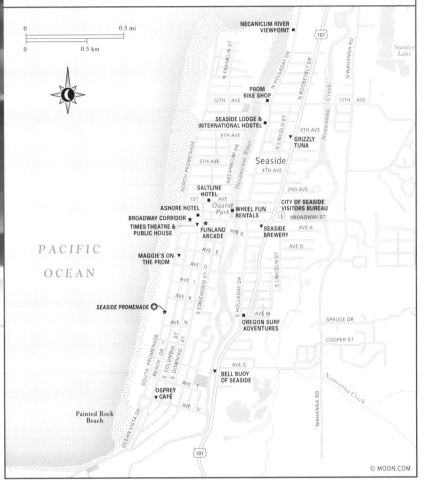

It's all a bit touristy, but it's fun to stroll up and down the street to soak up the festive atmosphere, which conjures the feeling of an old-school beach boardwalk. That it ends at the Pacific Ocean doesn't hurt, either.

Beaches

You'll have no shortage of opportunities to get on the beach at Seaside, but one stands out. **Painted Rock Beach** (Ocean Vista Dr. & Avenue W) is exactly what it sounds like: a small section of beach full of colorful rocks—painted with memorials, eye-catching designs, inspirational messages, and more. Most of the rocks can be found along a walkway between Ocean Vista Drive and the sandy beach itself, as well as on logs surrounding the trail. Visitors are asked not to take any rocks—but are invited to decorated unpainted rocks if the mood strikes. Access to Painted Rock Beach comes via a paved pathway near the intersection; since it's a quiet neighborhood with little

room for parking, consider walking south along the Prom and, beyond its southern terminus, walking another five minutes.

Recreation
Paddling and Water Sports

The quiet Necanicum River runs north-south through Seaside, so paddling offers a fun way to see the city's sights—from the hustle and bustle of visitors milling about to the shorebirds that nest in the wetlands at the northern edge of town. A slow flow makes the river an ideal destination for families and new paddlers.

Wheel Fun Rentals at Quatat Park (493 Oceanway St.; 503/738-8447; www.wheelfun-rentals.com; 11am-sunset Sat.-Sun. and holidays March 19-May 27, 11:30am-7:30pm daily May 28-Sept. 5, noon-sunset Sat.-Sun. and holidays Sept. 7-Oct. 10) offers a variety of watercraft rentals in the heart of downtown. Choose among single or double kayaks ($15-20 per hour), stand-up paddleboards ($15 per hour), or a variety of pedal-powered crafts—including a tricycle-like craft with massive wheels ($30-45 per hour). Rentals include a paddle (if necessary) and personal floatation device.

Bicycling

Whether you're cycling the Prom, riding on the beach, or dawdling around town, Seaside makes a fine place to explore on two wheels. The locally owned **Prom Bike Shop** (622 12th Ave.; 503/738-8251; www.prombike-shop.com; noon-5pm Thurs.-Sun.) offers a wide range of rentals to suit your group and desired experience. Options include cruiser bikes, mountain bikes, and road bikes ($10-15 per hour); three-wheeled bikes ($15-20 per hour); four-wheeled surrey bikes that seat up to nine ($20-40 per hour); and beach-friendly bikes ($15-25 per hour) and recumbent tricycles ($15 for 1.5 hours). Extended rentals are also available, as are tune-up and repair services.

Wildlife-Watching

The blink-and-you'll-miss-it **Necanicum River Viewpoint** (1901 N. Holladay Dr.; free) isn't much to look at—just a small parking area with room for a handful of cars. But a wooden viewing platform, along with a set of stairs to the Necanicum River shoreline, offers surprisingly robust opportunities to spy some of the more than 300 species of bird that spend at least part of the year in Seaside. Perched just south of where the Necanicum River meets the Neawanna Creek before flowing into the Pacific Ocean, visitors might see bald eagles (which winter in nearby spruce trees), sandpipers, snowy plovers, and other shorebird species—not to mention the area's resident elk.

Surfing

Believe it or not, surfing is a popular pastime on the northern Oregon Coast. Sure, the water might be chilly, even in midsummer, but the area's sandy beaches and headlands create ideal conditions for epic breaks and year-round surfing. The best conditions can usually be found between late June and early September, though wetsuits make it possible to comfortably surf year-round.

If you want to learn, a pair of schools offer lessons around Seaside. **Oregon Surf Adventures** (1116 S. Roosevelt Dr.; 503/436-1481; www.oregonsurfadventures.com) has been teaching new surfers since 2005 and offers a mix of lessons and summer camps—the latter for kids 9-15. Three-hour beginner lessons ($109, $30 for 24-hour equipment rental) are generally offered March-October, weather permitting, and focus on ocean awareness, how to use the equipment, water safety, etiquette, and more; semi-private and private lessons ($159-199, $30 for 24-hour equipment rental) are also available. Little ones can also enroll in summer camps ($399-649 for two to four days, July-Aug.) that cover the basics of surfing, include marine biology lessons, and

---

1: beach views from along the Seaside Promenade
2: Wheel Fun Rentals at Quatat Park

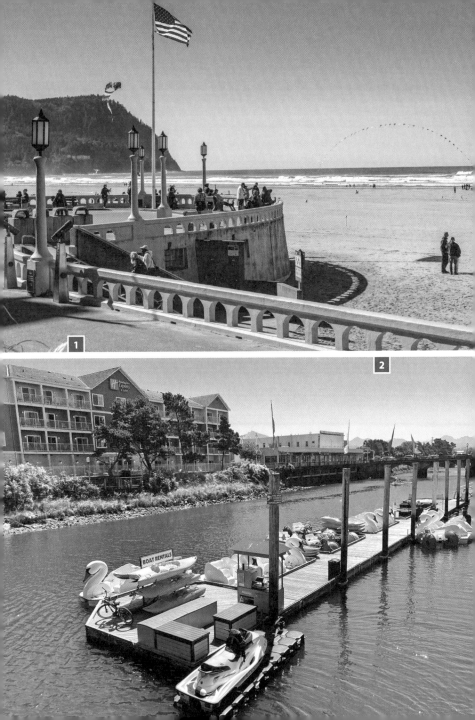

offer kid-friendly beach games; camps include equipment, food, and a goodie bag.

Another solid local school is **Northwest Women's Surf Camps & Retreats** (www. nwwomenssurfcamps.com). The local institution gears most of its classes and lessons toward women—women-only surf and bodyboard lessons run $130-350—but co-ed bodyboarding clinics ($130) and co-ed group lessons ($130) are available on select spring and summer weekends. Three-day family surf camps ($259 for the first day, $175 for the second and third days) are also available.

Beer, Wine, and Nightlife

Seaside Brewery (851 Broadway; 503/717-5451; www.seasidebrewery.com; 11am-9pm daily) has earned notoriety over the years for being housed in the city's former jail and city hall. The brewpub specializes in creative takes on classic styles; one blonde ale, for instance, was brewed with ginger root and Japanese hops, while an IPA was crafted with orange peel for a zesty kick. The brewpub's food menu leans heavily on pub favorites (burgers, fish-and-chips) alongside barbecue classics (such as smoked brisket and pulled pork). If the weather's nice, imbibe on the outdoor area, ideally around the fire pit, along Broadway.

Seaside's other brewery—Sisu Brewing Co.—can be found just down the street, its taps pouring at the **Times Theatre and Public House** (133 Broadway St.; 503/739-7188; timestheatre.com; 11am-10pm daily). Sisu's easy-drinking takes on classic styles (lagers, IPAs, and a few dark beers) can be enjoyed at a pub within the vintage movie theater—which, yes, still shows second-run movies and sporting events. The restaurant's food trends toward pub-fare favorites (fish-and-chips, sandwiches, and burgers), while the theater's concession stand serves bagged candy and caramel corn from a local candymaker.

Food
Pacific Northwest Cuisine

If you were any closer to the beach at **Maggie's on the Prom** (580 Beach Dr.; 503/738-6403; www.maggiesontheprom. com; 4pm-9pm Thurs.-Mon.; $22-50), you'd go home with sand in your shoes. The restaurant, sitting on the Seaside Promenade and affording wide-open ocean views, brings a touch of fine dining to town with pan-seared steelhead, truffled mushroom risotto, and other elegant dishes. Maggie's sources its ingredients from roughly two dozen fisheries, foragers, farmers, bakeries, and craft beverage producers in Oregon and Washington—so the menu changes seasonally. A garden-like patio offers outdoor seating in spring and summer.

Since 1946, **Bell Buoy of Seaside** (1800 S. Roosevelt Dr.; market 800/529-2722, restaurant 503/738-6348; www.bellbuoyofseaside. com; market 9:30am-5pm daily, restaurant 11am-4:45pm daily; $10-22) has been dishing some of the city's freshest seafood. Today, the family-owned restaurant and seafood market specializes in sustainable fare, with a menu that includes wild-caught fish-and-chips, melts, and a wide range of local, fresh seafood to cook back at your campsite or in your room. Razor clams for Bell Buoy's chowder are caught within a mile of the restaurant. A few picnic tables line the Necanicum River out back.

Seafood

Get your fish-and-chips to go at **Grizzly Tuna** (850 N. Roosevelt Dr.; 503/440-1039; 11am-7pm daily; $8-12), which dishes its fresh-caught albacore out of a drive-thru kiosk just north of downtown. The light, crisp breading never gets greasy or soggy, and the lean cuts of tuna are mildly flaky. Enjoy the dish (or a pair of fish tacos, the only other item on Grizzly Tuna's menu) in your vehicle—or at a pair of uncovered picnic tables in the parking lot.

Breakfast and Brunch

Osprey Café (2281 Beach Dr.; 503/739-7054; 8am-2pm Thurs.-Mon.; $8-12) is a popular

stop among locals for bringing some international flair to its lineup of classic American breakfast and lunch dishes. Highlights include arepas (stuffed cornmeal cakes, popular in South America), chilaquiles, a burger crafted with a koji marinade, and Korean fried chicken—but the local, wild-caught seafood dishes are nothing to sneeze at. Limited outdoor seating is available in spring and summer.

Accommodations

Just north of the community's bustling downtown core sits **Seaside Lodge & International Hostel** (930 N. Holladay Dr.; 503/738-7911; www.seasidehostel.net; $59 for a dorm bed, $194-269 for a private room) alongside the Necanicum River. A mix of basic private rooms and dorm beds are available; amenities include a common kitchen (stocked with herbs grown on the property), laundry service, canoe and kayak rentals ($9-25 for up to a full day for guests, $18-50 for up to a full day for day visitors), and an outdoor fire pit.

The hip, 22-room **Ashore Hotel** (125 Oceanway St.; 503/568-7506; www.ashore-hotel.com; $359-478) boasts simple rooms with comfortable beds and minimalist décor. Away from the room, guests can take a spin on the hotel's loaner bikes; stop by the on-site bar for light bites and regionally sourced beverages; take a dip in the indoor heated pool; or kick back around an outdoor fire pit. The hotel offers a variety of packages for travelers of all stripes—including the Bonfire Package, which gives guests all the tools they need (canned wine, a s'mores kit, firewood, newspaper, and a beach blanket) for enjoying one of Seaside's beloved pastimes.

Treat yourself to a touch of luxury at the clean, modern (pet-friendly) ★ **Saltline Hotel** (250 1st Ave.; 971/601-1082; www.salt-linehotel.com; $509-649), just a few steps from the Seaside Promenade and the beach itself. Rooms include chic furnishings, comfortable bedding, private balconies (in select rooms), and handcrafted works from local artists;

hotel-wide perks include free loaner bikes, an outdoor patio (home to a small playground, fire pit, and bocce court), an electric vehicle charging station, spa services, and a saltwater pool.

Information and Services

Get the lowdown on what to do and where to go at the **City of Seaside Visitors Bureau** (7 N. Roosevelt Dr.; 503/738-3097; www.seasideor.com; 9am-5pm Mon.-Sat.). After you've taken a selfie on the massive beach chair just outside, head indoors for brochures, pamphlets, and souvenirs for sale. You'll also find a public restroom in the building.

CANNON BEACH
Sights

TOP EXPERIENCE

★ Haystack Rock

There may be no more photographed site in all of Oregon than **Haystack Rock,** a 235-foot (72-m) basalt sea stack rising from the edge of the shore near downtown Cannon Beach. The rock was formed up to 17 million years ago by lava flows (which were also responsible for creating outcrops, headlands, bluffs, and other iconic formations along the Oregon Coast) and is today designated as one of seven Oregon Marine Gardens along the Oregon Coast *and* protected as part of the Oregon Islands National Wildlife Refuge.

That protected status makes Haystack Rock a haven for wildlife, both above and below the water. At low tide, visitors can walk right up to the rock and spot starfish, anemones, crabs, and other marine creatures in the tidepools at its base. At high tide, try to spot tufted puffins nesting on the rock (Apr.-July), along with other species of bird including the western gull, peregrine falcon, and black oystercatcher. (Just note that removing creatures or materials from within 300 yards/275 m of Haystack Rock, along with climbing the rock above the barnacle line, is prohibited.)

Cannon Beach

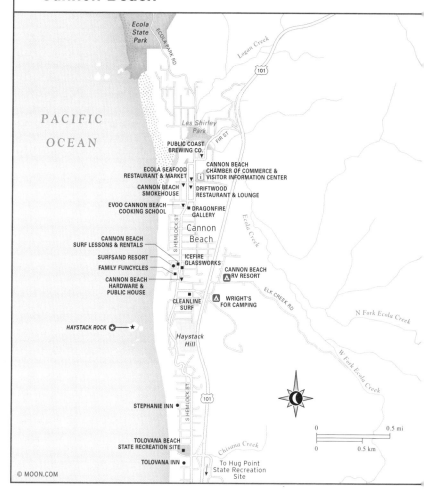

Ecola
State
Park

ECOLA PARK RD

Logan Creek

101

PACIFIC

OCEAN

Les Shirley
Park

FIR ST

PUBLIC COAST
BREWING CO.

CANNON BEACH
CHAMBER OF COMMERCE &
VISITOR INFORMATION CENTER

ECOLA SEAFOOD
RESTAURANT & MARKET

CANNON BEACH
SMOKEHOUSE

DRIFTWOOD
RESTAURANT & LOUNGE

EVOO CANNON BEACH
COOKING SCHOOL

DRAGONFIRE
GALLERY

Cannon
Beach

Ecola Creek

S HEMLOCK ST

CANNON BEACH
SURF LESSONS & RENTALS

SURFSAND RESORT

ICEFIRE
GLASSWORKS

FAMILY FUNCYCLES

CANNON BEACH
RV RESORT

CANNON BEACH
HARDWARE &
PUBLIC HOUSE

CLEANLINE
SURF

WRIGHT'S
FOR CAMPING

ELK CREEK RD

N Fork Ecola Creek

HAYSTACK ROCK

Haystack
Hill

W Fork Ecola Creek

STEPHANIE INN

S HEMLOCK ST

101

0   0.5 mi

TOLOVANA BEACH
STATE RECREATION SITE

Chisana Creek

0   0.5 km

TOLOVANA INN

To Hug Point
State Recreation
Site

© MOON.COM

If you'd like to learn more, keep an eye out for volunteers, clad in red jackets, with the **Haystack Rock Awareness Program** (503/436-8060; www.ci.cannon-beach.or.us). Between mid-February and October, volunteers head out at low tide to educate visitors about the sea creatures around Haystack Rock, offer tips for spotting wildlife, and help visitors stay safe.

Haystack Rock is readily accessible. Just about every east-west street in town offers beach access at its western terminus, and parking is plentiful at Tolovana Beach State Recreation Site in southern Cannon Beach—just a 15-minute walk away.

Ecola State Park

One of the most celebrated state parks anywhere on the Oregon Coast is the majestic **Ecola State Park** (end of Ecola State Park

Rd.; 503/812-0650; www.stateparks.oregon. gov; $5 day-use fee; sunrise-sunset daily). In all, the park covers nine miles (14.5 km) of coastline between Cannon Beach and Seaside, with several hiking trails, view points, picnic tables, and beach access spots for admiring the Pacific Ocean, watching for migrating gray whales, and photographing scenic sea stacks to the south.

Of the stops and view points in Ecola State Park, two stand out. The southernmost is the Ecola Point Day-Use Area, which hosts informational panels, a picnic area, drinking water, and restrooms; there is no beach access from Ecola Point, but the ocean views are spectacular. Farther north, the Indian Beach Day-Use Area hosts vault toilets and a picnic area, as well as easy access to what's known as Indian Beach—a popular spot to explore tidepools and go surfing; this is where the climax of the 1991 film *Point Break* was shot (filling in admirably for Bells Beach in Australia). From Indian Beach, visitors can hike to Hikers' Camp on Tillamook Head (2.6 mi/4.2 km round-trip), home to a World War II radar station and views of Tillamook Rock Lighthouse (more popularly known as "Terrible Tilly")—which sits on a basalt sea stack 1.2 miles (1.9 km) offshore. The trail eventually traverses all of Tillamook Head and ends at the southern edge of Seaside.

Ecola State Park was created in the 1930s on top of still-active landslides; as such, it's not unheard of for park roads or trails to be closed for repair, especially after heavy rains in winter and spring. Call ahead or visit the Oregon State Parks website to confirm the park is accessible. The road leading to Ecola State Park also has many turns with little shoulder room; motorhomes and trailers are not recommended. From Cannon Beach, the 3-mile (5-km) drive to Ecola State Park takes about 10 minutes via northbound Ecola State Park Road.

Beaches

The easiest ocean access in Cannon Beach comes at **Tolovana Beach State Recreation Site** (end of W. Warren Way; 503/812-0650; www.stateparks.oregon.gov; sunrise-sunset daily; free). Here you can watch the sunset, build a sandcastle, go for a stroll (Haystack Rock is just 15 minutes away), or relax on the sand. One popular pastime here is to build a beach bonfire on the area's dry, open sand; supplies are available in nearby convenience stores, and visitors should take care not to burn logs or driftwood piles. The wayside's

sunset at Haystack Rock

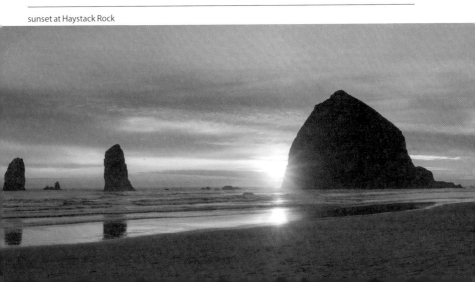

spacious parking lot fills up on sunny summer weekends, so try arriving by 10am or close to sunset. A small playground abuts the parking lot, as does a restroom.

Just south of Cannon Beach, **Hug Point State Recreation Site** (between mileposts 33 and 34, US-101; 503/812-0650; www.state-parks.oregon.gov; 6am-10pm daily; free) offers both easy beach access and a quirky look at Oregon history. Attractions in the small cove—bordered to the north by a sandstone headland—include a waterfall that tumbles onto the beach in winter and spring, tidepools (which can be accessed at low tide), forested picnic tables, and caves carved into the cliffside. At low tide, visitors can walk onto a ledge around the headland, which was an old stagecoach road; drivers had to "hug" the point to keep from falling into the ocean, hence the name. Ruts are still visible today. A short, steep paved walkway descends from the parking area to the beach and is not wheelchair accessible. Restrooms are available on-site. From Cannon Beach, the 4.5-mile (7.2-km) drive to Hug Point takes about seven minutes via US-101.

Recreation
Bicycling
Explore Cannon Beach in style with help from **Family FUNCycles** (1164 S. Hemlock St.; 503/436-2247; March-mid-Sept., daily schedule varies with the tides). The locally owned shop rents three-wheeled recumbent tricycles, also known as funcycles, as well as beach cruisers ($30 for 90 minutes), with toddler trailers available for $10.

Surfing
The friendly folks at the woman-owned **Cannon Beach Surf Lessons & Rentals** (1042 S. Hemlock St.; 503/791-3515; www.cannonbeachsurflessonsandrentals.com; hours vary by season) offers, well, surf lessons and rentals in the heart of Cannon Beach. If you're ready to get on the water, rentals include surfboards ($40 per day), boogie boards ($20 per day), wetsuits ($25 per day), and booties,

gloves, and hoods ($5 each)—with complete surf packages ($45) and boogie board packages ($35) available. Newbies, meanwhile, can sign up for one-on-one lessons ($175) and two-day lessons ($350), with an optional yoga add-on ($25 per person). All lessons include the necessary gear, and private group lessons are also available.

If you're an experienced surfer but need to grab some gear, **Cleanline Surf** (171 Sunset Blvd.; 503/436-9726; www.cleanlinesurf.com; 9am-5pm Sun.-Fri., 9am-6pm Sat.) sells wetsuits, surfboards, fins, bags, and more—and offers a wide range of rentals, including surfboards ($25-40), wetsuits ($15-20), and other accessories.

Art Galleries
Cannon Beach boasts a celebrated creative culture, as evidenced by the many art galleries around town. Gallery maps are available at the Cannon Beach Chamber of Commerce and Visitor Information Center (207 N. Spruce St.).

Check out ornate glass bowls, plates, vases, and other items—and see how it's all made at **Icefire Glassworks** (116 East Gower Ave.; 503/436-2359; www.icefireglassworks.com; 10am-5pm Sat.-Mon., noon-5pm Tues. and Thurs.-Fri.). The gallery and working studio features work from founder Jim Kingwell, as well as several regional artists. Time your visit right and you might even see your next favorite piece being crafted.

If you're not ready to commit to an expensive piece, never fear: **DragonFire Gallery** (123 S. Hemlock St.; 503/436-1533; www.dragonfiregallery.com; 10am-5pm daily, closed for lunch 1pm-1:30pm) prides itself on displaying and selling affordable works from artists throughout the Pacific Northwest. No matter your taste, chances are good you'll find something to love; the gallery showcases glass works, ceramic pieces, mixed media, paintings, fiber art, and even stylish clocks.

Festivals and Events
Each summer, more than 1,000 artists compete

in the community's annual **Sandcastle Contest** (www.cannonbeach.org; June)—and many more admire their handiwork, which often leads to complex, inventive creations; it is free to spectate, but builders must pay a $25 entrance fee to take part.

Every fall, the creative culture of Cannon Beach is spotlighted throughout the **Stormy Weather Arts Festival** (www.cannonbeach. org; first weekend of Nov.); events include paint-and-sip nights, painting classes, demonstrations, and live performances from regional musicians.

Beer, Wine, and Nightlife

Public Coast Brewing Co. (264 3rd St.; 503/436-0285; www.publiccoastbrewing. com; noon-8pm Thurs.-Mon.) pours a mix of house-made ales, lagers, and even hard seltzers. Visitors will enjoy classic styles (such as a crisp blonde ale and a bitter West Coast IPA) alongside more unconventional offerings (including a coconut brown ale and a peanut butter milk stout brewed with blueberry jam). Whenever possible, beers and food items incorporate ingredients from the Public Coast Farm just outside Portland—producing hops, blueberries, honey, and more. Outdoor seating is available.

Where else in Oregon can you enjoy a beer *and* buy a box of nails? At **Cannon Beach Hardware and Public House** (1235 S. Hemlock St.; 503/436-4086; www.cannonbeachhardware.com; 10am-8pm daily), you can do both. Also known as the Screw & Brew, the part-pub, part-hardware store pours a curated selection of about a half-dozen craft beers and ciders, mostly from Pacific Northwest producers. A full menu of pub-food favorites—mostly sandwiches, burgers, and fish-and-chips—rounds out the experience ($14-20).

Food
Pacific Northwest Cuisine
Since 1944, the stylishly old-school **Driftwood Restaurant & Lounge** (179 N. Hemlock St.; 503/436-2439; www.

driftwoodcannonbeach.com; restaurant 11:30am-9pm Sun.-Thurs. and 11:30am-10pm Fri.-Sat., bar 11:30am-midnight daily; $14-39) has served steaks and seafood dishes in the heart of downtown Cannon Beach. Coho salmon, Willapa Bay oysters, and Northwest halibut show up in a variety of seafood and pasta dishes, which share the menu with steak and ribs. A cozy fire pit resides on the restaurant's patio.

Cannon Beach Smokehouse (131 2nd St.; 503/436-4035; www.cbsmokehouse4u. com; 4:30-9:30pm Thurs., 11:30am-9:30pm Fri.-Wed.; $14-39) offers a meat-heavy break from seafood eateries around town, specializing in a wide range of house-smoked meats. Sausage, pulled pork tacos, and tender brisket sandwiches are just some of the restaurant's many highlights; wash it all down with cold beer produced by a craft brewery in town.

There's nothing quite like **EVOO Cannon Beach Cooking School** (188 S. Hemlock St.; 503/436-8555; www.evoocb.com; 6pm-9pm Fri.-Sat. and 4pm-7pm Sun. Jan.-March and Oct.-Dec., 6pm-9pm Thurs.-Sat. and 4pm-7pm Sun. Apr.-Sept.; $225) anywhere on the Oregon Coast. EVOO offers what it calls "dinner shows"—part dinner, part cooking show. Guests are seated around an open-air kitchen while chefs prepare three seasonal entrees from local ingredients, as well as dessert. Prices include wine pairings with each course. Seats are limited and fill up fast; reservations are recommended.

Seafood
Owned and operated by a family that's been fishing the Oregon Coast since 1977, **★ Ecola Seafood Restaurant and Market** (208 N. Spruce St.; 503/436-9130; www.ecolaseafoods.com; hours vary by season; $14-30) dishes a mix of fresh and prepared seafood, all of it wild-caught, in a casual environment. Highlights include the lightly battered cod and chips, homemade clam chowder, and (when in season) Dungeness crab. Outdoor dining is available, but you're also just a three-minute walk from the beach.

Accommodations

Cannon Beach is among the busiest destinations anywhere on the Oregon Coast; as such, reservations at the town's lodgings are recommended at least 6-8 months out, if possible. Alternately, vacation rentals are available through the likes of **Beachcombers NW** (www.beachcombersnw.com), **Oregon Beach Vacations** (www.oregonbeachvacations.com), and **Meredith Lodging** (www.meredithlodging.com). Wherever you stay, keep in mind that a minimum stay of up to three or four nights may be required in summer—especially on weekends.

At the southern edge of town sits the **Tolovana Inn** (3400 S. Hemlock St.; 503/436-2211; www.tolovanainn.com; $163-443), a budget-friendly lodging that nevertheless delivers a wide range of amenities and easy beach access. Guests can choose between suites and standard rooms—some pet-friendly, some with full kitchens, and some with ocean views. Other amenities include gas fireplaces (in suites), comfortable bedding, an indoor pool and sauna, an on-site fitness center, and charging stations for Teslas and other electric vehicles.

Since 1977, families have flocked to **Surfsand Resort** (148 W. Gower Ave.; 503/436-2274; www.surfsand.com; $446-653) for amenities that appeal to travelers young and old. The 95-room hotel sports 53 pet-friendly rooms (with treats and bowls for Fido), in-room soaking tubs and gas fireplaces, loaner bicycles, a fitness center (stocked with exercise bikes and a sauna), nightly bonfires with s'mores cookouts in summer, ice cream socials every Saturday, DVDs to rent, on-site spa services, and even tidepool walks with local guides.

The Oregon Coast is home to countless unfussy hotels and motels, which is what makes the ★ **Stephanie Inn** (2740 S. Pacific Ave.; 855/977-2444; www.stephanieinn.com; $669-1,029) so remarkable. The opulent, resort-style hotel boasts in-room jetted tubs, steam showers, gas fireplaces, and private patios or balconies—all with outstanding views of Haystack Rock and the Pacific Ocean. Away from your room, the hotel offers on-site spa and massage services, loaner bikes (in summer), and electric vehicle charging stations. The Stephanie Inn is largely geared toward couples on a romantic getaway; as such, pets and children younger than 12 are not permitted. The hotel's restaurant (dinner seatings at 5:30pm nightly and at 8pm Fri.-Sat.; $89, $129 with a wine flight) is among the most sought-after eateries in town, thanks to an ever-changing, five-course prix fixe menu that reflects whatever's fresh, in-season, and available locally.

Camping

Budget-minded tent campers love **Wright's for Camping** (334 Reservoir Rd.; 503/436-2347; www.wrightsforcamping.com; $45-57 Memorial Day-June and post-Labor Day, $48-60 July-Labor Day; campground closed Oct.-Memorial Day), a family-run campground since 1959. Wright's sits on the east side of US-101 and hosts 22 tent sites (although RVs of up to 25 feet can fit into some of the sites) in the heart of a spruce forest; each campsite includes a campfire grill and picnic table, bathrooms (with hot showers) are available, and firewood is for sale on-site.

RV campers, meanwhile, can opt for the well-appointed **Cannon Beach RV Resort** (340 Elk Creek Rd.; 503/436-2231; www.cbrvresort.com; $49 Nov.-Feb., $59 Mar.-Memorial Day weekend and Oct., $64 Memorial Day weekend-Sept.). The pet-friendly resort hosts 99 paved, full-hookup sites for RVs up to 47 feet long (including 11 pull-through sites); amenities include picnic tables and campfire grills at each site, an indoor heated pool and spa, an on-site convenience store, and full-service restrooms.

Information and Services

Stop by the **Cannon Beach Chamber of Commerce and Visitor Information Center** (207 N. Spruce St.; 503/436-2623; www.cannonbeach.org; 9am-6pm daily June 15-Sept. 15, 10am-5pm daily Sept. 16-June 14)

for recommendations on where to go, where to eat, what to do, and how best to enjoy the Cannon Beach area. Resources include brochures, maps, and pamphlets.

GETTING THERE

Seaside and Cannon Beach are pretty centrally located within the region—from both nearby communities *and* Portland. No wonder they're among the most popular destinations anywhere on the Oregon Coast.

Coming from downtown Portland, the 78-mile (125-km) drive to Seaside takes about 90 minutes via westbound US-26 and, where the highway ends at the coast, northbound US-101.

From Astoria, the 17-mile (27-km) drive to Seaside takes about 30 minutes via southbound US-101. From Seaside, the 9-mile (14-km) drive to Cannon Beach takes about 15 minutes via southbound US-101.

From Manzanita, the 15-mile (24-km) drive to Cannon Beach takes about 20 minutes via northbound US-101. From Cannon Beach, the 9-mile (14-km) drive to Seaside takes about 15 minutes via northbound US-101.

Visitors can also take the bus to Seaside and Cannon Beach via **The Point** (888/846-4183; www.oregon-point.com; $18 each way), which runs twice-daily bus service between the Astoria Transit Center (900 Marine Dr.) and Union Station in downtown Portland. Once in town, bus service between Seaside, Cannon Beach, and other communities on the north coast is available via **NW Connector** (503/861-7433; www.nworegontransit.org).

GETTING AROUND

Seaside and Cannon Beach both boast compact, walkable downtown cores with easy beach access. Well-signed street parking is available in both communities, as are public parking lots (though overnight parking is not permitted). Parking can be difficult to come by at midday on June-September weekends, so arrive by 10am or close to sunset to easily find a spot.

NW Connector (503/861-7433; www.nworegontransit.org; $1 per ride) offers 13 round trips Mon.-Fri. between Seaside and Cannon Beach, with multiple stops in both cities.

Oswald West State Park and Nehalem Bay Area

The Nehalem Bay area sits between Cannon Beach (to the north) and Tillamook (to the south), and is centered around where the Nehalem River meets the Pacific Ocean. Just north of the bay is Oswald West State Park—a towering rainforest that's home to scenic headlands and picturesque beaches—and the quiet getaway community of Manzanita. The fishing community of Wheeler sits just inland at a bend in the Nehalem River, and Rockaway Beach is just south of the Nehalem River. The quaint towns here are bound by their working-class connection to the coast and quiet Main Street charm, making them popular destinations for families.

★ OSWALD WEST STATE PARK

Named for the governor who first promoted public beaches in Oregon, **Oswald West State Park** (along US-101, 6.5 mi/10.5 km south of Cannon Beach; 800/551-6949; www.stateparks.oregon.gov; sunrise-sunset daily; free) spans 4 miles (6.5 km) of rugged shoreline from north to south—and packs in some of the most celebrated sites anywhere on the Oregon Coast. Towering forests of western red cedar, western hemlock, and Sitka spruce lead to bustling beaches, scenic headlands, and even secret waterfalls. Legend has it that treasure was buried centuries ago on the

towering Neahkahnie Mountain at the southern edge of the park, just north of modern-day Manzanita.

Oswald West State Park isn't a park where you'll find picnic areas or stunning roadside viewpoints; if you want to get the most out of the park, you'll have to put in at least a little work on the park's network of trails.

Hiking
Cape Falcon
Distance: 5.8 miles (9.3 km) round-trip
Duration: 3 hours
Elevation Gain: 640 feet (195 m)
Effort: Easy/moderate
Trailhead: Cape Falcon trailhead, along southbound US-101
Directions: From Cannon Beach, head southbound on US-101 for 9.5 miles (15.3 km). Turn right into the parking area at milepost 39, following a sign for the Cape Falcon trailhead. Additional parking is available along the other side of the highway just a bit farther south along US-101; take care when crossing the highway.

The out-and-back **Cape Falcon** trail begins on a mostly level path heading west through a forest of spruce and fir. After 0.5 mile (0.8 km), you arrive at a T-shaped junction; to the left is a 0.2-mile (0.3-km) spur to the **Day Use Picnic Area** and Short Sand Beach. This is well worth a side trip at the end of your hike, but continue right to head toward **Cape Falcon.** The oft-muddy trail ascends gradually, switchbacking a few times before arriving after 2.4 miles (3.9 km) at an unsigned junction with the Oregon Coast Trail; turn left to continue west on the Cape Falcon Trail. After 0.3 mile (0.5 km), you'll arrive at a grassy, exposed viewpoint atop Cape Falcon; keep an eye out for migrating gray whales below in winter and spring. Views encompass Neahkahnie Mountain to the south, as well as Short Sand Beach and Smugglers Cove below.

Neahkahnie Mountain
Distance: 5.9 miles (9.5 km) round-trip
Duration: 3 hours
Elevation Gain: 1,110 feet (335 m)

Effort: Easy/moderate
Trailhead: Neahkahnie Mountain trailhead, along southbound US-101
Directions: From Cannon Beach, head southbound on US-101 for 10.8 miles (17.4 km). Turn right into the Neahkahnie Mountain gravel parking area past milepost 40. Take care crossing the highway to the trailhead.

An out-and-back trail heads to the summit of **Neahkahnie Mountain.** From the **North Neahkahnie Mountain Trailhead,** you'll ascend an open hillside covered in thick salal bushes; views of Cape Falcon and Smugglers Cove to the north open up after 0.3 mile (0.5 km). Following the wide-open views, the trail enters a forest of Sitka spruce and western red cedar, ascending steadily throughout; in another 1.25 miles (2 km), it evens out before arriving at a viewpoint just below the mountain's summit. From here, you'll enjoy top-down views of Manzanita and Nehalem Bay to the south.

Beaches
Short Sand Beach (along US-101, 10 mi/16 km south of Cannon Beach; 800/551-6949; www.stateparks.oregon.gov; 6am-10pm daily; free) sits within Smugglers Cove, protected from high winds and harsh weather by Cape Falcon to the north and Neahkahnie Mountain to the south. With relatively mild, consistent weather, the beach is popular with picnickers, surfers, boogie boarders, and nature enthusiasts. Blumenthal Falls cascades onto the shore, over a rock wall, at the northern edge of the beach, and tidepools can be explored at low tide. Even with a short hike from the parking area, Short Sand Beach gets crowded on sunny summer weekends; try to visit in autumn or even winter for a bit more solitude (and to watch hardy surfers ride the waves). From the main parking area, follow signs for the mostly flat, 1-mile/1.6-km (round-trip) Short Sand Beach Trail.

1: Short Sand Beach at Oswald West State Park
2: view from the summit of Neahkahnie Mountain

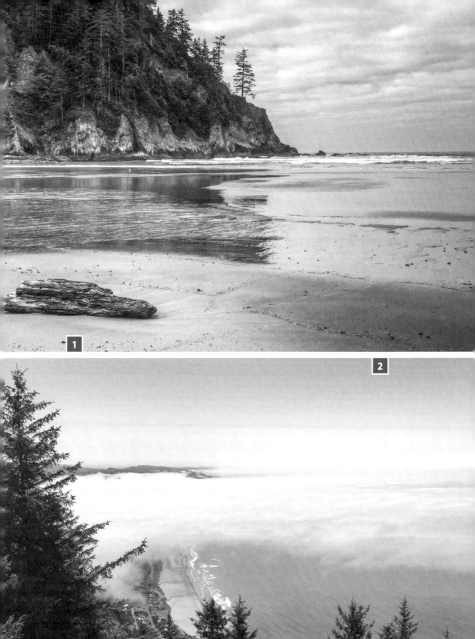

Getting There

From Cannon Beach, the 10-mile (16-km) drive takes about 15 minutes via southbound US-101. From downtown Portland, the 88-mile (142-km) drive takes about 1 hour, 35 minutes via westbound US-26 and, where the highway ends at the coast, southbound US-101. From Manzanita, the 4.5-mile (7.2-km) drive takes about 7 minutes via northbound US-101. Signs reading "Beach Access" announce your arrival at the large parking area.

Trails crisscross the entirety of Oswald West State Park—so a good starting point is the large parking area on the east side of US-101 (home to flush toilets, drinking water, and easy access to most of the park's sites). This parking area also offers the easiest, quickest access to Short Sand Beach.

NEHALEM BAY AREA

The tiny community of **Manzanita** (pop. 400) sits between the southern flank of Neahkahnie Mountain and Nehalem Bay, the former sheltering the city from some of the fog and rainfall more common in the likes of Tillamook and Seaside. As such, Manzanita feels very much like a classic beach town—complete with a charming, one-street downtown (Laneda Ave.) lined with restaurants and quiet inns. Easy access to the oft-sunny coast, never more than a short walk away, doesn't hurt, either.

At the southern edge of the Nehalem Bay area sits **Wheeler** (pop. 350), a quiet fishing community at a bend in the Nehalem River. Its close proximity to the river makes Wheeler a popular spot to catch crab—an Oregon Coast pastime—and get on the water, where you might spy birds and other wildlife.

Long before US-101 opened, forever changing travel along the Oregon Coast, train after train brought families to **Rockaway Beach** (pop. 1,170) for old-school fun on this easy-going stretch of shoreline. Decades later, the community retains its family-friendly charm with seafood shacks, roadside eateries, and spacious vacation rentals.

Sights

Dungeness crab is an Oregon Coast specialty, and **Kelly's Brighton Marina & Campground** (29200 US-101, Rockaway Beach; 503/368-5745; www.kellysbrightonmarina.com; hours vary by season) offers a variety of ways to enjoy the delicacy—whether catching your own or buying some to-go. Throw your crab ring or crab pot into the water with a two-hour boat rental ($120) or from the marina's dock ($17); both options include baited crab rings, a bucket, measuring tools, personal floatation devices, necessary instruction, and cooking of whatever you catch. Grab a three-day shellfish license for $10-19 at the marina's on-site store. Tent and RV campsites are also available if you'd like to make a night of it ($42-49 per night), and fresh seafood is available at the marina's market if you're pressed for time ($14 per pound for live Dungeness crab, $15-17 for a dozen Netarts oysters).

Recreation

Surfing and Bicycling

Whether you want to ride the waves or ride the shoreline, **Bahama Mama's** (411 Laneda Ave., Manzanita; 503/368-2453; www.bahamamamasbeachfare.com; 10am-5pm daily) offers bike and surfboard rentals. If you want to get on the water, the shop's rentals include wetsuits ($30), surfboards ($30), boogie boards ($15), skim boards ($15), and wetsuit accessories ($10). Cyclists, meanwhile, can ride the beach on three-wheeled "funcycles" ($15 per hour) or more traditional beach cruisers ($15 per hour, $40 for 24 hours), which are suitable for riding on the beach or street, as well as the paved paths at nearby Nehalem Bay State Park.

Paddling and Water Sports

The Nehalem River watershed through Wheeler is celebrated for its scenery and natural wonder; forested hillsides roll into the distance, herds of elk frolic in the meadows along its shore, and bald eagles soar overhead in winter. Enjoy the quiet stretch of river with

help from **Wheeler Marina** (278 Marine Dr., Wheeler; 503/368-5780; www.wheeler-marina.com; 6:30am-dusk June-Oct., hours vary Nov.-May). Selections include single and tandem kayaks, canoes, and stand-up paddleboards for anywhere from one hour ($22-28) up to a full day ($44-50).

Camping

Nehalem Bay State Park (end of Grey St., 2.5 mi/4 km south of Manzanita; 503/812-0650; www.stateparks.oregon.gov; $24-44, $43-64 for yurts) packs 265 electrical sites and 18 yurts (9 of which are pet-friendly) into a 4-mile-long (6.4-km) sand spit between the Pacific Ocean and Nehalem Bay. Each site sits surrounded by shore pine and includes a picnic table and campfire grill; more broadly, the campground hosts restrooms with showers, easy beach access, hiking and biking trails, and a pair of playgrounds. Visitors with their own canoes, kayaks, or stand-up paddleboards can put into Nehalem Bay via boat dock (mid-May-mid-Oct.)—and a life jacket loaner station offers personal floatation devices of various sizes. One- and two-hour horseback rides (which head through the surrounding dunes and onto the beach) are available from **Oregon Beach Rides** (971/237-6653; www.oregonbeachrides.com; $100-200; Memorial Day-Labor Day); corrals are located at the park's day-use area. From Manzanita, the 2.5-mile (4-km) drive to the park takes about eight minutes via Classic and Garey Streets.

Food
Pacific Northwest Cuisine

Sitting on the shore of the Nehalem River is **The Salmonberry** (380 S. Marine Dr., Wheeler; 503/714-1423; https://thesalmonberry.fun; 4pm-8pm Fri.-Sun.; $16-26), a hip restaurant that showcases regional flavors in myriad creative ways. The handmade bucatini, for instance, incorporates clams from Willapa Bay and dulse seaweed from nearby Garibaldi; the side of bread, meanwhile, is naturally fermented with wild yeast in

Nehalem. Pasta dishes and wood-fired pizza round out the eclectic menu. Outdoor dining is available along the river.

Seafood

The cozy **Old Oregon Smoke House** (120 US-101, Rockaway Beach; 503/355-2817; noon-7pm Thurs.-Sat. and Mon.-Tues., noon-6pm Sun.; $13-25) dishes all manner of classic (mostly fried) seafood dishes—fish-and-chips, crab cakes, melts, and sandwiches—alongside a hearty clam chowder. The shop also sells dozens of hot sauces, most of which you won't find elsewhere on the Oregon Coast. Plenty of outdoor dining opens up in spring and summer. A second location is open in Tillamook, just across the highway from the Tillamook Creamery.

Casual Fare

Legend has it the pronto pup—a close sibling of the corn dog—was invented in Rockaway Beach; naturally, the tasty snack gets its due at **Rockaway Pronto Pup** (602 US-101, Rockaway Beach; 971/306-1616; www.rockawayprontopup.com; 10am-5pm Fri.-Sat., 10am-4pm Sun.; $2-8). The only difference between pronto pups and corn dogs? The former uses pancake batter, while the latter is dipped in cornmeal batter. Visitors can taste the difference in beef and vegetarian "pups," as well as in fried zucchinis and pickles.

Breakfast and Brunch

The bright, airy, and thoroughly modern **Yolk** (503 Laneda Ave., Manzanita; 503/368-9655; https://yolkmanzanita.square.site; 8am-2pm Fri.-Mon.; $10-18) dishes all your favorite breakfast and lunch items—just with a twist. Its huevos rancheros, for instance, trade tortilla chips for grilled cornmeal cakes that give the dish a crisp, flavorful texture; Yolk's lemon ricotta pancakes, meanwhile, can be ordered with marionberries—creating a joyful blend of sweet and sour. Scrambles, hash dishes, burgers, and sandwiches round out the menu. Outdoor seating is available when the weather cooperates.

Accommodations

You'll find a few family-friendly motels in the Nehalem Bay area with the same basic amenities. If staying in one of these towns, consider a vacation rental; **Beachcombers NW** (www.beachcombersnw.com), **Oregon Beach Vacations** (www.oregonbeachvacations.com), and **Meredith Lodging** (www.meredithlodging.com) all offer rentals, as do the usual suspects—such as **Vacasa** (www.vacasa.com) and **VRBO** (www.vrbo.com).

With a name like **Ocean Inn** (32 Laneda Ave., Manzanita; 503/368-7701; www.oceaninnatmanzanita.com; $179-260), you know you're in for dramatic views and easy beach access. The modern lodging boasts eight fully equipped suites and a pair of smaller rooms; all suites come with fully stocked kitchens, while some include jetted tubs and wood stoves. Amenities include at least partial ocean views in most rooms, loaner fat-tire bikes, free chocolates from a Cannon Beach candymaker, and loaner beach chairs and umbrellas.

Just across the street from the Nehalem River, **Old Wheeler Hotel** (495 US-101, Wheeler; 503/368-6000; www.oldwheelerhotel.com; $169-249) sits along Wheeler's main drag and offers a quiet respite away from the region's busier communities. The space has been welcoming guests since the early 1900s and has enjoyed upgrades in recent years that preserve its charming Victorian aesthetic. Hardwood floors, antiques, and ornate rugs recall an earlier era, while jetted tubs and fireplaces place the charming inn firmly in the modern day.

Information and Services

Enthusiastic volunteers help out at the **Manzanita Visitor Center** (31 Laneda Ave., Manzanita; 503/812-5510; www.exploremanzanita.com; 11am-3pm Thurs.-Sun.) and are happy to provide tips, recommendations, suggestions, maps, brochures, and more. Visitors can even check out free beach wheelchairs, each equipped with large tires designed to handle the rugged terrain; reservations are recommended.

Half the fun of the **Rockaway Beach Chamber of Commerce Visitor Center** (103 S. 1st St., Rockaway Beach; 503/355-8108; www.rockawaybeach.net; 10:30am-4:30pm daily) is its location, housed inside a red caboose. Head inside and you can pick up brochures, maps, pamphlets, and more—and get information and recommendations from friendly staff members.

Getting There and Around

From Cannon Beach, the 14-mile (23-km) drive to Manzanita takes about 20 minutes via southbound US-101. From Manzanita, it's a farther 5 miles (8 km) and 10 minutes via southbound US-101 to Wheeler, and 12 miles (19 km) and 20 minutes via southbound US-101 to Rockaway Beach.

From Tillamook, the 15-mile (24-km) drive to Rockaway Beach takes about 25 minutes via northbound US-101. From Rockaway Beach, it's a farther 8 miles (13 km) and 10 minutes via northbound US-101 to Wheeler, and 12 miles (19 km) and 20 minutes via northbound US-101 to Manzanita.

And coming from downtown Portland, the 93-mile (150-km) drive to Manzanita takes about 1 hour, 40 minutes via westbound US-26 and, where the highway ends at the coast, southbound US-101.

Once in town, bus service between Manzanita, Nehalem, and other communities in the Tillamook area is available via **NW Connector** (503/861-7433; www.nworegontransit.org).

Tillamook Bay and the Three Capes Scenic Loop

Just inland from the Oregon Coast, the Tillamook Valley has long been noted for a cool, damp climate that produces lush, green grasses—the perfect environment for raising dairy cows. The first European settlers arrived in the Tillamook Bay in the early 1850s, and the region has been ground zero for dairy farming in Oregon ever since. Today, more than 100 farmers raise cows just outside the community of Tillamook, and a pair of creameries show off the local specialties.

Tillamook itself sits where OR-6 meets US-101 and feels very much like a crossroads; even with all there is to do, eat, and see in town, Tillamook makes a fine setting-off point for exploring nearby attractions—thundering waterfalls, quiet inlets, prime wildlife-watching, and more.

As the name implies, the Three Capes Scenic Loop comprises three scenic headlands stretching south from Tillamook Bay; each rewards visitors with sweeping Pacific Ocean views, whale-watching opportunities, and plenty of natural wonder. The northernmost of the three, Cape Meares, is home to the shortest lighthouse on the Oregon Coast and the so-called Octopus Tree—a Sitka spruce with no central trunk, but rather a series of sprawling limbs. Continuing south, a hiking trail to the westernmost tip of Cape Lookout offers some of the best whale-watching anywhere on the Oregon Coast, as well as a popular campground just steps from the Pacific Ocean. And the southernmost of the three capes is Cape Kiwanda, offering incredible ocean views in the heart of Pacific City.

TILLAMOOK

Just inland from the bay's southernmost reach, Tillamook is noted for fresh-caught seafood and a bustling dairy farming industry, as well

as myriad waterways that have given rise to a plethora of outdoor opportunities.

Sights

TOP EXPERIENCE

★ Tillamook Creamery

You'll find Tillamook cheese and ice cream all over the Pacific Northwest—but it never tastes better than from the source, which is one of the busiest tourist attractions anywhere on the Oregon Coast. **Tillamook Creamery** (4165 US-101; 503/815-1300; www.tillamook.com; 10am-6pm daily; free admission), owned by about 80 local dairy farming families, invites visitors to enjoy grilled cheese sandwiches, macaroni and cheese, fried curds, and nearly two dozen flavors of ice cream at its spacious café ($4-14); learn about the creamery's history through several interpretive exhibits; and see how cheese is made from high above the factory floor. At the end of it all, visitors can peruse a gift shop for all manner of Tillamook goodies—including cheeses not typically available in grocery stores.

Blue Heron French Cheese Company

The Tillamook Coast's wet, rainy climate is perfectly suited to dairy cows, so it's no surprise the region has given rise to not just one but two celebrated creameries. **Blue Heron French Cheese Company** (2001 Blue Heron Dr.; 800/275-0639; www.blueheronoregon.com; 8am-7pm daily in summer, 8am-6pm daily in winter) sits in a converted Jersey farm barn and offers cheese samples, wine pairings, a petting zoo for little ones, and an on-site deli dishing fresh-baked bread, soups, salads, and more. A gift shop sells Blue Heron delicacies, as well as wine and regionally sourced food items.

Tillamook Bay and Three Capes Scenic Loop

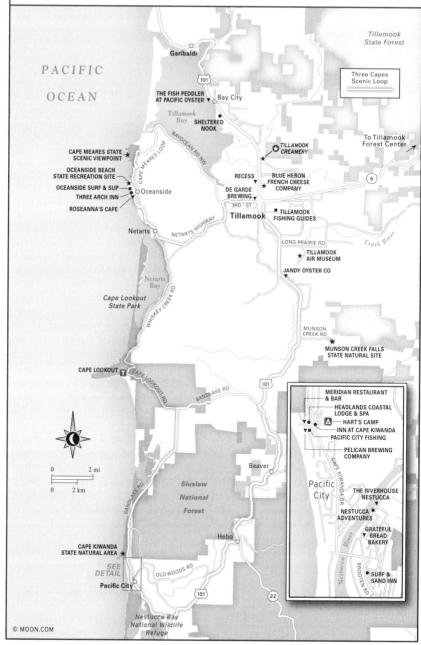

PACIFIC OCEAN

Tillamook State Forest

Garibaldi

THE FISH PEDDLER AT PACIFIC OYSTER ▼ · Bay City

Tillamook Bay

SHELTERED NOOK

Three Capes Scenic Loop

To Tillamook Forest Center

TILLAMOOK CREAMERY

CAPE MEARES STATE SCENIC VIEWPOINT

RECESS ▼
BLUE HERON FRENCH CHEESE COMPANY

OCEANSIDE BEACH STATE RECREATION SITE
OCEANSIDE SURF & SUP
THREE ARCH INN
ROSEANNA'S CAFE

DE GARDE BREWING ▼

Oceanside

3RD ST

Tillamook

TILLAMOOK FISHING GUIDES

Netarts

NETARTS HIGHWAY

LONG PRAIRIE RD

Trask River

TILLAMOOK AIR MUSEUM

Netarts Bay

JANDY OYSTER CO

Cape Lookout State Park

WHISKEY CREEK RD

MUNSON CREEK RD

MUNSON CREEK FALLS STATE NATURAL SITE

CAPE LOOKOUT

CAPE LOOKOUT RD

SANDLAKE RD

101

MERIDIAN RESTAURANT & BAR

HEADLANDS COASTAL LODGE & SPA

HART'S CAMP

INN AT CAPE KIWANDA

PACIFIC CITY FISHING

PELICAN BREWING COMPANY

Beaver

0   2 mi
0   2 km

Siuslaw National Forest

Pacific City

THE RIVERHOUSE NESTUCCA

NESTUCCA ADVENTURES

GRATEFUL BREAD BAKERY ▼

SURF & SAND INN

BROOTEN RD

Nestucca River

SANDLAKE RD

CAPE KIWANDA STATE NATURAL AREA

SEE DETAIL

Pacific City

OLD WOODS RD

Hebo

101

22

Nestucca Bay National Wildlife Refuge

© MOON.COM

Tillamook Forest Center

Between 1933 and 1951, a series of horrific wildfires struck the forests east of Tillamook. The three fires became collectively known as the Tillamook Burn—and its legacy is chronicled in great detail at the **Tillamook Forest Center** (45500 Wilson River Hwy.; 503/815-6800; www.tillamookforestcenter. org; 10am-4pm Wed.-Sun. Mar.-Memorial Day and Labor Day-Nov., 10am-5pm Wed.-Sun. Memorial Day-Labor Day; $5 suggested donation). A short film discusses the wildfires and their impacts on the forest, exhibits detail the region's ecology and reforestation efforts, and visitors can climb the steps of a 40-foot-tall fire lookout. From Tillamook, the 22-mile (35-km) drive east on OR-6 takes about 30 minutes.

Munson Creek Falls
State Natural Site

Gaze upon the tallest waterfall in the Oregon Coast Range at **Munson Creek Falls State Natural Site** (Munson Creek Rd., 1.6 mi/2.6 km west of US-101; 503/842-3182; www.state-parks.oregon.gov; sunrise-sunset daily; free), where an impressive, multi-tiered waterfall tumbles more than 300 feet (91 m) into a creek below. Trillium, corydalis, and other wildflowers bloom in the forest surrounding Munson Creek Falls each spring and summer, while autumn foliage displays light up with big-leaf maple and alder tree leaves turning red, yellow, and orange. In late fall and winter, spawning salmon can be seen in the creek near the base of the falls. A 0.5-mile/0.8-km (round-trip) hiking path (which can be reached year-round but is not wheelchair-accessible) leads from the parking area to a dramatic viewpoint. From Tillamook, the 8.7-mile (14-km) drive takes about 15 minutes via US-101 and Munson Creek Road.

Tillamook Air Museum

One of Tillamook's most iconic sites—and most cherished family attractions—is the **Tillamook Air Museum** (6030 Hangar Rd.; 503/842-1130; www.tillamookair.com; 10am-4pm Tues.-Sun.; $11, $9.50 for seniors 65 and older, $8.50 for military (active duty, veterans, or retired), $7.50 for children 7-18, $3.50 for children 1-6, free for children younger than 1, $65 for a family pass that covers two adults and up to four children 18 and younger). Housed in an enormous hangar that dates back to World War II, the museum is home to more than two dozen historic aircraft and a handful of vintage firefighting vehicles. Several exhibits cover World War II and the history of aviation in the United States. From Tillamook, the 4-mile (6.4-km) drive to the museum takes about seven minutes via southbound US-101 and Long Prairie Road.

Recreation
Kings Mountain Trail

Distance: 5.4 miles (8.7 km) round-trip
Duration: 3 hours
Elevation Gain: 2,370 feet (722 m)
Effort: Moderate
Season: March-November
Trailhead: Kings Mountain Trailhead, along OR-6
Directions: From Tillamook, head east on OR-6 for 25 miles (40 km). Just past milepost 25, turn left into the parking lot at a sign for the Kings Mountain Trailhead.

The thigh-busting, out-and-back **Kings Mountain Trail** takes you up to the summit of a mountain in the heart of the Oregon Coast Range—but sweeping views of the Pacific Ocean and Cascade peaks alike make the hard work worth it. Roughly 0.2 mile (0.3 km) beyond the trailhead, continue straight at the **Wilson River Trail Junction** as you begin a relentless ascent through a forest of alder and Douglas fir. In another 1.9 miles (3 km), reward yourself with a break on a quick spur trail to a **viewpoint** that affords vistas of the surrounding Oregon Coast Range. Back on the trail, continue another 0.6 mile (1 km) to the summit, noted by a sign and trail register. Views range from Tillamook Bay and the Pacific Ocean to the west to Mount Hood and Mount Adams to the east.

Wildlife-Watching

Nestucca Bay National Wildlife Refuge (7000 Christiansen Rd., Cloverdale; 541/867-4550; www.fws.gov; sunrise-sunset daily; free) sits on a peninsula where the Nestucca and Little Nestucca Rivers meet before flowing into the Pacific Ocean. That unique location creates a wide range of ecosystems (such as meadows, mudflats, marshes, and forests) that host a wide range of wildlife—most notably six species of Canada geese, which winter on the refuge late October-early April. In all, Nestucca Bay hosts more than 200 species of wildlife—including herons, pelicans, bald eagles, river otters, Roosevelt elk, black bears, and more. Roughly 2.5 miles (4 km) of nature trails offer ample wildlife-watching opportunities, as well as views of Haystack Rock, Nestucca Bay, and the Pacific Ocean. From Tillamook, the 28-mile (45-km) drive south takes 35 minutes via US-101.

Fishing

Several bays, lakes, rivers, and creeks crisscross the Tillamook Valley, so it's no wonder angling is a year-round activity. Enjoy a thrilling introduction to the area's angling with a trip through **Tillamook Fishing Guides** (3407 Hawthorne Ln.; 503/300-0024; www.tillamookfishingguide.com; $250). Cordial guides are happy to help newcomers with ideas for where to go, what to fish for, and what's biting at that time. Full-day trips include fish preparation and storage, as well as gear, bait, tackle, and safety equipment.

Paddling and Water Sports

The bays, estuaries, and rivers snaking through the Tillamook Bay ecosystem are prime paddling destinations—and there is no better-known outfitter 'round these parts than **Kayak Tillamook** (503/866-4808; www.kayaktillamook.com). The outfitter offers 2.5-hour guided tours (with 30 minutes of instruction and two hours of paddling) on lakes, rivers, and other flatwater destinations throughout the region ($75-85). Paddlers can also take excursions to pluck their own clams

out of Netarts Bay ($95). Custom and specialty outings, such as moonlight tours, are also available ($85-160)—as are lessons ($85). Trips are geared toward a wide range of fitness and experience levels.

Brewpubs

★ **De Garde Brewing** (114 Ivy Ave.; 503/815-1635; www.degardebrewing.com; noon-7pm Thurs.-Sat., 11am-5pm Sun.) has earned international acclaim over the years for its inventive offerings, which use wild yeast from the air of Tillamook County and are aged for up to five years in oak barrels. So instead of lagers, IPAs, and the like, you'll find farmhouse and wild ales crafted with Oregon black truffles, cider apples, cranberries, and other unusual ingredients. The results resemble a good wine more than beer, with crisp, funky, slightly tart flavor profiles.

Food

Tillamook and the surrounding communities are home to several fisheries, markets, and even a cannery. Sample the best of the region's output at ★ **The Fish Peddler at Pacific Oyster** (5150 Hayes Oyster Dr., Bay City; 503/377-2330; www.pacificseafood.com; 10am-5pm daily; $8-16) in nearby Bay City. The family-owned, laid-back eatery (which doubles as a fresh fish market—with signs indicating where each piece was caught) covers all the classic seafood dishes: fish-and-chips, a creamy (house-made) clam chowder, and more. Much of what you'll enjoy was caught in the Tillamook Bay, just across the parking lot from The Fish Peddler. A small outdoor seating area affords scenic views. From Tillamook, the 6-mile (10-km) drive north via US-101 takes about 10 minutes.

Kids of all ages find plenty to love at the appropriately named **Recess** (1910 Main Ave. N., Tillamook; 503/812-0308; https://recess-101088.square.site; 11am-7pm Tues.-Sat.; $10-17). The teal food truck boasts a

---

1: Tillamook Creamery **2:** view from the summit of Kings Mountain

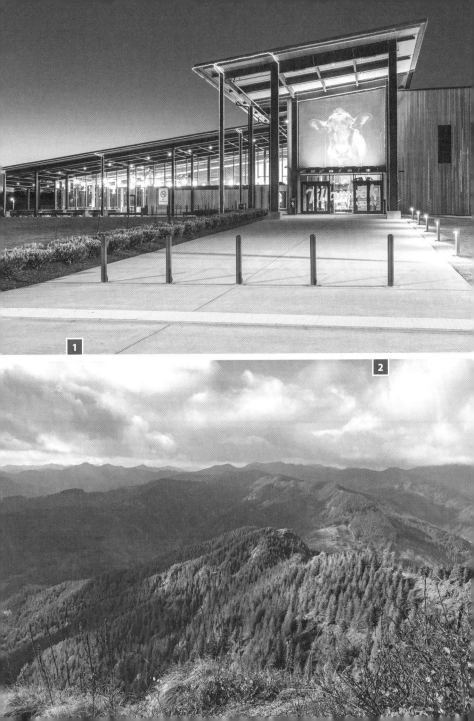

playful menu of burgers, wraps, salads, and comfort-food fare—all crafted with local ingredients whenever possible. Ordering at Recess is almost as much fun as eating: Hand-cut fries are called pick-up sticks, for instance; other creatively named dishes include the Foursquare Waffle (topped with pulled pork) and King of the Playground burger (with bacon, grilled onions, and barbecue sauce).

The exceptionally clean Netarts Bay, just 10 minutes west of Tillamook, is regionally renowned for its plentiful oyster beds. For a fine introduction to the local delicacy, head to **JAndy Oyster Co.** (6760 South Prairie Rd., Tillamook; 503/842-1197; www.jandyoyster. com; 11am-5pm Wed.-Thurs., 11am-7pm Fri., 10am-7pm Sat.; $10-20). The oyster bar and restaurant sustainably sources its oysters from Netarts Bay and serves them raw, fried, smoked, and in sandwiches; other seafood dishes, such as fish tacos and steamer clams, round out the menu. From downtown Tillamook, the 4-mile (6.5-km) drive south via US-101 takes about five minutes.

Accommodations

Tillamook may be one of the larger communities along the northern Oregon Coast, but it boasts little in the way of accommodations—aside from a few chain motels. For a stylish stay just outside town, spend a night at **Sheltered Nook** (7882 Warren St., Bay City; 877/299-6665; www.shelterednook.com; $350) in the tiny enclave of Bay City. The lodging comprises six tiny homes, each boasting a fully stocked kitchen, three comfortable beds, locally crafted furniture, and even full-sized showers. Each tiny home is dog-friendly and comes with a private deck and barbecue, while a communal space boasts a fire pit and picnic tables. From Tillamook, the 5-mile (8-km) drive to Sheltered Nook takes about 10 minutes via northbound US-101.

Getting There and Around

From Cannon Beach, the 41-mile (66-km) drive to Tillamook takes about 1 hour via southbound US-101. From Lincoln City, the 44-mile (71-km) drive takes about 1 hour via northbound US-101. From downtown Portland, the 72-mile (116-km) drive takes about 1 hour, 20 minutes via westbound US-26 and OR-6.

NW Connector (503/861-7433; www. nworegontransit.org; $15 each way, $20 round-trip) offers twice-daily bus service between the Tillamook Park & Ride (near the intersection of 3rd St. & Linden Dr.) and Portland's Union Station (800 NW 6th Ave.), with several stops in communities on US-26 and OR-6 along the way.

NW Connector also offers a variety of routes in and around Tillamook. One stays in town and includes stops downtown and at the Tillamook Creamery ($1.50); another provides service to the communities of Netarts and Oceanside ($1.50); another serves Port of Tillamook Bay and the Tillamook Air Museum ($1.50); and the other heads all the way north to Cannon Beach—with stops in Bay City, Garibaldi, Rockaway Beach, Wheeler, Nehalem, and Manzanita along the way ($1.50-4.50). All fares are one-way.

THREE CAPES SCENIC LOOP

West of Tillamook, the Three Capes Scenic Loop is made up of three scenic headlands that afford wide-open vistas—along with an up-close look at the shortest lighthouse on the Oregon Coast, epic whale-watching spots, and a playful sand dune that's a thrill for kids of all ages. Without stops, it takes about one hour to drive from Tillamook to all three capes.

From Tillamook, the 31-mile (50-km) drive to all three capes takes about one hour, without stops, via westbound OR-131, southbound Netarts Bay Road, and southbound Sandlake Road. All three capes can be viewed in a day, but plentiful accommodations surround Cape Lookout and Cape Kiwanda if you'd rather make a weekend of it.

Before heading out, note that the drive isn't currently a loop—despite signs and outdated maps indicating otherwise. Your best bet for exploring all three capes is to head west from

Tillamook to Oceanside via OR-131, make the quick drive north to Cape Meares, backtrack to Oceanside, and continue south to the other two capes along this route.

Sights

Cape Meares State Scenic Viewpoint

The northernmost of the scenic loop's three capes is **Cape Meares State Scenic Viewpoint** (3500 Cape Meares Loop, Tillamook; 800/551-6949; www.stateparks. oregon.gov; 7am-7pm daily; free), home to both the shortest lighthouse on the Oregon Coast and perhaps the most unique tree anywhere in the state—all just a short walk from the parking area.

A paved, occasionally steep, 0.4-mile /0.6-km (round-trip) loop trail heads downhill from the parking area to the **lighthouse** at the western tip of Cape Meares; the lighthouse dates back to 1887 and stands just 38 feet (11.5 m) tall, some 217 feet (66 m) above the ocean below. The lighthouse interior (which also houses a gift shop) is open 11am-4pm Monday-Friday May-September, with longer hours on the weekend, as well as 11am-6pm daily June-August. Tours of the lighthouse tower are free and available on a first-come, first-served basis. Even from its base, the lighthouse is a great place to watch for migrating gray whales.

Back at the parking area, visitors can hike 0.2 mile/0.3 km (round-trip) to the so-called Octopus Tree. This large Sitka spruce, thought to be more than 200 years old, is named for its unusual appearance; instead of one central trunk, it has several limbs growing upward from its base.

You'll also find a few interpretive panels on local ecology at the parking area, as well as restrooms and picnic tables.

From Tillamook, the 11.5-mile (18.5-km) drive takes about 20 minutes via westbound OR-131 (which turns north when it arrives at Netarts Bay); from Pacific City, the 25-mile (40-km) drive takes about 45 minutes via northbound Sandlake Road. Cape Lookout Road, Whiskey Creek Road, and OR-131.

Cape Lookout State Park

Centered around a windswept headland, **Cape Lookout State Park** (13000 Whiskey Creek Rd., Tillamook; 503/842-4981; www. stateparks.oregon.gov; $5 day-use fee; sunrise-sunset daily) is a popular getaway for beachgoers from Portland, visitors exploring the Three Capes Scenic Loop, and as a spot to spy migrating gray whales.

At the northern edge of the park sits a sprawling campground, a scenic day-use site with easy beach access, and a short (family-friendly) nature trail that explains the ecology of forests on the Oregon Coast. Farther south, visitors can hike to the far western edge of Cape Lookout, famously one of the best sites to spot migrating gray whales anywhere on the Oregon Coast December-early February and March-October.

Cape Lookout State Park sits at the southern edge of Netarts Bay, between the communities of Tillamook (to the north) and Pacific City (to the south). From Tillamook, the 10-mile (16-km) drive takes about 15 minutes via westbound OR-131 and southbound Netarts Bay Road (which becomes Whiskey Creek Road). From Pacific City, the 13-mile (21-km) drive takes about 20 minutes via northbound Sandlake Road and Cape Lookout Road.

Cape Kiwanda State Natural Area

A sweeping dune and sandstone headland sits the heart of **Cape Kiwanda State Natural Area** (33180 Cape Kiwanda Dr., Pacific City; 503/842-3182; www.stateparks. oregon.gov; sunrise-sunset daily; $10 parking fee) near the northern edge of Pacific City. At low tide, visitors can walk along the shore, but the real fun requires some work. A steep climb up the 230-foot (70-m) dune (give yourself plenty of time to make the ascent) rewards visitors with sweeping views of Pacific City below, Haystack Rock to the west, and the Pacific Ocean all around. If it's early in the day, watch for Pacific City's famed flat-bottom dory boats skidding onto the shore to the south; in late February-May and mid-December-mid-January, watch for

gray whales just offshore. The best (most fun) way to descend is by rolling down or sliding on your butt. Observe all signs, and stay behind the fence line at all times; the sandstone cliffs are always eroding, and several people have died after climbing over the fences. From Tillamook, the 23-mile (37-km) drive takes about 30 minutes via southbound US-101 and Sandlake Road.

Beaches

Easy beach access can be found at **Oceanside Beach State Recreation Site** (Netarts Oceanside Hwy. W. & Rosenberg Loop, Tillamook; 503/842-3182; www.state-parks.oregon.gov; 7am-8pm daily; free) in the heart of Oceanside, a small beach community immediately south of Cape Meares near the northern edge of the Three Capes Scenic Loop. The site affords ample access to the bustling stretch of shoreline, popular for wintertime agate hunting (the small rocks, made with quartz and other materials, are quite colorful—and common along the Oregon Coast), summertime tidepool exploration, and year-round views of the Three Arch Rocks National Wildlife Refuge just offshore. Walk to the northern edge of the beach, and you'll arrive at a small, man-made tunnel that heads through the bluff at Maxwell Point and to an even more isolated beach just beyond.

The beach is also popular with surfers, as well as adventurous kayakers and stand-up paddleboarders. Gear up at **Oceanside Surf & SUP** (1505 Pacific Ave., Oceanside; 503/354-5481; www.oceansidesurfco.com; 8am-8pm daily), which offers a variety of rentals—including surf boards ($80 per day or $20 per hour, includes all necessary gear), wet suits ($40 per day), stand-up paddleboards ($80 per day), skim boards ($40 per day), and even body boards ($40-60 per day). Two-hour lessons are also available ($150, discounts available for groups of two or more) and include all necessary gear and equipment. The shop also sells beach towels, surf wax, and other accessories.

From Tillamook, the 9-mile (14.5-km) drive takes about 15 minutes via westbound OR-131.

Recreation
Cape Lookout Trail
Distance: 5.5 miles (8.9 km) round-trip
Duration: 2.5 hours
Elevation Gain: 1,370 feet (418 m)
Effort: Moderate
Trailhead: Cape Lookout trailhead, along Cape Lookout Rd.
Directions: From Tillamook, head west on 3rd St. for 5.1 miles (8.2 km). At a fork in the road, turn left onto Whiskey Creek Rd. Follow the road as it heads south for 7.8 miles (12.6 km), and turn right at a sign for the Cape Lookout Trail parking area.

The out-and-back **Cape Lookout Trail** takes you to the western tip of the cape, where some of the best views anywhere on the Oregon Coast await—as do regular whale-watching opportunities. Soon after leaving the trailhead, stay right at a junction to remain on the Cape Trail, descending through a forest of Sitka spruce and western hemlock. As it progresses, the oft-muddy trail switchbacks several times before heading onto short stretches of boardwalk; keep an eye out in this area for views of Cape Kiwanda and Haystack Rock to the south. After about 2.7 miles (4.3 km), you leave the forest and begin the quick home stretch to the western edge of Cape Lookout. There, 270-degree views await.

Paddling and Water Sports
Explore the quiet Nestucca River, before it flows into the Pacific Ocean, with some help from **Nestucca Adventures** (34650 Brooten Rd., Pacific City; 503/965-0060; www.nestuccaadventures.com; 10am-4pm Thurs.-Mon.). Kayak rentals run $30-65 per hour, while stand-up paddleboard rentals run $30-40; each rental includes paddles and personal flotation devices.

Fishing
Pacific City's angling community is synonymous with flat-bottom dory boats, so do as the

locals do with **Pacific City Fishing** (33180 Cape Kiwanda Dr., Pacific City; 503/320-3476; www.pacificcityfishing.com; $225-325). Captain Mark Lytle offers trips for all the usual species—rockfish, lingcod, salmon, and crab—with cleaning, bagging, vacuum sealing, and ice included. But perhaps the highlight of each trip is the launch and landing, both of which occur not from a dock but by heading through the waves that crash into the shore at the foot of Cape Kiwanda. Up-close views of Haystack Rock are included at no additional charge. Tours depart from the parking area at Pelican Brewing Company.

Brewpubs

There may be no more scenic brewery in Oregon than ★ **Pelican Brewing Company** (33180 Cape Kiwanda Dr.; 503/965-7007; www.pelicanbrewing.com; 11am-10pm daily) in Pacific City. Since 1996, the award-winning brewery has been churning out some of Oregon's best-loved beers, from an easy-drinking cream ale to the chocolate-tinged Tsunami Stout. The pub sits literally steps from the Pacific Ocean and Haystack Rock, making its sand-covered patio the hottest seat in town on spring and summer weekends. You'll also find Pelican outposts in Cannon Beach, Tillamook, and Lincoln City.

Food

Seafood and Pacific Northwest Cuisine

Roseanna's Cafe (1490 Pacific Ave., Oceanside; 503/842-7351; www.roseannascafe.com; 3pm-8pm Thurs.-Sun.; $13-28) is a family-owned eatery that serves a filling lunch and dinner menu leaning heavily on freshly caught, locally sourced seafood—such as fried oysters, a shrimp melt, salmon filets, and rich pasta dishes (topped with shrimp, prawns, and scallops).

The bounty of the Tillamook Bay is on full display at **The Riverhouse Nestucca** (34450 Brooten Rd., Pacific City; 503/483-1255; www.

riverhousenestucca.com; 4pm-9pm Wed.-Sun.; $19-33). The laid-back, airy restaurant overlooks the Nestucca River and celebrates local cuisine with fresh-shucked oysters from nearby Netarts Bay, as well as a wide range of seafood items that includes grilled rockfish tacos and macaroni and cheese prepared with Dungeness crab and wild-caught shrimp. The eatery's menu changes seasonally to reflect what's fresh, and outdoor seating is available in summer.

Meridian Restaurant and Bar (33000 Cape Kiwanda Dr., Pacific City; 503/483-3000; www.headlandslodge.com; 4pm-9pm daily; $24-65) earns the rare distinction of being a hotel restaurant that's as much a destination as the hotel itself. The chic, airy restaurant (housed in Headlands Coastal Lodge & Spa) serves a mix of Pacific Northwest fare and elegant seafood dishes, sourcing its ingredients from the Tillamook Bay region whenever possible; farmers and purveyors are mentioned by name on the Meridian menu, and herbs are plucked from an on-site garden. Popular choices include chargrilled octopus, crab cakes, fresh clams and pasta, and sturgeon—but the menu changes regularly to reflect what's fresh and in season. Diners can also opt for a pre-selected, seasonal four-course meal with an optional Oregon wine pairing for even more local flavor ($100-125).

Bakeries and Cafés

Grateful Bread Restaurant & Bakery (34805 Brooten Rd., Pacific City; 503/965-7337; www.gratefulbreadbakery.com; 8am-2pm Thurs.-Mon.; $13-15) is as much a tribute to the Grateful Dead as it is a delightful café. Servers wear tie-dyed shirts adorned with imagery inspired by the legendary jam band while dishing a hearty selection of scrambles, omelets, lunch sandwiches, tacos, wraps, and more (some of which come topped with locally caught fish). On your way out, grab a loaf of bread, fresh-baked scone, or surprisingly large cookie for the road.

Building a Beach Campfire on the Oregon Coast

The Pacific Ocean might be too cold for swimming in Oregon, but we know how to make the most of our time at the coast. If the weather cooperates, that means building a beach campfire—yes, even in December. If you'd like to build your own campfire on the beach, here's how to get started and stay safe:

- **Location, location, location:** You can technically build a beach campfire almost anywhere on the Oregon Coast, but the communities of Seaside, Cannon Beach, Manzanita, and Pacific City on the northern coast are uniquely suited to nights around the fire—thanks to easy beach access and well-stocked convenience stores close by.

- **Supplies:** All you really need to get started is a bundle of logs, some kindling (or old newspaper), and a lighter. S'mores are optional but encouraged. Having a can of Oregon wine or locally made beer doesn't hurt, either. Just about every coastal community hosts convenience stores near the beach that sell these supplies.

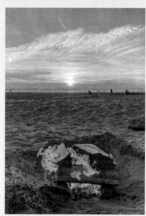

beach bonfire

- **Fire danger level:** Burn bans may be in effect in summer and early fall, especially if conditions are dry and wildfire activity is high around Oregon. Check with your hotel, campground host, the Oregon State Parks website, or your local visitor center before planning a fire.

- **Getting started:** Dig enough sand to create a small pit at your preferred spot; ideally, the logs will be just below the rest of this beach. This minimizes the potential for your fire to spread *and* protects the base of your fire from the Oregon Coast's ever-present wind gusts.

- **Safety:** Note that fires must remain small—roughly the size of a lawn chair—and should be set on dry, open sand west of the vegetation line (far enough away so a stray spark won't cause a grass fire). Burn only small logs, and use plenty of water and sand to completely douse your fire when finished; it should be cool enough to touch.

Accommodations
Oceanside

Each of the six rooms at **Three Arch Inn** (1505 Pacific Ave.; 888/406-8795; www.three-archinn.com; $174-235) offers sweeping ocean views afforded by large windows, but the fun doesn't end there. Amenities include cozy seating areas, free Wi-Fi, jetted tubs, and (in the suite) a full kitchen.

Pacific City

Pacific City's secluded location, away from US-101, preserves no shortage of small-town charm, even on summer weekends. But that means fewer lodgings—which leads to higher prices and more competition for rooms. Book at least three to four months out if angling for a specific summer weekend, and prepare for minimum stays of at least two nights.

Sitting at the base of Cape Kiwanda is Pacific City's most opulent lodging:

(33000 Cape Kiwanda Dr.; 503/483-3000; www.headlandslodge.com; $675-750). Headlands straddles the line between hotel and resort by hosting 33 modern oceanfront lodge rooms, 18 spacious cottages (all with ocean views), in-room racks for bikes and surfboards, pillowtop mattresses, gas fireplaces, Bluetooth speakers, and stylish furnishings. Other amenities include an on-site fitness center, spa treatments, and two Tesla charging stations. Guests can even link up with Headlands' so-called adventure coaches, who can help plan and execute a wide range of local outings (from beach bonfires to kayaking trips).

Just across the highway from the Pacific Ocean, the **Inn at Cape Kiwanda** (33105 Cape Kiwanda Dr.; 888/965-7001; www.in-natcapekiwanda.com; $369-459) blends class and comfort in a variety of ways. Every room boasts an oceanfront view and gas fireplace, while some come with jetted tubs. Other highlights include coffee and pastry deliveries from the café downstairs, free beach chairs and beach towels, free loaner bikes, and free DVD rentals from the front desk. Some rooms are pet-friendly and come with dog towels, blankets, and treats; a pet wash station is available on site.

Sitting on the east side of the Nestucca River, away from the Pacific Ocean, is the quiet **Surf & Sand Inn** (35215 Brooten Rd.; 503/965-6366; www.surfandsandinn.com; $155-175). The charming, one-story inn was a World War II-era U.S. Coast Guard station—but today boasts 15 playfully decorated, no-frills rooms that are far cheaper than premium lodgings elsewhere in town. Secure bicycle storage is available.

Camping

Sitting just north of Cape Lookout proper is the expansive **Cape Lookout State Park campground** (13000 Whiskey Creek Rd., Tillamook; 503/842-4981; www.stateparks. oregon.gov), with sites suited to campers of all comfort levels. In all, the park hosts 38 full-hookup sites ($26-47), 170 tent sites ($17-23), 1 electrical site with water ($24-44), 13 yurts, 6 of which are pet-friendly ($43-64), and 6 deluxe cabins, 3 of which are pet-friendly ($89-108). Sites fill up fast in summer; try to book your preferred site when the reservation window opens six months in advance if planning a trip in July or August.

The campground is separated from the Pacific Ocean by a dune; tent sites closest to the ocean have less shade than the sites farther inland, which sit in a forest of spruce and pine. Amenities include flush toilets and showers, a small interpretive center, an amphitheater where ranger-led programs are held, and easy access to the beach.

When you want to spend a night around the fire but long for a little luxury, make haste for **Hart's Camp** (33145 Webb Park Rd., Pacific City; 503/965-7006; www.hartscamp. com; $349-396). The camp hosts eight luxurious Airstream trailers, each with full (indoor) kitchens, private yards (outfitted with picnic tables, chairs, gas grills, and fire pits), and restrooms with showers. An outdoor common area boasts a large fire pit, outdoor games, and a covered picnic area—and an on-site general store stocks the essentials. Hart's Camp also hosts a shade-free RV park ($65-90) with full hookup sites for RVs or trailers of up to 30 feet (9.1 m); sites come with campfire grills and picnic tables, as well as access to nearby showers and restrooms.

Central Coast

Oregon's central coast runs from Lincoln City to

Winchester Bay—and along the way it packs a wide range of awe-in-spiring natural beauty into seemingly every bend, headland, wayside, and viewpoint.

Travel the central coast and you'll encounter tidepools in the midst of ancient lava flows, where sea stars and other marine life can be viewed up-close; historic lighthouses resting atop windswept headlands and offering wide-open views out to sea; rocky capes butting up against the raging Pacific Ocean; and the always-shifting Oregon Dunes, one of the longest stretches of coastal sand dunes in North America. And that's to say nothing of the many viewpoints where you can watch

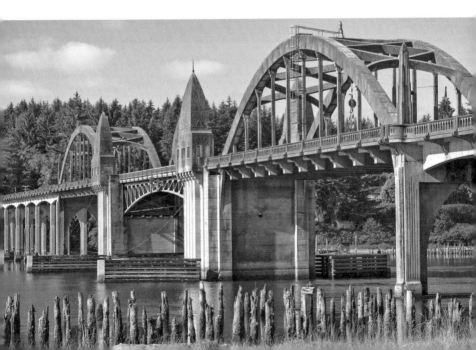

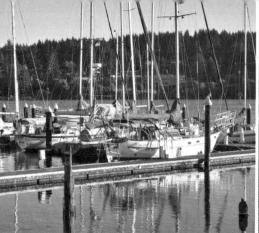
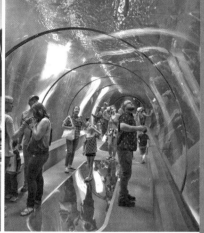

Highlights

Look for ★ to find recommended sights, activities, dining, and lodging.

★ **Visit the Whale Watching Center:** The onshore viewing station offers sweeping vistas in the heart of Depoe Bay (page 126).

★ **Experience the splendor of Yaquina Head Outstanding Natural Area:** Get up close with marine creatures at vibrant tidepools, watch for migrating whales from atop a wide-open headland, and stand at the base of the tallest lighthouse on the Oregon Coast (page 133).

★ **See marine life at the Oregon Coast Aquarium:** Fish, seabirds, and other Oregon Coast wildlife all call the massive aquarium home (page 135).

★ **Marvel at Cape Perpetua:** Tidepools, dramatic rock formations, hiking trails, and scenic viewpoints come together at this sprawling headland (page 142).

★ **Stroll Historic Old Town Florence:** Enjoy family-friendly eateries, charming inns, and more on the Siuslaw riverfront (page 146).

★ **Hike to Heceta Head Lighthouse:** A short stroll ends at one of the Oregon Coast's most-photographed lighthouses (page 148).

★ **Check out the Sea Lion Caves:** Descend to the base of a cave that's home to hundreds of clamoring sea lions (page 148).

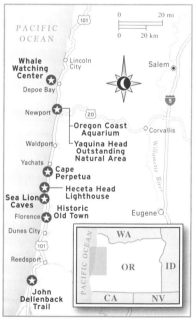

★ **Hike the John Dellenback Trail:** The dramatic hike showcases one of the longest stretches of coastal dunes in the world (page 154).

migrating gray whales or caves where you can gawk at the coast's resident sea lions.

The variety of outdoor beauty is matched only by the disparate communities you may find yourself in while traveling the central coast. Lincoln City welcomes families with twice-yearly kite festivals and plenty of coastline for building sandcastles, while the likes of Newport and Florence boast historic old towns—home to locally sourced seafood restaurants and enchanting attractions. The region's smaller communities of Depoe Bay and Yachats, meanwhile, offer an unhurried look at life on the Oregon Coast through mom-and-pop restaurants, boutique inns, and uncrowded (but no less scenic) views.

PLANNING YOUR TIME

Most visitors will find that a weekend on the central coast is enough time to see some of the region's outdoor attractions, enjoy locally sourced seafood, indulge in the sights, and (with luck) see a breathtaking sunset or spy migrating gray whales.

But trying to cover the entire central coast in one weekend will entail more driving than you'd prefer; it's two hours from **Lincoln City** (at the northern edge of the region) to **Winchester Bay** (in the south), but opportunities to stop present themselves almost the entire way.

Rather, consider making Lincoln City or Newport your home base if trying to see the central coast's top sights on a **two- or three-day trip;** these are the region's largest communities and boast the most hotel rooms, eateries, and tourist services. **Lincoln City** sits at the northern edge of the area and is near **Depoe Bay,** a cozy fishing community, as well as **Neskowin,** home to scenic beach access and a beloved hiking trail.

Some 30 minutes south of Lincoln City, **Newport** boasts plenty to do in its own right—and is the most centrally located of the area's communities, with easy access to the likes of **Yachats** (30 minutes south) and **Florence** (60 minutes south), the latter of which sits at the northern edge of the **Oregon Dunes Natural Scenic Area.** That central location makes Newport the best option for visitors hoping to cover a bit of ground.

That said, you'll find plenty of small-town charm in **Depoe Bay,** home to a handful of thoughtful inns and lauded restaurants, and **Yachats,** surrounded by immense natural beauty. And if the Oregon Dunes are your ultimate goal, **Florence** is the largest community nearby—and is just across the **Siuslaw River** from the northernmost dunes. Farther south, the working-class communities of **Reedsport** and **Winchester Bay** sit just inland and offer easy access to the dunes and other natural attractions.

Summer is the best time to visit Oregon's central coast, with little rainfall June-September; this is also when families flock to the coast in droves, filling campgrounds and leading to long waits at the area's most popular restaurants. If you're looking for a quieter experience with off-season lodging rates, consider a trip in April-May or October, when crowds are a bit thinner; the weather can be unpredictable at this time but is generally mild. November-March is the height of stormy season, with overcast skies and rain showers a regular occurrence—which makes it a fine time to watch storms roll in off the Pacific Ocean and batter the coast's rocky headlands. Migrating gray whales are another draw, and are most common in Dec.-Jan. and March-June.

Previous: Siuslaw River Bridge in Florence; ships docked on the waterfront in Historic Old Town Florence; Oregon Coast Aquarium exhibit.

Central Coast

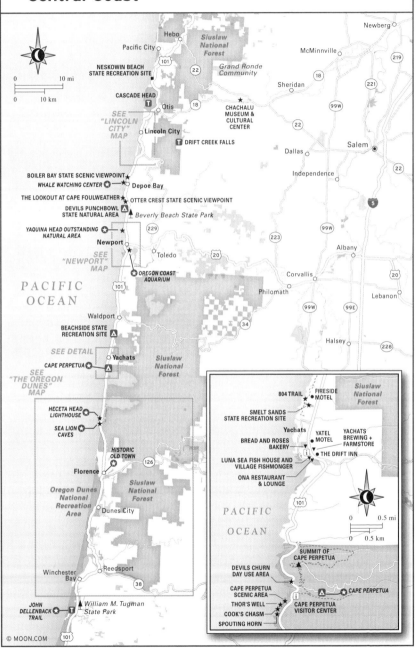

Newberg

Hebo

Siuslaw National Forest

Pacific City

McMinnville

(219)

101

NESKOWIN BEACH
STATE RECREATION SITE

22

Grand Ronde Community

Sheridan

18

221

CASCADE HEAD

Otis

18

★ CHACHALU
MUSEUM &
CULTURAL
CENTER

99W

22

Salem

SEE
"LINCOLN
CITY"
MAP

Lincoln City

DRIFT CREEK FALLS

Dallas

Independence

22

BOILER BAY STATE SCENIC VIEWPOINT
WHALE WATCHING CENTER ● Depoe Bay

THE LOOKOUT AT CAPE FOULWEATHER ★ Otter Crest State Scenic Viewpoint

DEVILS PUNCHBOWL
STATE NATURAL AREA ▲ *Beverly Beach State Park*

5

YAQUINA HEAD OUTSTANDING
NATURAL AREA

229

Newport

223

99W

SEE
"NEWPORT"
MAP

Toledo

Albany

20

20

**PACIFIC
OCEAN**

OREGON COAST
AQUARIUM

101

Corvallis

Philomath

Lebanon

Waldport

34

99W

99E

BEACHSIDE STATE
RECREATION SITE

Halsey

228

SEE DETAIL

Yachats

Siuslaw National Forest

CAPE PERPETUA ▲

SEE
"THE OREGON
DUNES"
MAP

*HECETA HEAD
LIGHTHOUSE*

*SEA LION
CAVES*

*HISTORIC
OLD TOWN*

126

Florence

*Oregon Dunes
National
Recreation
Area*

Dunes City

*Siuslaw
National
Forest*

Winchester
Bay

Reedsport

38

*JOHN
DELLENBACK
TRAIL*

William M. Tugman
State Park

101

© MOON.COM

Inset detail map

Siuslaw National Forest

804 TRAIL ★ FIRESIDE
MOTEL

SMELT SANDS
STATE RECREATION SITE

Yachats

YATEL
MOTEL

YACHATS
BREWING +
FARMSTORE

BREAD AND ROSES
BAKERY

THE DRIFT INN

LUNA SEA FISH HOUSE AND
VILLAGE FISHMONGER

ONA RESTAURANT
& LOUNGE

101

**PACIFIC
OCEAN**

0   0.5 mi
0   0.5 km

SUMMIT OF
CAPE PERPETUA

DEVILS CHURN
DAY USE AREA

CAPE PERPETUA ★ CAPE PERPETUA
SCENIC AREA

THOR'S WELL ▲ CAPE PERPETUA
VISITOR CENTER

COOK'S CHASM

SPOUTING HORN

N   10 mi
N   10 km

Lincoln City

By Oregon Coast standards, Lincoln City (pop. 9,800) is a remarkably *young* community. Between the late 1800s and mid-1950s, the city as we know it today was actually five smaller townships—all sharing a seven-mile stretch of sandy shoreline on the central Oregon Coast. The community of Oceanlake, for instance, was named as such because it sat between the Pacific Ocean and Devil's Lake. To the south, Taft was the social and economic heart of the area at the northern edge of Siletz Bay.

But in 1964, the five communities decided to join together as one: Lincoln City was officially incorporated in March 1965.

In the years since, the sprawling Lincoln City has enjoyed success as a bustling tourist destination, with year-round fun that ranges from outdoor adventure to more art-oriented fare. Hiking and beachgoing are both popular pastimes, and you don't need to leave town to find a picturesque campground or wildlife refuge teeming with critters. The city's celebrated art scene, meanwhile, revolves around glass art—from glasswork you can craft yourself to colorful floats that get placed along the coastline year-round. A handful of refreshing brewpubs and filling restaurants are ready to serve when you're done adventuring for the day.

SIGHTS
Siletz Bay National Wildlife Refuge

Enjoy a rich variety of wildlife and ecosystems at **Siletz Bay National Wildlife Refuge** (along US-101, 5 mi/8 km south of Lincoln City; 541/867-4550; www.fws.gov; sunrise-sunset daily; free), which occupies the eastern shore of Siletz Bay and the southern shore of the Siletz River. The quiet refuge sits on the site of a former cow pasture that's been reclaimed by Mother Nature; today, visitors can follow the short, flat 1-mile/1.6-km (round-trip) Alder Island Nature Trail

through forests, marshland, mudflats, meadows, and other ecosystems—where wildlife sightings are not an uncommon occurrence. In spring and fall, migrating shorebirds feed on the estuary's clams, crabs, worms, and other critters; by summer, osprey and brown pelicans feed in the wetlands. All year long, visitors might spot elk, deer, river otters, and (less frequently) bobcats, coyotes, and even black bears. A boat launch is available to non-motorized craft next to the parking area (bring your own canoe, kayak, or stand-up paddleboard; rentals aren't available).

Chachalu Museum and Cultural Center

Just east of Lincoln City, the Confederated Tribes of Grand Ronde honors its past and present in a variety of fascinating ways at the **Chachalu Museum and Cultural Center** (8720 Grand Ronde Rd., Grand Ronde; 503/879-5211; grandronde.org; 10am-4pm Tues.-Fri.; free). The museum spotlights cultural artifacts, wall-size photographs of important natural spaces, and interpretive panels that describe the many tribes of western Oregon, traditional foods, and more. From Lincoln City, the 26-mile (42-km) drive takes about 35 minutes via US-101 north and OR-18 east toward Salem/Portland.

BEACHES

Just north of town, **Neskowin Beach State Recreation Site** (along US-101, 13 mi/21 km north of Lincoln City; 541/994-7341; www.stateparks.oregon.gov; sunrise-sunset daily; free) hosts some of the area's most distinctive natural features near the community of Neskowin. Chief among them: the Neskowin Ghost Forest, comprising the remnants of a Sitka spruce forest that dates back 2,000 years; when the tide is low, roughly 100 stumps peek through the sandy shoreline. Immediately north of the ghost forest is Proposal Rock,

Lincoln City

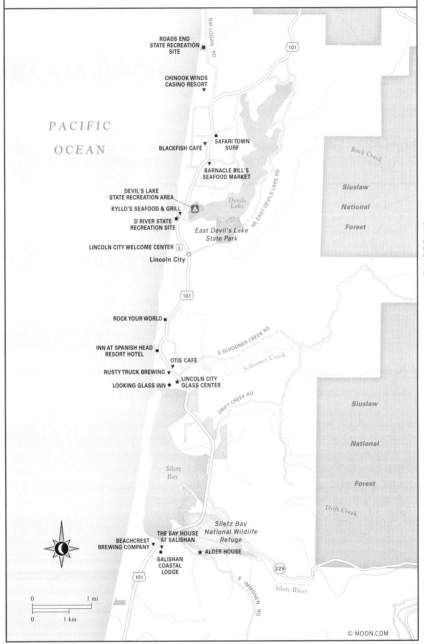

PACIFIC

OCEAN

ROADS END
STATE RECREATION
SITE

NW LOGAN RD

101

CHINOOK WINDS
CASINO RESORT

SAFARI TOWN
SURF

BLACKFISH CAFÉ

BARNACLE BILL'S
SEAFOOD MARKET

NE EAST DEVILS LAKE RD

Rock Creek

Siuslaw

National

Forest

DEVIL'S LAKE
STATE RECREATION AREA

KYLLO'S SEAFOOD & GRILL

D RIVER STATE
RECREATION SITE

Devils
Lake

East Devil's Lake
State Park

LINCOLN CITY WELCOME CENTER

Lincoln City

101

ROCK YOUR WORLD

S SCHOONER CREEK RD

INN AT SPANISH HEAD
RESORT HOTEL

OTIS CAFÉ

Schooner Creek

RUSTY TRUCK BREWING

LOOKING GLASS INN

LINCOLN CITY
GLASS CENTER

DRIFT CREEK RD

Siuslaw

National

Forest

Siletz
Bay

Drift Creek

Siletz Bay
National Wildlife
Refuge

THE BAY HOUSE
AT SALISHAN

BEACHCREST
BREWING COMPANY

ALDER HOUSE

SALISHAN
COASTAL
LODGE

229

101

S IMMONEN RD

Siletz River

0   1 mi

0   1 km

© MOON.COM

a towering island just offshore. And at the southern edge of the beach sits Cascade Head, a massive headland that dwarfs the surrounding forest. Note that reaching the ghost forest involves crossing a small stream that empties into the ocean; the water is rarely more than ankle-high, but it is chilly all year long—so take caution when doing so. Flush restrooms are available at the parking area.

Still something of a local secret, **Roads End State Recreation Site** (NE Sal La Sea Dr. & NE Logan Rd.; 541/994-7341; www.stateparks.oregon.gov; sunrise-sunset daily; free) is partially protected from the elements by a headland to the north; as a result, it consistently boasts calmer, less windy conditions than other nearby beaches. Rocky outcrops just offshore are the remnants of an ancient lava flow—and provide habitat for several species of shorebird. Flush restrooms are available at the parking area.

Found in the heart of town, **D River State Recreation Site** (US-101 & SE 1st St.; 541/994-7341; www.stateparks.oregon.gov; sunrise-sunset daily; free) sits where the D River flows into the Pacific Ocean—completing a journey of just 120 feet from nearby Devil's Lake. (Some contend it's the shortest river in the world, though that remains a matter of dispute.) The windy conditions here are usually favorable to kite flying, even if you'll likely share the shore with heavy crowds staying at surrounding motels. Flush restrooms are available at the parking area.

While exploring beaches around Lincoln City, keep an eye out for glass floats—the colorful centerpiece of the community's **Finders Keepers** (www.oregoncoast.org) event. Each year, more than 3,000 spherical floats crafted by local artisans are placed along public beaches around Lincoln City; if you find a float, it's yours to keep. Floats are placed throughout the year, but additional (typically themed) floats are generally dropped on select dates, usually tied to holidays and celebrations; additional red, white, and pink floats might be placed on the beach around Valentine's Day, for instance.

RECREATION
Hiking
Cascade Head

Distance: *5.2 miles (8.4 km) round-trip*
Duration: *2.5 hours*
Elevation Gain: *1,150 feet (351 m)*
Effort: *Easy/moderate*
Trailhead: *Knight County Park, roughly 8.5 miles (13.7 km) north of Lincoln City via US-101 and N. Three Rocks Rd.*

The out-and-back **Cascade Head Trail** ascends nearly to the summit of a sweeping headland near the mouth of the Salmon River. The hike starts near an informational sign board before crossing North Three Rocks Road almost immediately; continue hiking through a forest of ferns, salal, and Sitka spruce. After about 0.4 mile (0.6 km), head left at a Y-shaped intersection to cross Savage Road, and follow the gravel path on the road's shoulder northward, following many signs that point the way. After 0.1 mile (0.2 km), cross the road again, returning to the forest at a sign for the **old Cascade Head Trailhead.** In another mile, you'll arrive at a meadow that offers your first views of the Pacific Ocean and (to the south) the Salmon River. The path continues ascending the exposed hillside, often through meadows of wildflowers (late May-mid-June) before arriving at a sweeping viewpoint marked by an unsigned metal post. The trail continues on, but this makes a fine turnaround point.

Drift Creek Falls

Distance: *4.4 miles (7.1 km) round-trip*
Duration: *2 hours*
Elevation Gain: *570 feet (174 m)*
Effort: *Easy/moderate*
Passes/Fees: *$5 or Northwest Forest Pass*
Trailhead: *Along Forest Road 17, roughly 16 miles (26 km) southeast of Lincoln City via US-101 and S. Drift Creek Camp Rd.*
Directions: *From Lincoln City, head 3.5 miles (5.6 km) south on US-101 to milepost 119, then turn left to head east on South Drift Creek Road for 1.6 miles (2.6 km). Turn right at a T-shaped junction to remain on the road. After 0.4 mile (0.7 km), head to the left at a fork,*

uphill, onto South Drift Creek Camp Road, which soon becomes Forest Road 17. Follow it for 10.2 (16.4 km) paved miles to the trailhead parking area, which will be on your right.

The **Drift Creek Falls Trail** descends from the trailhead through a forest of Douglas fir, vine maple, alder, ferns, and salal before crossing Homer Creek in 1.2 miles (1.9 km). Over the next 0.4 mile (0.6 km), the trail continues descending through a forest of western red cedar and Sitka spruce before arriving at a 240-foot (73-m) suspension bridge that spans Drift Creek; here the scenic waterfall at the end of your hike comes into view. Continue another 0.25 mile (0.4 km) down to the base of the 75-foot (23-m) waterfall, flanked by columnar basalt that formed 55 million years ago. On your return ascent, consider a detour through the **North Loop,** which winds through an old-growth forest for 1 mile (1.6 km) before returning to the **Drift Creek Falls Trail** and climbing back to the trailhead.

Paddling and Water Sports

Right in town, **East Devil's Lake State Park** (205 NE East Devil's Lake Rd.; 541/994-2002; www.stateparks.oregon.gov; sunrise-sunset daily; free) sits on the eastern shore of Devil's Lake and hosts a boat launch where kayakers, canoers, and stand-up paddleboarders can get on Devil's Lake. The inland location shelters the J-shaped lake from Lincoln City's famous winds, creating pleasant conditions for new and relaxed paddlers; wetlands and stands of Douglas fir surround the lake, offering a nice buffer from nearby city life. The lake technically empties into the Pacific Ocean via the D River, but this river is far too shallow to ford. Watch for bald eagles, snowy plovers, and great blue herons hunting for their next meal. A restroom is available at the parking area.

If you didn't bring your own gear, rent what you need from **Safari Town Surf** (3026 NE US-101, Ste. 3; 541/996-6335; www.safaritownsurf.com; 9am-7pm Mon.-Sat. and noon-7pm Sun. mid-June-Labor Day; 1pm-5pm Mon., 10am-5pm Wed.-Sat., noon-5pm Sun. Labor Day-mid-June), which offers single

kayaks ($50 per day) and tandem kayaks ($60 per day); rentals include a paddle, seat back, and life jacket. Delivery to the lake is available ($100-130), as are soft racks ($5 per day) for hauling your rental to and from the shop. Paddlers can sign up for a two-hour, family-friendly guided kayak tour ($99), as well.

The shop also leads private and group stand-up paddleboarding lessons on Devil's Lake ($119-150); each lesson includes necessary instruction along with a board, paddle, leash, life jacket, and wetsuit rental—all for up to 24 hours.

Fat Tire Biking

With so much shoreline, Lincoln City has fast become a destination for fat tire biking—which uses bicycles outfitted with extra-wide tires to gain traction and tackle difficult terrain, such as sandy beaches. Around town, **Roads End State Recreation Site** is a great place for beginners to give the activity a try, thanks to minimal elevation gain, little foot traffic to contend with, and close proximity to Lincoln City proper.

If you want to give the fun activity a shot, the family-owned-and-operated **Safari Town Surf** (3026 NE US-101, Ste. 3; 541/996-6335; www.safaritownsurf.com; 9am-7pm Mon.-Sat. and noon-7pm Sun. mid-June-Labor Day; 1pm-5pm Mon., 10am-5pm Wed.-Sat., noon-5pm Sun. Labor Day-mid-June) offers rentals ($50 per day), which include a helmet. For a more challenging ride, book a guided, 10.5-mile/16.9-km (round-trip) outing to Siletz Bay ($139 per person, two-person minimum).

BREWPUBS AND NIGHTLIFE
Brewpubs

Rusty Truck Brewing (4649 SW US-101, Lincoln City; 541/994-7729; www.rustytruckbrewing.com; 3pm-9pm Wed., noon-9pm Thurs.-Fri. and Sun., noon-11pm Sat.) offers an old-school craft beer experience in the heart of Lincoln City. You'll find plenty of traditional yet expertly brewed ales and lagers

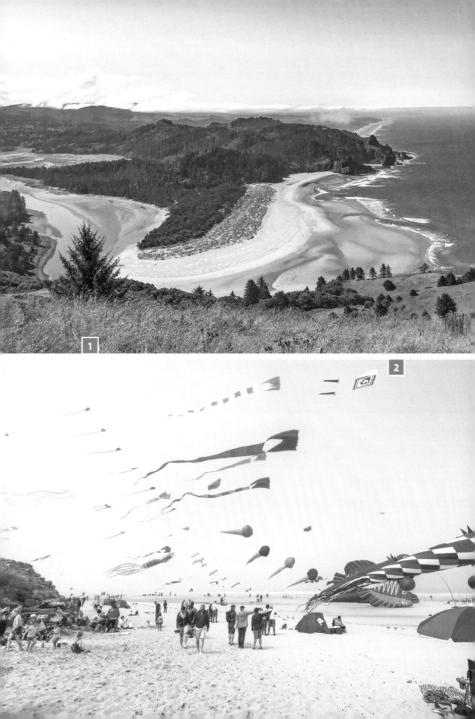

on the menu—with an amber ale, German-style pilsner, and a slightly bitter Pacific Northwest IPA leading the way. Some of Rusty Truck's more creative efforts include a golden ale brewed with Oregon-grown blackberries and a toffee porter sporting strong notes of chocolate and—surprise!—toffee.

South of Lincoln City, at the sprawling Salishan Coastal Lodge complex, is one of the newer breweries on the Oregon Coast. ★ **Beachcrest Brewing Company** (7755 N. US-101, Gleneden Beach; 541/234-4013; www.beachcrestbrewing.com; 1pm-6pm Mon.-Thurs., noon-8pm Fri.-Sat., noon-6pm Sun.) offers 12 house-made beers on tap at its family-friendly pub, usually sporting a creative mix of small-batch seasonal offerings—which means the tap list will change from visit to visit. Beachcrest offers plenty of outdoor seating, including a covered and heated tent that occasionally hosts live music.

Casinos

A pair of tribal casinos sit within (and near) Lincoln City—and are undeniable draws for regional visitors.

Chinook Winds Casino Resort (1777 NW 44th St., Lincoln City; 888/244-6665; www.chinookwindscasino.com; 8am-4pm daily) is owned and operated by the Confederated Tribes of Siletz Indians—and features a wide range of table games, slots, sports betting, bingo, keno, and more; other attractions at the resort include overnight accommodations, several on-site eateries, a golf course, and regular entertainment (from sporting event watch parties to stand-up comedy sets).

Roughly 28 miles (45 km) east of Lincoln City sits **Spirit Mountain Casino** (27100 SW Salmon River Hwy., Grand Ronde; 503/879-2350; www.spiritmountain.com; 24 hours daily), owned and operated by the Confederated Tribes of Grand Ronde. The casino specializes in table games, slots, and

keno; an on-site hotel offers overnight stays, a handful of on-site eateries serve a variety of cuisines, and an entertainment hall hosts live events.

ART GALLERIES

For many, Lincoln City has long been synonymous with glass art. In the early to mid-20th century, glass fishing floats would routinely wash ashore around town, having floated all the way from Japan. These days, the city's **Finders Keepers** (www.oregoncoast.org) promotion invites beachcombers to find glass floats that are designed by local artists and deliberately placed on the shore. It's no wonder the city hosts a handful of galleries, shops, and studios devoted to glass art today.

Lincoln City Glass Center (4821 SW US-101; 541/996-2569; www.lincolncityglasscenter.com; 10am-6pm daily) is the heart of glassblowing in Lincoln City; it hosts two galleries, offers a wide variety of colorful glass artwork for sale (such as votives, floats, and paperweights), and invites visitors to watch glassblowers ply their trade in the workshop. Visitors can even craft their own pieces ($65-225) alongside friendly artists and instructors.

Away from town, **Alder House** (611 Immonen Rd.; 541/996-2483; www.alderhouse.com; 10am-5pm daily May-Oct.) is a glassblowing studio where visitors can watch pieces being created in real time. Visitors can watch the entire glassblowing process, chat with artists about how it all works, and even have custom pieces crafted (for a fee); predesigned pieces (such as vases, pendants, and floats) are also available for purchase.

FESTIVALS AND EVENTS

Predictable winds and plenty of sand make Lincoln City a popular spot to fly kites. It's only natural, then, that the city holds not one but two **Kite Festivals** (www.oregoncoast.org; free) each year—one in June, right around the summer solstice, and the other in early October. The festivals, both taking place at the D River State Recreation Site, usually include

1: views from Cascade Head 2: Kite Festival in Lincoln City

kite-making workshops, performances, a parade on the beach, and demonstrations with massive kites. If you'd like to fly kites on your own, no matter the season, find them at several gift shops and souvenir stores throughout Lincoln City.

SHOPPING

Since 2011, the woman-owned **Rock Your World** (3203 SW US-101; 541/351-8423; www.rockyourworldgems.com; 11am-5pm Sun.-Thurs., 11am-6pm Fri.-Sat.) has carried rocks, gems, minerals, jewelry, and more—with much of that selection sourced from the Pacific Northwest; even if you're not a rockhound, you'll be amazed by the intricate designs and colorful specimens on display. The shop also offers what it calls **Beachcombing Exploriences** (Jan.-Apr.; free); each two-hour guided trip invites amateur rockhounds to comb the Lincoln City coastline for agates, fossils, gemstones, shells, petrified wood, and other items that wash ashore after winter and spring storms.

Barnacle Bill's Seafood Market (2174 NE US-101; 541/994-3022; www.barnaclebillsseafoodmarket.com; 9:30am-5pm Sun.-Thurs., 9:30am-5:30pm Fri.-Sat.) is an open-air market where visitors can purchase fresh-caught seafood to prepare back at their hotel or campsite, as well as smoked and packaged food to enjoy back home. The market has been a mainstay since 1949, thanks in part to an ever-changing lineup of fresh seafood (including Chinook salmon, albacore tuna, lingcod, and Dungeness crab) and prepared items (such as smoked salmon and canned tuna). Fried fish-and-chips are also available; everything is cash only, but an ATM is on-site.

FOOD
Seafood

For decades, ★ **Blackfish Café** (2733 NW US-101, Lincoln City; 541/996-1007; www.blackfishcafe.com; 11:30am-3pm and 5pm-8pm Wed.-Sun.; $14-40) has effortlessly walked a fine line between "casual eatery" and "upscale, sit-down dining experience"—earning acclaim for its inventive dishes and fresh seafood in the process. (In some cases, the seafood in your meal may have been caught just hours earlier.) Fish-and-chips are prepared with a batter featuring Oregon-brewed beer, rockfish is sourced from nearby Pacific City, oysters come from Yaquina Bay in Newport, and ocean-caught salmon fillets are basted with a fennel lime butter for an elegant touch.

Both the view and the seafood come highly recommended at **Kyllo's Seafood & Grill** (1110 NW 1st Ct., Lincoln City; 541/994-3179; www.kyllosseafoodandgrill.com; 11:30am-8pm Sun.-Thurs., 11:30am-9pm Fri.-Sat.; $16-49). The menu leans heavily on seafood, with an emphasis on locally sourced ingredients; oysters come from Willapa Bay, and the crab linguine is made with Dungeness crab—a local specialty. And sitting at the edge of the surf, Kyllo's also has some of the best sunset views in Lincoln City. Reservations aren't accepted, so be prepared to wait for a table at dinnertime, especially on summer weekends.

Long a Lincoln City fine-dining institution, **The Bay House at Salishan** (7760 N. US-101, Gleneden Beach; 541/996-3222; www.thebayhouse.org; 5:30-9pm Wed.-Sun.; $74-100) moved in 2020 to the Salishan Coastal Lodge in nearby Gleneden Beach—but has lost none of what made the original so special. The restaurant serves a three- or four-course menu, as well as a six-course tasting menu, with the likes of pork belly (topped with salted caramel apple butter) and smoked Muscovy duck being just some of the highlights. The curated wine list features some of Oregon's best, as well.

Classic American

Since the 1920s, **Otis Café** (4618 SE US-101; 541/994-2813; www.otiscafe.com; 7am-3pm daily; $11-16) has been a popular stop for down-home cooking. The diner's original location (just north of town) burned down in 2019, and it reopened the following year in Lincoln City proper; fans still line up on summer weekends for filling portions of its

omelets, griddle fare, and burgers. In 1989, no less than the *New York Times* called the Otis Café's German potatoes, hand-peeled and cooked to order, "legendary." Meat and seafood are sourced from regional producers, and all breads and baked goods are made in-house.

ACCOMMODATIONS

Inn at Spanish Head Resort Hotel (4009 SW US-101, Lincoln City; 541/996-2161; www.spanishhead.com; $259-399) looks as if it were built into a cliffside on the shore of the Oregon Coast—and, in turn, offers guests what feels like their own private stretch of shoreline. Each of the hotel's 120 rooms boast ocean views with floor-to-ceiling windows, and most come with private balconies; some have full kitchens. On-site amenities include a restaurant and bar, an outdoor heated pool, and an indoor hot tub—all with ocean views, naturally.

Lincoln City's historic Taft neighborhood brims with historic buildings at the edge of Siletz Bay, and the cozy **Looking Glass Inn** (861 SW 51st St., Lincoln City; 541/996-3996; www.lookingglassinn.com; $149-239) sits in the heart of it all. Several rooms and suites boast bay and ocean views, and thoughtful amenities include an outdoor crab cooking station, an outdoor fire pit, in-room kitchens, and gas fireplaces. Dogs of all sizes are welcome—and will receive towels, two bowls, treats, and more at check-in.

The **Salishan Coastal Lodge** (7760 N. US-101, Gleneden Beach; 541/764-3600; www.salishan.com; $314-1,262) makes it possible to spend a weekend at the Oregon Coast without ever visiting the Oregon Coast. Just a short drive south of Lincoln City, the resort hosts an 18-hole golf course (designed by PGA golfer Peter Jacobsen), a full-service spa (offering facials, massages, enhancements, private yoga sessions, and more), on-site nature trails, a tennis center, three on-site restaurants, and even a thrilling aerial adventure park. The rooms and suites, meanwhile, evoke the Pacific Northwest with plenty of stone, locally sourced timber, and natural light; fireplaces and private balconies are in each room, as well. A three-night stay may be required on summer weekends.

Camping

You don't even have to leave town for a great camping experience around Lincoln City. **Devil's Lake State Recreation Area** (1452 NE 6th Dr.; 541/994-2002; www.stateparks.oregon.gov; $7-64) sits in town, just a minute or two from US-101 and along the southern shore of its namesake lake. Campers can choose from 28 full-hookup sites, 5 electrical sites, 54 tent sites, 10 yurts (5 of which are pet-friendly), and a hiker-biker camp area; none of the sites sit directly on the lakeshore, but a wide trail leads to a dock on the water. (Two campsites and two yurts are wheelchair accessible.) Flush toilets and hot showers are available, and firewood is for sale from a camp host. Portions of the campground close in winter due to flooding; closures can last into June, weather depending. Given its location within Lincoln City, sites routinely fill up on summer weekends; make reservations six months out, when the reservation window opens—especially if you have your heart set on a specific site or yurt.

INFORMATION AND SERVICES

The **Lincoln City Welcome Center** (801 SW US-101, fourth floor; 541/996-1274; www.oregoncoast.org; 8am-5pm Mon.-Fri.) offers maps, brochures, pamphlets, and visitor guides for exploring the community—and its staff members are happy to provide recommendations for making the most of your time in town.

GETTING THERE AND AROUND

From Tillamook, the 44-mile (71-km) drive to Lincoln City takes about 1 hour via southbound US-101. From Newport, the 25-mile (40-km) drive to takes about 35 minutes via northbound US-101. From Salem, the 58-mile (93-km) drive takes about 1 hour, 10 minutes

via westbound OR-22 and OR-18, as well as southbound US-101. And from Portland, the 88-mile (142-km) drive takes about 1 hour, 50 minutes via I-5 southbound, as well as OR-99W and OR-18 westbound.

US-101 is the primary north-south thoroughfare through Lincoln City. Given that the community occupies such a long stretch of coastline—and hosts such a high volume of visitors—traffic can slow to a crawl on summer weekends; give yourself plenty of time, and consider avoiding US-101 at peak travel times (3pm-7pm Fri.-Sat. and 11am-3pm Sun.).

For car-free travel, **NW Connector** (503/861-7433; www.nworegontransit.org; $1-5) and **Lincoln County Transit** (541/265-4900; www.co.lincoln.or.us/transit) run four buses daily (and another bus Mon.-Sat.) between Lincoln City and surrounding communities, with stops in Depoe Bay and at Beverly Beach State Park. Another route loops through town Monday-Saturday ($1). Visitors can also take one of three daily buses (each way) between Lincoln City and Salem in the Willamette Valley ($1.50-6), with a stop along the way at Spirit Mountain Casino.

Depoe Bay

The community of Depoe Bay (pop. 1,800) is a popular stop roughly halfway between Lincoln and Newport. West of US-101, a sidewalk follows the top of a rock wall where waves tumble onto the shore and upward through a rocky fissure (creating a blowhole-like display); during winter storms, raging waves can crash over the wall and onto the highway. East of US-101, visitors stroll a strip of souvenir shops, seafood eateries, and outfitters; fishing and whale-watching are both popular pastimes around town, and guides are happy to help you enjoy both.

Speaking of those pastimes: Charters leave from the cozy confines of Depoe Bay, which city officials claim is the world's smallest natural navigable harbor; at its narrowest point, Depoe Bay is just 50 feet wide. The main sidewalk through town offers a viewpoint of ships coming and going, as well as the seals and sea lions lazing on its banks.

SIGHTS

TOP EXPERIENCE

★ **Whale Watching Center**
Every year, nearly 25,000 gray whales pass the Oregon Coast on their migrations between Alaska and Mexico. If you're interested

in spying the majestic creatures, the **Whale Watching Center** (119 SW US-101; 541/765-3304; www.stateparks.oregon.gov; hours vary by season; free) is an essential stop in the heart of Depoe Bay. Sitting atop a seawall and home to an expansive viewing deck, the center delivers wide-open ocean views—along with binoculars, interpretive panels about whales, and other helpful resources. Oregon State Parks staff and volunteers are happy to provide tips for seeing whales, updates on when they were most recently spotted, and recommendations for other stops to go whale-watching. Some resident gray whales linger year-round, but the best time to see them is mid-December-mid-January and late March-June; even if gray whales aren't migrating, you might spot humpback whales, orcas, dolphins, and other species.

Boiler Bay State Scenic Viewpoint
A basalt-rimmed viewpoint affords spectacular views of the Pacific Ocean, as well as the eponymous bay, at **Boiler Bay State Scenic Viewpoint** (1.2 mi/1.9 km north of Depoe Bay along US-101; 541/265-4560; www.stateparks.oregon.gov; sunrise-sunset daily; free)

1: the harbor at Depoe Bay **2:** The Lookout at Cape Foulweather gift shop **3:** Devils Punchbowl State Natural Area

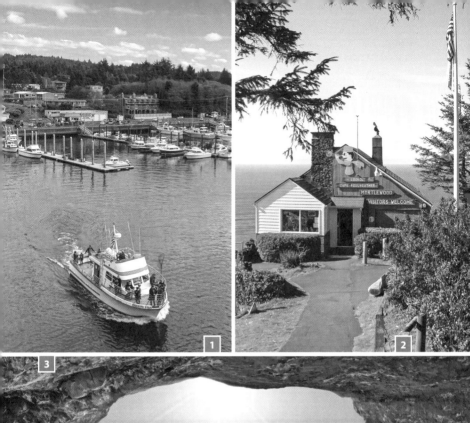

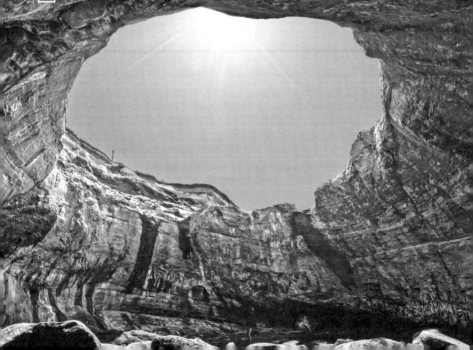

just north of town. At low tide, peer down into the bay to see if you can spy the boiler from the *J. Marhoffer,* a ship that exploded and sank here in 1910; predictably, this is the boiler that gives the bay its name. In winter, furious waves pound the headland and shoreline around the viewpoint; in spring, migrating whales come close to shore; and all year long, a variety of birds (including pelicans and oystercatchers) can be seen around the viewpoint. Restrooms are available, and several picnic tables invite visitors to linger.

Otter Crest State Scenic Viewpoint

Otter Crest State Scenic Viewpoint (3.8 mi/6.1 south of Depoe Bay along Otter Crest Loop; 541/765-2270; www.stateparks.oregon. gov; sunrise-sunset daily; free) offers spectacular views of some of the Oregon Coast's most distinctive landmarks: the headland and rocky outcrops of Cape Foulweather to the north and Devils Punchbowl (a bowl-shaped headland) to the south. In addition to sweeping views from 500 feet above the shore, you may spy some of the area's wildlife—such as bald eagles, gray whales, harbor seals, pelicans, and gulls. An on-site gift shop—**The Lookout at Cape Foulweather** (541/765-2270; www.stateparks.oregon.gov; 10am-4pm Wed.-Sun.)—sells all manner of coast-related trinkets and souvenirs; park staff are also on hand to offer whale-watching assistance, and benches invite visitors to sit and sightsee through massive windows.

Devils Punchbowl State Natural Area

Year-round fun abounds at **Devils Punchbowl State Natural Area** (5.5 mi/9 km south of Depoe Bay along 1st St.; 541/265-4560; www.stateparks.oregon.gov; sunrise-sunset daily; free). The heart of the park is a bowl-shaped collapsed sea cave. At low tide, visitors can descend to the beach below and enter the rocky base of the cave; at high tide (and during winter storms), churning waves thrash about, creating a dramatic sight.

Tidepools can be explored on the north side of the cave, as well. Flush toilets and picnic tables are available. The viewpoint is surrounded by homes and businesses, so take care to park in designated spots only. Devils Punchbowl gets busy on summer weekends, so try to arrive by 9am or after 4pm to miss the biggest crowds.

RECREATION
Whale-Watching

Depoe Bay is home to a few whale-watching outfitters that offer up-close views of the massive creatures—as well as other wildlife that calls the area home.

Tradewinds Charters (118 SE US-101; 541/765-2345; www.tradewindscharters.com; $30-50, $15-30 for children 12 and younger) has been offering tours since 1938, bringing decades of expertise to every one- or two-hour whale watching trip. Each trip includes facts and insights from a knowledgeable captain—and is tailored to where whales are most likely to be that day. Boats are outfitted with heated cabins for when conditions are less than ideal.

Also in town, **Whale Research EcoExcursions** (234 SE US-101; 541/912-6734; www.oregonwhales.com; $49, $39 for children 2-12; Jan.-Oct.) offers 90-minute whale-watching tours led by a marine biologist and a team of trained naturalists—with facts about gray whales, seals, sea lions, shorebirds, and other local wildlife. Blankets, hats, jackets, gloves, and rain gear are available if the weather doesn't cooperate. Tours include admission to the Whale, Sealife and Shark Museum in downtown Depoe Bay; small exhibits showcase wildlife that can be found along the Oregon Coast, artwork, shark displays, and educational films made by Carrie Newell (who runs both operations).

Fishing

In addition to its whale-watching expeditions, **Tradewinds Charters** (118 SE US-101; 541/765-2345; www.tradewindscharters. com; $100-320) offers fishing charters geared toward new and experienced anglers alike. Outings allow anglers to fish for lingcod,

Whale-Watching on the Oregon Coast

Every year, nearly 25,000 gray whales migrate between the warm waters of Mexico (their winter home) and the cooler waters of Alaska (their summer home). Roughly 200 gray whales remain along the Oregon Coast all year long—and are most visible when they feed near the shore in summer and fall—but your best bet for spying the whales comes between mid-December and mid-January, as well as late March-June. You might also see humpback whales (Aug.-Sept.), orcas (Apr.-June), and—on occasion—blue whales, dolphins, and porpoises.

Each December and March, Whale Watching Spoken Here (www.orwhalewatch.org) hosts events along the entire Oregon Coast that help visitors spy the whales offshore and learn more about the majestic creatures. But no matter the time of year, there are plenty of spots to spy gray whales on the Oregon Coast; here are a few favorite sites (just don't forget your binoculars and rain gear):

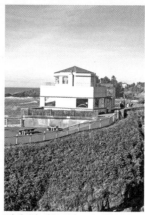

Whale Watching Center in Depoe Bay

NORTH COAST

· **Cape Meares State Scenic Viewpoint:** Sweeping ocean views are aided by coin-operated viewing machines—bring quarters (page 109).

· **Cape Lookout State Park:** A hike to the tip of the cape ends at a dramatic viewpoint that offers views up and down the coast—as well as into the waters below (page 109).

CENTRAL COAST

· **Whale Watching Center:** The outpost in Depoe Bay offers incredible views, as well as tips from Oregon State Parks staff and volunteers (page 126).

· **Boiler Bay State Scenic Viewpoint:** Gray whales come extremely close to shore, especially in spring, near this headland (page 126).

· **Otter Crest State Scenic Viewpoint:** This viewpoint's perch, high above the coastline, makes it easy to spot whales farther out at sea; a small gift shop offers benches and binoculars if you'd rather watch from indoors (page 128).

· **Cape Perpetua Scenic Area:** Watch for whales from rocky headlands, inside an on-site visitor center, or from atop the cape—which boasts views from 800 feet (245 m) above the Pacific Ocean (page 142).

SOUTH COAST

· **Shore Acres State Park:** A fully enclosed structure near the rocky shoreline allows for easy whale-watching in all conditions (page 166).

· **Cape Sebastian State Scenic Corridor:** A pair of viewpoints high above the shore afford views far out to sea (page 190).

rockfish, coho and chinook salmon, halibut, albacore tuna, and crab for five to eight hours; each trip includes gear, tackle, instruction, hot coffee, and rain gear.

Dockside Charters (270 Coast Guard Dr.; 541/765-2545; www.docksidedepoebay. com; $100-320) is another popular charter, with outings for rockfish, lingcod, coho salmon, halibut, and albacore tuna that last five to eight hours. The Dockside fleet has several types of vessels to meet the needs of your group and includes rods, reels, and necessary gear with each trip. Crabbing is also available on rockfish charters ($25), and cleaning services ($1.50-6) are available if you'd rather someone else do the messy work.

Anglers should purchase a single-day **fishing license** (www.myodfw.com; $23 per license) before hitting the water; if fishing *and* crabbing, purchase a single-day **angling and shellfish combo license** (www.myodfw. com; $32.50 per license).

Surfing

Experienced surfers enjoy catching waves on the stretch of beach just north of Devils Punchbowl, which is protected from uncooperative weather by the small headland. **Pura Vida Surf Shop** (845 1st St., Otter Rock; 541/264-8793; www.pvsurfshop.com) offers everything you need to get started. If you're ready to surf, the shop's range of rentals includes surfboards ($30-60), skim boards ($25-30), wetsuits ($25-30), and more—all available in half-day or full-day increments. Bodyboard packages are also available ($40-55), as are surfboard packages ($45-65); both options include a board, wetsuit, booties, and other gear. Two-hour lessons are also available ($100) and include a surfboard (with leash), wetsuit, booties, equipment fittings, and safety precautions.

BREWPUBS

Depoe Bay is home to exactly one brewery—the aptly named Depoe Bay Brewing Company—and you can find its beers on tap at **The Horn Public House and Brewery** (110 SE US-101; 541/764-6886; www.thehorn. pub; 11am-9pm Sun.-Thurs., 11am-10pm Fri.-Sat.). The always bustling brewpub pours nearly a dozen beers, with styles ranging from the classic (including a hazy IPA and a crisp hefeweizen) to the less common (such as an Irish red ale and a ginger beer); an upstairs dining room offers dramatic ocean views, and The Horn's seafood offerings (including clam chowder and fish-and-chips) are quite popular.

FOOD
Pacific Northwest Cuisine

Just south of town, overlooking a small cove, sits the acclaimed ★ **Restaurant Beck** (2345 S. US-101; 541/765-3220; www.restaurant-beck.com; 5pm-8pm Sun.-Thurs., 5pm-9pm Fri.-Sat.; $24-36) at The Whale Cove Inn. The eatery sources most of its ingredients from nearby growers, so the creative menu of upscale seafood and Pacific Northwest-inspired dishes is always changing; pork belly might be served with oregano ice cream, while locally caught sea bass might come topped with sun-dried, Oregon-grown blueberries. Reservations are accepted, but all window seats are available on a first-come, first-served basis.

Seafood

The menu at **The Sticks** (16 US-101; 541/614-4137; www.thesticksrestaurant.com; noon-7pm Fri.-Mon.; $7-17) might trend toward conventional seafood fare—fish-and-chips, seafood sandwiches, and chowder—but the preparation is anything but. Beer for the fish's crispy batter comes from Rogue Ales in nearby Newport, and all sauces (from tartar sauce to hot sauce) are made in-house.

Seemingly every community on the Oregon Coast has a restaurant that's been slinging clam chowder for decades—and in Depoe Bay, that's **Gracie's Sea Hag** (58 US-101; 541/765-2734; www.theseahag.com; 8am-8pm Sun.-Thurs., 8am-9pm Fri.-Sat.; $7-24). Open since 1963, Gracie's fresh seafood selections include oysters from nearby Yaquina

Bay, fish-and-chips, melts, and more—but its clam chowder sits atop the menu for good reason. The chowder is thick, with a stew-like consistency, and is scratch-made daily.

Just north of town, **Tidal Raves** (279 N. US-101; 541/765-2995; www.tidalraves.com; 11am-8pm daily; $16-38) pairs its upscale seafood menu with incredible ocean views. While you'll see plenty of seafood favorites, seemingly every dish is prepared with a thoughtful twist: The tuna melt is made with sustainably harvested albacore and house-baked bread; macaroni and cheese is stuffed with Dungeness crab; and wild-caught shrimp is barbecued and covered in a spicy red curry glaze.

ACCOMMODATIONS

Just a few miles south of town, **Inn at Otter Crest** (301 Otter Crest Dr., Otter Rock; 800/452-2101; www.innatottercrest.com; $220-250) hosts some of the most dramatic views anywhere on the Oregon Coast—from Cape Foulweather (in the north) to Yaquina Head Lighthouse (in the south), all from a forested hillside above the Pacific Ocean. The inn is made up of individually owned condos, so each room features unique decor—but all rooms and suites come with a balcony and cable television. Some rooms include a full kitchen. Note that pets are not permitted in guest rooms.

★ **Channel House** (35 Ellingson St., Depoe Bay; 541/765-2140; www.channel-house.com; $175-395) sits atop an oceanfront bluff and at the foot of Depoe Bay, pairing its epic views with welcome amenities. Channel House's 15 well-appointed rooms and suites include Tempur-Pedic mattresses and free Wi-Fi; some come with in-room fireplaces and private decks that boast outdoor hot tubs. Breakfast—usually a mix of fresh fruit, cereal, oatmeal, granola, and yogurt—is served each morning. The hotel is geared toward couples on romantic getaways more than families; as such, children younger than 17 are not permitted.

Sitting just across the street from the bay for which it is named, **SCP Depoe Bay** (235 SE Bayview Ave., Depoe Bay; 541/765-2350; www.scphotel.com; $357-465) hosts 13 cozy guest rooms—all boasting scenic harbor views. Choose among standard rooms (some with in-room hammock chairs, others with in-room fireplaces) and rooms with bunk beds that sleep up to four. Eco-friendly, thoughtful touches include homemade granola, teas and coffee from regional producers, and locally sourced, sustainability harvested materials. The hotel also hosts a small fitness and yoga space, as well as a quiet co-working area.

GETTING THERE

From Lincoln City, the 12-mile (19-km) drive to Depoe Bay takes about 17 minutes via southbound US-101. From Newport, the 13-mile (21-km) drive takes about 18 minutes via northbound US-101.

NW Connector (503/861-7433; www.nworegontransit.org; $1-5) and **Lincoln County Transit** (541/265-4900; www.co.lincoln.or.us/transit) run four buses daily (and another bus Mon.-Sat.) between Lincoln City and Newport, with stops in Depoe Bay and at Beverly Beach State Park.

Newport

Ever since the first European-American settlers arrived at Yaquina Bay in the 1860s, Newport has been synonymous with industry (specifically: fishing) and tourism. That continues today, with the working-class community (pop. 10,250) still a hub for anglers and commercial fisheries, as well family-friendly entertainment.

Much of the city's lauded seafood restaurants, family attractions, and outdoor opportunities is centered around Yaquina Bay, which is fed by the Yaquina River before

Newport

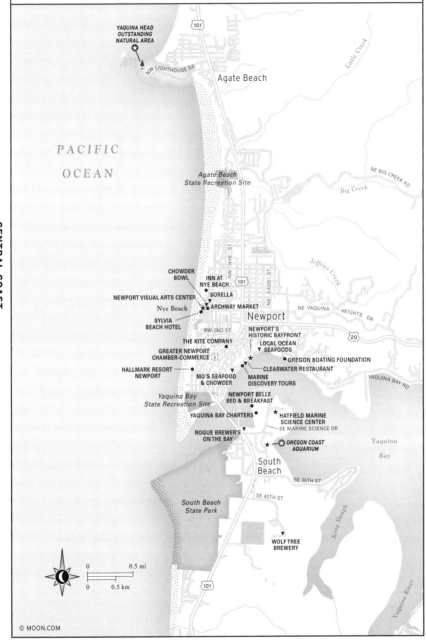

YAQUINA HEAD
OUTSTANDING
NATURAL AREA

NW LIGHTHOUSE DR

Agate Beach

PACIFIC

OCEAN

NE BIG CREEK RD

Agate Beach
State Recreation Site

Big Creek

Little Creek

Jeffries Creek

NW NYE ST

NE EADS ST

CHOWDER
BOWL
INN AT
NYE BEACH
NEWPORT VISUAL ARTS CENTER
SORELLA
Nye Beach
ARCHWAY MARKET
SYLVIA
BEACH HOTEL

NE YAQUINA HEIGHTS DR

Newport

SW 2ND ST

THE KITE COMPANY
NEWPORT'S
HISTORIC BAYFRONT
LOCAL OCEAN
SEAFOODS
GREATER NEWPORT
CHAMBER-COMMERCE
OREGON BOATING FOUNDATION
HALLMARK RESORT
NEWPORT
CLEARWATER RESTAURANT
MO'S SEAFOOD
& CHOWDER
MARINE
DISCOVERY TOURS
YAQUINA BAY RD

Yaquina Bay
State Recreation Site
NEWPORT BELLE
BED & BREAKFAST

YAQUINA BAY CHARTERS
HATFIELD MARINE
SCIENCE CENTER
SE MARINE SCIENCE DR

ROGUE BREWER'S
ON THE BAY
OREGON COAST
AQUARIUM

Yaquina
Bay

South
Beach

SE 35TH ST

SE 40TH ST

South Beach
State Park

WOLF TREE
BREWERY

Kings Slough

Yaquina River

0   0.5 mi

0   0.5 km

© MOON.COM

emptying into the Pacific Ocean. The bay is also home to Newport's Historic Bayfront, which offers a glimpse at the community's past and present. Interpretive panels along the bayfront explain different types of fishing vessels.

Away from Yaquina Bay, the Nye Beach neighborhood remains a popular tourist draw, much as it has since the 1880s. Here, a few walkable blocks host excellent restaurants and offer easy beach access. And at the northern edge of Newport, Yaquina Head Outstanding Natural Area occupies a windswept headland—home to the tallest lighthouse on the Oregon Coast, not to mention some of the region's best wildlife-watching opportunities and tidepool exploration.

SIGHTS
★ Yaquina Head Outstanding Natural Area
The attractions at **Yaquina Head Outstanding Natural Area** (750 NW Lighthouse Dr.; 541/574-3100; www.blm.gov; 8am-5pm Sun.-Thurs., 8am-sunset Fri.-Sat.; $7 for a three-day pass) are numerous. The windswept headland, jutting out from the shoreline at the northern edge of Newport, is home to the state's tallest lighthouse, some of its most popular tidepools, incredible wildlife-watching opportunities, an engaging interpretive center, hiking trails, and wide-open ocean views.

A good place to start is the **interpretive center** (10am-4pm daily), which hosts exhibits on local marine life and cultural history of the headland, as well as a full-scale replica of the Yaquina Head lighthouse lantern and a small gift shop. Restrooms and drinking water are available at the interpretive center.

Parking areas around the various sites at Yaquina Head are plentiful (though can fill on spring and summer weekends, especially when the sun comes out); if you'd rather explore by foot, several hiking paths connect Yaquina Head's attractions and ascend the area's hillsides for sweeping views. Pick up a map at the entrance station or in the interpretive center to get started.

Note that dogs must be kept leashed at all times, and that pets are not permitted near the lighthouse, in buildings, or around the tidepools at Yaquina Head.

Yaquina Head Lighthouse
The **Yaquina Head lighthouse** is one of the stars of the show on Yaquina Head, standing 93 feet (28 m) tall as the tallest lighthouse on the Oregon Coast; it was first lit in 1873, and the last keeper departed in 1966. A short, paved path leads from the parking area to its base; along the way, a few interpretive panels discuss the history of the lighthouse—and the importance of lighthouses on the Oregon Coast.

Lighthouse tours are offered throughout the year. September-June, tours are offered as conditions, weather, and staffing permit; if visiting at this time, check the Yaquina Head Outstanding Natural Area website (www.blm.gov), or pop into the interpretive center for the latest on whether tours are being offered that day. July-August, tours are offered daily, and reservations can be made up to 90 days in advance (877/444-6777; www.recreation.gov; $1) for a limited number of outings. Tours typically last about 45 minutes and require visitors to climb 114 steps; children must be at least 42 inches tall to take the tour.

At the western edge of Yaquina Head, in the shadow of its mammoth lighthouse, views extend far out to sea; in winter and spring, this is a popular place to watch migrating gray whales. Just offshore, immediately to the west, **Colony Rock** is covered each spring with upward of 65,000 common murres; bald eagles, western gulls, brown pelicans, and peregrine falcons are just some of the other species of bird that live or hunt at Yaquina Head.

Restrooms are available at the Yaquina Head lighthouse parking area.

Tidepools
Kids of all ages love exploring the **tidepools** at Cobble Beach and Quarry Cove, both home

Oregon's Celebrated Lighthouses

Up and down the Oregon Coast, lighthouses recall a by-gone era and reflect the rugged nature of the region's coastline; the lighthouses were largely erected, after all, to help mariners navigate Oregon's rocky coastline and pass safely through the area's grumpy winter storms.

Even if these lighthouses aren't occupied today, they remain some of the coast's most popular tourist attractions. In all, 11 lighthouses still stand along the Oregon Coast, though some are closed to the public. If you want to see these structures up close, here are a few of the most popular to get started.

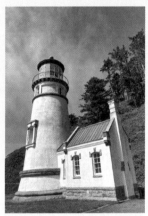

Heceta Head Lighthouse

- **Cape Meares:** The shortest lighthouse on the Oregon Coast was first lit in 1890 and was the most powerful of its time; today, visitors can look out to sea from its base and take tours of the tower (page 109).

- **Yaquina Head:** The tallest lighthouse on the Oregon Coast sits near the edge of a windswept bluff and was first lit in August 1873 (page 133).

- **Heceta Head:** Perched on a bluff overlooking the Pacific Ocean, the lighthouse dates back to 1894 and is believed to have the strongest beam on the Oregon Coast (page 148).

- **Umpqua River:** The lighthouse at the mouth of the Umpqua River is noted for its unique beams of red and white light (page 153).

- **Cape Blanco:** The southernmost lighthouse on the Oregon Coast accessible to visitors *also* sits on a headland at the state's westernmost point (page 185).

to a rich variety of marine life—including sea stars, anemones, urchins, crabs, snails, and more. If you're unfamiliar, tidepools are small pockets of water on rocky stretches of shoreline that get inundated when the tide comes in—and revealed when the tide recedes. At low tide, visitors can (carefully) walk on the rocky shore to see the marine life up close, revealing an unusual look at life below the surface of the sea. These exist all over the Oregon Coast, but few tidepools are as accessible as the ones at Yaquina Head.

Driving in, the first tidepools you come to are at **Quarry Cove,** accessible by a short, paved (but not wheelchair-accessible) path to the shoreline. Quarry Cove is actually a man-made set of tidepools, sitting on the site of a former rock quarry. At the western edge of

Yaquina Head is **Cobble Beach,** whose basalt rock tidepools can be reached via a set of wooden stairs. Just offshore from Cobble Beach is **Seal Rock,** where harbor seals hang out fairly often.

Tidepools are best explored at low tide; visit the official Yaquina Head Outstanding Natural Area website (www.blm.gov) for an updated calendar of estimated tidepool "discovery times"—essentially when marine life is visible and the tidepools are ripe for exploration. Tidepools are usually pretty docile in decent weather, but precautions should always be taken; keep small children within arm's reach, never turn your back on the ocean, watch for sneaker waves, and stay at least 150 feet away from seals and birds at all times.

★ Oregon Coast Aquarium

The **Oregon Coast Aquarium** (2820 SE Ferry Slip Rd.; 541/867-3474; www.aquarium.org; 10am-6pm daily Memorial Day-Labor Day, 10am-5pm daily Labor Day-Memorial Day; $24.95, $19.95 seniors 65 and older and children 13-17, $14.95 children 3-12, free for children 2 and younger) is home to roughly 15,000 birds, mammals, fish, invertebrates, and plants—almost all native to the Oregon Coast. These creatures are on display in captivating exhibits (indoors and out) that take visitors up close with replica tidepools, undersea sites, shorelines, and more. Highlights are numerous, but the Passages of the Deep exhibit takes visitors through a 200-foot-long (60-m) underwater tunnel that showcases roughly 3,500 sea creatures; as you progress, the replica landscapes gradually transition from Oregon's rocky coastline to the open waters of the Pacific Ocean. The grounds are exceptionally well-maintained, a series of rotating exhibits offer different looks at marine life, and a spacious play area invites little ones to run around.

Newport's Historic Bayfront

No trip through town is complete without a stroll along **Newport's Historic Bayfront,** which borders Yaquina Bay and has been the heart of the community's commercial fishing industry for more than 150 years. Most of the area's fisheries, brewpubs, and restaurants can be found along a 0.6-mile (1-km) stretch of SW Bay Boulevard, roughly between SW Bay Street (to the west) and SW Eads Street (to the east).

Heading west to east, the working-class nature of the district is apparent. You'll pass still-operating fisheries (and will smell the warehouses long before you see them), as well as the pub where **Rogue Ales & Spirits** brewed its first beers way back in 1989; the brewing outfit moved across Yaquina Bay some years ago, but a friendly pub pours roughly three dozen house-made beers today. You'll also pass several seafood restaurants, most serving fresh fare straight from the docks of Yaquina Bay.

Toward the eastern edge of the neighborhood, a wooden boardwalk follows the bayfront, hosts interpretive panels on fishing vessels and fish species native to the area, and offers an up-close look at the docks where anglers come and go. If stopping to eat and ambling in and out of shops, give yourself two or three hours to explore the neighborhood; parking is limited on summer weekends.

Hatfield Marine Science Center

A nice companion to the Oregon Coast Aquarium, **Hatfield Marine Science Center** (2030 SE Marine Science Dr.; 541/867-0100; hmsc.oregonstate.edu; 10am-4pm Thurs.-Mon.; $3, free for children 4 and younger) is part of a research institute led by Oregon State University. From the middle of Yaquina Bay, the science center offers a variety of interactive exhibits—including a simulator that lets children navigate a vessel through Yaquina Bay, tidepool touch tanks (home to sea stars, abalones, sea anemones, and other creatures), crustacean displays, and the science behind sustainable fishing.

Yaquina Bay State Recreation Site

Yaquina Bay State Recreation Site (SW Government St. & SW Mark St.; 541/265-5679; www.stateparks.oregon.gov; 6am-9pm daily; free) sits on the north side of Yaquina Bay and offers fine views, along with an introduction the city's second-most-famous lighthouse. The small park sits on a bluff and hosts a handful of turnouts that afford fantastic views of Yaquina Bay, the iconic Yaquina Bay Bridge, and the Pacific Ocean; parking areas on the park's west side lead to footpaths down to the coastline, as well. If it's open, be sure to ascend two flights of stairs to **Yaquina Bay lighthouse** (noon-4pm daily March-Sept., noon-4pm Wed.-Sun. Oct.-Feb.), Oregon's only wooden

lighthouse still standing; visitors can check out the watch room, as well as some interpretive panels and a video about the lighthouse's history in the basement.

Nye Beach

The centrally located **Nye Beach** neighborhood offers a decidedly more modern, hipper vibe than its counterpart on the bayfront. Even if many of the compact district's buildings date back decades, this is where you'll find curated markets, cutting-edge eateries, a captivating art gallery, and easy coastal access.

The main north-south route through Nye Beach is NW Coast Street, and the main east-west thoroughfare is the C-shaped NW Beach Drive. The road heads west for about 0.1 mile (0.2 km) before turning north at a turnaround and continuing east, back toward Coast Street for another 0.1 mile (0.2 km). Even with a stop for food and frolic on the beach, you can explore the entirety of the compact neighborhood in about two or three hours.

Near the western edge of Nye Beach, the **Newport Visual Arts Center** (777 NW Beach Dr.; 541/265-6540; www.coastarts.org; noon-4pm Wed.-Sat.) hosts four art galleries that showcase rotating exhibits from new and established regional artists, as well as a media room that hosts digital art and installations (such as video, light, and sound).

Next to the Visual Arts Center is a vehicle turnaround at the edge of the shoreline; a few concrete benches here offer wide-open views, and a short path offers access down to the beach, where Nye Creek trickles into the Pacific Ocean.

BEACHES

Beverly Beach State Park (198 NE 123rd St.; 541/265-9278; www.stateparks.oregon.gov; sunrise-sunset daily; free) hosts a spacious day-use area with easy beach access between Cape Foulweather and Yaquina Head. From the parking area, a paved pathway heads under US-101 and alongside the trickling Spencer Creek—ending at a typically busy

yet beautiful beach area, where views to the south extend, on a clear day, to Yaquina Head Lighthouse. Away from the shore, you'll find picnic tables, flush restrooms, and a campground with more than 275 campsites (including full-hookup sites, electrical sites with water, and basic tent sites) and yurts.

Agate Beach State Recreation Site (NW Oceanview Dr. & Agate Beach State Wayside; 541/265-4560; www.stateparks.oregon.gov; sunrise-sunset daily; free) is a popular stretch of shoreline at the northern edge of Newport. A pedestrian tunnel heads from the parking area, under an old stretch of US-101 (now NW Oceanview Dr.), and ends at the coast—where Yaquina Head stands tall to the north. As the name implies, this is a great place to find agates—colorful pieces of quartz that wash ashore after winter storms.

The miles-long **South Beach State Park** (along US-101, 3 mi/5 km south of Newport; 541/867-4715; www.stateparks.oregon.gov; sunrise-sunset daily; free) begins at the southern edge of Newport and packs plenty of outdoor recreation into its forested setting. Though it's mostly known as a bustling campground, South Beach hosts several miles of walking and biking paths (some paved), horseshoe pits, a nine-hole disc golf course (loaner discs are available at the campground's **Hospitality Center** (10am-6pm daily), and—of course—beach access.

RECREATION
Paddling and Water Sports

Chances are good you'll see the Yaquina Bay from Newport's Historic Bayfront or while driving across the Yaquina Bay Bridge—but what about seeing Newport from the bay itself? The nonprofit **Oregon Boating Foundation** (600 SE Bay Blvd.; 800/806-4882; www.oregonboatingfoundation.org; Tues.-Sun. late June-Labor Day; $50), which works to get people on the water safely and improve waterway access, hosts regular guided kayak tours of Yaquina Bay all summer long. Each two-hour outing showcases

the landmarks of Yaquina Bay and offers up-close views of the area's wildlife.

Fishing

Newport's anglers stay busy all year long, fishing for the likes of albacore tuna, salmon, Dungeness crab, halibut, and more. If you'd like to join the fun, book a trip with **Yaquina Bay Charters** (2128 SE Marine Science Dr.; 541/265-6800; www.yaquinabaycharters.com; $90-270). The outfitter takes anglers of all experience levels on deep-sea fishing trips that last up to a full day; outings are geared toward coho salmon (June-Sept.), albacore tuna (June-Sept.), halibut (June-Sept.), and lingcod (year-round). Those wishing to catch crab can do so on a joint crabbing and whale-watching tour ($60) or through a three-hour crabbing trip ($450 for up to 12 people). Yaquina Bay Charters provides bait, tackle, and coffee—and can sell anglers the appropriate fishing license before heading out; fish filleting and crab cooking is available back at the dock for an additional fee.

Whale-Watching and Wildlife-Viewing

The family-owned-and-operated **Marine Discovery Tours** (345 SW Bay Blvd.; 541/265-6200; www.marinediscoverytours.com; $55, $30 for children 12 and younger; Mar.-Oct.) offers two-hour cruises on Yaquina Bay and the Pacific Ocean (conditions permitting), with naturalists explaining Newport's rich wildlife and even catching the occasional crab for educational demonstrations. Depending on the season, visitors might see gray whales, seals, sea lions, bald eagles, and other species of wildlife.

BREWPUBS AND NIGHTLIFE

Rogue Ales & Spirits launched in 1988 in southern Oregon—but expanded into Newport the following year and has called the city home ever since. Today, Rogue's Dead Guy Ale (a sweet, malty Maibock-style ale) is the brewery's flagship offering—but you can try dozens of Rogue beers and house-made spirits at three pubs around town. Craft beer geeks gravitate toward ★ **Rogue Brewer's on the Bay** (2320 OSU Dr., Newport; 541/819-0202; www.rogue.com; 11am-8pm daily), the brewery's headquarters and where its popular ales and lagers are brewed; here visitors can enjoy roughly 40 Rogue beers on tap, as well as a menu of pub fare (burgers, sandwiches, seafood, and salads) and incredible views of Yaquina Bay. Other Rogue locations in town include Rogue Spirits Sunset Bar (a cocktail bar not far from the brewery) and Rogue Bayfront Public House on Newport's Historic Bayfront.

Just south of town, **Wolf Tree Brewery** (4590 SE Harborton St., South Beach; 458/868-9151; www.wolftreebrewery.com; noon-9pm Wed.-Sun.) crafts small-batch ales and lagers from natural spring water and uses locally sourced ingredients whenever possible; every spring, for instance, the Wolf Tree team harvests Sitka spruce tips and uses them (in lieu of hops, a more traditional ingredient) in a handful of beers—including a saison and a sour beer. The dog-friendly and family-friendly brewpub boasts a tap list of 12 beers (including some from Pacific Northwest breweries), a food menu of pub favorites, and a large patio.

FESTIVALS AND EVENTS

Winter might be the Oregon Coast's slow season—but don't tell that to the **Newport Seafood and Wine Festival** (www.newportchamber.org; Feb.; $10-48). The long-running festival routinely features more than 150 vendors providing pours from dozens of regional wineries, offering light bites from local chefs, and showcasing artisan goods from local crafters.

SHOPPING

Since 1991, **The Kite Company** (407 SW Coast Hwy.; 541/265-2004; www.thekitecompany.com; 9am-5:30pm Mon.-Sat., 9am-4pm Sun.) has sold a wide range of kites to

families looking to enjoy the popular coastal pastime. The family-owned-and-operated shop claims to test fly everything it sells and prides itself on selling a thorough selection of kites—along with windsocks, wind spinners, and other toys.

At the eastern edge of Nye Beach, stop into the women-owned **Archway Market** (701 NW Beach Dr.; 541/264-8372; www.archwaymarket.com; 9am-9pm daily), named for the concrete arch that spans NW Beach Dr. and welcomes visitors to Nye Beach; far more than a simple convenience store, the surprisingly robust market carries artisan food products, local beer and wine, smoked seafood, saltwater taffy, locally themed gifts, reusable picnic supplies, and more.

FOOD
Seafood

Newport is a classic fishing community where chefs routinely source fresh ingredients from local anglers. You'll find seafood all over town, but these are a few of our favorite eateries.

Perhaps the most celebrated restaurant in Newport (if not the entire Oregon Coast) is the woman-owned ★ **Local Ocean Seafoods** (213 SE Bay Blvd.; 541/574-7959; www.localocean.net; 11am-8pm Sun.-Thurs., 11am-8:30pm Fri.-Sat.; $15-37), which sources most of its seafood from anglers working the Yaquina Bay docks just across the street. Popular dishes include flaky Dungeness crab cakes, pan-fried Yaquina Bay oysters, and fish-and-chips (which is grilled, rather than fried); the rest of the menu includes seafood sandwiches, stews, and more—all of it cooked to perfection. Fresh seafood is available to-go from an on-site market, as well. Reservations are recommended on weekends all year long and are almost mandatory on summer weekends.

For a more down-home experience, check out **Chowder Bowl** (728 NW Beach Dr.; 541/265-7477; www.newportchowderbowl. com; 11am-8pm Sun.-Thurs. and 11am-9pm Fri.-Sat. in winter, 11am-9pm daily in summer; $13-27) in the heart of Newport's Nye Beach neighborhood. Just a short walk from the beach, Chowder Bowl could easily rest on its laurels as a tourist trap—but the family-friendly eatery sources its oysters from Yaquina Bay, gets its bread from a bakery nearby, and dishes a satisfying menu of sandwiches and fried seafood. Outdoor seating is available.

The chic **Clearwater Restaurant** (325 SW Bay Blvd.; 541/272-5550; www.clearwaterrestaurant.com; 11am-9pm daily; $15-46) sits on Yaquina Bay, offering outstanding views (with outdoor seating) alongside a seafood menu that blends longtime favorites and more modern fare. That means you'll find classic dishes like fried fish-and-chips and seafood pasta—as well a tuna poke bowl, a macaroni and cheese dish crafted with crab and infused with an earthy truffle oil, and a seafood stew made with coconut curry. Much of it is sourced fresh from local anglers on Yaquina Bay.

Any discussion of Newport seafood joints is incomplete without a nod to **Mo's Seafood and Chowder** (622 SW Bay Blvd.; 541/265-2979; www.moschowder.com; 11am-9pm daily; $13-23), an Oregon Coast mainstay since 1946. Many seafood shacks claim to make "world-famous" chowder, but Mo's might actually live up to the billing; its chowder base is sold in grocery stores throughout the Pacific Northwest and spurs hour-long waits on sunny summer weekends. The chowder is fine, as is a thorough menu of casual seafood favorites, but the real draw is the experience; fishing nets, glass floats, and other marine-themed bric-a-brac adorns the walls of this family-friendly outpost. You'll find other Mo's restaurants in several coastal communities (such as Astoria, Seaside, Cannon Beach, Lincoln City, and Florence) and at the Portland International Airport—as well as just across the street.

1: Local Ocean Seafoods 2: fishing boats on Newport's Historic Bayfront 3: Yaquina Head lighthouse

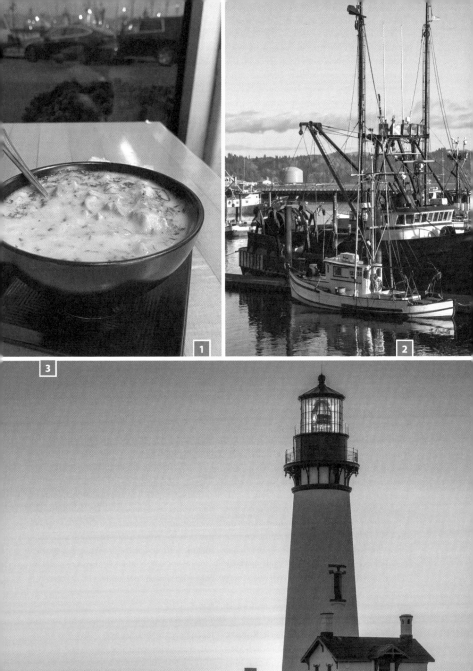

Get a closer look at Newport's fishing industry through a free, guided outing with **Shop at the Dock Tours** (tours meet at the Port of Newport, 600 SE Bay Blvd., next to Dock 5; 541/737-2714; seagrant.oregonstate. edu; July-Aug.; free). The 90-minute, small-group tours head behind the scenes of commercial fisheries, with insight on regional species and the community's history as a fishing town. Tours are offered Fridays periodically throughout the summer; tours are free and offered on a first-come, first-served basis.

Italian

Sorella (526 NW Coast St., Ste. C; 541/265-4055; www.sorellanyebeach.com; 3pm-8pm Sun.-Thurs., 3pm-9pm Fri.-Sat.; $16-21) is the brainchild of the husband-and-wife team behind Restaurant Beck in Depoe Bay and excels in fresh, hearty northern Italian dishes. That translates to filling dishes with handmade pasta (such as baked rigatoni, spaghetti and meatballs, and lasagna) and a rotating selection of pizzas that changes with what's fresh and in season.

ACCOMMODATIONS

All of the 21 literary-themed rooms at **Sylvia Beach Hotel** (267 NW Cliff St.; 541/265-5428; sylviabeachhotel.com; $180-300) are dedicated to various authors from throughout history—including J. R. R. Tolkien, Jane Austen, and Oregon's own Ken Kesey; you'll find books from each author in their room, along with a sizeable collection in the on-site library. The hotel's literary bent means you won't find Wi-Fi, televisions, radios, or telephones in your room. Several rooms boast views of the Pacific Ocean and Yaquina Head Lighthouse; three have in-room fireplaces and private decks. Breakfast comes with the room and usually includes house-made pastries and granola, along with other light bites.

Every room at ★ **Hallmark Resort Newport** (744 SW Elizabeth St.; 855/391-2484; www.hallmarkinns.com; $234-394) boasts an oceanfront view, but the attractions and amenities don't stop there: Spacious

rooms and suites (some with gas fireplaces and spa tubs) open up to private patios and balconies, and pillowtop mattresses provide plenty of comfort. Pet-friendly amenities include on-site exercise areas and wash stations; a portion of each pet fee is earmarked for local animal shelters. The on-site restaurant, **Georgie's Beachside Grill** (541/265-9800; www.georgiesbeachsidegrill.com; 7:30am-9pm daily; $13-45) pairs its eclectic seafood menu (featuring locally sourced seafood dishes, often served with tropical flourishes) with sweeping ocean views.

Stay in the heart of Newport's hippest neighborhood at **Inn at Nye Beach** (729 NW Coast St.; 541/265-2477; www.innatnyebeach. com; $434-624). The boutique hotel is mere steps from the shore (select rooms offer unobstructed ocean views) and boasts a variety of comfortable amenities—such as fireplaces and soaking tubs in select rooms, eco-friendly bath toiletries, coffee and tea from regional producers, and more. Away from your room (some of which are pet-friendly), highlights include an infinity spa overlooking the ocean, outdoor fire pits, and scratch-made breakfast each morning.

As far as location and creativity goes, **Newport Belle Bed and Breakfast** (2126 SE Marine Science Dr.; 541/867-6290; www. newportbelle.com; $330-350) can't be beat. The romantic, adults-only B&B is housed in a paddlewheel boat and sits in Yaquina Bay, showcasing impressive views of the arched Yaquina Bay Bridge and surrounding fishing docks. Each of the five rooms features memory foam mattresses, and amenities throughout the boat include a three-course breakfast served each morning, a fully enclosed sunroom, and daily happy hour with beer, wine, and snacks.

Camping

The most popular campground around Newport is **South Beach State Park** (US-101, 3 mi/5 km south of Newport; 541/867-4715; www.stateparks.oregon.gov; $17-44 for campsites, $43-54 for yurts), which sits just south of where the Yaquina River flows

into the Pacific Ocean. Campers can choose among 227 RV-friendly electrical sites with water, 60 tent sites, and 27 yurts; in all, 5 sites and 24 yurts are wheelchair-accessible. Amenities include flush toilets, hot showers, and firewood for sale. The coastline is up to 0.5 mile (0.8 km) from the campground, giving this park a secluded vibe despite its close proximity to Newport.

INFORMATION AND SERVICES

The **Greater Newport Chamber of Commerce** (555 SW Coast Hwy.; 541/265-8801; www.newportchamber.org; 9am-4pm Mon.-Fri.) sits along the main drag through town and hosts plenty of resources for enjoying your time—such as brochures, maps, pamphlets, and recommendations for where to eat, sleep, and play.

GETTING THERE AND AROUND

From Lincoln City, the 25-mile (40-km) drive to Newport takes about 35 minutes via southbound US-101. From Florence, the 49-mile (79-km) drive to takes about 1 hour, 5 minutes via northbound US-101. And from Corvallis, the 49-mile (79-km) drive takes about 1 hour via westbound OR-20.

NW Connector (503/861-7433; www.nworegontransit.org; $1-5) and **Lincoln County Transit** (541/265-4900; www.co.lincoln.or.us/transit) run four buses daily (and another bus Mon.-Sat.) between Lincoln City and Newport, as well as daily service around Newport (with stops at hotels and popular attractions along the way).

NW Connector (503/861-7433; www.nworegontransit.org; $1-6) and **Benton Area Transit** (541/766-6700; www.co.benton.or.us/ridethebat) also run four buses daily between Newport and the communities of Corvallis and Albany in the Willamette Valley.

Yachats and Cape Perpetua

The community of Yachats (pop. 550—and pronounced "YAH-hots") surrounds the mouth of the Yachats River, which empties into the Pacific Ocean near the base of the mammoth Cape Perpetua. Here sandy shores give way to a rougher basalt shelf, lending an air of ruggedness to the oceanfront. The community sits within a short drive of several larger coastal communities, giving it an overlooked, unhurried, and oft-uncrowded vibe.

To the south, the Cape Perpetua Scenic Area is perhaps more famous for its fascinating natural features than its namesake headland, which lords roughly 800 feet (245m) over the surrounding shoreline and offers some of the Oregon Coast's best views; no matter—it's all worth at least a day of exploration.

SIGHTS AND RECREATION
804 Trail

Unlike most of its peers along the Oregon Coast, the coastline in Yachats isn't sweeping and sandy; instead, it's noted for numerous basalt outcrops that formed up to 56 million years ago—and which butt up against the Pacific Ocean. So while you won't spend your summer weekend lounging on the beach in Yachats, the shoreline offers a different (starker) kind of beauty.

Perhaps the best way to see this up-close is from along the **804 Trail** (www.yachatsoregon.org; sunrise-sunset daily; free), which follows the path of a disused road along the rocky coastline. In all, the flat path (mostly paved, with some stretches of gravel) runs 1.4 miles (2.3 km) round-trip, darting in and out of a small coastal forest while offering impressive views

out to sea. Benches invite walkers to enjoy the vista at points along the trail, and occasional descents allow access to the rugged shoreline—but should be undertaken with extreme caution, in good weather, and only at low tide. It's not uncommon to see shorebirds looking for their next meal or harbor seals milling about; at low tide, visitors might see sea stars, mussels, and anemones clinging to the outcrops.

With a few parking spots and on-site restrooms, **Smelt Sands State Recreation Site** (804 Lemwick Ln.; 541/867-7451; www.stateparks.oregon.gov; sunrise-sunset daily; free) makes a fine access point at the south end of the path. The 804 Trail's northernmost terminus is just north of NW Perch St., ironically enough, at a sandy stretch of shoreline at the northern edge of Yachats. If you want to descend to the beach there, you may do so via a set of wooden steps (which are removed in winter) or with the assistance of a rope; take caution, as conditions can be quite slippery.

★ Cape Perpetua Scenic Area

There is nowhere else on the Oregon Coast quite like the **Cape Perpetua Scenic Area** (US-101, 3 mi/5 km south of Yachats; 541/547-3289; www.fs.usda.gov; sunrise-sunset daily; $5 day-use fee per vehicle or Northwest Forest Pass). The namesake headland, a forested monolith, towers 800 feet (245 m) over the Pacific Ocean, delivering some of the most scenic views on the Oregon Coast and hosting some of the region's most famous—and unusual—natural features.

Driving from Yachats, the first stop you come to is the **Devils Churn Day Use Area** and **Devils Churn Information Center** (10am-4pm Thurs.-Sun.). Devils Churn is a narrow inlet, surrounded on all sides by the basalt shoreline, where waves crash into the surf and can seem to explode, shooting spray dozens of feet in the air. Spy the dramatic site from an overlook next to the parking lot, or follow the paved **Trail of the Restless Waters** (0.4 mi/0.6 km round-trip) to the base of the inlet; the first portion of the trail is wheelchair-accessible. People have died after

getting hit by waves at Devils Churn, so be careful, and keep your distance—especially in stormy conditions. Rangers are on hand to sell passes and provide tips and recommendations at the information center, which is also home to a coffee bar and snack stand (selling pastries and sandwiches).

Just 0.2 mile (0.3 km) south is the **Cape Perpetua Visitor Center** (2400 US-101, Yachats; 9:30am-4:30pm daily Memorial Day Labor Day, 10am-4pm daily Labor Day-Memorial Day), which shows short films, offers educational presentations, hosts guided hikes, and more; the center's massive windows and wheelchair-accessible dock show off incredible ocean views—great for whale-watching (in early winter and spring) and storm-watching (in winter). A gift shop within the visitor center sells books, postcards, and other souvenirs. This is also where you can access most of the 26 miles (42 km) of hiking and biking trails throughout Cape Perpetua. Potable water and restrooms are available at the Cape Perpetua Visitor Center.

From the visitor center, take the 0.8-mile/1.3-km (round-trip) **Captain Cook Trail,** a mostly mellow, paved path that shows off some of Cape Perpetua's most beloved sites; without stops, the well-signed hike takes about 30-45 minutes. Along the way, you'll see **Cook's Chasm,** a rocky inlet; **Spouting Horn,** a partially collapsed sea cave that appears to erupt when waves crash into it (especially at high tide and during winter storms); **Thor's Well,** a circular sinkhole in the rocky shoreline that seems to swallow waves as they tumble into surf; and several **tidepools** that invite exploration at low tide (sturdy shoes and walking sticks are recommended). The rocks around Thor's Well are jagged and slippery; if taking an up-close look, keep an eye out for sneaker waves—and never turn your back on the ocean or walk onto the shoreline in stormy conditions or at high tide.

1: fish-and-chips at Luna Sea Fish House and Village Fishmonger **2:** Spouting Horn at Cape Perpetua **3:** summit views from atop Cape Perpetua

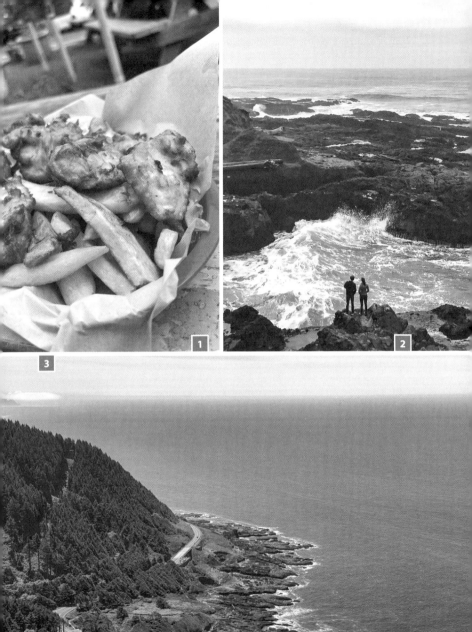

Another popular jaunt is the **Giant Spruce Trail,** a 2-mile/3.2-km (round-trip) footpath that parallels Cape Creek and ends at the foot of a massive, 500-year-old Sitka spruce tree. The trail departs from the visitor center and takes about one hour to complete.

Visitors can also hike or drive to **the summit of Cape Perpetua,** the highest point accessible to vehicles anywhere on the Oregon Coast. Views comprise Cape Cove Beach and the rocky shoreline below, the wide-open expanse of the Pacific Ocean to the west, and the community of Yachats—faintly visible through a stand of Sitka spruce to the north. A short, mostly flat loop trail circles the summit and passes through a stone shelter built in the 1930s by the Civilian Conservation Corps; picnic tables and restrooms are available at the summit parking area.

FOOD
Breweries and Pubs
Since opening in 2013, **Yachats Brewing + Farmstore** (348 US-101 N; 541/547-3884; www.yachatsbrewing.com; noon-8pm Thurs.-Fri., noon-9pm Sat., 10am-5pm Sun.) has made a name for itself with creative ales and lagers, many using regional ingredients. The Salal Sour, for instance, is a mixed-culture saison made with salal berries that grow in abundance along the Oregon Coast; the briny Smoked Oyster Stout, meanwhile, is crafted with smoked oysters. The brewpub's food menu leans heavily on internationally inspired vegetarian dishes. A patio out front affords outdoor dining.

Seafood
If you're wondering where to find the best fish-and-chips on the Oregon Coast, ★ **Luna Sea Fish House and Village Fishmonger** (153 US-101; 541/547-4794; www.lunaseafishhouse.com; 10:30am-8pm Mon.-Thurs., 9am-9pm Fri.-Sun.; $13-22) is routinely part of the conversation. The house specialty at the angler-owned eatery is wild-caught fish-and-chips; flaky lingcod is perhaps the most popular selection, but you can't go wrong with

fresh tuna, halibut, or salmon. Sandwiches, fish tacos, and a few vegetarian-friendly items round out the menu. A covered, heated outdoor seating area is available, and Luna Sea occasionally hosts local musicians. A second location in Seal Rock, just south of Newport, opened in 2021.

For something more upscale, stop by **Ona Restaurant & Lounge** (131 US-101 N; 541/547-6627; www.onarestaurant.com; 2pm-8pm Wed.-Sun.; $26-40), whose globally inspired menu incorporates local, seasonal ingredients whenever possible. That means you'll find ramen (loaded with seasonal vegetables) alongside oysters from nearby Yaquina Bay, locally caught halibut and chips (served with a light Asian slaw), and albacore tuna seared with a Japanese spice blend. A covered, heated patio affords views of the Yachats River and Pacific Ocean.

Bakeries and Cafés
For being such a small town, Yachats sure boasts a robust selection of early-morning bakeries and cafés. One of the most popular is **Bread and Roses Bakery** (238 4th St.; 541/547-4454; www.bnrbakery.com; 8am-1pm Thurs.-Sun.; $2-8), which makes all of its baked goods in-house with organic flour from an Oregon producer—and crafts a variety of mouth-watering cakes, breads, pastries (both sweet and savory), soups, and more. If your schedule works out, the bakery's weekly pizza offerings (3pm-6pm Thurs. and Sat.; $21-24) is well worth trying; a variety of inventive pies make good use of creative toppings (such as a savory squash sauce, broccoli, pepperoncini, and sharp white cheddar cheese).

ACCOMMODATIONS
The Drift Inn (124 US-101 N; 541/547-4477; www.driftinnlodging.com) hosts 20 rooms for overnight travelers. In all, you'll find 15 stylish if occasionally cozy rooms ($115-250), each with themed décor and pleasant amenities (such as private decks, clawfoot tubs, and tiled showers). The inn also rents out 5 hostel-style rooms ($57) with private

sleeping quarters but shared bathrooms and showers. Common amenities include outdoor fire pits, bike racks, an on-site game room (with pool and shuffleboard), laundry facilities, free Wi-Fi, and room service from the on-site pub.

From the highway, the one-story, U-shaped **Yatel Motel** (640 US-101 N; 541/547-3225; www.yatelmotel.com; $109-149) resembles a lot of rustic inns you'll pass along the Oregon Coast. But the refurbished motel, which dates back to 1948, sets itself apart with modern amenities that mingle well with vintage, beach-themed décor: Televisions come connected to popular streaming services, for instance, in rooms where upcycled wooden pallets are used for bed headboards and rocking chairs invite relaxation on rainy days. The eight-room inn is dog-friendly.

Yachats has a few oceanfront lodgings—including the **Fireside Motel** (1881 US-101 N; 541/547-3636; www.firesidemotel.com; $164-289), which butts up against a rocky stretch of shoreline at the northern edge of town. Rooms with a view boast balconies and fireplaces, and all rooms are named for resident species of bird (bald eagle, brown pelican, osprey, and so forth). The pet-friendly motel offers towels, sheets, and pooper scoopers; custom picnic kits are available for an added fee; an electric vehicle charging station is on-site; and the motel's market stocks grab-and-go food items, locally crafted souvenirs, and more.

Camping

The well-maintained **Beachside State Recreation Site** (off US-101, 5.3 mi/8.6 km north of Yachats; 541/563-3220; www.stateparks.oregon.gov; Mar. 15-Oct.; $7-64) sits within an easy drive of several attractions and communities along the central coast, including Yachats—making it a popular, pleasant stop for campers on this stretch of shoreline.

The campground hosts 32 electrical sites with water, 42 tent sites, two yurts (one of which is pet-friendly), and a hiker/biker camp area for cyclists riding US-101 and backpackers hiking the Oregon Coast Trail; flush toilets and hot showers are available, and firewood is for sale on-site. A small stand of trees shields campers from the shoreline, but several short paths head to the beach. From Yachats, the 5.3-mile (8.6-km) drive via US-101 northbound takes about 10 minutes.

Cape Perpetua Campground (2200 US-101 S, Yachats; 541/547-4580; www.fs.usda. gov; Mar.-Sept.; $26) is the only option for spending the night at Cape Perpetua. The scenic campground can be found along Cape Creek—and in the mossy shadow of Sitka spruce, Douglas fir, and alder trees; all 37 tent and RV sites come with a campfire ring and picnic table, and flush toilets and potable water are available. No hookups are available.

INFORMATION AND SERVICES

Stop into the **Yachats Area Chamber of Commerce and Visitors Center** (241 US-101 N; 541/547-2345; www.yachats.org; 10am-4pm daily) for maps, brochures, and all kinds of recommendations from friendly volunteers.

GETTING THERE AND AROUND

From Newport, the 24-mile (39-km) drive to Yachats takes about 30 minutes via southbound US-101. From Florence, the 25-mile (40-km) drive takes about 35 minutes via northbound US-101.

NW Connector (503/861-7433; www. nworegontransit.org; $1-4) and **Lincoln County Transit** (541/265-4900; www. co.lincoln.or.us/transit) run four buses Monday-Saturday between Yachats and Newport.

The Oregon Dunes

This stretch of Oregon Coast is defined less by the shoreline than what's *next* to the shore: specifically, the Oregon Dunes, an otherworldly attraction that runs roughly 40 miles (64 km) along this bustling stretch of the coast. The occasionally forested, sometimes wind-whipped sand dunes are all west of US-101 and can extend two miles or more inland, creating a buffer from the ocean—and the perfect environment for camping, off-highway vehicle riding, hiking, paddling, and other fun adventures. You'll enjoy far fewer oceanfront outings than you might elsewhere along the coast, but the scenery in this neck of the woods is like nowhere else in the region.

At the northern edge of the region is Florence (pop. 9,400), a classic coastal community that sits at a bend in the Siuslaw River. The former fishing town teems today with a variety of restaurants, parks, and close proximity to all kinds of fun natural sites. Just outside town, you'll find Heceta Head Lighthouse, one of the most visited attractions anywhere on the Oregon Coast, and the Oregon Dunes National Recreation Area. In town, meanwhile, Historic Old Town Florence is the town's beating heart—and packs a bevy of parks, eateries, hotels, and more into just a few busy blocks.

Farther south, Reedsport (pop. 4,000) is the first of two communities you'll encounter after crossing the Umpqua River. The working-class town sits inland from the Pacific Ocean and offers little in the way of tourist services, but has seen a waterfront revitalization project bear fruit with an engaging museum and a handful of homegrown eateries leading the way.

A few minutes southwest, Winchester Bay (pop. 350) sits where the Umpqua River meets the Pacific Ocean—and near the heart of the Oregon Dunes. The community's bustling Salmon Harbor Marina is ground zero for nearby outdoor recreation—led by crabbing, fishing (for salmon, bass, steelhead, sturgeon, and more), and tearing through the dunes on off-highway vehicles (OHVs). Wherever you are around town, keep an eye out for the distinctive red and white beams of the Umpqua River Lighthouse.

SIGHTS
Florence
★ Historic Old Town Florence

Florence is certainly a coastal town in the sense that it's located along the Oregon Coast, but some of the city's best sites are found inland—at a bend in the Siuslaw River, which drains into the Pacific Ocean at the western edge of town. It's at this U-shaped curve that visitors can stroll **Historic Old Town Florence,** the onetime home of Florence's fishing industry—but today where you'll find the community's best eateries, charming inns, and delightful sites (many of them hosted in buildings that date back to the early 1900s).

Most of the district's public parking stalls and popular sites can be found along Bay Street (between Juniper St. and Nopal St.), which runs parallel to the Siuslaw River.

The **River House Inn** (page 157) sits at the western edge of Old Town, showcasing views of the Siuslaw River and Oregon Dunes in the shadow of the arched Siuslaw River Bridge. Walking eastward, warm up with a cup of locally roasted coffee at **River Roasters** (1240 Bay St.; 541/997-3443; www. coffeeoregon.com; 7am-5pm daily, $2-6), home to a kitschy café and partially covered patio overlooking the river; or enjoy locally sourced Pacific Northwest cuisine at **Waterfront Depot** (page 156). At the eastern edge of the stately district, shop for locally crafted gifts, award-winning chocolate, and regional artwork at **Wind Drift Gallery** (1395 Bay St.; 541/997-9182; www.oregoncoastgalleries.net; 10am-5:30pm daily).

The Oregon Dunes

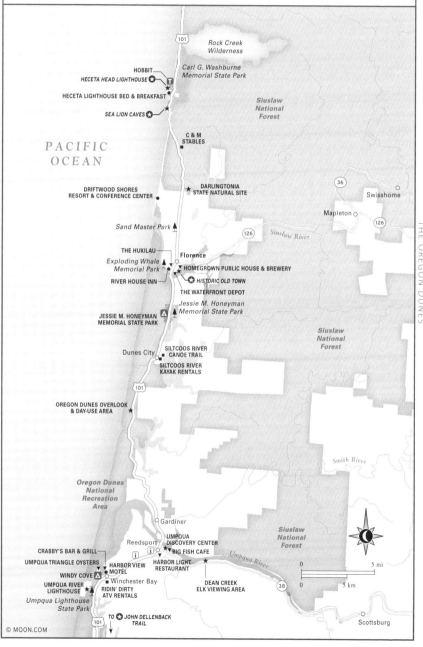

PACIFIC OCEAN

Rock Creek Wilderness

Carl G. Washburne Memorial State Park

Siuslaw National Forest

HOBBIT
HECETA HEAD LIGHTHOUSE ✪
HECETA LIGHTHOUSE BED & BREAKFAST
SEA LION CAVES ✪

C & M STABLES

DRIFTWOOD SHORES RESORT & CONFERENCE CENTER

★ DARLINGTONIA STATE NATURAL SITE

36
Swisshome

Mapleton

Sand Master Park

126

Siuslaw River

THE HUKILAU
Florence
Exploding Whale Memorial Park
HOMEGROWN PUBLIC HOUSE & BREWERY
RIVER HOUSE INN
HISTORIC OLD TOWN
THE WATERFRONT DEPOT

Jessie M. Honeyman Memorial State Park

JESSIE M. HONEYMAN MEMORIAL STATE PARK

Dunes City
SILTCOOS RIVER CANOE TRAIL
SILTCOOS RIVER KAYAK RENTALS

Siuslaw National Forest

101

OREGON DUNES OVERLOOK & DAY-USE AREA ★

Smith River

Oregon Dunes National Recreation Area

Gardiner

Reedsport
UMPQUA DISCOVERY CENTER
BIG FISH CAFE
CRABBY'S BAR & GRILL
UMPQUA TRIANGLE OYSTERS
HARBOR VIEW MOTEL
HARBOR LIGHT RESTAURANT
WINDY COVE
UMPQUA RIVER LIGHTHOUSE ★
RIDIN' DIRTY ATV RENTALS
Winchester Bay
Umpqua Lighthouse State Park

Umpqua River

Siuslaw National Forest

DEAN CREEK ELK VIEWING AREA ★

38

TO ✪ JOHN DELLENBACK TRAIL

101

Scottsburg

0   5 mi
0   5 km

© MOON.COM

Along the way, several small parks and docks showcase Siuslaw River views, display public art, and offer interpretive panels that explain regional history.

★ Heceta Head Lighthouse

Sitting atop a windswept bluff just north of Florence is **Heceta Head Lighthouse State Scenic Viewpoint** (US-101, 12 mi/19 km north of Florence; 541/547-3416; www. stateparks.oregon.gov; sunrise-sunset daily; $5 day-use fee). The lighthouse sits on a headland that rises 1,000 feet (1,600 m) above the Pacific Ocean and first lit up in 1894; more than a century later, it is considered the strongest light on the Oregon Coast. Guided tours through the base of the lighthouse and the first floor of the tower are available 11am-3pm daily in summer and 11am-2pm daily in winter. Even without a tour, Heceta Head is a worthy stop; a sandy beach below the lighthouse makes a delightful place to relax on clear days—and seals, sea lions, and gray whales can be seen from the base of the lighthouse. A wide, 1-mile/1.6-km (round-trip) hiking path ascends roughly 150 feet (240 m) to the lighthouse, passing the Heceta Lighthouse Bed & Breakfast along the way. Picnic tables and restrooms are available at the parking area.

From Florence, the 12-mile (19-km) drive via US-101 northbound takes about 20 minutes.

★ Sea Lion Caves

Since 1932, the roadside attraction **Sea Lion Caves** (91560 US-101; 541/547-3111; www. sealioncaves.com; 9am-4pm daily; $16, $15 seniors, $10 children 5-12, free for children 4 and younger) has offered access to the largest sea cave anywhere in the United States—which also happens to host a colony of hundreds of Steller sea lions. Just beyond the gift shop, visitors can look for sea lions lounging on rocky formations around the cave below (where they spend most of their summers)—and then walk down to an elevator that descends to the sea cave itself; sea lions can largely be found in the cave throughout winter and spring, and during storms.

From Florence, the 11-mile (18-km) drive via US-101 northbound takes about 15 minutes. Note that a large parking area is on the east side of US-101; visitors must cross the highway (near a bend in the road) to access the Sea Lion Caves. Take extreme caution when doing so.

Darlingtonia State Natural Site

Stop by the small botanical garden at **Darlingtonia State Natural Site** (5400 Mercer Lake Rd.; 541/997-3851; www.stateparks.oregon.gov; sunrise-sunset daily; free) to walk through a grove of *Darlingtonia californica* plants—the only carnivorous plant in Oregon. More commonly known as cobra lilies, the plants have hidden openings that attract (and eventually trap) unsuspecting insects, which soon decompose and turn into nitrogen that is absorbed by the plant. The plants bloom between late spring and early summer—but are worth a quick trip year-round. A short, flat walking path (part dirt, part wooden boardwalk) connects the parking area to the grove, where an interpretive panel explains the plant. Restrooms and picnic tables are available at the parking area. From Florence, the 4.5-mile (7.2-km) drive via northbound US-101 takes about seven minutes.

Exploding Whale Memorial Park

In November 1970, a dead sperm whale washed ashore on the beach in Florence. The carcass was too large to remove through conventional means, so state officials opted to dynamite the whale—figuring it would mostly disintegrate and leave behind small chunks for other animals to feed on. Instead, the explosion was so large that hulking chunks of blubber pelted nearby vehicles, buildings, and—yes—curious onlookers.

Naturally, the incident entered local lore—it's still a touchy subject around town today—and was recognized in 2020 with the creation of **Exploding Whale Memorial Park** (612

Where to See Seals and Sea Lions

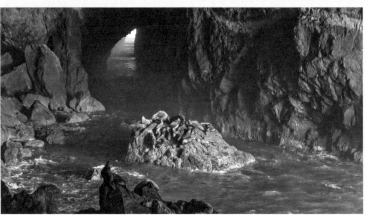

Sea Lion Caves

In all, two species of seal and three species of sea lion live on rocky outcrops, sandy beaches, and in various bodies of water along the Oregon Coast—with most calling Oregon home all year long. In some areas, you'll hear the roars and barks of sea lions; in others, you'll see seals flopping on land or poking their head above water. However it happens, it's always a treat to see (and hear) these awe-inspiring creatures.

Keep your eyes peeled, and you'll almost certainly see seals and sea lions frolicking on your travels up and down the Oregon Coast. But if you want to make a point of seeing seals and sea lions in their natural environments, here are five safe bets for doing exactly that. Just be sure to stay at least 150 feet (50 m) away from the animals, and never try to approach, feed, or pet them.

- **Astoria Riverwalk:** You'll hear the resident sea lions barking long before you see them along the boardwalk on the Columbia River, especially around the Bowline Hotel (page 73).

- **Cape Meares State Scenic Viewpoint:** Enjoy south-facing views of Three Arch Rocks National Wildlife Refuge, the only pupping site of Steller sea lions on the north Oregon coast (page 109).

- **Yaquina Head Outstanding Natural Area:** Watch seals lounging on rocks or swimming in the surf from up on Yaquina Head, or walk down to the shore for a closer look (page 133).

- **Sea Lion Caves:** The name is a dead giveaway: The largest sea cave in the United States hosts a colony of Steller sea lions that live in the area throughout winter, spring, and summer (page 148).

- **Cape Arago State Park:** The park's overlook at Simpson Reef and Shell Island (both part of the Oregon Islands National Wildlife Refuge) peers down on offshore colonies of seals and sea lions (page 167).

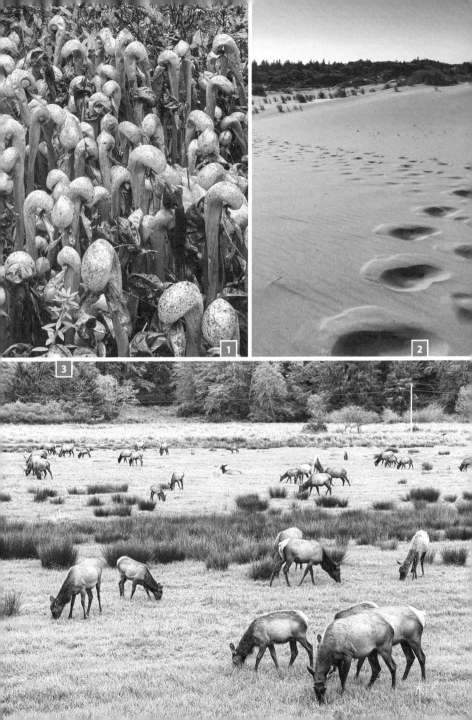

Rhododendron Dr.; 541/997-4106; www. ci.florence.or.us; sunrise-sunset daily; free) along the Siuslaw River. The park doesn't offer a view of where the infamous whale blew up—but still hosts a lovely picnic area, views of the nearby dunes and the Siuslaw River Bridge, easy river access, and interpretive panels on local ecology.

Jessie M. Honeyman Memorial State Park

Just south of Florence, **Jessie M. Honeyman Memorial State Park** (US-101, 4 mi/6.5 km south of Florence; 541/997-3851; www.state-parks.oregon.gov; sunrise-sunset daily; $5 day-use fee) straddles the east and west sides of US-101 (with an overpass providing safe passage for cyclists and pedestrians) and hosts a whole weekend worth of fun—including a pair of inland freshwater lakes, easy access to the Oregon Dunes, and several walking paths. With so much to do, it's a good thing the park has a mammoth campground.

A good place to start is the **Cleawox Lake Day-Use Area,** which sits along the north shore of its namesake lake and is home to **Honeyman Lodge** (10am-5pm daily Memorial Day-Labor Day), constructed in the late 1930s by the Civilian Conservation Corps.; today, the lodge hosts interpretive displays and a small gift shop, as well as canoe, pedal boat, and stand-up paddle-board rentals (June-Sept.; $10 per hour) if you want to get on the calm waters of Cleawox Lake. Sandboard rentals are also available (June-Sept.; $10 per day) for "surf-ing" the dunes of the adjacent **Sand Dunes Day-Use Area.** Young kids enjoy splashing around in the shallow lake, but lifeguards are not present. In spring, colorful rhodo-dendron blooms crowd the footpath around Cleawox Lake—and in fall, huckleberry and blackberry bushes invite visitors to pick a fresh, juicy snack.

On the south side of Cleawox Lake is the **Dunes North parking area,** which hosts a restroom and provides access to the dunes that butt up against the lake; a sandy hillside offers fun opportunities if you brought a sled or just want to roll down the dunes.

East of US-101, you'll find **Woahink Lake,** popular with paddlers, picnickers, and swim-mers (though no lifeguard is present). Bring your own canoe, kayak, or stand-up paddle-board, as rentals are not available.

Note that you won't find easy beach access anywhere within the park, which is separated from the Pacific Ocean by two miles of dunes. Hiking across the dunes is not recommended.

Oregon Dunes Overlook and Day-Use Area

As one of the northernmost stretches of dune accessible to the public, the **Oregon Dunes Overlook and Day-Use Area** (81100 US-101, Gardiner; 541/271-6000; www.fs.usda. gov; 7am-7pm daily; $5 day-use fee per ve-hicle or Northwest Forest Pass) offers a fine introduction to the otherworldly landscape.

From the day-use area, take in views of the dunes (extending all the way to the Pacific Ocean) from wheelchair-accessible viewing platforms, learn about how the dunes formed through on-site interpretive panels, enjoy daily ranger-led talks, or join guided hikes on most summer weekends. The viewpoint also offers access to several miles of hiking trails that descend to the dunes and head westward to the coastline; in particular, the first 0.5 mile (0.8 km) of the 2-mile (3.2-km) round-trip Oregon Dunes Loop Trail is paved and wheelchair accessible. Flush toilets and potable water are available at the overlook at day-use area.

Note that beach access from the Oregon Dunes Overlook is limited March 15-September to protect the western snowy plover; if hiking at this time, stay on the trail, and walk only on wet sand once at the beach.

1: Darlingtonia State Natural Site 2: Oregon Dunes Overlook and Day-Use Area 3: Dean Creek Elk Viewing Area

Dogs are not permitted on the trail during this time.

From Florence, the 11.5-mile (18.5-km) drive via southbound US-101 takes about 15 minutes.

Reedsport
Oregon Dunes National Recreation Area

Looking at the mythical Oregon Dunes is like peering back in time. For millennia, sedimentary rock from the Oregon Coast Range moved downstream through coastal rivers—slowly eroding into sand along the way. Some 6,000 years ago, the sand-covered shoreline took shape—and the Oregon Dunes were born. Today, the Oregon Dunes tower up to 500 feet (150 m) in places and make up one of the largest stretches of coastal dunes anywhere in the world. The ever-shifting hillsides of sand surround (and are surrounded by) forests, lakes, bays, and more—creating a landscape unlike anywhere else on the Oregon Coast.

Even if the dunes look placid and peaceful, they're always changing; winds are constantly shaping and reshaping the dunes, which stretch about 40 miles (65 km) between Florence (in the north) and Coos Bay (in the south), and ocean currents dredge sand from the ocean floor before depositing it onto the beach—where wind whips it onto the dunes. Writer Frank Herbert was so inspired by the Oregon Dunes, he created an entire planet covered in sand—Arrakis—in his seminal 1965 novel *Dune*.

In 1972, the United States Congress designated the Oregon Dunes a national scenic area, preserving the vast expanse for all manner of outdoor recreation; today, almost every grain of sand is open to the public. Popular activities include camping, hiking, riding off-highway vehicles, and even "surfing" the sand throughout the **Oregon Dunes National Recreation Area.**

Sitting in the heart of the Oregon Dunes, you'll find the **Oregon Dunes National Recreation Area Visitor Center** (855 US-101, Reedsport; 541/271-6000; www.fs.usda.gov; 8am-4pm Mon.-Fri.). The center, located about 15 minutes from the nearest dune access, offers passes, permits, maps, and brochures—and hosts a small gift shop and interpretive exhibits. Friendly rangers are happy to offer advice and recommendations. Potable water and flush toilets are available. From Florence, the 22-mile (35-km) drive via southbound US-101 takes about 30 minutes.

Dean Creek Elk Viewing Area

Just outside Reedsport, the **Dean Creek Elk Viewing Area** (48819 OR-38, Reedsport; 541/756-0100; www.blm.gov; sunrise-sunset daily; free) offers the chance to spy a herd of 60 to 100 Roosevelt elk that live on the preserve all year long. Several pullouts along the highway afford safe viewing opportunities—bull elk can reach 1,000 pounds (450 kg), after all—as does a fenced viewing area with interpretive panels and restrooms. Your best bet to view elk is in the early-morning and early-evening hours, when the animals are more active. The viewing is especially enchanting during the elk rut between mid-September and mid-October, when bulls unleash their bugle calls and lock antlers for the chance to mate with female elk. From Reedsport, the 3.2-mile (5-km) drive via eastbound OR-38 takes about four minutes.

Umpqua Discovery Center

Reedsport and Winchester Bay sit where the Umpqua River collides with the Pacific Ocean, which has informed the area's natural and cultural history since time immemorial. **Umpqua Discovery Center** (409 Riverfront Way, Reedsport; 541/271-4816; www.umpqua-discoverycenter.com; 10:30am-4:30pm Tues.-Sat. and noon-4pm Sun. June 15-Sept., 10:30am-4pm Tues.-Sat. Oct.-June 15; $8, $4 for children 5-16) showcases this history—from the Native American tribes who have long called the region home to the area's more recent industrial legacy—through interpretive panels, models, multimedia exhibits, artifacts,

Where to See Winter Storms

Between November and March, winter storms occasionally pound Oregon's famously rocky shoreline. And when they do, the results can be dramatic—with waves tumbling over headlands, crashing into seawalls, and engulfing sea stacks. When conditions are especially fraught, waves can shoot 100 feet (30 m) or more in the air.

Storm-watching has become a popular winter activity on the Oregon Coast, with parks (both protected from and exposed to the elements) brimming with eager visitors. If you'd like to see Mother Nature's fury for yourself, here are five parks for doing just that. Be sure to dress for the elements with layers and waterproof gear, keep a safe distance from waves at all times, stay off jetties, and never turn your back on the ocean.

- **Fort Stevens State Park:** An elevated (but uncovered) platform stands at the northwest corner of the park, boasting views of where winter storms punish a jetty at the mouth of the Columbia River (page 84).

- **Whale Watching Center:** Nominally a small outpost for spying migrating gray whales, the enclosed building sits just above a seawall that gets pounded by winter storms (page 126).

- **Boiler Bay State Scenic Viewpoint:** Sitting high above its namesake bay, the wayside offers dramatic views of waves crashing into the shore (page 126).

- **Cape Perpetua Scenic Area:** Watch storms roll in from the comfort of a fully enclosed visitor center, or brave the elements at the likes of Devils Churn and Cook's Chasm (page 142).

- **Shore Acres State Park:** A fully enclosed observation building stands on a sandstone cliff high above the Pacific Ocean, offering sweeping views of the waves and massive rock formations below (page 166).

and more. Locally made goods are for sale in the gift shop, and the museum's back deck offers views of the Umpqua River.

Winchester Bay
Umpqua River Lighthouse
Standing over where the Umpqua Lighthouse meets the Pacific Ocean, the **Umpqua River Lighthouse** (1020 Lighthouse Rd., Winchester Bay; 541/271-4631; www.umpqua-valleymuseums.org; 10am-5pm daily; $8, $4 for children 5-17, free for children 4 and younger) dates back to 1894 and stands 65 feet (20 m) tall. Lighthouse tours are offered daily, year-round, with docents from the Umpqua River Lighthouse Museum next door; the attraction hosts photographs, artifacts, and other materials that tell the story of the lighthouse. Just across the street, a small parking area and viewing platform offer views of the Umpqua River and Pacific Ocean, along with interpretive panels that explain the region's

gray whale population—and offer tips for seeing whales from the perch.

RECREATION
Hiking
Hobbit Trail
Distance: *1 mile (1.6 km) round-trip*
Duration: *1 hour*
Elevation Gain: *170 feet (50 m)*
Effort: *Easy*
Trailhead: *Hobbit Trailhead, 1 mile/1.6 km north of Heceta Head Lighthouse*
Directions: *From Florence, drive northbound on US-101; after 12.5 miles (20 km), turn right into a small parking area for the Hobbit Trailhead. The trailhead itself is on the west side of US-101, just north of the parking area.*

The creatively named (out-and-back) **Hobbit Trail** evokes an enchanting world—and lives up to the billing with an easy, family-friendly hike through a lush coastal forest. From the trailhead, the path descends through fern and

Sitka spruce (the latter draped in moss), and even on sunny days, the trail can feel quite dark owing to the richness of vegetation. As it descends, the path heads through a tunnel of salal that feels straight out of a fairy tale before ending at a quiet stretch of coastline in Carl G. Washburne Memorial State Park. This trail has grown in popularity in recent years, thanks largely to its name, so try timing your visit to a weekday (if possible), and try to hit the trail for a short outing by 9am.

★ John Dellenback Trail

Distance: *5.5 miles (8.9 km)*
Duration: *3 hours*
Elevation Gain: *300 feet (90 m)*
Effort: *Easy/moderate*
Passes/Fees: *$5 day-use fee per vehicle or Northwest Forest Pass*
Trailhead: *John Dellenback Trailhead, 6.8 mi/11 km southeast of Winchester Bay*
Directions: *Follow US-101 south of Winchester Bay; after 6.8 miles (11 km), turn right into the signed parking area.*

There are plenty of opportunities to hike the Oregon Dunes, but the lauded **John Dellenback Trail** invites hikers to walk across the widest stretch of dunes anywhere on the Oregon Coast.

The trail begins in a forest of Douglas fir, pine, rhododendron, and salal as a well-signed, 1-mile (1.6-km) lollipop loop that splits just as soon as you cross a small footbridge over Elk Creek, mere steps from the trailhead. Head right at the intersection, and continue through a forest for roughly 0.5 mile (0.8 km); along the way, you'll cross a road in the nearby Elk Creek Campground. At the next junction, head right to follow a sign for the **sand dunes.** This takes you, almost immediately, out onto the dunes themselves.

Once on the dunes, you'll see several wooden posts with blue rims acting as trail markers that guide you toward a sandy marshland (which often floods Nov.-Mar.) and, eventually, the shore. (It can help to track this hike using a mobile GPS app to keep from getting lost.) Once you arrive at the ocean, feel free to head north or south along the shoreline, if so you choose. Otherwise, retrace your steps to return to the trailhead.

The elevation change can vary, depending on recent winds and shifting dunes—but hiking across sand can wear out even the heartiest of hikers; know your limits, give yourself plenty of time, and bring enough water for the outing. This trail is best done by 11am to avoid the day's windiest conditions. And note that

John Dellenback Trail

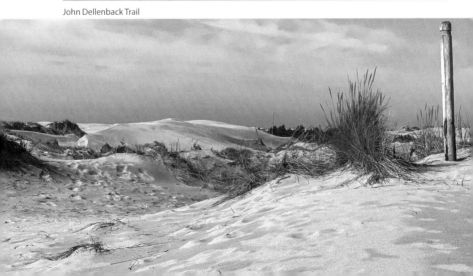

beach access is limited March 15-September to protect the western snowy plover; if hiking at this time, stay on the trail, and walk only on wet sand once at the beach. Note that dogs are not permitted on the trail during this time, either. And since the trail markers can be buried by sand (depending on recent winds), hikers should download a PDF map from the U.S. Forest Service website (www.fs.usda.gov) before heading out.

Vault toilets are available at the trailhead.

Sandboarding

There are seemingly countless ways to enjoy the Oregon Dunes—and one of the more creative pursuits is sandboarding. For the uninitiated, sandboarding entails (surprise!) surfing down dunes on what looks like a snowboard. If you have the equipment, you can sandboard on dunes all over the region—but the best place to start (and gear up) is **Sand Master Park** (4981 US-101, Florence; 541/997-6006; www.sandmasterpark.com; 10am-6pm daily summer, 10am-5pm Mon.-Tues. and Thurs.-Sat. and noon-5pm Sun. winter), just south of Florence.

If it's your first time out, instruction is available ($45 per hour, gear not included) on a private park within the dunes. Rental sandboards run $10-25 for up to 24 hours, with goggles and helmets running $5 over that same time period; all rentals include access to the park—and its many ramps, rails, and jumps for a more thrilling outing. From Florence, the 2-mile (3.2-km) drive via southbound US-101 takes about five minutes.

OHV Riding

When the weather's nice, the buzzing of off-highway vehicles (OHVs) cuts through the air around Winchester Bay, and puffs of sand kick up behind speeding buggies within earshot of the Pacific Ocean. Given the community's close proximity to the Oregon Dunes National Recreation Area, Winchester Bay is a popular destination for riders.

If you want to get on the dunes, consider a rental through **Ridin' Dirty ATV Rentals**

(75293 US-101, Winchester Bay; 541/500-0744; www.ridindirtyrentals.com; 9am-5pm Tues.-Sat.). The shop offers rides for the whole family, from ATVs geared toward younger riders ($50-360) and beginner riders ($65-400) to dune buggies that seat up to five ($125-1,200); rentals are available for up to 24 hours and include safety training, fitted helmets, transport to the dunes, and recommendations for where to ride.

Paddling and Water Sports

Hiking and ATV riding might be the most popular ways to experience the Oregon Dunes, but the **Siltcoos River Canoe Trail** offers another perspective. Starting just west of the quiet Siltcoos Lake, paddlers can follow the 6-mile/10-km (round-trip) river trail as it winds through a forest of Sitka spruce, through the dunes, and into an estuary before arriving at the Pacific Ocean; along the way, paddlers might spot wildlife—including river otters, deer, harbor seals, and several species of bird. The calm waters and Class I rapids are easy to navigate, though paddlers should keep an eye out for downed trees and river debris that can impede progress. In all, give yourself three to five hours for the peaceful trip.

If you don't have your own craft, rentals are available through **Siltcoos River Kayak Rentals** (Siltcoos Lake Resort, 82855 Fir St., Westlake; 541/999-6941; www.siltcoosriver.com; 10am-9pm daily mid-May-early Oct.). Single kayaks run $45 per day, and tandem kayaks run $65 per day; life jackets and paddles are included with each rental. From Florence, the 7.5-mile (12-km) drive via southbound US-101 takes about 10 minutes.

Beach access is limited March 15-September to protect the western snowy plover; if paddling at this time, paddlers should stay in (or on) their craft and off the shoreline at the Pacific Ocean.

Horseback Riding

C&M Stables (90241 US-101, Florence; 541/997-7540; www.oregonhorsebackriding.com) offers a variety of horseback rides

in the Florence area—but none are quite as ethereal as its Dune Trail Rides ($75-95); each beginner-friendly outing lasts 60-90 minutes and heads through a mixture of forested dunes and wide-open stretches of sand that are constantly shifting with the wind. Since the sand is so soft, your horse will have no choice but to take it easy—leading to a laid-back ride and giving you plenty of time to enjoy the scenery. Other rides through C&M Stables include beach rides lasting 90 minutes to two hours ($95-125) and two-hour beach rides ($185) tailored to more experienced riders.

Fishing

The lower Umpqua River is an angler's paradise; get on the water with **Living Waters Guide Service** (541/430-1736; www.fishinglivingwaters.com; $300-400). Led by guide Todd Harrington, trips cover the lower Umpqua and several coastal rivers nearby—wherever the fish are biting—and offer the chance to catch smallmouth bass, chinook, coho salmon, and more; each outing includes gear and tackle, flies (if fly fishing), fish filleting and packaging, snacks, and refreshments.

Rippin Drag Guide Service (541/817-4782; www.rippindragguideservice.com; $75-325) is another popular guide service, with trips (around Winchester Bay, along the Umpqua River, and in the Pacific Ocean) geared toward the region's marquee species—including salmon, rockfish, sturgeon, tuna, halibut, and crab.

Anglers should purchase a single-day **fishing license** (www.myodfw.com; $23 per license) before hitting the water; if fishing *and* crabbing, purchase a single-day **angling and shellfish combo license** (www.myodfw.com; $32.50 per license).

BEER, WINE, AND NIGHTLIFE

At **Homegrown Public House & Brewery** (294 Laurel St., Florence; 541/997-4886; www.homegrownpublichouse.com; noon-7pm Fri.-Tues.), it's all about community. The Florence natives behind the pub seek to bring friends and visitors together over locally sourced pub fare (including Oregon-grown mushrooms and flatbread, Cajun-fried oysters, and beer-battered fish-and-chips) and house-made brews you won't find anywhere else—all in a spacious, airy pub and on a relaxing patio. The pub also hosts occasional live music and fundraiser nights for worthy causes.

FESTIVALS AND EVENTS

Every spring, the **Oregon Divisional Chainsaw Carving Championship** (www.oregonccc.com; Father's Day weekend; $5-15) invites skilled chainsaw artists to Reedsport to turn otherwise ordinary logs into dramatic works of art—and the general public to watch them do so. Food and beverage vendors are on hand, and select pieces are auctioned off.

FOOD

Florence

Florence is home to several restaurants that lean heavily on the community's commercial fishing industry—with many situated near the Siuslaw River in Historic Old Town Florence. A handful put their own creative spin on traditional seafood cuisine, incorporating Asian and Italian influences into their dishes.

★ **The Waterfront Depot** (1252 Bay St.; 541/902-9100; www.thewaterfrontdepot.com; 3pm-9pm daily; $13-27) is among the area's most popular eateries, thanks to an elegant seafood menu that includes Dungeness crab cakes, locally caught oysters, crab-encrusted Alaska halibut, and other seasonal dishes. The dimly lit restaurant, perfect for a romantic night out, is housed in an old train station and features a full bar, along with a curated selection of regional wines and suggested wine pairings. Outdoor seating is available when the weather cooperates.

Away from the Siuslaw River waterfront, **The Hukilau** (185 US-101; 541/991-1071; www.hukilauflorence.com; 11am-6:30pm Wed.-Sat.; $18-30) dishes a variety of sushi offerings, Hawaiian-Asian fusion items,

and a full tiki bar brimming with tropical drinks. The wide-ranging menu includes more than 30 types of sushi rolls (including a dozen house specialties), some made from locally sourced seafood, as well as the likes of Japanese pork katsu and pineapple teriyaki chicken. Daily specials are offered, and outdoor seating is available.

Reedsport

Reedsport is best known for stick-to-your-ribs diner fare, but **Big Fish Cafe** (345 Riverfront Way; 541/361-6331; www.bigfishcafereedsport.com; 4:30pm-8pm Tues.-Sun., 9am-noon Sun.; $15-23) is changing all that with an internationally inspired menu that spotlights pasta dishes, chicken tikka masala, and more—along with locally caught seafood dishes. The eatery is housed in a converted Coast Guard ship on the Umpqua River; outdoor seating is available.

Away from the waterfront, the woman-owned **Harbor Light Restaurant** (930 US-101; 541/271-3848; www.harborlightrestaurant.com; 11:30am-8pm Sun.-Thurs., 11:30am-9pm Fri.-Sat.; $13-20) serves locally sourced seafood dishes that draw on family recipes; the restaurant has been owned by the same family for more than 40 years, and the chef and owner often buys albacore tuna, salmon, lingcod, and other fresh seafood straight from the dock in nearby Winchester Bay. Chicken, turkey, and other meats are smoked on-site.

Winchester Bay

The Salmon Harbor Marina on Winchester Bay hosts a few popular eateries, chief among them **Crabby's Bar & Grill** (196 Bayfront Loop; 541/271-3474; www.keepitcrabby.com; 11am-7:30pm Sun.-Thurs., 11am-9pm Fri.-Sat.; $17-30). Enjoy locally sourced seafood dishes (Dungeness crab Rangoon, fresh fish-and-chips, tuna burgers, and more) in the wood-paneled restaurant or on its outdoor dining area, kept warm by fire pits and boasting views of Winchester Bay.

If you want some local oysters to prepare back at your campsite or hotel room, stop by **Umpqua Triangle Oysters** (723 Ork Rock Rd.; 541/271-5684; www.umpquatriangleoysters.com; 9am-5pm Thurs.-Mon.; $12-13 per dozen). Umpqua Triangle's oysters flourish in a protected growing area inside Winchester Bay that boasts the right mix of freshwater and salt water (as well as just the right temperature). The resulting delicacy bypasses the grainy texture common with most oysters; instead, the meat is sweet, with a mild touch of saltiness. Umpqua Bay's farm store sells oysters in a variety of sizes, as well as condiments, local wine, and beer.

ACCOMMODATIONS
Under $250

Anglers fishing out of Salmon Harbor Marina appreciate the simple, friendly **Harbor View Motel** (540 Beach Blvd., Winchester Bay; 541/271-3352; www.harborviewmotel.org; $100-140)—just across the street from the water. The motel hosts 14 basic rooms, including one suite with a full kitchen, dining table, couch, and separate bedroom. The motel's innkeepers sure know their clientele: on-site, outdoor crab cooking is available for guests.

The clean, well-kept ★ **River House Inn** (1202 Bay St., Florence; 541/997-3933; www.riverhouseflorence.com; $180-220) offers plenty of amenities—in-room lounge chairs and work desks, white noise machines, plenty of outlets, electric vehicle and Tesla charging stations, and more—but the hotel's location might be its biggest draw. The inn sits along the Siuslaw River; several rooms showcase views of the river and (across the water) the Oregon Dunes. It's not uncommon to see river otters, seals, sea lions, and birds right outside your window. The River House Inn is also a short walk to Historic Old Town Florence.

Over $250

Speaking of great locations, **Driftwood Shores Resort & Conference Center** (88416 1st Ave., Florence; 541/997-8263; www.

Is the Oregon Coast Pacific Passport Right for You?

The most-visited public lands along the Oregon Coast are all managed by a hodgepodge of state and federal government groups; Oregon State Parks runs dozens of state park and state recreation sites, while the U.S. Forest Service, National Park Service, and Bureau of Land Management run many *other* sites along the coast. What's more, only some of these require admission. It can get confusing fast, especially if you're from out of the area and don't understand the different types of public lands.

But the **Oregon Coast Pacific Passport** (800/551-6949; www.fs.usda.gov; $10 for a five-day passport, $35 for an annual passport) seeks to change all that by offering admission to 16 of the most popular sites along the entire Oregon Coast—regardless of who runs it. So the pass covers entry at Fort Stevens State Park (page 84), Lewis and Clark National Historical Park (page 74), Yaquina Head Outstanding Natural Area (page 133), Heceta Head Lighthouse State Scenic Viewpoint (page 148), Jessie M. Honeyman Memorial State Park (page 151), and Shore Acres State Park (page 166), among other sites.

If you plan on visiting at least two of these sites on your trip to the coast, the five-day passport will pay for itself. Passes are available at visitor centers, participating state parks, and U.S. Forest Service offices along the Oregon Coast; head online (www.fs.usda.gov) for a complete list of participating sites and where to purchase passes on your visit.

driftwoodshores.com; $164-412) boasts the *only* oceanfront lodging in Florence. Each of the hotel's 124 rooms offers unfettered ocean views, along with a private deck or balcony; some rooms include full kitchens, as well. Other amenities include an indoor pool (with adults-only hours each night), an aquatic play area for children, electric vehicle and Tesla charging stations, and pet-friendly rooms.

Spend the night in a lightkeeper's cottage with **Heceta Lighthouse Bed & Breakfast** (92072 US-101 S, Dunes City; 866/547-3696; www.hecetalighthouse.com; $430-619)—perched at the base of Heceta Head Lighthouse. Guests can choose among six opulent rooms within the keeper's house—one with an ocean view, another with views of the lighthouse, and others with views of the surrounding forest. Amenities throughout the Victorian-inspired property include family-style breakfasts, daily wine and cheese socials, a fully equipped kitchen, cozy common areas with spectacular views, handcrafted fireplaces, and a wraparound porch. Note there is a two-night minimum if staying

on a Saturday, pets are not allowed, and children must be 10 or older.

Camping
Florence

Just north of Florence is the popular **Carl G. Washburne Memorial State Park** (US-101, 14 mi/22.5 km north of Florence; 541/547-3416; www.stateparks.oregon.gov; $7-54). The spacious, well-kept campground sits in a lovely forest of pine and spruce; the bubbling China Creek runs through one loop and alongside another. In all, visitors can choose among 41 full-hookup sites, 14 electrical sites with water, 7 (secluded) walk-in tent sites (open May-Sept.), a hiker/biker camp, and 2 yurts—1 of which is pet-friendly; 1 electrical site is considered wheelchair-accessible.

Just south of Florence, **Jessie M. Honeyman Memorial State Park** (US-101, 4 mi/6.5 km south of Florence; 541/997-3641; www.stateparks.oregon.gov; $7-64) hosts the state's second-largest campground, at the northern edge of the Oregon Dunes. In all, the forested campground hosts 47 full-hookup

sites, 121 electrical sites with water, 187 tent sites, 10 yurts (5 of which are pet-friendly), and a hiker/biker camp area. The sites are spread across several loops on the west side of US-101, with several trails leading to the Oregon Dunes and Cleawox Lake nearby; within the campground, amenities include hot showers, flush toilets, a playground, and firewood for sale.

Both campgrounds are situated near some of the region's best-loved attractions—and routinely fill up on summer weekends. Make reservations six months out, when the reservation window opens, especially if you have your heart set on a specific site or yurt.

Winchester Bay

Winchester Bay's close proximity to the Oregon Dunes makes it a popular stop among off-highway vehicle (OHV) riders—many of whom camp at the bucolic, county-run **Windy Cove Campground** (541/957-7001; www.yourdcparks.com), which is broken into two loops. **Loop A** (380 Salmon Harbor Dr., Winchester Bay; $35-40) hosts 29 full- and partial-hookup sites, while **Loop B** (684 Salmon Harbor Dr., Winchester Bay; $30-50 for campsites, $99 for cabins) offers 39 full-hookup sites, 28 tent sites, and 2 cabins. Both campgrounds boast flush toilets, restrooms, and potable water—as well as dedicated OHV routes to reach the dunes nearby; Loop B also includes a playground.

Not far from the mouth of the Umpqua River, **Umpqua Lighthouse State Park** (460 Lighthouse Rd., Winchester Bay; 541/271-4118; www.stateparks.oregon.gov; $17-92) hosts a bevy of year-round camping options not far from the shore of Lake Marie. Choose among nearly 50 tent and RV sites (12 of which are full-hookup sites), 9 yurts (4 of which are pet-friendly—and 1 of which is wheelchair-accessible), and 2 log cabins (1 of which is pet-friendly); some include views of Lake Marie. Showers and flush toilets are available.

And just south of town, the quiet **William M. Tugman State Park** (72549 US-101, Lakeside; 541/759-3604; www.stateparks.oregon.gov; $24-64) offers nearly 100 sites with water and electrical hookups, as well as 16

Heceta Head Lighthouse and Heceta Lighthouse Bed & Breakfast

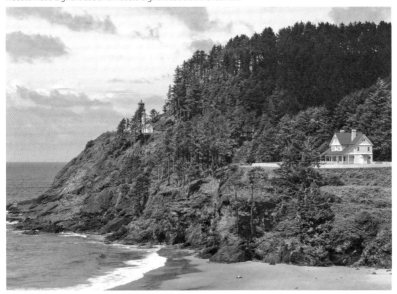

yurts (8 of which are pet-friendly) in a shady forest of shore pine along Eel Lake. Anglers fish for largemouth bass, rainbow trout, steelhead, coho salmon, and other species in the lake; anyone fishing should purchase a single-day **fishing license** (www.myodfw.com; $23 per license). Two campsites and 11 yurts are wheelchair-accessible; flush toilets and showers are available, and campers can purchase firewood from the camp host. All sites are open year-round.

INFORMATION AND SERVICES

Stop by the **Florence Area Chamber of Commerce and Visitors Center** (290 US-101; 541/997-3128; www.florencechamber.com; 11am-3pm Mon.-Sat., 11am-3pm Sun. June-Oct.) for brochures, maps, recommendations, and more. The **Reedsport Winchester Bay Chamber of Commerce** (2741 Frontage Rd., Reedsport; 541/271-3495; www.reedsportcc.org; 8am-5pm Mon.-Fri.) offers brochures, maps, and recommendations for where to eat, sleep, and play in the Reedsport and Winchester Bay area.

GETTING THERE AND AROUND

From Newport, the 49-mile (79-km) drive to Florence takes about 1 hour, 10 minutes via southbound US-101. From Coos Bay, the 49-mile (79-km) drive to takes about 1 hour via northbound US-101. And from Eugene, the 61-mile (98-km) drive takes about 1 hour, 15 minutes via westbound OR-126.

From Florence, the 22-mile (35-km) drive to Reedsport takes about 30 minutes via southbound US-101. From Coos Bay, the 23-mile (37-km) drive to Winchester Bay takes about 30 minutes via northbound US-101.

Winchester Bay is about 5 miles (8 km) southwest of Reedsport; both communities are along US-101, and driving between the two takes just less than 10 minutes.

Pacific Crest Bus Lines (541/344-6265; www.pacificcrestbuslines.com; $16-35 each way) runs one bus (each way) daily between Coos Bay and Eugene, with stops in Florence and Reedsport.

South Coast

The stretch of Oregon coastline between Coos

Bay and the California border doesn't see the same crowds as its northern counterparts—but it nevertheless boasts a working-class charm that's rich in natural wonder. Working harbors dish some of the state's best seafood, much of it caught that morning; hiking trails ascend to sweeping overlooks and descend to quiet beaches; viewpoints can be enjoyed from world-class golf courses and speeding jet boats alike; and some of the state's best-loved parks traffic in an unusual blend of windswept beaches and stately gardens. The Samuel H. Boardman State Scenic Corridor, meanwhile, may be the most scenic stretch of coastline in Oregon—and packs no shortage of wide-open bluffs, secluded

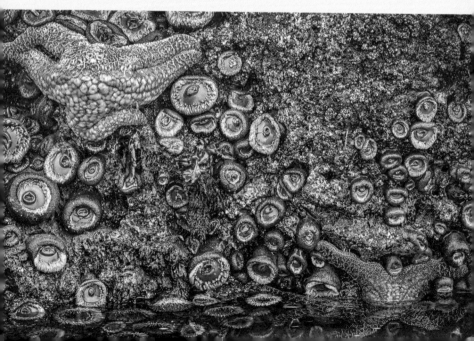

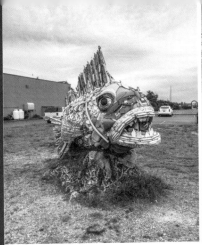
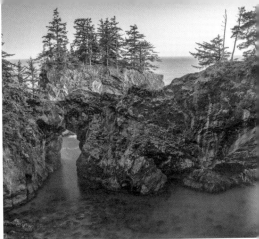

Highlights

Look for ★ to find recommended sights, activities, dining, and lodging.

★ **Admire the beauty of Shore Acres State Park:** The regal gardens enchant visitors from around the world, and its clifftop storm-watching station is second to none on the Oregon Coast (page 166).

★ **Stroll the Historic Old Town Bandon neighborhood:** Bandon's Historic Old Town sits along the Coquille River and is home to locally made treats, myriad seafood shacks, and more (page 174).

★ **Enjoy a round at Bandon Dunes Golf Resort:** Thanks to their views, natural hollows, and Scottish-influenced design, the six courses that cover this resort are routinely cited as some of the best in the world (page 177).

★ **Enjoy the views at Cape Blanco State Park:** Sitting at Oregon's westernmost point, the popular park is home to the oldest lighthouse on the Oregon Coast, hiking trails, and expansive ocean views (page 185).

★ **Explore the Rogue River with a jet boat ride:** Take a thrilling jet boat tour along a forested stretch of the 215-mile (346-km) Rogue River, home to all manner of wildlife, rugged natural features, and heart-racing whitewater rapids (page 187).

★ **Gawk at the Samuel H. Boardman State Scenic Corridor:** The 12-mile (19-km)

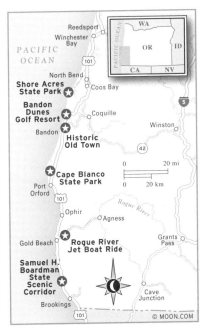

stretch of highway is considered by many to be the most beautiful part of the Oregon Coast—and is home to dramatic rock formations, craggy cliffs, and quiet beaches (page 197).

beaches, fascinating rock formations, and photo-worthy sunset views into just 12 dramatic miles (19 km).

PLANNING YOUR TIME

Broadly speaking, a weekend on Oregon's southern coast is plenty of time to enjoy outdoor recreation, sample the region's seafood, and spy some of the wildlife that calls the quiet corner of Oregon home.

You can drive the entire stretch of the southern coast—from the city of **North Bend** (in the north) to **Brookings** (in the south)—in just 2 hours, 15 minutes without stopping. But doing so sells short the region's natural attractions, passionate chefs, and scenic sites. So your best bet is to spend a night or two in one community and immerse yourself in that area's offerings.

A cluster of three cities sits at the northern edge of the region: **North Bend** sits at a bend in the Coos River and acts as a connective tissue to the surrounding communities of **Charleston** (to the southwest) and **Coos Bay** (to the southeast); here a weekend trip rewards visitors with thundering waterfalls, peaceful paddling, fresh seafood, and scenic state parks. It's at these parks, along the **Cape Arago Beach Loop,** that the Oregon Coast turns rockier and more rugged—with sea stacks, reefs, and other natural wonders just offshore extending all the way the Oregon-California border.

A half-hour south of Charleston and Coos Bay is **Bandon,** a small town that nevertheless hosts a world-class golf resort, excellent seafood shacks, the charming **Historic Old Town Bandon** district, and other fun attractions. In spring and summer, the community's **Circles in the Sand** art demonstrations bring curious travelers in droves.

Another 30 minutes south of Bandon, US-101 returns from an inland detour at **Port Orford.** Other than the charmingly quaint **Prehistoric Gardens,** the small town is refreshingly bereft of the tourist traps so common elsewhere on the Oregon Coast.

It's another 35 minutes south to **Gold Beach,** which sits at the mouth of the Rogue River and is known for its close connection to the waterway; **commercial fishing** is a popular activity, **jet boat tours** take visitors up the forested river gorge, and several **eateries** dish locally sourced seafood.

It's only another 30 or so minutes south to **Brookings-Harbor,** the southernmost beach communities in Oregon, but that assumes you don't stop at the many viewpoints along the 12-mile (19-km) **Samuel H. Boardman State Scenic Corridor**—which can lay claim to being the most scenic stretch of coastline anywhere in Oregon. Give yourself at least half a day to stop at viewpoints, enjoy a picnic, and tackle a hike or two.

Summer is the best time to visit Oregon's south coast, with little rainfall June-September, but that doesn't mean the rest of the year is all rain and wind; the farther south you go, the closer you are to Oregon's so-called "banana belt"—where more sunshine, fewer showers, and warmer-than-average temperatures may surprise visitors all year long. Even so, rainfall is common November-March—an occasionally gloomy time that nevertheless dovetails with opportunities to watch storms ravage the coastline and spy migrating gray whales out at sea.

SOUTH COAST

Previous: tidepool on the Oregon Coast; street art made from discarded materials in Historic Old Town Bandon; coastline views from along the Samuel H. Boardman State Scenic Corridor.

South Coast

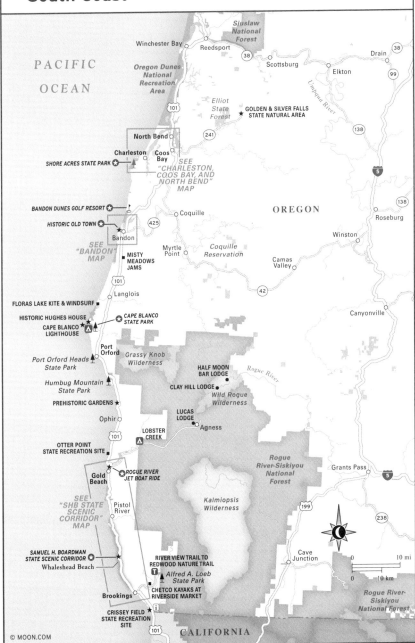

PACIFIC

OCEAN

Siuslaw
National
Forest

Winchester Bay
Reedsport
Drain
38
38
Scottsburg
Elkton
99
Oregon Dunes
National
Recreation
Area
Umpqua River

Elliot
State
Forest
GOLDEN & SILVER FALLS
STATE NATURAL AREA
138

101
North Bend
241

Charleston
Coos
Bay
SEE
"CHARLESTON,
COOS BAY, AND
NORTH BEND"
MAP
OREGON
5
SHORE ACRES STATE PARK

138

BANDON DUNES GOLF RESORT
425
Coquille
Roseburg

HISTORIC OLD TOWN
Bandon
Winston

SEE
"BANDON"
MAP
MISTY
MEADOWS
JAMS
Myrtle
Point
Coquille
Reservation
Camas
Valley

101
Langlois
42
Canyonville

FLORAS LAKE KITE & WINDSURF

HISTORIC HUGHES HOUSE
CAPE BLANCO
STATE PARK
CAPE BLANCO
LIGHTHOUSE
Port Orford
Port Orford Heads
State Park
Grassy Knob
Wilderness
Rogue River
HALF MOON
BAR LODGE

Humbug Mountain
State Park
CLAY HILL LODGE
Wild Rogue
Wilderness

PREHISTORIC GARDENS
LUCAS
LODGE
Ophir
101
LOBSTER
CREEK
Agness

OTTER POINT
STATE RECREATION SITE
Rogue
River-Siskiyou
National
Forest
Grants Pass

Gold
Beach
ROGUE RIVER
JET BOAT RIDE
5

SEE
"SHB STATE
SCENIC
CORRIDOR"
MAP
Pistol
River
Kalmiopsis
Wilderness
199
238

SAMUEL H. BOARDMAN
STATE SCENIC CORRIDOR
Whaleshead Beach
RIVER VIEW TRAIL TO
REDWOOD NATURE TRAIL
Alfred A. Loeb
State Park
Cave
Junction
0   10 mi
0   10 km

Brookings
CHETCO KAYAKS AT
RIVERSIDE MARKET
Rogue River-
Siskiyou
National Forest

CRISSEY FIELD
STATE RECREATION
SITE
101
CALIFORNIA

© MOON.COM

Charleston, Coos Bay, and North Bend

You can travel between the cities of North Bend (pop. 9,650), Coos Bay (pop. 16,200), and Charleston (pop. 800) without ever realizing you've left one for the other—but the working-class communities (occasionally referred to as Oregon's Bay Area) are truly greater than the sum of their parts, offering little of the touristy sheen so common at some of the more polished cities along the Oregon Coast.

North Bend describes the city's literal location at a northern bend in the Coos River as it turns south and empties into the Pacific Ocean; naturally, it's the northernmost of the three cities here. Immediately southeast of North Bend is Coos Bay, which sits where the Coos River enters—you guessed it—Coos Bay; a close proximity to outdoor adventure, working waterfront, and creative culinary scene are all breathing new life into the onetime lumber town. And to the southwest of North Bend—and due west of Coos Bay—is Charleston; the community is far smaller than its regional counterparts but nevertheless dishes some of the area's best seafood and makes a

great gateway to the Cape Arago Beach Loop, home to some of the most scenic state parks in Oregon.

SIGHTS
Cape Arago Beach Loop
The Cape Arago Beach Loop packs a lot of scenic beauty into a short drive—one that can be done, with stops, in just a couple of hours. Following the Cape Arago Highway west from Charleston, the two-lane loop takes visitors past a handful of parks that boast epic sunset views and wildlife-watching opportunities all year long—along with seasonal attractions, such as storm-watching in winter and garden viewing at Shore Acres State Park in spring and summer.

Sunset Bay State Park
Coming from Charleston, the first of the three scenic state parks you arrive at is **Sunset Bay State Park** (OR-540, 3 mi/4.8 km west of Charleston; 541/888-3732; stateparks.oregon.gov; sunrise-sunset daily; free). The centerpiece of the park's day-use area is a small

Sunset Bay State Park

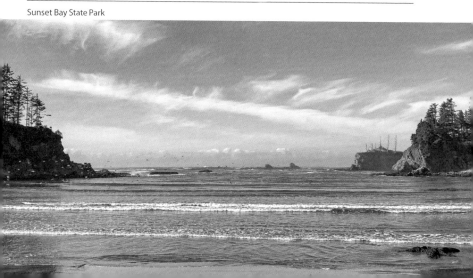

Charleston, Coos Bay, and North Bend

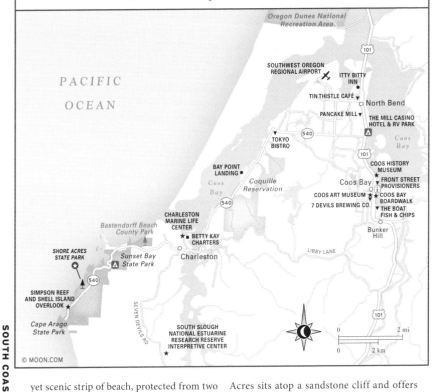

© MOON.COM

yet scenic strip of beach, protected from two forested cliffs that jut into Sunset Bay itself—thus protecting the shoreline from the elements. Given the park's name, this is an excellent place to watch the sunset (especially in spring); the cove is also a popular place to watch boogie-boarders and surfers waiting on the perfect wave, as well as harbor seals and sea lions splashing about. Flush restrooms are available.

★ Shore Acres State Park

The next park visitors arrive at along the Cape Arago Beach Loop is undoubtedly the centerpiece of the area: **Shore Acres State Park** (OR-540, 4.1 mi/6.6 km west of Charleston; 541/888-3778; stateparks.oregon.gov; sunrise-sunset daily; $5 day-use fee). One of the most beautiful state parks in all of Oregon, Shore

Acres sits atop a sandstone cliff and offers plenty of natural wonder both near and away from the water.

Near the shore, high above the Pacific Ocean, the park is renowned for its winter whale-watching and storm-watching opportunities, when thunderous waves can crash into cliffsides and rock formations below, sending swells up to 50 feet (15 m) in the air. The nature-viewing opportunities are made all the more pleasant by a fully enclosed **observation building,** which hosts a few benches and interpretive panels—and offers sweeping views out to sea.

Away from the cliffs and rugged beauty is another kind of natural attraction: a colorful **flower garden** that dates back to when the park was a home for an area timber baron in the early 20th century. A fire

in 1936 destroyed most of the buildings, as well as the garden—but the latter was re-planted in the 1970s. Today, you'll typically see flowers from around the world in bloom all year long; the first spring bulbs appear in late February, hundreds of rhododen-drons and 8,000 tulips bloom March-May, 800 rose bushes bloom June-September, and so forth. An on-site **information and gift center** (10:30am-4:30pm daily) offers loaner wheelchairs, informative brochures, recom-mendations from friendly volunteers, and a variety of items for sale—walking sticks, granola bars, books, child-friendly science kits, toys, and more.

The **Friends of Shore Acres** (www.sho-reacres.net), an advocacy group for the park, maintains the gardens, installs interpretive panels, crafts brochures, and updates its web-site with information on what's in bloom at any given time. The group also puts on the annual **Holiday Lights at Shore Acres event** (4pm-9:30pm nightly Thanksgiving-Dec.; free with $5 park admission), where more than 300,000 lights cover sculptures, 26 Christmas trees, and more throughout the park; appearances from Santa Claus, choral performances, and other fun events round out the festivities.

Cape Arago State Park

At the end of the Cape Arago Beach Loop, you'll find **Cape Arago State Park** (OR-540, 5.3 mi/8.5 km west of Charleston; 541/888-3778; stateparks.oregon.gov; sunrise-sunset daily; free). The park hosts viewpoints of the Cape Arago headland, the wider Pacific Ocean, and short trails descending to the base of two coves—North Cove and South Cove, as they're known—within the park; at low tide, South Cove hosts dramatic tide-pools, while the North Cove offers excellent wildlife-watching opportunities of nearby Shell Island. (Note that the North Cove trail is closed March-June to protect seal pups.) Picnic tables and a gazebo shelter are found at the park, as well.

Simpson Reef and Shell Island Overlook

Technically part of Cape Arago State Park, the **Simpson Reef and Shell Island Overlook** (OR-540, 4.8 mi/7.7 km west of Charleston; 541/888-3778; stateparks.oregon.gov; sunrise-sunset daily; free) is a wheelchair-accessible viewpoint that affords views of sea stacks and jagged rock formations in the ocean below. Shell Island, just offshore, is home to im-pressive colonies of seals and sea lions late August-June; even from up on this cliff, you can occasionally hear the chatter of barking California sea lions over the crashing waves. A variety of birds (such as osprey and black oystercatchers) rest and nest on surrounding islands, as well. Keep an eye out for migrating gray whales in winter and spring. Interpretive panels explain the wildlife that inhabits the ecosystems before you—and discuss how to tell the difference between the various species of seals and sea lions that call the area home. Volunteers from the nonprofit Shoreline Education for Awareness are on hand 10am-4pm Saturdays and Sundays (and holiday Mondays) Memorial Day-Labor Day to help visitors spy wildlife and better understand the ecosystem.

Golden and Silver Falls State Natural Area

Sitting in the Oregon Coast Range, **Golden and Silver Falls State Natural Area** (end of OR-241, 25 mi/40 km east of Coos Bay; 541/888-3778; stateparks.oregon.gov; sunrise-sunset daily; free) hosts a pair of impressive waterfalls in adjacent gorges, both around 250 feet (75 m) tall. In all, three short hiking trails crisscross the park: One (0.6 mi/1 km round-trip) heads to the base of Silver Falls, another (0.6 mi/1 km round-trip) heads to the base of Golden Falls, and a third (1.8 mi/2.9 km round-trip) ascends to a viewpoint halfway up Silver Falls *and* to the top of Golden Falls. All three trailheads depart from the parking area, which hosts a few picnic tables and vault toilets. The best time to visit is March-May, when winter runoff and seasonal rains fill the

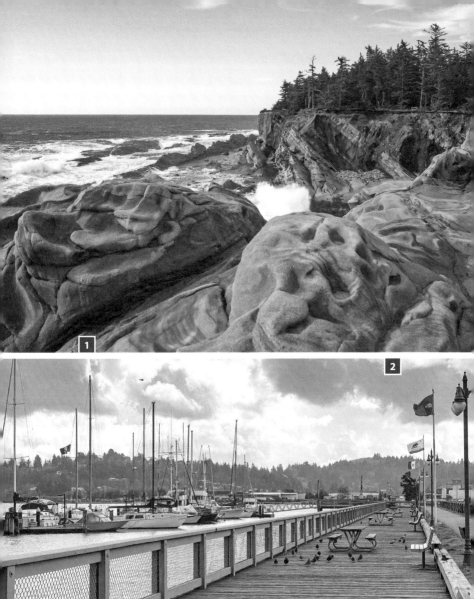

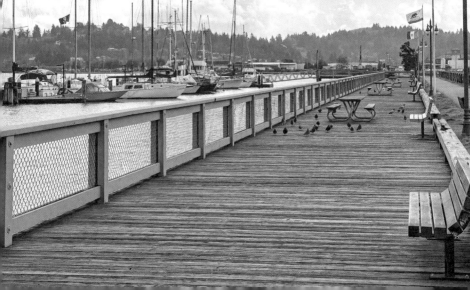

thundering waterfalls; Silver Falls, especially, slows to a trickle in summer. Note that the final 3 miles (5 km) of the road to Golden and Silver Falls narrows to a single lane and turns to gravel; RVs are not recommended for visiting the park.

Coos History Museum
Dive into the cultural, industrial, and social history of Oregon's south coast at the **Coos History Museum** (1210 N. Front St., Coos Bay; 541/756-6320; www.cooshistory.org; 11am-5pm Tues.-Sat.; $7, $3 for children 5-17, free for children 4 and younger and active-duty military). Exhibits on two floors explore the region's rich history through photographs, artifacts, and in-depth exhibits; maritime history and notable shipwrecks, for instance, are explored through boats, a ship wheel, lighthouse lantern, and other items. The museum's Native American exhibits include baskets, tools, stories, and more from the Coquille and Confederated Tribes of Coos, Lower Umpqua and Siuslaw Indians.

Coos Art Museum
In downtown Coos Bay, the **Coos Art Museum** (235 Anderson Ave., Coos Bay; 541/267-3901; www.coosart.org; 10am-4pm Tues.-Fri., 1pm-4pm Sat.; $5, $2 for students and seniors) hosts a robust permanent collection of more than 600 works, mostly from Pacific Northwest artists, and offers a wide range of rotating exhibits, typically centered around themes of local interest (such as maritime-inspired artwork and nature photography).

Of particular note is the second-floor Prefontaine Gallery, dedicated to the life of Coos Bay native and American long-distance runner Steve Prefontaine; "Pre," as he was commonly known, competed at the 1972 Summer Olympics and set numerous American running records—but his life was tragically cut short when he died in a car accident at just 24 years old. The gallery pays tribute to the local legend through photographs, trophies, and other memorabilia.

Coos Bay Boardwalk
Step back in time with a trip along the charming, 0.2-mile (0.3-km) **Coos Bay Boardwalk** (US-101, between Curtis Ave. and Commercial Ave.), a wooded pathway that parallels US-101 and hugs the city's waterfront. Views abound the entire way and may include great blue herons, ospreys, bald eagles, and other birds looking for their next meal. Three **covered pavilions** (US-101 and Anderson Ave.; sunrise-sunset daily; free) host picnic tables, interpretive panels on the community's industrial history and long-running relationship with the timber industry, and even an old tugboat display.

In the middle of the three pavilions, which run north-south and are adjacent to each other, are support beams made with different types of wood that are native to Oregon; educational panels explain the characteristics of each, what they're used for, how to spot the various trees in the wild, and how often they're harvested for lumber.

Charleston Marine Life Center
Learn all about the marine life and underwater ecosystems of the Coos Bay area at the **Charleston Marine Life Center** (63466 Boat Basin Rd., Charleston; 541/346-7280; cmlc.uoregon.edu; 11am-3pm Fri., 11am-5pm Sat.; $5, $4 for senior citizens, free for children and students). The interpretive center is part of the University of Oregon's marine biology research and teaching field station in Charleston—and includes hands-on, interactive experiences that showcase local marine life through aquariums, underwater videos from Oregon's marine reserves, whale skeletons, and more.

South Slough National Estuarine Research Reserve Interpretive Center
The name of the attraction may be a

mouthful, but the **South Slough National Estuarine Research Reserve Interpretive Center** (61907 Seven Devils Rd., Charleston; 541/888-5558; www.southsloughestuary.org; 10am-4pm Tues.-Sat.; free) is an impressive site that helps visitors understand and explore the South Slough Reserve (as it's more commonly known). The interpretive center hosts educational materials on the ecologically unique estuaries of Coos Bay—comprising wetlands, riparian forests, and other habitats that host a wide range of wildlife (such as birds, shellfish, and more). Away from the center, visitors can hike a number of short trails (some through towering forests, others along the South Slough's marshland) and paddle the estuaries (bring your own boat); water trail maps are available in the interpretive center's bookstore ($4) or for free online. Occasional guided paddles are offered with trained naturalists. Note that trails are open sunrise-sunset daily. Restrooms are available.

RECREATION
Paddling and Water Sports
With inlets, estuaries, creeks, and more, Oregon's Bay Area is a popular paddling destination.

The shallow, namesake bay at **Sunset Bay State Park** (page 165) is protected by rocky cliffs on two sides from whipping winds and harsh weather, making it a fine place to go kayaking and stand-up paddleboarding when the waves are calm. Rentals aren't available at or near the park, so bring your own craft.

Elsewhere, the **South Slough Reserve** (page 169) is an estuary within Coos Bay that showcases a variety of ecosystems and is home to several species of bird—including great blue herons, bald eagles, and ospreys. You'll want to bring your own craft, and paddling maps are available online (free) and at the South Slough National Estuarine Research Reserve Interpretive Center ($4). Naturalist-led guided paddling trips are made each spring and summer; dates are available online (www.southsloughestuary.org).

Alternately, paddlers can book a kayaking trip through the South Slough Reserve with **South Coast Tours** (541/373-0487; www.southcoasttours.net; May-Sept.; $85, $165 for two paddlers). The local outfitter leads a 2.5-hour tour that's timed around the incoming and outgoing tide for easier paddling; along the way, a knowledgeable guide points out the many birds that call the area home and explain what makes the environment so special. South Coast Tours also offers paddling trips around Brookings-Harbor, Port Orford, and other communities along the south coast.

Fishing
In all, Coos County (in which Coos Bay, North Bend, and Charleston are all located) hosts more than 30 freshwater lakes and rivers, not to mention Coos Bay itself—leading to a bustling commercial fishing industry that teems with anglers all year long. All the usual suspects can be found in the Coos Bay area, including Chinook salmon (Aug.-Oct.), steelhead (Nov.-Mar.), bottomfish (year-round), and Dungeness crab (year-round).

If you want to take a guided trip, **Betty Kay Fishing Charters** (90389 Albacore Ave., Charleston; 800/752-6303; www.bettykaycharters.com; Apr.-Oct.) is a beloved local outfitter that leads five-hour rockfish outings ($100, $80 for children 5-11) and day-long tuna trips ($250)—both in the waters around Charleston and in the Pacific Ocean.

Anglers should purchase a single-day **fishing license** (www.myodfw.com; $23 per license) before hitting the water; if fishing *and* crabbing, purchase a single-day **angling and shellfish combo license** (www.myodfw.com; $32.50 per license).

BREWPUBS
Since 2013, the family-owned ★ **7 Devils Brewing Co.** (247 S. 2nd St., Coos. Bay; 541/808-3738; www.7devilsbrewery.com; 11am-9pm Sun.-Mon. and Wed.-Thurs., 11am-10pm Fri.-Sat.) has churned out one excellent beer after another in downtown Coos Bay. The tap list is refreshingly old school, bypassing the latest trends for tried-and-true

styles that include a biscuity amber ale, a slightly spicy red ale, and a coffee-tinged porter. 7 Devils' food menu, meanwhile, is full of classic pub fare—but with locally caught seafood, seasonal salads, and cheese curds from nearby Face Rock Creamery. The lively pub hosts occasional live music inside and offers comfortable patio seating outside. A second (waterfront) outpost affords wide-open views of Coos Bay.

FESTIVALS AND EVENTS

The **Prefontaine Memorial Run** (www.prefontainerun.com; Sept.; $15-45) honors the memory of Coos Bay's hometown hero Steve Prefontaine with an annual 10K run that follows one of his old training courses, as well as a 2-mile (3.2-km) fun run and walk.

FOOD

Given that North Bend and Coos Bay are the area's largest communities, it's no surprise that's where you'll find most of the region's eateries; Coos Bay's downtown, especially, is chockablock with restaurants. But when you want fresh-from-the-boat seafood, Charleston offers a few well-regarded stops mere steps from the docks.

Charleston

Housed in a former church, **Miller's at the Cove** (63346 Boat Basin Rd.; 541/808-2404; www.millersatthecove.rocks; 11am-9pm daily; $10-24) is today a sports bar that serves up some of the area's best-loved seafood. Melts are made with fresh Dungeness crab and Oregon pink shrimp; local oysters can be served on the half shell, broiled, or fried; grilled or beer-battered fish-and-chips is made with local rockfish; and on it goes. Baja tacos are the house specialty, stuffed with cod, halibut, bay shrimp, prawns, or crab. In winter, the most coveted seats are around the fireplace.

It's hard to miss **Monkey Business Food to Go** (90378 Albacore Ln.; 541/778-3650; 11am-4pm Thurs.-Tues.; $7-18), housed in a bright yellow food cart at the Charleston Marina Complex. The eatery's wide-ranging menu includes a selection of hearty burgers and grill fare (such as chicken strips and a hot dog)—but its seafood, sourced fresh from local anglers, is worth seeking out. The fish is lightly battered to crispy perfection, the clam strips are tender, and the clam chowder is thick and chunky—the perfect balm for a chilly coastal evening. As the name implies, Monkey Business is takeout-only—but hosts a few picnic tables if you'd like to linger.

Coos Bay

Shark Bites Café (240 S. Broadway; 541/269-7475; www.sharkbites.cafe; 11am-9pm Mon.-Thurs., 11am-9:30pm Fri.-Sat.; $12-20) churns out all the classic casual seafood dishes—but does it better than most in downtown Coos Bay. Sandwiches are stuffed with oysters from Coos Bay, house-made Dungeness crab cakes are popular entrées, and fish tacos are prepared five different ways with cod, halibut, and shrimp.

Yes, ★ **The Boat Fish & Chips** (102 Hall Ave.; 541/808-9500; 11am-8pm Wed.-Mon., 11am-7pm Tues.; $9-25) dishes its oysters, clam chowder, and other seafood favorites from a landlocked houseboat mere steps from the water in Coos Bay. The menu at the woman-owned eatery includes all the local favorites—fish sandwiches, fried oysters, shrimp, hand-cut filets, fish-and-chips, and more—all sourced from local anglers whenever possible. Covered outdoor seating is available.

If you're hankering for good sushi, make your way to **Tokyo Bistro** (525 Newmark Ave.; 541/808-0808; www.tokyocoosbay.com; 11am-9pm Sun. and Tues.-Thurs., 11am-10pm Fri.-Sat.; $12-25). The eatery crafts its excellent sushi and other Japanese dishes with locally sourced seafood and fresh produce; that includes tuna poke salad, amaebi from local spot prawns, and blackened tuna sashimi. If sushi doesn't sound right, you'll find teriyaki dishes, sesame chicken katsu, ramen, and

more. Local musicians perform on Sunday evenings.

If you've had your fill of seafood, try the Neapolitan-style wood-fired pizzas at **Front Street Provisioners** (737 N. Front St.; 541/808-3420; https://frontstreetprovisionersmenu.square.site; 11am-9pm daily; $12-25) near the waterfront in Coos Bay. The woman-owned eatery serves nearly 20 creative pies adorned with fresh, local ingredients whenever possible; other highlights include seasonal salads (crafted with local ingredients), a handful of filling pasta dishes, and hearty calzones. Outdoor seating is available in summer.

North Bend

Fuel up for a day of adventure at **Pancake Mill** (2390 Tremont St.; 541/756-2751; www.pancakemill.com; 6am-3pm daily; $12-25), a longtime favorite among locals for its wide-ranging breakfast selection. You'll find all the breakfast classics here—egg dishes, waffles, omelets, and so forth—but pancakes in their many forms (crepes, Swedish pancakes with lingonberry filling, Dutch babies, potato pancakes, and more) are the star of the show here.

Vegan-friendly fare can be hard to come by on the Oregon Coast, owing to the region's love affair with seafood and all, so leave it to **Tin Thistle Café** (1972 Sherman Ave.; 541/267-0267; 11am-4pm Tues.-Sat.; $8-12) to craft a menu of 100 percent vegan cuisine that will please even the most ardent meat-eater in your crew. The menu includes veggie burgers prepared three ways, a lineup of hearty salad bowls and wraps, savory pasties, smoothies, and more—even nachos with white sauce and nondairy cheese.

ACCOMMODATIONS AND CAMPING

You'll find accommodations all over the area—and that includes Coos Bay—but the region's standout lodgings are concentrated around Charleston and North Bend. The former makes an ideal overnight destination if you're exploring the area's state parks and want to spend a night under the stars; and the latter hosts a few charming inns within a quick drive of nearby attractions.

Charleston

A few well-maintained campgrounds sit near (or along) the Cape Arago Beach Loop—and are popular stops for outdoor enthusiasts wanting to immerse themselves in this scenic stretch of coastline.

The Boat Fish & Chips

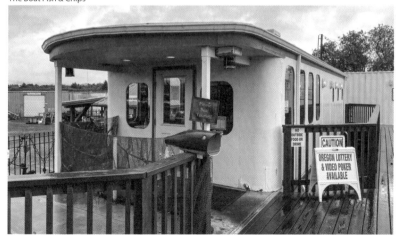

The sprawling campground at **Bastendorff Beach County Park** (63379 Bastendorf Beach Rd.; 541/396-7755; www.co.coos.or.us; $22-60) hosts 74 RV sites with water and electric hookups, 25 tent sites, and a pair of cabins with electricity and heat; each site comes with a campfire grill and picnic table, and flush restrooms and showers are available. One site is wheelchair accessible. Some sites reside in a wide-open meadow, boasting little privacy, while others are set amid a forest of Sitka spruce. Note that a two-night minimum stay is required. Away from the campground, the park's day-use area hosts a horseshoe pit, basketball court, spacious lawn, and massive playground.

Sunset Bay State Park (OR-540, 3 mi/5 km west of Charleston; 541/888-3778; stateparks.oregon.gov; $7-64) is the most centrally located of the campgrounds along the Cape Arago Beach Loop. It sits on the east side of the road, away from Sunset Bay, which affords the forested park some modicum of protection from the elements. In all, the campground hosts 30 full-hookup sites, 35 electrical sites with water, 65 tent sites, 8 yurts (4 of which are pet-friendly), and a hiker/biker camp area; 3 campsites and 3 yurts are wheelchair-accessible. Flush toilets and hot showers are available. The crowded campground is busy, and sites routinely fill up on summer weekends; make reservations six months out, when the reservation window opens—especially if you have your heart set on a specific site or yurt.

The high-end ★ **Bay Point Landing** (92443 Cape Arago Hwy.; 541/351-9160; www.baypointlanding.com; $306-408 for cabins and trailers, $93-180 for RV campsites) sits along Coos Bay and brings a decidedly modern touch to the old-school experience of camping. The trendy resort hosts 17 sleek, fully furnished cabins that boast comfortable linens, full bathrooms, kitchenettes, and outdoor patios; brand-new Airstream trailers that come with skylights, kitchenettes, private bathrooms, and outdoor fire pits; and

full-hookup RV campsites, some next to Coos Bay, that include picnic tables and stone fire pits, access to restrooms and laundry facilities, and more. The resort's luxe clubhouse, open to all guests, hosts a bocce ball court, playground, fitness center (complete with indoor pool), communal fire pits, and a general store that stocks the basics (such as s'mores ingredients and local beers—which guests can order via text message for delivery to their site).

North Bend

Sitting next to its namesake casino, **The Mill Casino Hotel & RV Park** (3201 Tremont St.; 541/756-8800; www.themillcasino.com; $275-$325 for hotel rooms, $60-95 for RV sites)—owned and operated by the Coquille Indian Tribe—hosts more than 200 well-appointed hotel rooms overlooking Coos Bay, as well as a pet-friendly RV park with more than 100 sites. Select hotel rooms (some of which are pet-friendly) offer in-room fireplaces and kitchenettes and jetted tubs—while all rooms boast comfortable beds (with linens made in Oregon); amenities include an on-site pool, hot tub, and fitness center. The RV park hosts back-in and pull-through full-hookup sites (some alongside Coos Bay), with plenty of room to accommodate slide-outs and additional vehicles.

It's not hyperbole to say that there's no lodging quite like the ★ **Itty Bitty Inn** (1504 Sherman Ave.; 541/756-6398; www.ittybittyinn.com; $165-210) anywhere on the Oregon Coast. The vintage motel boasts five themed rooms—complete with appropriate décor—devoted to, among other subjects, the Oregon Trail, tiki lounges of the 1950s and '60s, and *Star Trek*; one room is decorated, floor to ceiling, to look like the bridge of the U.S.S. Enterprise, complete with screen-accurate stage props. Regionally made soaps and locally roasted coffee are stocked in each room—and bicycles, record players, and even rebuilt Atari 2600 video game systems are available for guest use.

INFORMATION AND SERVICES

The friendly folks who staff the **Coos Bay Visitor Information Center** (50 Central Ave., Coos Bay; 541/269-0215; www.oregonsadventurecoast.com; 9am-5pm Mon.-Fri. and 10am-2pm Sat. year-round, 10am-2pm Sun. Memorial Day-Labor Day) are happy to provide recommendations, information, brochures, and maps for enjoying the area. Public restrooms are also available.

GETTING THERE AND AROUND

From Winchester Bay, the 20-mile (32-km) drive to North Bend (which offers easy access to Charleston and Coos Bay) takes about 25 minutes via southbound US-101. From Bandon, the 27-mile (43-km) drive takes about 35 minutes via northbound US-101.

Charleston, the gateway to the Cape Arago Beach Loop, is about 20 minutes from North Bend (via OR-540) and about 15 minutes from Coos Bay (via Ocean Blvd. SE and OR-540).

Coos Bay can be reached from Roseburg (along the Interstate 5 corridor) via OR-42 westbound and US-101 northbound; the 68-mile (109-km) drive takes about 2 hours, 15 minutes.

North Bend can be reached by air at **Southwest Oregon Regional Airport** (OTH, www.cooscountyairportdistrict.com); United Airlines serves the airport with year-round flights to San Francisco (SFO) and seasonal service (May-Sept.) to Denver (DEN). Two multinational rental car companies operate from the airport, but taxi and ride-share service is available, as well.

Curry Public Transit (541/412-8806; www.currypublictransit.org; $4-24) runs its **Coastal Express** Monday-Saturday, with stops in several south coast communities—including Coos Bay and North Bend.

Bandon and Vicinity

The community of Bandon (pop. 3,100) sits at the mouth of the Coquille River and has made a name for itself with a wide range of attractions geared toward seemingly every kind of traveler.

Foodies enjoy visiting Face Rock Creamery, sampling the cranberry-infused cider at Bandon Rain, and seeing who makes the best fish-and-chips in Historic Old Town Bandon. Outdoor enthusiasts appreciate the sea stacks at Coquille Point, the quiet wetlands of the Bandon Marsh National Wildlife Refuge, and the windswept dunes at Bullard Beach State Park. And golfers the world over flock to Bandon Dunes Golf Resort, which hosts six links-style courses that head through some of the most scenic headlands, dunes, and forests in Oregon.

SIGHTS

★ Historic Old Town Bandon

Just about everything you'll want to do in town can be found around **Historic Old Town Bandon,** a compact district of about six city blocks between the banks of the Coquille River (to the north) and a coastal bluff (to the south); its western border is roughly Alabama Avenue SE, and its eastern border is Delaware Avenue SE.

The walkable nature of the neighborhood makes it a fun place to grab a bite, window-shop, watch anglers at work, and admire Bandon's artsy side (a handful of sculptures, carved from myrtlewood native to southern Oregon, line a wooden sidewalk along the Coquille River). Several of Old Town's wood-sided buildings date back to the years immediately following 1936, when a fire swept through Bandon, adding a touch of historical charm.

Bandon

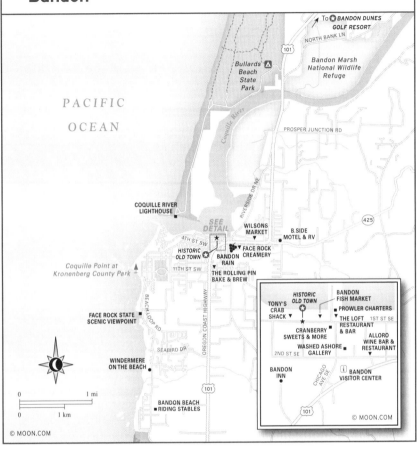

Just west of the heart of Historic Old Town, a small park hosts a **memorial for the Nasomah people** (1st Ave. SW & Cleveland Ave. SE) who lived along the Coquille River for more than 3,000 years; it includes a poetic interpretive panel that describes life in the village that once stood where Bandon now sits today.

Coquille Point

Coquille Point, located at **Kronenberg County Park** (1490 11th St. SW; 541/347-2437; sunrise-sunset, free), showcases dramatic views of the wider Pacific Ocean and

Bandon's rocky sea stacks; the latter are part of the **Oregon Islands National Wildlife Refuge,** which comprises nearly 2,000 rocks, reefs, and islands along the entire Oregon Coast. Several flat, wheelchair-accessible walking paths crisscross the headland, pass interpretive panels that explain the area's wildlife, and lead to benches with scenic views; a wooden staircase descends to the shore, though this isn't advised at high tide. Watch for harbor seals in the surf, migrating gray whales in winter, and a variety of seabirds that nest on the rocks just offshore.

BEACHES

Just north of Bandon, **Bullards Beach State Park** (US-101, 2.5 mi/4 km north of Bandon; 541/347-2209; stateparks.oregon.gov; sunrise-sunset daily; free) occupies two very different ecosystems near the mouth of the Coquille River. The northern edge of the park, dotted with walking and cycling paths (both paved and unpaved), is heavily forested, with spruce and pine dominating the landscape. Farther south, a sand spit separates the Pacific Ocean from the Coquille River; here visitors can stroll among nearly 5 miles of coastline and check out the **Coquille River Lighthouse,** which was constructed in 1896, was decommissioned in 1939, and sits at the mouth of its namesake river. The lighthouse's signal room is open 11am-5pm daily mid-May-September.

High above the surf, **Face Rock State Scenic Viewpoint** (US-101, 2.5 mi/4 km south of Bandon; 541/347-2209; stateparks.oregon.gov; sunrise-sunset daily; free) boasts views of Bandon's picturesque sea stacks. A short walking path heads down to the shore where, at low tide, visitors can walk among the jagged rock formations—and inside a few that have eroded over the years. The park's namesake rock sits offshore and resembles the profile of a human face looking skyward. Restrooms and picnic tables are available, as well.

Every spring and summer, Face Rock State Scenic Viewpoint is the site of **Circles in the Sand** (May-Aug.; free), where local artists trace labyrinths, detailed designs, and other artwork in the sand. Those labyrinths can be walked for about two hours before the tide begins to return, making it a popular, if fleeting attraction. Parking fills to capacity quickly whenever the designs are created, usually about seven times per month May-Aug.; check the website for full schedules of when the designs will be on display, and try to arrive close to the beginning of the event—and on weekdays, if possible.

RECREATION
Horseback Riding
The sea stacks and rock formations that dot

Bandon's stretch of shoreline demand a closer look—and **Bandon Beach Riding Stables** (54629 Beach Loop Rd.; 541/347-3423; www.bandonstables.com) offers several memorable opportunities for doing just that. Riders can choose among hour-long daytime outings ($65, year-round) or 90-minute sunset rides ($85, Mar.-Sept.)—all of which includes instruction, a short trail ride, and plenty of time on the beach.

Wildlife-Watching
Bandon Marsh National Wildlife Refuge (83673 North Bank Ln.; 541/347-1470; www.fws.gov; sunrise-sunset daily; free) sits along the Coquille River and across the highway from Bullards Beach State Park—and is home to riparian forests, salt marshes, and rich mudflats that attract thousands of migrating waterfowl and other shorebirds every spring and fall. This has long been an important site for the Coquille people, who spent generations fishing for coho and Chinook salmon, as well as steelhead and cutthroat trout, in the river. A few short walking paths traverse the refuge's various ecosystems; note that dogs are not permitted on the refuge.

If you'd like to paddle the refuge but don't have the gear, sign up for a tour with **South Coast Tours** (541/373-0487; www.southcoasttours.net; Apr.-early Oct.; $90, $170 for two paddlers). The local outfitter leads a two-hour, beginner-friendly tour that explores the culture, history, wildlife, and ecology of the national wildlife refuge and the Coquille River. South Coast Tours also offers paddling trips around Brookings-Harbor, Port Orford, and other communities along the south coast.

Fishing
Bandon sits at the mouth of the Coquille River, right where it empties into the Pacific Ocean, and the community's waterways are angling destinations all year long. Clams, salmon, tuna, and bottom-feeding fish can be caught in spring-summer, while fall heralds the arrival of Dungeness crab.

Join the local pastime with a trip via

Prowler Charters (325 1st St. SE; 541/347-1901; www.prowlercharters.com; $90-240, $80-230 for children 14 and younger), which offers outings for all the most popular species. Individual trips focus on halibut, bottom-feeding fish, and tuna—and include bait and tackle. Visitors can also add a crab pot ($30) if they'd like try to catch Dungeness crab on certain trips. Filleting and vacuum packing is available for an additional fee.

Anglers should purchase a single-day **fishing license** (www.myodfw.com; $23 per license) before hitting the water; if fishing *and* crabbing, purchase a single-day **angling and shellfish combo license** (www.myodfw.com; $32.50 per license).

Golf
★ **Bandon Dunes Golf Resort**
The community of Bandon is, in some circles, synonymous with **Bandon Dunes Golf Resort** (57744 Round Lake Rd.; 844/981-0830; www.bandondunesgolf.com; $100-295 for resort guests, $140-$395 for non-guests)—routinely cited as the top resort in Oregon, and one of the best golf resorts in the United States.

In all, the sprawling resort hosts six links-style courses on a windswept stretch of shoreline high above the Pacific Ocean, with courses traversing dunes, meadows, pine forests, bluffs, and native vegetation; every hole on the 18-hole Sheep Ranch course, for instance, boasts open ocean views. The Bandon Dunes course, meanwhile, was designed by renowned architect David McLay-Kidd and is famous (or infamous) for its windy conditions. Perhaps the resort's only drawback is that carts aren't permitted; golfers must either carry their own bags or hire a caddie (541/347-5909; $100 per bag, per round, $40-60 per player for a group caddie).

Away from the links, golfers can improve their game at The Punchbowl, an 18-hole putting course that heads through a series of natural hollows, or at the Practice Center—which hosts two full ranges, one green, a bunker practice area, and other landscapes. The resort also hosts seven eateries, a wide range of lodging options, gift shop, and massage center.

CIDER MAKERS
Since 2016, **Bandon Rain** (640 2nd St. SE; 541/972-3101; www.bandonrain.com; 2pm-6pm Mon. and Thurs., noon-7pm Fri.-Sat., noon-5pm Sun.) has been pouring an exciting blend of ciders along the main drag through town; one highlight (of many) is a slightly tart cider that's crafted with locally grown cranberries. Several of the cidermaker's seasonal selections draw inspiration from Bandon's location on the south coast; the summer and fall special, for instance, is made with gorse—an invasive plant that imbues the cider with floral notes and tinges of tea. Bandon Rain's industrial taproom affords views of the production area, and a few tables provide covered outdoor seating.

ART GALLERIES
The beautiful yet tragic **Washed Ashore Gallery** (640 2nd St. SE; 541/972-3101; www.bandonrain.com; 2pm-6pm Mon. and Thurs., noon-7pm Fri.-Sat., noon-5pm Sun.) is a powerful art gallery where all the pieces—such as a massive starfish, salmon, and a whale rib-cage—are made from bottles, toys, cans, packaging, and other debris that has washed up on ocean beaches. Interpretive panels explain the gallery's mission, describe the animals represented with each piece, and list the specific pieces of debris that went into each piece. Washed Ashore pieces can also be found around Historic Old Town Bandon if you'd like to see more of the gallery's work.

FESTIVALS AND EVENTS
The **Bandon Cranberry Festival** (www.bandon.com; Sept.) has been a community mainstay since 1947 and bills itself as the longest-running festival on the Oregon Coast; the event pays tribute to its namesake crop with a parade, cranberry-eating contest, art exhibits, and other events.

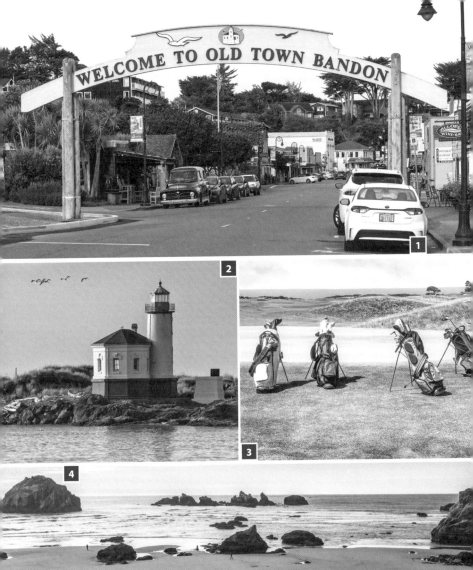
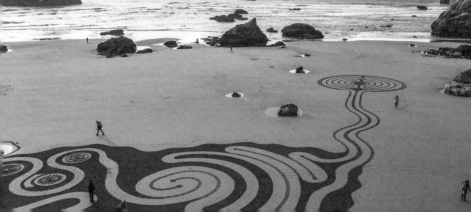

SHOPPING

The family-owned **Cranberry Sweets & More** (280 1st St. SE; 541/347-9475; www.cranberrysweets.com; 10am-5pm daily) launched in 1962 with a lineup of cranberry-infused candies—and has expanded in the decades since to produce all kinds of sweet treats: cookies, fruit candy, caramel corn, and more are all made in small batches, by hand. Even so, anything with locally sourced cranberries is sure to please. The company also runs a factory store in Coos Bay.

Along those same lines, **Misty Meadows Jams** (48053 US-101 S; 541/347-2575; gotjam.com; 9am-5pm daily) got its start producing jam with locally grown cranberries—but has expanded its output over the years into other jams, jellies, salsas, and more. Homemade selections today include cranberry-infused ketchup, mustard, and even salsa—as well as more than a dozen jams and jellies made with Oregon-grown berries.

FOOD
Pacific Northwest Cuisine
Bandon has a rich cheese-making tradition that dates back to the 1880s. Yet in 2000, the dairy co-op behind Tillamook Cheese purchased the Bandon Cheese Factory and shut it down soon after. From the ashes rose ★ **Face Rock Creamery** (680 2nd St. SE; 541/347-3223; www.facerockcreamery.com; 10am-6pm daily; $5-8) in 2013, reigniting the community's love affair with cheese. Today, the creamery acts as a part-eatery, part-retail shop. In addition to watching cheese being made, visitors can sample several lunch dishes in the on-site café (including cheesy panini and house-made macaroni and cheese) and even grab a scoop of Umpqua ice cream. The creamery's market, meanwhile, sells specialty cheeses, curds, regional wine, and beer to-go. You'll also find a Face Rock shop in Coos Bay.

River and ocean views are in short supply at

1: Historic Old Town Bandon **2:** Coquille River Lighthouse at Bullards Beach State Park **3:** golf bags at Bandon Dunes Golf Resort **4:** Circles in the Sand at Face Rock State Scenic Viewpoint

eateries around Bandon, which is part of the considerable allure of **The Loft Restaurant and Bar** (315 1st St. SE; 541/329-2552; 10am-4pm Wed.-Sat., 10am-3pm Sun.; $6-18). The restaurant overlooks a marina on the Coquille River and pairs its views with an excellent menu that blends Pacific Northwest fare and classic seafood dishes. The appetizing brunch menu includes a smoked salmon benedict, while lunch and dinner selections include clam chowder, fish sandwiches, and several burgers.

Seafood
★ **Tony's Crab Shack** (155 1st St.; 541/347-2875; www.tonyscrabshack.com; 10:30am-7pm daily; $11-26) started in 1989 as an offshoot of the bait-and-tackle shop next door, a place where owner Tony Roszkowski could steam crabs for visitors. But it's grown over the years into a full-fledged (if cozy) restaurant that's among the most acclaimed anywhere on the coast. You'll still find locally caught Dungeness crab, but the restaurant's menu also includes fish tacos, sandwiches, crab cakes, oysters, chowder, and other seafood delicacies—none of it deep-fried. Outdoor seating is available.

Fish-and-chip shops are common around Historic Old Town Bandon, but **Bandon Fish Market** (249 1st St. SE; 541/347-4282; www.bandonfishmarket.com; 11am-6pm daily; $10-20) deserves plaudits for variety (cod, lingcod, rockfish, and halibut are all available), a menu that changes with what's in season, and for crafting a house-made coleslaw with locally sourced cranberries. Oysters, clam strips, prawns, clam chowder, and other seafood classics round out the menu.

Mexican
From the outside, **Wilsons Market** (90 June Ave. SE; 541/347-3083; www.wilsonsmarket.com; 7am-10pm daily; $5-17) doesn't look like much—just a ramshackle convenience store that stocks soda, snacks, beer, and the like. But the shop's deli counter dishes some of the best-loved Mexican food anywhere on the south

coast, all of it piled high with house-smoked meats. Tacos are made with pork shoulder, smoked chicken, and carne asada, while the burritos are stuffed with meats, beans, a house-made barbecue sauce, and even seasoned curly fries. The decadent nachos are seemingly the size of a small child. Outdoor seating is available.

Italian

Calling **Alloro Wine Bar & Restaurant** (375 2nd St. SE; 541/347-1850; www.allorowinebar. com; 4:30pm-7pm Fri.-Sat. and Mon.-Tues.; $32-47) "just" a wine bar sells the upscale bistro short: Sure, Alloro boasts a wine cellar stocked with curated selections from throughout the Pacific Northwest, Italy, France, and beyond—some of which you won't find anywhere else in Oregon. But the restaurant also serves what it calls "Italian-inspired coastal cuisine" that elegantly blends fresh seafood, house-made pasta, and (whenever possible) locally sourced vegetables.

Bakeries and Cafés

You'll find a few bakeries and cafés around Bandon, but **The Rolling Pin Bake & Brew** (215 10th St.; 541/252-5244; www.therolling-pinbb.com; 8:30am-2pm Fri.-Tues.; $4-12) stands out for its towering, scratch-made biscuits (baked daily) that go just as well with the eatery's homemade jam as they do house-made sausage gravy. Soups, salads, and wraps comprise the light lunch menu, and Rolling Pin's selection of pastries—including cookies and cupcakes—make an excellent dessert or on-the-go treat.

ACCOMMODATIONS

The woman-owned **B.side Motel & RV** (1175 2nd St. SE; 541/347-3421; www.bandonway-sidemotelrv.com; $199 for motel rooms, $100 for RV sites, $44 for tent sites) brings together a vintage motel and compact RV park away from Bandon's hustle and bustle. B.side's updated motel rooms include organic cotton linens made in the Pacific Northwest, comfortable mattresses, pour-over coffee with locally roasted beans, in-room shrubbery, and other elegant touches; some rooms are dog-friendly. The basic RV park, meanwhile, wraps around the motel and includes full-hookup spaces with electric, water, and sewer connections—as well as restrooms, showers, and on-site laundry. A few tent sites are also available and include access to charcoal grills, private restrooms, showers, and coin-operated laundry.

Closer to the ocean, near the southern edge of town, is **Windermere on the Beach** (3250 Beach Loop Rd.; 541/347-3710; www.winder-mereonthebeach.com; $165-249). Every room offers an ocean view and easy beach access near a quiet stretch of shoreline. Some rooms include a fireplace, fully equipped kitchen or kitchenette, and private deck; family-friendly cottages, meanwhile, come with up to three beds, a kitchen, deck, and plenty of space for lounging. Some rooms are pet friendly.

Bandon Inn (355 US-101; 541/347-4417; www.bandoninn.com; $269-279) sits atop a bluff that overlooks Historic Old Town and affords views of both the Coquille River and Pacific Ocean—making it one of the more popular stops in town. Amenities are pretty basic—and include flat-screen televisions, free Wi-Fi, and complimentary DVD players—but the beds are comfortable, and the location is excellent.

If you're coming to town to hit the links, chances are good you'll want to spend a night or two at **Bandon Dunes Golf Resort** (57744 Round Lake Rd.; 844/981-0830; www.bandon-dunesgolf.com; $290-1,950). The luxurious resort hosts lodge rooms and secluded cottages near its three lakes and ponds, all amid forested settings. Rooms may afford views of the resort's courses, nearby dunes, forestland, or the Pacific Ocean; beyond the views, on-site amenities include a massage center, fitness center, sauna, hot tub, several miles of hiking and biking trails, and more.

1: Face Rock Creamery **2:** Tony's Crab Shack
3: Windermere on the Beach

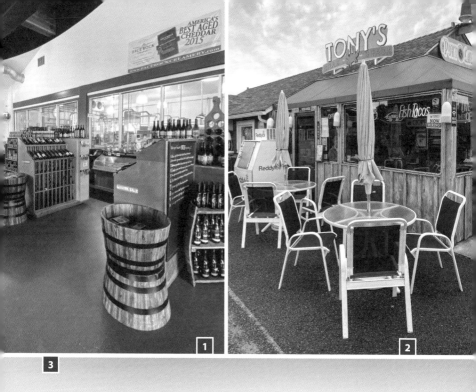

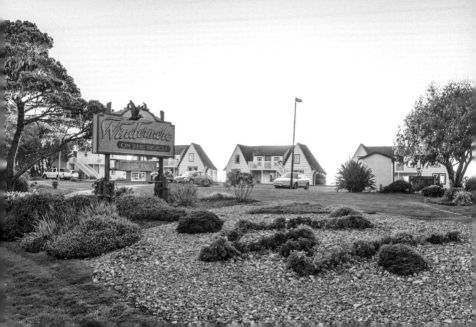

Camping

Just north of Bandon, **Bullards Beach State Park** (US-101, 2.5 mi/4 km north of Bandon; 541/347-2209; stateparks.oregon.gov; $7-64) hosts a large campground near the mouth of the Coquille River. In all, the park has 103 full-hookup sites, 82 electrical sites with water, 13 yurts (6 of which are pet-friendly), and a hiker/biker camp area—all sandwiched between US-101 and the Pacific Ocean in a forest of spruce and pine. Six campsites and three yurts are wheelchair accessible. Flush toilets and showers are available, and the beach can be reached via a 0.25-mile (0.4-km) flat path.

INFORMATION AND SERVICES

Stop into the **Bandon Visitor Center** (300 2nd St.; 541/347-9616; www.bandon.com; 11am-3pm daily), at the edge of Historic Old Town, for pamphlets, brochures, maps, recommendations, and tips for making the most of your time in Bandon.

GETTING THERE AND AROUND

From Coos Bay, the 24-mile (39-km) drive to Bandon takes about 30 minutes via southbound US-101. From Port Orford, the 27-mile (43-km) drive takes about 30 minutes via northbound US-101.

Curry Public Transit (541/412-8806; www.currypublictransit.org; $4-24) runs its **Coastal Express** Monday-Saturday, with stops in several south coast communities—including Bandon.

Port Orford and Vicinity

The cozy community of Port Orford (pop. 950) sits in the heart of Oregon's south coast and takes pride in offering a home-grown experience for out-of-towners; that means no fast-food joints, no strip malls, no stoplights, and—perhaps most importantly—no crowds.

That means quiet dinners over locally sourced seafood, exhilarating bike rides to some of the region's most scenic vistas, beaches dotted by sea stacks, coastal campgrounds at the base of towering mountains and on windswept headlands, and sightseeing from the foot of a majestic lighthouse at Cape Blanco State Park—the westernmost point in Oregon.

SIGHTS

Prehistoric Gardens

The old-school **Prehistoric Gardens** (36848 US-101 S., Port Orford; 541/332-4463; www.prehistoricgardens.com; 9am-6pm daily; $12, $10 for seniors 60 and older, $8 for children 3-12, free for children 2 and younger) is one of the most beloved family attractions on the Oregon Coast. The roadside attraction opened in 1955 and today hosts 23 life-size dinosaur replicas—all accessible via a self-guided walk through a lush forest. All your kids' favorites are accounted for here, from the long-necked Brachiosaurus to the fearsome Tyrannosaurus rex, and a series of interpretive panels offer a dash of education to the fun attraction. The gravel trail is wheelchair- and stroller-accessible. From Port Orford, the 12-mile (19-km) drive takes about 15 minutes via southbound US-101.

Port Orford Heads State Park

Shipwrecks were a fact of life along the Oregon Coast in the late 1800s and early 1900s, a development that spurred the U.S. Coast Guard to construct a lifeguard station on a headland just west of Port Orford. The Coast Guard kept watch over a stretch of coastline between 1934 and 1970; today, a handful of buildings survive as part of **Port Orford Heads State**

Park (Port Orford Hwy., 1 mi/1.6 km west of Port Orford; 541/332-6774, ext. 0; stateparks. oregon.gov; sunrise-sunset daily May-Oct.; free). One such building is the former crew headquarters, now the **Port Orford Lifeboat Station Museum** (10am-3pm Thurs.-Sat.; donations accepted); there, historical artifacts and interpretive panels explain the nature of shipwrecks along with the history of the lifeguard station. Visitors can also get an up-close look at an unsinkable lifeboat and enjoy dramatic ocean views from along the park's trails; one trail leads to views of structures (and the remnants of former buildings) where the Coast Guard launched its craft at the base of a cove.

BEACHES

Battle Rock Wayside Park (520 Jefferson St., Port Orford; 541/332-4106; www.enjoy-portorford.com; sunrise-sunset daily; free) is a scenic spot that's named for a bloody chapter in local history. The modern-day park sits where explorer William Tichenor landed in 1851, hoping to establish a settlement on land already occupied by the Qua-to-mah band of the Tututni people. A battle between the local tribe and Tichenor's men ensued, with the latter prevailing after several weeks. Today, the park hosts an interpretive panel that explains the tragic battle, as well as a few benches and short walking paths down to the coastline—where the craggy, tree-covered Battle Rock juts out to sea from the shore.

RECREATION
Hiking
Humbug Mountain

Distance: *5.5 miles (8.9 km) round-trip*
Duration: *3 hours*
Elevation Gain: *1,730 feet (527 m)*
Effort: *Moderate*
Trailhead: *Humbug Mountain Trailhead, along US-101*
Directions: *From Port Orford, follow US-101 south. After 5.6 miles (9 km), soon after the highway curves inland, turn right into a parking area for the Humbug Mountain Trailhead.*

The lollipop-shaped **Humbug Mountain Trail** takes you up to the summit of the headland with a steady ascent—but rewards hikers with towering forests and views that range from Port Orford (in the north) to Gold Beach (in the south). From the parking area, hikers steadily rise through a lush forest of old-growth spruce and Douglas fir before arriving at a loop that ascends to the summit. Turn right and head counterclockwise on

Battle Rock Wayside Park and Port Orford

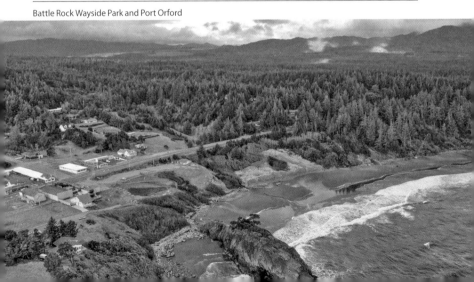

the loop, following the **West Trail**—which quickly brings you to a north-facing viewpoint that shows off Port Orford and Cape Blanco; farther up the well-maintained trail, a short spur heads to the tree-free summit of Humbug Mountain—where southward views toward Gold Beach await. It's not uncommon for low-lying fog to obscure the best views, especially in the morning, but the towering trees and ever-present greenery make it an epic hike all year long.

Bicycling

The south coast boasts plenty of scenery, and the 61-mile/98-km (round-trip) **Wild Rivers Coast Scenic Bikeway** (www.traveloregon. com) offers a fun (if thigh-burning) way to see the sites. Port Orford sits along the vaguely Y-shaped bike route, making it an ideal home base for exploring some (or all) of the scenic route as it travels along the Elk River and into the Oregon Coast Range, heads westward to Cape Blanco State Park, and visits a few parks around town.

Note that you'll need to bring your own bike; road-bike rentals are not available in town, but **Pineapple Express Adventure Rides** (832 Oregon St., Ste. 1, Port Orford; 541/655-0233; www.pineappleexpress.bike; 10am-4pm Tues.-Sat.) can assist with repairs, tune-ups, and other services. The shop also offers fat bike rentals ($60 per day) and beach cruiser rentals ($30 per day) for low-key rides on the surf and closer to town.

Windsurfing and Kiteboarding

The freshwater Floras Lake, ever so slightly inland from the Pacific Ocean, enjoys steady winds throughout summer and fall—and has become a popular windsurfing and kiteboarding destination on the southern coast. **Floras Lake Kite & Windsurf** (92850 Boice Cope Rd., Langlois; 541/236-5046; www.floraslakekiting.com; 10am-5pm daily Apr.-mid-Sept.) helps enthusiasts and newbies alike get on the water through a variety of lessons and gear rentals.

Three-hour kiteboarding lessons ($300-400)

include instruction, a wetsuit, harness, a kite, a helmet equipped with Bluetooth for remote instruction, kiteboard, and Jet Ski support; beginners should take at least three lessons (one on land, two on water) before getting on the water themselves.

Windsurfing lessons ($100 for a 90-minute beginner lesson, $100 per hour for all subsequent lessons) include equipment, wetsuits, booties, and instruction; experienced windsurfers can also rent gear ($20 per hour, $40 for three hours, $55 per day) and get right on the water without the instruction.

And if you'd like a calmer way to experience Floras Lake, kayak and stand-up paddleboard rentals are available ($15 per hour, $35 for three hours, $50 per day).

All lessons should be booked 3-4 weeks ahead of time, especially between Memorial Day and Labor Day. Note that there is a $5 day-use fee to park at Boice Cope Park, where a short walking trail leads to the Floras Lake kite and windsurfing school.

FOOD

Seafood

★ **The Crazy Norwegian's Fish & Chips** (259 6th St., Port Orford; 541/332-8601; noon-7pm Wed.-Sun.; $11-16) is a regional icon, noted for its (surprise!) fish-and-chips. The Alaskan cod is perfectly flaky and slightly crispy without ever feeling greasy—but keep an eye out for locally caught rockfish whenever it appears on the menu; both are dished with a house-made tartar sauce. Wash it all down with a homemade lemonade that's infused with locally sourced cranberries. Given the dearth of dining options in Port Orford, wait times may top an hour on busy summer weekends—but "Crazy's" (as it's known around town) is worth it. Outdoor seating is available.

If you're looking for something a bit more elegant, make haste for **Redfish** (517 Jefferson St., Port Orford; 541/366-2200; www.redfishportorford.com; 11am-9pm Wed.-Fri., 10am-9pm Sat.-Sun.; $15-32), which specializes in upscale seafood dishes and Pacific

Northwest-inspired fare—all made with fish, produce, and meats from local, sustainable sources. The fish tacos are made with whatever's in-season, for instance, and clams come from nearby Charleston. A selection of burgers and sandwiches rounds out the menu. Outdoor seating is available, and views of the Pacific Ocean are breathtaking.

ACCOMMODATIONS

Castaway by the Sea (545 5th St., Port Orford; 541/332-4502; www.castawaybythe-sea.com; $300-480) sits on a hillside overlooking the Pacific Ocean—every room has an ocean view—and boasts a down-home atmosphere that makes it well-suited to families. Accommodation choices include standard rooms (some with enclosed porches), condos with fully stocked kitchenettes, a spacious two-bedroom suite, and two-story townhomes.

Slow down and unwind at the delightfully laid-back ★ **WildSpring Guest Habitat** (92978 Cemetery Loop Rd., Port Orford; 866/333-9453; www.wildspring.com; $348-378), which hosts five ornate cabins in a forest high above the Pacific Ocean. The cabins come with heated floors, comfortable mattresses, vintage furnishings, a massage table, and more—all designed to help visitors disconnect and relax. (You won't find phones or TV reception in any of the cabins.) Guests can reflect and meditate along a walking labyrinth, enjoy an indoor common area, and even take a dip in an open-air jetted tub that offers scenic ocean views. Note there is a two-night minimum if staying on a Saturday July-September.

Camping

A cozy campground at **Humbug Mountain State Park** (US-101, 6 mi/10 km south of Port Orford; 541/332-6774; stateparks.oregon.gov; $7-44) sits at the base of one of the tallest headlands anywhere on the Oregon Coast, with a short trail leading under US-101 and to a quiet stretch of coastline. Campers can choose among 39 electrical sites with water

(2 of which are wheelchair-accessible) and 56 tent sites, as well as a hiker/biker camp area; one of the campground's loops closes Nov.-Apr. Flush toilets and showers are available, and Junior Ranger activities may be offered in summer.

GETTING THERE AND AROUND

From Bandon, the 27-mile (43-km) drive to Port Orford takes about 30 minutes via southbound US-101; from Gold Beach, the 28-mile (45-km) drive takes about 30 minutes via northbound US-101.

Curry Public Transit (541/412-8806; www.currypublictransit.org; $4-24) runs its **Coastal Express** Monday-Saturday, with stops in several south coast communities—including Port Orford.

★ CAPE BLANCO STATE PARK

Cape Blanco State Park (Cape Blanco Rd., 10 mi/16 km northwest of Port Orford; 541/332-6774; stateparks.oregon.gov; sunrise-sunset daily; free) sits at the westernmost point in Oregon and blends local history with outdoor opportunities like almost nowhere else in the region. The windswept headland hosts the oldest standing lighthouse on the Oregon Coast, more than 8 miles (13 km) of hiking and equestrian trails (leading to the beach and to sweeping vistas), a ranch home that dates back to 1898, and a well-maintained campground.

Sights
Cape Blanco Lighthouse
It's not a visit to Cape Blanco without a trip to the **Cape Blanco Lighthouse.** Constructed in 1870, the lighthouse is notable for a variety of reasons. (Among them: In 1903, it employed Mabel Bretherton, the first female lighthouse keeper in Oregon.) Its prominence, alone on a headland that was once covered in Sitka spruce, makes the lighthouse an especially striking sight. A welcome center near its base is open 10am-3pm Thurs.-Sat.; lighthouse

tours ($2; free for children 15 and younger) are offered 10am-3:30pm Wed.-Mon. Apr.-Oct. Note that a locked gate prevents access to the 0.3-mile (0.5-km) one-way road leading to the lighthouse whenever the lighthouse is closed; while it's fair game to walk along the gated road for a closer look, time your visit to when it's open for the best views.

Historic Hughes House

Get a look at local life in the late 19th century with a walk through the **Historic Hughes House.** The 11-room Victorian home was constructed from locally sourced cedar in 1898 for a family of ranchers and dairy farmers—and remains open seasonally for tours (donations accepted), offered 10am-3:30pm Wednesday-Monday May-September.

Camping

A forest of spruce and pine protects campers from the wind at a spacious **campground** (541/332-6774; stateparks.oregon.gov; $24-62), which is centrally located within the park and offers easy access to several hiking and equestrian trails. In all, the park hosts 52 electrical sites with water, 4 cabins (2 of which are pet-friendly), and a hiker/biker camp; 6 sites and 1 cabin are wheelchair-accessible. Flush toilets and hot showers can be found in the heart of the campground's primary loop.

Getting There

From Port Orford, the 10-mile (16-km) drive to Cape Blanco State Park takes about 15 minutes via US-101 northbound and Cape Blanco Road westbound. The route to the park (and its attractions) is exceptionally well-signed.

Gold Beach and Vicinity

No discussion of Gold Beach (pop. 2,250) is complete without acknowledging the community's name: Yes, gold was discovered near the mouth of the Rogue River (at the northern edge of the present-day city) in 1853. Given the township's close proximity to California, this ignited a miniature gold rush that lasted several years.

Even after the last of the gold had been found, locals stuck around to take advantage of the area's abundant salmon and trout runs—giving birth to a commercial fishing industry that remains an economic driver around town today. Sitting where the Rogue River flows into the Pacific Ocean, much of the community's economy centers around these bodies of water. Anglers may still enjoy bountiful fishing, but jet boat tours take visitors deep into the Rogue River canyon, and lodges welcome hikers along the Rogue River Trail.

BEACHES

Beach access is plentiful around Gold Beach, but a few parks and viewpoints stand out.

Just north of town, the crowd-free **Otter Point State Recreation Site** (Old Coast Rd., 4.5 mi /7.2 km north of Gold Beach; 541/332-6774; stateparks.oregon.gov; sunrise-sunset daily, free) offers several easy walking trails (including one out to the Otter Point headland), a few tougher paths down to the shore, photogenic sandstone rock formations, and scenic viewpoints in almost any weather. Come prepared for the whipping winds that are synonymous with this area. From Gold Beach, the 5.5-mile (9-km) drive via US-101 northbound and Old Coast Road westbound takes about 10 minutes.

The scenic **Pistol River State Scenic Viewpoint** (US-101, 10.7 mi/17.2 km south of Gold Beach; 541/469-0224; stateparks.oregon.gov; sunrise-sunset daily; free) sits just south of where the Pistol River flows into the Pacific Ocean. The sandy stretch of shoreline, typically littered with driftwood, is noted

for its dunes (which tend to grow in spring and summer). The Pistol River has changed course several times in recent years, leaving behind small "pothole" lakes that attract shorebirds and waterfowl. Beachcombing is a popular activity here, with agates and fishing floats washing ashore on occasion; the steady winds here also mean you might spy windsurfers catching some air in the waves just offshore. From Gold Beach, the 10.7-mile (17-km) drive via US-101 southbound takes about 15 minutes.

RECREATION
★ Rogue River Jet Boat Ride

The 215-mile (346-km) Rogue River begins its journey high in the Cascade Range, spilling out of a hillside in Crater Lake National Park, winding through forests and gorges, and eventually flowing into the Pacific Ocean just north of Gold Beach. For a fun look at the mighty river, take a jet boat tour through **Jerry's Rogue Jets** (29980 Harbor Way, Gold Beach; 800/451-3645; www.roguejets. com; May-Oct. 15; $42-129, $26-69 for children 4-11), which started as a mail-delivery service in 1895 and has expanded into a popular attraction.

Visitors can choose among four tours of varying lengths, each with a unique focus. The seven-hour Wilderness Whitewater Tour, for instance, heads deep into the Rogue River canyon and showcases the area's wildlife (such as elk, black bears, and bald eagles); the thrilling, 4.75-hour Express Whitewater Tour, meanwhile, traverses whitewater rapids and swift currents while explaining the history of the Rogue River area. Most tours include restroom breaks and barbecue lunches.

Fishing

Anglers love Gold Beach for the plentiful fishing opportunities (a handful of rivers sit within a one-hour drive of town), prolific winter steelhead runs, and mild winter weather that's generally warmer and less rainy than the central and north coast.

With a mix of ocean-going vessels and river-ready boats, **Five Star Charters** (29957 Harbor Way, Gold Beach; 888/301-6480; www.5starcharters.com; $250, two-person minimum) can take you wherever the fish are biting. Tours last anywhere from four hours to a full day and focus on crab and bottom-feeding fish ($200 per person, four-person minimum), salmon ($150-300 per person, two-person minimum), and steelhead

Otter Point State Recreation Site

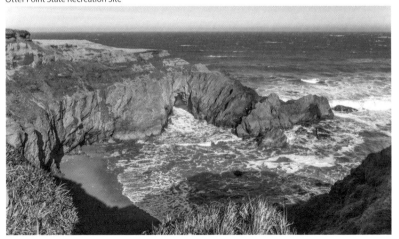

($300 per person, two-person minimum). All fishing gear and tackle is provided, and fish cleaning and crab cooking comes with the bottom-feeding trip.

Anglers should purchase a single-day **fishing license** (www.myodfw.com; $23 per license) before hitting the water.

BREWPUBS

The award-winning ★ **Arch Rock Brewing Company** (28779 Hunter Creek Rd., Gold Beach; 541/247-0555; www.archrockbeer.com; 11am-6pm Tues.-Fri. and 11am-5pm Sat.) pours its trio of exemplary beers in a cozy tasting room that's no larger than your childhood bedroom. (On busy days, crowds may spill into the production brewery next door.) Grab a glass (or fill your growler) with Arch Rock's German-style lager, a hoppy pale ale, and a chocolatey porter; seasonal selections are only occasionally offered (and in extremely limited batches), but no matter: The brewery's three flagship beers are all standard-bearers for their styles and are among the best on the Oregon Coast.

SHOPPING

The mighty myrtlewood tree grows only on the southern Oregon and northern California coasts—and is prized for its colorful wood and intricate grain patterns. See all that beauty up close at **Rogue River Myrtlewood Shop** (29750 Ellensburg Ave., Gold Beach; 541/247-2332; 9am-4pm Mon.-Sat. and 10am-4pm Sun. Oct.-Mar., 9am-5pm daily and 10am-4pm Sun. Apr.-Sept.), which manufactures most of what it sells; a window from the gift shop even invites visitors to peer in on carvers plying their trade. You'll find plenty of bowls, boxes, cutting boards, and carvings, but the shop specializes in intricate lighthouses of varying sizes; naturally, the carvings light up.

FOOD

Pacific Northwest Cuisine

A favorite among locals, **Spinner's Seafood Steak & Chop House** (29430 Ellensburg Ave., Gold Beach; 541/247-5160; www.spinnersrestaurant.com; 4:30-9pm Thurs.-Mon.; $17-48) delivers the kind of fine-dining experience you'd expect from an old-school steakhouse. The menu leans heavily on aged steaks, locally sourced seafood, pasta dishes, and a few burgers. Oregon-grown ingredients are used whenever possible—such as in the Dungeness crab cakes, cedar-planked salmon, and a chicken dish that's topped with toasted hazelnuts. Some tables boast ocean views, and outdoor dining is available.

Seafood

The lively **Barnacle Bistro** (29805 Ellensburg Ave., Gold Beach; 541/247-7799; www.barnaclebistro.com; noon-8:30pm Tues.-Sat.; $11-21)—housed in an octagon-shaped building—prides itself on serving freshly prepared, locally sourced seafood in a comfortable environment. The perfectly crispy fish-and-chips is made with local rockfish, a tuna melt spotlights Oregon albacore, Dungeness crab cakes are infused with Oregon bay shrimp—and on it goes. A selection of burgers rounds out the menu. Most ingredients, if not made in-house, are sourced from local anglers, farmers, bakers, and breweries. Outdoor seating is available.

Barbecue

Seafood might be the dominant cuisine up and down the Oregon Coast, but **Gold Beach BBQ** (29545 Ellensburg Ave., Gold Beach; 541/425-5460; www.goldbeachbarbq.com; 11am-6pm Sun.-Tues. and Thurs., 11am-7pm Fri.-Sat.; $10-25) offers a filling alternative if you need a break from fish-and-chips. The usual smoked meats are accounted for here: ribs, tri-tip, pulled pork, chicken, and more—all prepared in a smoker in the eatery's parking lot. Get the meat on its own, in a sampler platter, or in sandwich form; be sure to save room for the restaurant's decadent Dirty Fries, topped with barbecued meats and house-made sauces. Of course, a thick clam chowder—infused with house-made bacon—is available (and is excellent).

ACCOMMODATIONS

Pacific Reef Hotel (29362 Ellensburg Ave., Gold Beach; 541/247-6658; www.pacificreef-hotel.com; $130-350) doesn't just offer well-kept rooms with basic amenities—it also hosts a unique attraction you won't find at any other hotel in Oregon. Accommodations include basic, budget-friendly rooms, family suites, and even an A-frame cabin; some rooms offer ocean views, patios, and full kitchens. Each night, guests can head to an outdoor theater area behind the hotel, where a large screen shows a short promotional video about the natural wonders of the south coast and another short, animated film—all while a captivating light show illuminates the surrounding trees.

Just inland, **Endicott Gardens Bed & Breakfast** (95768 Jerry's Flat Rd., Gold Beach; 541/425-5483; www.endicottgar-densgoldbeach.com; $205-450) sits near the Rogue River in a pastoral, garden-like setting—the perfect getaway for couples on a romantic retreat. Guests can choose among a luxury spa suite, three thoughtfully decorated hotel rooms, and an apartment on the second floor of the B&B's farmhouse (boasting views of an on-site garden). Farm-to-table breakfasts (featuring ingredients from the B&B's orchards, as well as organic produce and local meats) come with most rooms, and an on-site spa offers a wide range of services. Note that the B&B is pet-free and does not permit children.

Seemingly every element is imbued with a sense of luxury at the lavish ★ **Tu Tu' Tun Lodge** (96550 N. Bank Rogue River Rd., Gold Beach; 800/864-6357; www.tututun.com; $325-1,465), situated in a forest on the banks of the Rogue River—about 8.5 miles (13.7 km) inland from Gold Beach. Overnight options include comfortable lodge rooms with riverside patios and wood-burning fireplaces, suites with fully stocked kitchens and cast-iron fireplaces, and a trio of full-size homes teeming with stylish charm—all boasting floor-to-ceiling windows for dramatic views. An on-site spa offers massage therapy and skin treatments, a heated lap pool is open May-October, and kayaks and stand-up paddleboards are available to rent in summer.

Rogue River Lodges

For an immersive Rogue River experience, consider an overnight stay in one of several lodges along the river—most of which can be accessed only by boat or hiking trail and are only open May-November. If you're not hiking, the lodges typically offer jet-boat shuttles from the Gold Beach area for an added fee. Most serve family-style meals of the meat-and-potatoes variety; three meals are typically included with nightly rates. Reservations are generally required and usually fill months in advance.

If hiking, note that temperatures along the Rogue River canyon can be unbearable in July-August; consider an overnight outing in May-June or September-October, when conditions are much more pleasant. And be sure to watch for rattlesnakes, black bears, and poison oak along the trail.

Each lodge has its own charm, but these are a few of our favorites.

If you're looking for an easy overnight trip, **Clay Hill Lodge** (541/373-2077; www.clay-hilllodge.com; $175, $100 for children 9 and younger) sits just 6 miles (10 km)—a roughly three-hour hike—from Foster Bar, near the western terminus of the Rogue River Trail (a 40-mile (64-km) hiking trail that parallels its namesake river through the Coast Range). Visitors can choose among Western-themed rooms or cabins, a covered deck overlooks the Rogue River, and nightly dinners (served buffet- or family-style) are crafted from organic produce and fresh-baked breads. The lodge also offers fishing trips ($500 per person, includes lodging and meals).

Some 14 miles (23 km) upstream of Foster Bar, **Half Moon Bar Lodge** (541/300-9112; www.halfmoonbarlodge.net; $200-600) offers comfortable cabins, suites, and lodge rooms at a bend in the Rogue River. Pillow-top beds, outdoor furniture, wide porches, an outdoor fire pit, and even summertime misters add

to the laid-back ambiance; some rooms have shared bathrooms. A full bar serves cocktails, Oregon beer, and regional wine when you're looking to unwind after a day outdoors.

If you'd rather drive, the century-old **Lucas Lodge** (3904 Cougar Ln., Agness; 541/247-7443; $50-100) is just over an hour inland from Gold Beach and is accessible by vehicle. In all, visitors can choose among six cabins and several lodge rooms (the latter of which have shared bathrooms).

Camping

You won't find much coastal camping around Gold Beach, but **Lobster Creek Campground** (Jerry's Flat Rd., 11.3 mi/18.2 km northeast of Gold Beach; 541/618-2200; www.fs.usda.gov; $15) offers a delightful alternative along the banks of the Rogue River. The quiet campground, perched in a bucolic forested setting, hosts just seven shady sites—three tent-only sites and four that accommodate small RVs—each outfitted with campfire grill and picnic table. A gravel bar abutting the Rogue River is just a few steps away. All sites are available on a first-come, first-served basis.

INFORMATION AND SERVICES

Check out the **Gold Beach Visitor Center** (94080 Shirley Ln., Gold Beach; 541/247-7526; www.visitgoldbeach.com; 9am-3pm daily) for maps, brochures, and other information—not just for Gold Beach but nearby communities, as well. Restrooms are available on-site, and a short walking path heads to the coast.

And if you need help planning your outdoor adventure, stop by the **Gold Beach Ranger District Office** (29279 Ellensburg Ave., Gold Beach; 541/618-2200; www.fs.usda. gov; 7:45am-4:30pm Mon.-Fri.). The small shop sells passes and permits for federally managed lands, offers maps, and hosts a few interpretive panels that touch on area history. Friendly rangers are happy to provide recommendations and suggestions for where to go, as well.

GETTING THERE AND AROUND

From Port Orford, the 28-mile (45-km) drive to Gold Beach takes about 35 minutes via southbound US-101. From Brookings-Harbor, the 28-mile (45-km) drive takes about 35 minutes via northbound US-101.

Once in Gold Beach, US-101 (sometimes written in addresses and referred to as Ellensburg Ave.) is the main north-south thoroughfare through town.

Curry Public Transit (541/412-8806; www.currypublictransit.org; $4-24) runs its **Coastal Express** Monday-Saturday, with stops in several south coast communities—including Port Gold Beach.

CAPE SEBASTIAN STATE SCENIC CORRIDOR

A pair of parking lots comprise most of the **Cape Sebastian State Scenic Corridor** (US-101, 10.7 mi/17.2 km south of Gold Beach; 541/469-0224; stateparks.oregon.gov; sunrise-sunset daily; free)—but what scenic parking lots they are. Views from the headland's impressive summit, some 650 feet (200 m) above the coastline, extend miles to sea, offering outstanding opportunities to watch for migrating gray whales in winter and spring. A hiking trail descends to the coast and leads to a semi-secret beach far from the area's crowds.

From US-101, you'll follow a paved entry road for about 0.2 mile (0.3 km) through a forest of Sitka spruce; take a right at the fork to visit the northernmost of the park's two viewpoints. This is the less scenic of the pair, but views nevertheless extend above the treetops and to the Pacific Ocean below.

Heading back to the fork, you'll continue straight for another 0.3 mile/0.5 km (remaining southbound), at which point you'll arrive at a parking area—and one of the most dramatic views anywhere on the south coast. On a clear day, views extend as far north as Humbug Mountain (near Port Orford) and as far south as Crescent City, California.

From Gold Beach, the 5.7-mile (9.2-km)

drive via US-101 southbound takes about 5 minutes; the entry road is well-signed.

Hiking
Cape Sebastian

Distance: *3.8 miles (6.1 km) round-trip*
Duration: *2 hours*
Elevation Gain: *590 feet (180 m)*
Effort: *Easy/moderate*
Trailhead: *Southern parking area at Cape Sebastian State Scenic Corridor*

The out-and-back **Cape Sebastian Trail** takes you to the base of the namesake cape and to the shore of the Pacific Ocean—where incredible views of sea stacks and wildlife await. On the trail's early stretch you'll hike through a hall of salal before entering a dense forest of Sitka spruce as you steadily descend toward the coastline. The forest thins, and the ocean comes into view as you follow a series of switchbacks; soon after, the path levels out about 50 feet (15 m) above the shoreline, with plenty of clearings that allow you to look out to sea—where you might see harbor seals and sea lions frolicking nearby, or migrating gray whales farther offshore. A series of cables provide assistance if you want to make the short, often muddy descent to the base of the quiet Hunters Cove.

Brookings-Harbor and Vicinity

The southernmost communities on the Oregon Coast are Brookings (pop. 6,400) and Harbor (pop. 1,950), separated only by the Chetco River (which flows out of the Kalmiopsis Wilderness in the Klamath Mountains and into the Pacific Ocean here).

Funny enough, the area might be most noted for its fantastic weather—a genuine rarity on the otherwise soggy Oregon Coast. Brookings-Harbor sit in the heart of what's called "Oregon's Banana Belt"—a stretch of coastline that's warmer and milder than surrounding areas. Temperatures can occasionally reach 60°F (16°C) in January-February, while towns just a few minutes north are mired in rainfall and high temperatures of around 45°F (7°C); rainfall is rare June-September, and high temperatures can even exceed that of inland Oregon. The towns' orientation at the mouth of the Chetco River (which runs north-south through Brookings-Harbor) protects them from maritime breezes, creating those warm, dry conditions.

The working-class towns don't have much in the way of charming neighborhoods or historic architecture—but make up for the nondescript look with easy access to outdoor adventure. A quiet harbor affords easy access to deep-sea fishing, a renowned state park sits at the northern edge of town, the nearby Samuel H. Boardman State Scenic Corridor offers some of the coast's most impressive views, and one of the northernmost groves of redwood trees grows just a short drive from the area.

SIGHTS
Azalea Park

Brookings has been growing colorful azaleas for more than 200 years—and there's no better place around town to see the vibrant shrubs than at **Azalea Park** (640 Old County Rd., Brookings; 541/469-2163; www.brookings.or.us; sunrise-sunset daily; free). Azaleas usually bloom April-May, making spring the best time to visit, but attractions at the park beckon families year-round; highlights include a stage that hosts live music, horseshoe pits, a large playground, a sandy volleyball court, and picnic tables. Every holiday season (5pm-9pm nightly, the day after Thanksgiving-Dec. 25), colorful light displays dazzle park visitors. Restrooms are available.

Crissey Field State Recreation Site

Stretching between the Winchuck River and the Oregon-California border, **Crissey**

Field State Recreation Site (US-101, 6 mi/10 km south of Brookings; 541/469-0224; stateparks.oregon.gov; sunrise-sunset daily; free) offers a fine introduction to the Oregon Coast's many ecosystems. Several short walking paths traverse the park's wetlands and forest—and offer access to the state's southernmost stretch of coastline. The site's **visitor center** hosts restrooms, brochures, and visitor information (8am-7pm daily)—and is staffed (9am-4pm Thurs.-Mon.) with folks happy to share recommendations, tips, insights, and more.

BEACHES

Brookings is a working-class harbor town, which means beach access isn't as plentiful as you might find in other coastal communities. So your best bet for enjoying the beach is at the enchanting **Harris Beach State Park** (US-101, 2 mi/3 km north of Brookings; 541/469-0224; stateparks.oregon. gov; 8am-7pm daily; free), which delivers up-close looks at a particularly rugged stretch of Oregon coastline. From the day-use area, several short walking paths head through the surrounding forests and down to the shore, which is dotted by several large sea stacks. Just offshore sits Bird Island, the largest island off the Oregon Coast and a breeding site for the tufted puffin and other species. Picnic tables afford sweeping ocean views, and a bevy of wildlife—from seals and sea lions to gray whales—can routinely be spotted. Interpretive panels explain the creatures you might see in the park's tidepools, with tips on staying safe and treating the animals with care. Restrooms are available.

RECREATION

Hiking

River View Trail to Redwood Nature Trail

Distance: *3.3 miles (5.3 km) round-trip*
Duration: *1.5 hours*
Elevation Gain: *590 feet (180 m)*
Effort: *Easy/moderate*

Trailhead: *Alfred A. Loeb State Park gravel parking area, just beyond the park entrance*

Directions: *From Brookings, head east on North Bank Chetco River Road, following a sign for Loeb State Park. After 7.7 miles (12.4 km), turn right into Alfred A. Loeb State Park. Continue through the first intersection and, after 500 feet (150 m), turn right into a small gravel parking area.*

The lollipop-shaped **River View Trail to Redwood Nature Trail hike** combines two different trails into one enchanting trek. The first is the **River View Trail,** a mostly flat path that heads along the banks of the Chetco River and through a grove of Oregon myrtle, which are native to southwestern Oregon and northwestern California. Across the road from where the trail ends, hikers can pick up the **Redwood Nature Trail,** a loop hike that passes through one of the northernmost redwood groves on Earth; the redwoods along this path are considered "young" at 300-800 years old, but some are more than 12 feet (4 m) in diameter and more than 200 feet (60 m) tall. After walking through the redwoods, hikers can return to the trailhead via the River View Trail.

Fishing

Guide Andy Martin runs **Wild Rivers Fishing** (541/813-1082; www.wildriversfishing.com; $250; two-person minimum), which combs the waterways around Brookings (including the Chetco, Rogue, and Umpqua Rivers), as well as the open ocean waters near town, for a variety of native species. Drift boat and jet boat trips on area rivers last eight hours and focus on steelhead (late Dec.-Mar.), chinook salmon (late Mar.-June and Aug.-Dec.), and more. Each trip includes bait, tackle, cleaning, and bagging of whatever you catch.

Martin also offers deep-sea fishing trips through **Brookings Fishing Charters** (541/813-1082; www.brookingsfishing.com;

1: Azalea Park in Brookings **2:** rocky coastline at Harris Beach State Park **3:** Redwood Nature Trail **4:** coastline views from along the Samuel H. Boardman State Scenic Corridor

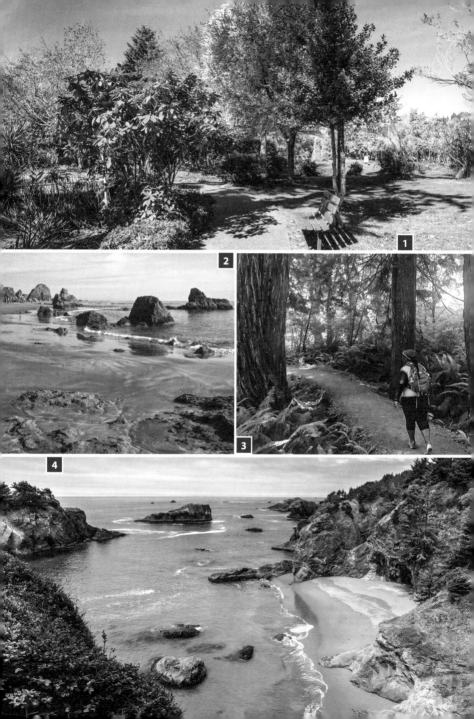

$175-375); the harbor at Brookings is protected from treacherous swells, making deep-sea fishing an easier (and more reliable) outing than at other points on the Oregon Coast. Trips are generally timed around seasonal runs of chinook salmon, albacore tuna, halibut, lingcod, and rockfish.

Anglers should purchase a single-day **fishing license** (www.myodfw.com; $23 per license) before hitting the water.

Paddling and Water Sports

The shallow, crystal-clear waters of the Chetco River are a popular paddling destination, especially in spring and summer. Rent your gear from **Chetco Kayaks** at **Riverside Market** (98877 N Bank Chetco River Rd., Brookings; 541/661-3213; www.chetcokayaks.com; $30-45 per day; May-Oct.), which offer single kayaks, tandem kayaks, and stand-up paddleboards. Shuttles are available for an additional fee.

BREWPUBS

The roughly two dozen beers on tap at any given time at ★ **Chetco Brewing** (830 Railroad St., Brookings; 541/661-5347; www.chetcobrew.com; noon-7pm Sun.-Mon. and Thurs., noon-8pm Tues. and Fri.-Sat.) offer a genuine taste of the Oregon Coast. For starters, the brewery grows various hops, fruits, and herbs for use in its inventive beers—and does so with organic practices. Classic and creative styles abound, from a crisp German pilsner to an ever-changing coffee stout recipe (crafted, of course, with organic beans). The dog-friendly brewpub hosts live music, an on-site food truck, trivia nights, and other fun community events.

You don't have to be a fan of J. R. R. Tolkien to find something to love at **Misty Mountain Brewing & Tap Haus** (625 Chetco Ave., Ste. 120, Brookings; 541/813-2599; www.misty-mountainbrewing.com; 1pm-8pm Tues.-Sat.), which pours eight small-batch beers. The small brewery focuses on easy-drinking takes on classic styles—think IPAs, pale ales, saisons, and stouts—with occasionally

inventive twists; a heavy-hitting Russian imperial stout, for instance, is imbued with pumpkins every fall. Each beer is named for a slice of *Lord of the Rings* lore, and Tolkien-inspired flourishes (such as trinkets and a colorful mural) dot the whimsical pub.

FOOD
Pacific Northwest Cuisine

Gastropubs are a dime a dozen in Oregon, but few put the thought and attention into their offerings like **Oxenfrē Public House** (631 Chetco Ave., Brookings; 541/813-1985; www.oxenpub.com; 4pm-11pm Mon.-Sat.; $14-29). The friendly watering hole sources its produce, cheese, beer, and other goods from local producers—all of which get shout-outs on the food menu. Food items include creative tacos, lasagna, steak, and fried chicken served atop a Belgian waffle; the latter is a local favorite and is served with bacon, a house-made chili honey mayonnaise, avocado, apple slaw, and aged white cheddar cheese. Cocktail fans, meanwhile, appreciate a creative drinks menu.

Italian

Black Trumpet Bistro (625 Chetco Ave., Ste. 200, Brookings; 541/887-0860; www.blacktrumpetbistro.net; 4pm-11pm Mon.-Sat.; $11-26) might sit in the heart of downtown Brookings but nevertheless delivers a classic bistro experience with a wide range of thoughtfully prepared, Italian-inspired dishes. Locally foraged mushrooms, house-made bread, and Oregon-produced meats go into a menu spotlighting Italian sandwiches, pasta dishes, and more.

Seafood

You won't find much sushi on the Oregon Coast—never mind sushi that comes from sustainable sources—but that's a testament to the thoughtfulness behind **Pacific Sushi & Grill** (613 Chetco Ave., Brookings; 541/251-7707; www.pacificsushi.com; 11:30am-9pm daily; $12-22). Locally caught crab, tuna, salmon, and other seafood goes into Pacific

The Oregon Coast Trail

The sea stacks, windswept headlands, lush forests, and iconic rock formations of the Oregon Coast are some of the state's most beloved sites—and backpackers can hike it all along what's known as the Oregon Coast Trail. The 380-mile (612-km) hiking path heads through state parks, forests, coastline, and more, traversing some of the coast's most scenic sites.

If you're interested in hiking the Oregon Coast Trail, here's what to know—and how to get started:

- **Season:** Conditions are ideal between spring and early fall (May-early Oct.), with late August-early October being the best time to hike; otherwise, hikers risk encountering miserable downpours, which can slow their progress considerably and deprive them of the most dramatic vistas. And since several campgrounds offer hiker/biker areas, backpackers don't have to sweat reservations during the busy season (June-Aug.).

- **Caution:** Most—but not all—of the Oregon Coast Trail traverses sandy shorelines and coastal forests; some sections of coastline may be inaccessible at high tide, so hikers should plan their outing around the day's tides. About 10 percent of the trail follows the shoulders of roads (such as city streets and US-101); hikers should take extreme caution when walking along roadsides. These gaps are identified as such on official trail maps, and hikers should have a plan to find safe passage between these stretches before setting out.

- **Overnight stays:** Most state parks with campgrounds offer walk-in hiker/biker camps ($7-8 per night) that usually come with flush toilets, hot showers, shared campfire grills, and picnic tables; some also include lockers to store gear and food. Sites are available on a first-come, first-served basis. Beach camping is available in some areas—but restrictions may apply in certain areas (such as within city limits of most major communities) and at certain times of year; specific beach camping rules can be found on the Oregon State Parks website (stateparks. oregon.gov).

- **Getting to and from the Oregon Coast Trail:** If flying into Portland International Airport (PDX), you can take your pack on TriMet's MAX light rail line (which stops at the airport). From there, hikers can take The Point bus to Astoria and begin their hike in nearby Fort Stevens State Park via NW Connector (503/861-7433; www.nworegontransit.org; $1 per ride). Getting back to Portland is a bit more difficult. Hikers can take The Point bus between Brookings and the community of Cave Junction in the southern Oregon Cascades, at which point they can take a bus, provided by Josephine Community Transit, to the city of Grants Pass; there, backpackers can take The Point to Medford and fly home from the Rogue Valley International-Medford Airport—or catch a Greyhound bus north back to Portland.

- **Maps:** Oregon State Parks (stateparks.oregon.gov) provides official Oregon Coast Trail maps that break down different segments of the trail—with planning tips, resources for drinking water and restrooms, tips for staying safe, recommendations for navigating gap sections, and more.

Sushi's nigiri, sashimi, and many rolls; vegetarian rolls are also available.

ACCOMMODATIONS

Slow down and unwind with a night or two at the **South Coast Inn Bed and Breakfast** (516 Redwood St., Brookings; 541/469-5557; www.southcoastinn.com; $119-159), housed in a craftsman-style home that dates back to 1917. The inn hosts six charming rooms, ranging from Victorian-era abodes with clawfoot tubs and vintage touches to a spacious cottage and a thoroughly modern apartment. Two rooms offer views of the Pacific Ocean. Most rooms come with a family-style breakfast (topped with garnish from the on-site garden), and common areas (one with a fireplace) invite guests to linger with a book or discuss

the day's adventures. Note that pets are not permitted at the B&B.

Sitting just south of where the Chetco River flows into the Pacific Ocean, **Beachfront Inn** (16008 Boat Basin Rd., Brookings; 541/469-7779; www.beachfrontinn.com; $317-426) is one of the only lodgings in town to boast sweeping ocean views, which come with every room. Choices range from basic yet clean rooms to bigger suites (some with sofa sleepers, jetted tubs, and full kitchens); both room types include private balconies or indoor nooks with excellent views. Pets are welcome for an additional fee.

Camping

The campground at **Harris Beach State Park** (US-101, 2 mi/3 km north of Brookings; 541/469-0224; stateparks.oregon.gov; $7-64) sits in a forest of spruce and fir, shielding campers from both the elements *and* traffic noise on nearby US-101. In all, campers can choose among 65 full-hookup sites, 25 electrical sites with water, 59 tent sites, 6 yurts (3 of which are pet-friendly—and 1 of which is wheelchair-accessible), and a hiker/biker camp area reserved for backpackers and cyclists. Amenities at the clean campground include a playground, flush toilets, and hot showers; most sites are level and offer some modicum of privacy, especially in the southernmost D loop. Note that generators are not allowed and that some campsites are closed November-April.

Just inland from Brookings, **Alfred A. Loeb State Park** (N. Bank Chetco River Rd., 8 mi/13.2 km northeast of Brookings; 541/469-7215; stateparks.oregon.gov; $24-52) sits amid a grove of myrtlewood trees along the Chetco River; in fact, three cabins and several campsites face the wide, slow-moving river. The campground offers 43 electrical sites with water, 5 non-reservable sites for RVs up to 20 feet (6 m) long, and 3 log cabins; flush toilets and hot showers are available. Anglers enjoy fishing for salmon and steelhead in fall and winter; bring your own gear if you'd like to try your luck. The

campground's location, away from the coast and US-101, means you'll enjoy a quieter experience than you might at other Oregon Coast campgrounds; the less-hurried nature brings about all manner of wildlife, including river otters, osprey, and owls. Most sites can be booked in advance for stays May 16-October; they are available on a first-come, first-served basis the rest of the year. From Brookings, the 8-mile (13-km) drive takes about 15 minutes via N. Bank Chetco River Road.

INFORMATION AND SERVICES

Stop into **Brookings City Hall and Visitor Information Center** (898 Elk Dr., Brookings; 541/469-1102; www.brookings.or.us; 10am-2pm Mon.-Fri.) for resources, recommendations, brochures, pamphlets, and more for making the most of your time in Brookings. Potable water and restrooms are available.

And just next to the Oregon-California border, you can find travel information for other communities along the Oregon Coast and throughout Oregon at **Crissey Field State Recreation Site** (US-101, 6 mi/10 km south of Brookings; 541/469-0224; stateparks.oregon.gov). The site's **visitor center** offers brochures and visitor information (8am-7pm daily)—and is staffed (9am-4pm Thurs.-Mon.) with folks happy to answer any questions you might have. Restrooms are available at the visitor center.

GETTING THERE AND AROUND

From Gold Beach, the 28-mile (45-km) drive to Brookings-Harbor takes about 30 minutes via southbound US-101. From Crescent City, California, the 26-mile (42-km) drive takes about 30 minutes via northbound US-101.

Once in town, US-101 (sometimes written in addresses and referred to as Chetco Ave.) is the main north-south thoroughfare through town.

Curry Public Transit (541/412-8806; www.currypublictransit.org; $4-24) runs its

Coastal Express Monday-Saturday, with stops in several south coast communities—including Brookings-Harbor.

TOP EXPERIENCE

★ SAMUEL H. BOARDMAN STATE SCENIC CORRIDOR

Don't get us wrong: Every grain of sand, windswept Sitka spruce, craggy rock formation, and weather-worn sea stack along the Oregon Coast is downright stunning. But one could certainly make the case that there is no more beautiful stretch of coastline than the 12-mile-long (19-km-long) **Samuel H. Boardman State Scenic Corridor** (541/469-0224; stateparks.oregon.gov; free).

The scenic stretch of US-101 sits between Gold Beach and Brookings, passing myriad waysides, viewpoints, and more—all of which showcase a rugged stretch of coastline dotted with headlands, sea stacks, rock formations, gurgling creeks, and craggy bluffs that demand more than a little awe. You can drive the entire corridor in about 15 minutes, without stopping, but doing so deprives you of some of the best viewpoints anywhere along the Oregon Coast.

Roughly a dozen parking areas along the corridor (named for Oregon's first state parks superintendent) offer beach access and/or sweeping vistas; each is signed and on the west side of the highway. We'd recommend stopping at as many as your schedule allows—but here are a few highlights, listed north-south in each section. In winter and spring, keep an eye out for migrating gray whales just offshore.

Sights

The northernmost stop on the corridor is the **Arch Rock Picnic Area** (sunrise-sunset daily), which offers a fine introduction to what the corridor is all about. From the parking area, views comprise a series of offshore sea stacks and craggy islands, some topped by hardy trees; elsewhere, a short, paved

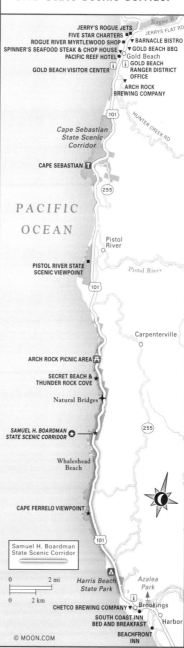

walking path descends to a viewpoint that affords views of the namesake rock, its interior eroded over the centuries by crushing waves. (The rock was a very important place to the Tolowa people, who lived along this section of coast long ago.) A few picnic tables can be found around the parking area, as can wheelchair-accessible vault toilets.

Farther south, a short trail leads to a viewpoint that shows off the region's **Natural Bridges** (sunrise-sunset daily). Here you can peer at seven collapsed sea caves, each looking like craggy, tree-lined overpasses in the heart of a windswept cove. Some steep, user-made hiking trails head down to the rocks and even cross one, but these are unsafe and not maintained; stick to the official viewpoint for the dramatic sites.

Near the southern edge of the corridor sits the **Cape Ferrelo Viewpoint** (sunrise-sunset daily). A 1-mile/1.6-km (round-trip) loop trail—surrounded by meadows of colorful wildflowers April-May—ascends to the top of the headland; from there, views of the jagged coastline abound in every direction. (On a clear day, views to the south extend all the way into California.) This headland, with wide-open vistas high above the Pacific Ocean, is an excellent place to watch migrating gray whales in winter and spring.

Beware when visiting viewpoints or hiking along the corridor: Poison oak is common in forests and along trails on the south coast; wear long pants, and try to keep your distance from the shiny, three-leafed plants.

Beaches

Several viewpoints sit along the Pacific Ocean, offering roadside beach access. Other sites demand a bit more work, most notably **Secret Beach and Thunder Rock Cove** (sunrise-sunset daily). An overlook from above the Pacific Ocean offers views of the area's breathtaking sea stacks, some of which are right on the beach at Thunder Rock Cove. For a closer look, follow a rocky, 1.6-mile/2.5-km (round-trip) trail as it descends about 350 feet (100 m) to the surf; to the south, just beyond the rock formations, Secret Beach hosts a few tidepools rich with marine life. If hiking to the shoreline, note that the coast is best accessed at low tide (and can be impassable at high tide); time your trip to coincide with low tide, and be aware of steep drop-offs and slippery conditions, for the safest possible experience.

Near the southern edge of the corridor sits the popular **Whaleshead Beach,** best accessed from the **Whaleshead Picnic Area** (sunrise-sunset daily). The beach is named for a sea stack that resembles a beached whale—and appears to emit a waterspout upward when hit with waves. From the picnic area, a flat path heads to the beach, bordered to the north by a massive headland and surrounded by craggy rock formations just offshore. Picnic tables and wheelchair-accessible vault toilets are available at the picnic area. (Just south of the parking area, **Whaleshead Viewpoint** shows off top-down views of the namesake rock—but a trail to the shore is steep.)

Background

The Landscape

GEOGRAPHY
Formation of the Oregon Coast

The Oregon Coast began to take shape (in one sense) hundreds of millions of years ago. As plates shifted beneath Earth's surface more than 200 million years ago, they sent lava flows cascading across the modern-day Pacific Northwest; these basalt flows left behind the rocks, sea stacks, and other natural features that would be carved by millions of years of erosion—like Tillamook Head, Arch Cape, and the Haystack Rocks in Cannon Beach and Pacific City. The last of those

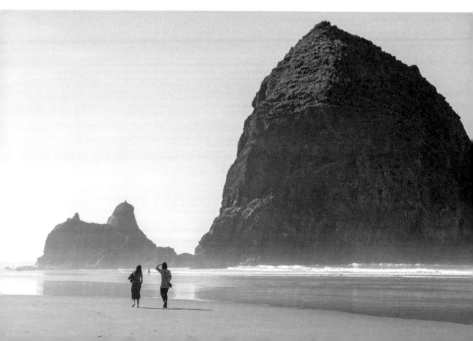

lava flows oozed some 15 million years ago, and the Oregon Coast Range began to rise about five million years later. Due to various ice ages, the Oregon Coast used to be much farther east—but sedimentary rock buildups, melting glaciers, and a warming climate created the modern-day coastline.

Earthquakes and Tsunamis

Oregon sits along the **Cascadia Subduction Zone,** a 600-mile-long (9,700-km) fault that runs between British Columbia and northern California; it sits up to 100 miles (160 km) west of the Pacific coast shore. More than 40 earthquakes have occurred from that fault over the past 10,000 years, with most coming anywhere between 200 to 1,200 years apart. (It is believed that the most recent earthquake coming from the Cascadia Subduction Zone occurred in 1700—and that it caused a tsunami in Japan.) Scientists predict that there is a 37 percent chance the fault produces a massive quake in the next 50 years.

CLIMATE
Portland

Portland is known in the popular imagination for having a rainy climate, but the reality is a bit more complicated. October-May, Portlanders typically see mostly cloudy skies with occasional rain showers; rarely does it rain all day in Portland. Portland sees 36 inches (1 m) of rain each year, with roughly half of that falling November-January. In the heart of winter, the region sees daily high temperatures of about 45-50ºF (7-10°C), with mostly rain showers but little snow.

Mild temperatures and spotty rain showers are the hallmarks of spring in the region, all of which gives way to warm, dry weather (with low humidity) as the season progresses. High temperatures hit about 81ºF (27°C) in August—but can frequently push to 90ºF (32°C) and warmer.

Oregon Coast

The **Oregon Coast** essentially has two seasons: rainy and dry. And even then, the dry season isn't immune from occasional showers or frequent cloud cover.

Rainy season more or less begins in October and extends into May or June, with the coast seeing 75-90 inches (1.9-2.3 m) of rainfall annually. Winter storms rolling in off the Pacific Ocean make storm-watching a popular pastime, but seasonal weather patterns mean most of the Oregon Coast's best sunsets occur December-March—on clear days, anyway. Daily high temperatures reach about 45-55ºF (7-13°C), and snow is almost unheard of on most of the coast. The sole exception to Oregon's rainy winter and spring weather is the so-called **Banana Belt**—a stretch of coastline between **Gold Beach** and **Brookings-Harbor** that's known for sunny skies and mild temperatures, even in winter.

July-September, meanwhile, are reliably dry up and down the Oregon Coast. Daily highs reach 60-70ºF, with warmer temperatures more common as you head south. You may wake to fog most mornings, especially on the north coast, but cloud cover typically breaks by midday. Summer rain is infrequent but not unheard of.

Previous: Haystack Rock in the background at Cannon Beach.

Plants and Animals

PLANTS
Coastal Plant Life

Along the Oregon Coast, the **Sitka spruce** boasts needles and bark that resist salty spray—making it one of the most common trees in the region. The tree can grow to 180 feet (55 m) tall and can live up to 800 years. You'll occasionally see Sitka spruce on its own, but it more commonly grows in forests of hemlock, cedar, and pine.

Other tree and plant species on the Oregon Coast include **shore pine,** which usually grows up to 35 feet (10 m) and is (similar to Sitka spruce) resistant to salt spray; **salal** bushes, with berries that have long been an important source of food, medicine, and more for Native American tribes along the coast; and **rhododendrons,** which can grow to 20 feet (6 m) tall and provide colorful pops of pink, white, and purple in spring along the Oregon Coast (as well as in the Cascade Range).

European beachgrass, introduced to help stabilize perpetually shifting sand dunes, is a species of grass common to beachy areas up and down the Oregon Coast; the grass crowds out native vegetation and, over time, introduces non-native plants—dramatically impacting ecosystems that have remained intact for decades or centuries.

ANIMALS
Tidepools and Coastal Animals

One of the great joys of the Oregon Coast is just how prevalent wildlife is—whether off the coast, in tidepools along the shore, or even around inland meadows and streams.

Perhaps there is no more famous animal on the Oregon Coast than the **gray whale.** Every year, roughly 25,000 gray whales migrate between Mexico and Alaska (Dec.-Jan. and Mar.-May), with a small number of residents lingering along the Oregon Coast all

year long. Less common sightings along the coast include **orcas, humpback whales,** and the occasional **blue whale.**

Closer to shore, Oregon is home to two species of sea lion and three species of seal; the **Stellar sea lion** is the most commonly spotted (and heard!) of Oregon's sea lions, from the **Sea Lion Caves** near **Florence** to waterfront harbors in **Astoria,** while **pacific harbor seals** and **northern elephant seals** are frequently spotted up and down the Oregon Coast. And in tidepools—pockets and pools of ocean water that form when tides recede over rocky stretches of coastline—you'll see an abundance of wildlife year-round; common sightings include **sea stars, sea lettuce, sea anemones, barnacles,** and even **hermit crabs.**

Fish

Across the state, keep an eye out in streams, rivers, and wetlands (as well as in the Columbia River's many tributaries) for **Chinook** (or king) **salmon, coho salmon, sockeye salmon,** and **steelhead.** In fall, a popular pastime is watching salmon as they return to their birthplace to spawn. Crowds gather around streambeds to watch salmon fighting their way upstream. Locally caught seafood is served in restaurants along the Oregon Coast and in Portland.

Mammals

Mammals are common throughout Oregon, though the sheer volume of visitors at popular outdoor destinations keeps them hidden and makes encounters rare. Consider yourself lucky if you see a **black-tailed deer, raccoon, skunk, bobcat, American beaver** (Oregon's state animal), **California ground squirrel,** or **yellow-bellied marmot.** All can be found throughout the state. Regal **Roosevelt elk** can also be found throughout the western portion of the

state—such as at **Dean Creek Elk Viewing Area,** just outside Reedsport, and along the northern Oregon Coast, largely between **Cannon Beach** and **Astoria.**

Birds

Bird-watching is a popular activity around Oregon. Some of the most common birds you'll see around Oregon include the **great blue herons** (noted for their S-shaped necks), soaring **ospreys,** and **bald eagles** (which can be seen all over the state—but feed on spawning salmon and are most commonly spotted Jan.-Feb.). And if you go hiking on the west side of the state, chances are good you'll hear a **pileated woodpecker** at some point. Areas of the Oregon Coast, meanwhile, are protected during the nesting season of the **snowy plover**—a short, stout shorebird with a white belly and sandy gray back.

Wherever you go, bring a field guide or mobile app for identification, a decent pair of binoculars, and a good camera for the best possible experience.

Amphibians and Reptiles

The common **garter snake** can be found throughout western Oregon, as can the **western pond turtle,** which lives in lowland ponds and lakes.

Insects and Arachnids

Perhaps the insect most commonly identified with Oregon is the simple mosquito. **Mosquitos** appear all over the state in late spring and early summer, especially around bodies of water, and reach their aggressive nadir in late June-July. **Yellowjackets** and **hornets** also live in Oregon.

History

EARLY HISTORY AND INDIGENOUS PEOPLES

More than 50 Native American tribes have fished, hunted, foraged, and lived throughout modern-day Oregon since time immemorial. Some of the earliest recorded evidence of human habitation in the region comes via the so-called Fort Rock sandals—footwear discovered near Fort Rock in 1938 that revealed fibers dating back nearly 10,000 years.

Over several millennia, these tribes fished in the legendary Celilo Falls in the Columbia River (which was submerged by the creation of the Dalles Dam in 1957); traded obsidian culled from Newberry Volcano; gathered berries and hunted elk in the Willamette Valley; foraged plants, fashioned tools, and crafted canoes on the Oregon Coast; and so forth. Nary a corner of modern-day Oregon hasn't been touched, in some impactful way, by Native American tribes.

But the arrival of white explorers and settlers, combined with the actions of the U.S.

government, led to the decimation and removal of the region's Indigenous communities. Disease brought by the incoming emigrants—to which the Indigenous peoples had no immunity (such as smallpox, measles, and influenza)—wiped out much of the area's Native American population in the early 1800s, and life was anything but easy for the survivors: By the mid- to late 1800s, the federal government had forced most of the region's Native American population onto inland reservations, far from their ancestral homes and traditional fishing villages. Several treaties signed in 1855 dealt another blow to regional tribes; the various treaties established what would become reservations throughout the state, but tribes ceded wide swaths of ancestral homeland in return.

Today, there are nine federally recognized tribes in Oregon. They are the Burns Paiute Tribe; the Confederated Tribes of Coos, Lower Umpqua and Siuslaw Indians; the Coquille Indian Tribe; the Cow Creek Band

of Umpqua Tribe of Indians; the Confederated Tribes of Grand Ronde; the Klamath Tribes; the Confederated Tribes of Siletz; the Confederated Tribes of the Umatilla Indian Reservation; and the Confederated Tribes of Warm Springs.

THE OREGON TRAIL

The door for white settlers to move to Oregon opened when Meriwether Lewis and William Clark arrived in the state in 1805 as part of their famed Corps of Discovery Expedition; the explorers camped in the Columbia River Gorge and wintered on the Oregon Coast, near present-day Astoria, while searching for a waterway across North America and seeking to understand the lands the United States had recently acquired in the Louisiana Purchase. Lewis and Clark were among the first European-Americans to visit this region, though rumors of a "great river of the West" (this would be the Columbia River) had brought explorers to the Oregon Coast for centuries.

Some of the area's first European-American emigrants settled in the nearby Willamette Valley in the mid-1800s, kicking off the largest mass migration of people in U.S. history. Thousands of emigrants from the East, Midwest, and South headed west via wagons on the 1,900-mile (3,000-km) Oregon Trail (primarily between 1843 and 1869, until the transcontinental railroad was completed), enticed by fertile soil and economic opportunities. The trail originated in Independence, Missouri, and ended in Oregon City, just south of Portland.

The Columbia River Gorge and Mount Hood played an important role in the Oregon Trail. In the early days, emigrants on this final stretch of the trail had no choice but to float the Columbia River once they reached The Dalles, a dangerous passage given pre-dam rapids near present-day Cascade Locks. Then, in 1846, Kentucky emigrant Sam Barlow established the tolled Barlow Road, offering an alternate inland route—though still tricky given dense forests and rocky

ridgelines—around the south slope of Mount Hood; the wagon road roughly parallels today's US-26.

Oregon Black Pioneers

Even before it was a state, Oregon was inhospitable and unwelcoming to Black residents—but that didn't stop determined Black pioneers from becoming pillars in their communities and making contributions that continue to be felt today.

The first known Black person to visit what we know as Oregon is Markus Lopius, who was a crew member aboard the American ship *Lady Washington*; Lopius reached the Tillamook area in August 1788 and allegedly died just a few days later after an argument in which he accused a member of the Tillamook tribe of stealing his cutlass. The next Black man to arrive in Oregon was York, an enslaved man who in 1805 came to Oregon as part of the Corps of Discovery Expedition with Lewis and Clark. Over the following decades, a number of enslaved or formerly enslaved Black people would start businesses and become beloved community members around Oregon—especially in the Willamette Valley.

When Oregon became a state in 1859, it attempted to erase these contributions with exclusion laws written to discourage Black Americans from living in the state. Even so, Black Oregonians persevered. In 1914, for instance, the National Association for the Advancement of Colored People created a Portland chapter—which is today the oldest continually chartered chapter of the civil-rights organization west of the Mississippi River. A few years later, 50 or so Black loggers worked in the now-defunct logging town of Maxville deep in the Wallowa Mountains. The state's last exclusion law would be repealed in 1926.

STATEHOOD

One of the thousands of westward travelers on the Oregon Trail was Marcus Whitman, a physician who arrived in Walla Walla in present-day Washington in 1835 to establish

Oregon's Racist Founding

It's not an exaggeration to say that racism and white supremacy were driving forces in the founding of Oregon. When Oregon was admitted to the United States in 1859, it was the only state with an exclusion law written into the state constitution—meaning that Oregon excluded all free Black people from living in the state, even as slavery was outlawed. Several cities around the state were known for decades as "sundown towns," where people of color were unofficially barred from being in town between dusk and dawn. Interracial marriage was banned in 1866 (a law that wouldn't be repealed until 1951), the Ku Klux Klan flourished in Oregon well into the 1920s, and racist language would remain in the state constitution until 2002.

Yet Oregon wouldn't be the state it is today without immigrants and communities of color. Japanese immigrants, for instance, were some of the first (and most successful) farmers in the Hood River Valley; Chinese immigrants, meanwhile, helped build the railroads that connected Oregon to the rest of the world. And Black Oregonians have been pillars of their communities since Oregon was technically a territory—long before it was a part of the union.

If you'd like to learn more about that history—and the communities of color that have been so central to the growth and success of Oregon since before its founding—you have several options for doing so. The **Oregon Black Pioneers** (oregonblackpioneers.org) celebrate Black Oregonians—and hold occasional interpretive events to showcase that history. And in Eugene, the **Strides for Social Justice mobile app** (peacehealth.org/strides-for-social-justice) offers digital walking tours that showcase the city's Black history. Other museums throughout the state, including the **Oregon Historical Society** (ohs.org) in Portland, share impactful stories through multimedia offerings and engaging exhibits.

a mission. He had little success in converting the Cayuse people who lived in the region, and a measles outbreak in 1847 led to the deaths of many locals—for which they blamed Whitman. Tensions built and, in an event that came to be known as the Whitman Massacre, Cayuse members killed him—along with his wife, Narcissa, and 11 others, leading to a war between the Cayuse people and the United States and spurring the U.S. government in 1848 to expand its control of the North American continent by formally establishing the Oregon Territory, which covered what would become Washington, Oregon, Idaho, and parts of Montana and Wyoming.

European settlement increased in the years that followed, largely thanks to the Oregon Donation Land Act, passed by Congress in 1850; the law granted free federal land to white male citizens 18 and older and set off a land rush that brought roughly 30,000 new settlers to the Oregon Territory. Native American communities, already besieged by disease and war, resisted the invasion of their lands, sparking conflicts throughout the region over the next several years.

Oregon achieved statehood in 1859. By the late 1800s, the federal government had forced most of the region's Native Americans onto inland reservations, far from their ancestral homes and traditional fishing villages.

OREGON'S ROLE IN WORLD WAR II

Given its location on the west coast of the United States, perhaps it's no surprise that Oregon played a somewhat hidden role in World War II. In June 1942, for instance, a Japanese submarine fired on Fort Stevens near the mouth of the Columbia River—the only time during World War II that enemy fire struck a military base in the contiguous United States; officers chose not to return fire, and little damage was done to the installation. Later that year, Nobuo Fujita became the only foreign pilot to successfully bomb the United States during World War II when he

dropped an incendiary bomb from a seaplane over the southern Oregon Coast (not far from Brookings-Harbor); much like the shelling at Fort Stevens, little damage was done—and Fujita was invited to Brookings 20 years later as a show of international unity.

In 1945, Japan began sending massive balloons, filled with hydrogen and armed with bombs, into the jet stream—hoping that each would make landfall in the United States, explode on impact, cause numerous wildfires, and send Americans into a panic. These "balloon bombs," as they were known, eventually landed as far east as Iowa, but the rainy forests on the Oregon Coast Range stopped most from ever igniting. That spring, one of the balloons killed a minister, his pregnant wife, and five children from their Sunday school class outside the small community of Bly in southern Oregon; it was the only time Americans were killed by enemy fire in the continental United States during World War II.

Against this backdrop, a city grew between the northern border of Portland and the Columbia River. Vanport was built in 1942 to house workers at nearby shipyards, many of them Black, and became the state's second-largest city in the process. Sitting on flood-prone lowlands along the Columbia River, the city was destroyed in 1948 when as massive flood broke through a railway berm that the government had previously declared safe. In all, 15 residents lost their lives in the devastating floods.

CONTEMPORARY TIMES

Post-World War II growth around the United States fueled Oregon's economy, which at the time was dominated by timber. Across the state, loggers and lumberjacks felled wide swaths of the state's old-growth forests to feed the country's insatiable desire for strong timber. At the industry's peak in the 1950s, 1960s, and 1970s, Oregon produced nearly 10 billion board feet of lumber each year.

But the industry's long, slow decline in Oregon began in the late 1970s, brought on by changing rules and regulations, increased environmental protections, more efficient technology, and overseas outsourcing. Today, Oregon's timber industry is a fraction of what it once was; in 2020, the industry produced fewer than 240 million board feet of lumber.

Even as Oregon's timber industry thrived, the state's progressive future was being written by Governor Tom McCall, a maverick Republican who led the state from 1967 to 1975. During his time as governor, McCall preserved protections for Oregon's beaches, took steps to manage growth through mandatory land-use planning, promoted energy conservation, and signed into law the Oregon Bottle Bill (an anti-littering law, a boon to recycling, and the first mandatory container deposit law in the United States). These days, Oregonians largely enjoy clean air, clean water, and easy access to scenic natural settings all over the state—and have McCall to thank for laying the groundwork.

Essentials

Transportation

AIR

Portland International Airport (PDX, 7000 NE Airport Way, Portland; 503/460-4234; flypdx.com) is the primary airport in the state, located just 10 miles (16 km) northeast of downtown. PDX welcomes nearly 20 million passengers each year, with 16 carriers serving the airport. The airport has earned well-deserved plaudits over the years for hosting local eateries and retailers rather than chains, and for offering "street pricing"—so vendors can't charge you more than they do elsewhere in Portland.

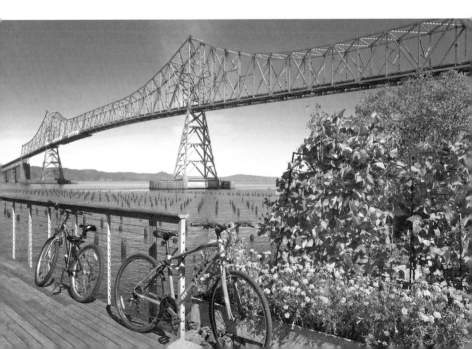

Airport Transportation

MAX Light Rail Red Line (trimet.org; 2.5-hour ticket $2.50, day pass $5) provides easy access between Portland International Airport and downtown Portland. Trains run every 15 minutes 5am-1:45am, and tickets can be purchased via debit cards and credit cards from on-site ticket machines or with mobile wallets and contactless cards at digital fare readers. Several taxi companies and rideshare services operate at the airport.

TRAIN

Amtrak (800/872-7245; amtrak.com) operates the *Cascades* route, which runs north-south along the I-5 corridor between Vancouver, British Columbia, and Eugene, with stops in Portland and Seattle, among others. The *Empire Builder* route runs from Portland to Chicago, with stops in Spokane, Minneapolis, and more. The *Coast Starlight* route runs north-south between Seattle and Los Angeles, with stops in Portland and other cities along the I-5 corridor.

BUS

Greyhound (800/231-2222; greyhound. com) offers service along the I-5 corridor—where stops include Portland, Salem, Eugene, Grants Pass, and Medford—and along I-84 (with stops in Hood River, Pendleton, Baker City, and other communities). Filling some of the considerable gaps in Greyhound's coverage, **POINT Intercity Bus Service** (888/846-4183; oregon-point.com) operates several routes throughout the state—with service between Portland and the northern coast, Portland and Eugene, and Brookings and Klamath Falls in southern Oregon. And the budget-minded **FlixBus** (855/626-8585; flixbus.com) offers regional connections to roughly a dozen cities throughout the Pacific Northwest—with Oregon stops including Portland, Salem, Corvallis, and Eugene.

CAR

An automobile is the most practical and efficient way of getting around the state; it would be challenging to rely on any other mode of transportation. Portland and most large cities (such as Bend, Salem, and Eugene) boast some form of mass transit, and regular bus service links Portland to many of those communities (especially across the Willamette Valley and throughout the northern Oregon Coast)—but the distance between destinations, sprawl of the state, and number of rural areas make it difficult to depend on mass transit for far-flung travel.

If visiting in winter, the Oregon Department of Transportation's **TripCheck** website (tripcheck.com) is an essential resource for current road conditions, updated webcams, closure information, alerts, and more.

Some Oregon traffic laws confuse those from out of state; one quirk, for instance, is that left turns are permitted at red lights—but only after stopping and yielding to traffic and pedestrians, and when turning onto a one-way street. Also note that U-turns are illegal in most cases across Oregon; U-turns are generally prohibited at intersections controlled by a traffic signal (unless a sign explicitly permits a U-turn) and when a vehicle cannot be seen when coming from either direction within 500 feet/150 m (within city limits) or 1,000 feet/300 m (outside city limits).

Major Highways

Major highways in the state include **I-5,** which runs north-south through Portland to the borders with Tijuana, Mexico, to the south and Vancouver, British Columbia, to the north, and connects the city to Los Angeles and San Diego in California and Seattle, Washington.

I-84 begins just east of downtown Portland and runs east-west, paralleling the Columbia River Gorge, before continuing southeast through eastern Oregon and Boise, Idaho, before ending near Salt Lake City, Utah.

US-26 begins on the Oregon Coast, between Seaside and Cannon Beach; it runs east-west through the state, heading through Portland, Mt. Hood, and the Painted Hills before eventually ending in Nebraska.

US-20 is the other thoroughfare that spans all of Oregon; the longest road in the United States begins in Newport, on the Oregon Coast, and heads through Corvallis, Bend, and the Oregon Outback, before continuing east—and eventually ending in Boston.

US-101 runs north-south along the Pacific coast; it begins on the Olympic Peninsula in Washington, covers the entire Oregon Coast, and ends in southern California.

Gas

Up until 2023, Oregon was one of two states that largely prohibited you from pumping your own gas. Now, you can choose to pump your own gas or have an attendant pump for you. If you opt for the attendant, pull up to the pumps, and the attendant will typically come to your vehicle, take your cash or card, and pump gas for you. (Tips of $1-2 are appreciated but not typically expected.)

Car and RV Rentals

Car rentals are widely available throughout Portland, but **Portland International Airport** (PDX, 7000 NE Airport Way; 503/460-4234; flypdx.com) is your most convenient option for rentals. The in-airport rental car pickup and drop-off is located on the first level of the short-term parking garage, easily accessible from the baggage claim area. The usual big chain companies are here: five operate on-site at the airport (Avis, Dollar Car Rental, Enterprise Rent-a-Car, Hertz, and National), and three are a quick shuttle ride away (Alamo, Budget, and Thrifty).

Ridesharing Services

Ridesharing services, such as **Lyft** and **Uber,** are typically only available in the state's largest cities—such as Portland, Salem, Eugene, Bend, and Medford—with some service to surrounding suburbs and communities. That said, almost every community in Oregon, no matter the size, has taxi service.

Electric-Vehicle Charging Stations

Oregon has nearly 1,600 public electric-vehicle charging stations across seven charging networks (such as ChargePoint, EVgo, and Tesla); these stations are available all over the state—including many rural communities—and more are being added all the time. The state of Oregon's **Charge on the Go** website (goelectric.oregon.gov/charge-your-ev) includes recommendations for mobile apps to help with finding public chargers, tips for a productive and enjoyable charging experience, and suggestions for travel itineraries through regions with an especially high number of charging stations.

BICYCLE

If you explore some of the Beaver State by bike, keep in mind that bicycles are legally considered vehicles—so cyclists have the same right of way as automobile drivers. Helmets are required for riders 15 and younger—but are a good idea for everyone. Similarly, lights are required for riding after dark; that means a white light on the front (visible at least 500 feet/150 m) and a red light or reflector (visible at least 600 feet/180 m) on the rear.

The **Oregon Department of Transportation** (888/275-6368; oregon.gov/odot) offers a number of excellent resources—including tips for cycling safety, maps, links to Scenic Bikeways, and more. **Travel Oregon** (traveloregon.com) brings together some of the state's best road riding and mountain biking routes—complete with maps and recommendations for where to stop along the way. And **BikePortland** (bikeportland.org) is a news site devoted largely to cycling-related matters in Portland; beyond the latest headlines, though, you'll find an events calendar and other tips for riding around Oregon's largest city.

Recreation

HIKING

Hiking is among the most popular outdoor activities anywhere in Oregon, and you'll find a hiking trail suited to your time constraints, skill level, and interests almost anywhere you go. On the western, more temperate side of the state, trails are often accessible year-round—even if they can become quite muddy in winter.

Trails proximate to the city of Portland tend to get crowded in summer, and parking lots can fill by 9am; elsewhere and out of season, this likely won't be an issue.

If hiking in summer, research wildfire conditions before heading out; hazy skies may obscure a particularly scenic view, polluted air may make it unhealthy to be outside, and public lands may be closed altogether due to fire danger or to help with recovery from a previous fire.

Also note that car break-ins at trailheads, especially around Portland, aren't uncommon. Carry valuables with you, and tuck bags and other goods away and out of sight; even innocuous-seeming items left visible in vehicles can attract the wrong kind of attention.

Recreation Passes and Fees

Wide swaths of public lands all over Oregon fall under state and federal management. In summer, many trailhead and day-use parking areas managed by the U.S. Forest Service require vehicles to display a **Northwest Forest Pass,** available online (fs.usda.gov; day pass $5, annual pass $30) or at regional retailers. Day passes can sometimes be purchased at trailhead pay stations, but there's no guarantee, so it's best to purchase ahead of time. Also note that **America the Beautiful Passes** (nps.gov; $80) are valid at sites where Northwest Forest Passes are accepted.

All year long, day-use permits are required at 26 of the most popular **Oregon State Parks** properties (stateparks.oregon.gov; $5);

these are typically available at pay stations at each park.

BICYCLING

Oregon has long been known as a bike-friendly state; in 1971, for instance, the state legislature passed the Oregon Bicycle Bill—which required at least 1 percent of the annual state highway fund to go toward bicycle infrastructure. (That law also required the inclusion of sidewalks and bikeways whenever a new road or highway is built or rebuilt.) More recently, Portland has earned international acclaim for its commitment to cycling; more than 6 percent of Portland workers commute by bike each year, protected pathways crisscross the city, and several events throughout the year—from the neighborhood-friendly Portland Sunday Parkways to the outlandish World Naked Bike Ride—celebrate that love affair with cycling.

But cycling is making inroads elsewhere around the state, as well. In 2009, Oregon became the first state in the nation to create a statewide **Scenic Bikeway program** (traveloregon.com); today, 17 curated routes showcase the best of the state—scenic views, quiet backroads, friendly communities, and more. Elsewhere around the state, Oakridge (which bills itself "the Mountain Biking Capital of the Northwest") sits surrounded by more than 300 miles (480 km) of single-track mountain biking trails—and the sprawling Phil's Trail Complex comprises dozens of miles of trails that fan out across the Deschutes National Forest near Bend.

CAMPING

You'll find public and private campgrounds all over Oregon.

Some of the best are run by **Oregon State Parks** (800/551-6949; stateparks.oregon.gov). These campgrounds, some of which remain open-year-round, are typically

well-maintained and feature amenities such as flush toilets, hot showers, and hook-ups; some include cabins and circular yurts (both of which come with electricity and heating). Expect to pay $17-47 for a tent or RV site, and $43-64 for cabins and yurts. Reservations are available six months out through **ReserveAmerica** (800/452-5687; oregonstateparks.reserveamerica.com); cabins and yurts fill up soon after the reservation window opens, especially on summer weekends, and many campgrounds (especially along the Oregon Coast) routinely fill to capacity July-August. Pets are permitted in most Oregon State Parks, but they must be physically restrained (whether you're holding them or they're on a leash up to six feet long) unless inside a tent, vehicle, or pet-friendly cabin or yurt.

The **U.S. Forest Service** (fs.usda.gov), meanwhile, manages hundreds of campgrounds throughout Oregon. Amenities are commonly limited to vault toilets and potable water, but the remote locations of many U.S. Forest Service campgrounds can't be beat. If driving an RV or hauling a trailer, research ahead of time whether a desired campground can accommodate your equipment; many campgrounds are on rural roads, and sites trend toward the small side. Sites typically run $10-25, and reservations are available six months in advance through **Recreation. gov** (877/444-6777); sites at popular destinations can fill within days of the reservation window opening up—especially on summer weekends. Pets are generally permitted in U.S. Forest Service campgrounds, but they must be physically restrained (typically on a leash up to 6 feet/2 m long) unless inside a tent or vehicle; dogs should also be kept inside a tent, RV, or trailer at night.

Wherever you camp, note that summertime campfire bans may be in effect, especially during the hottest part of the season (late July-mid-Sept.). Such campfire bans are enacted to stop human-caused wildfires and keep campers safe; if camping in summer, please research possible campfire restrictions in advance and plan accordingly.

FISHING AND HUNTING

The **Oregon Department of Fish and Wildlife** (myodfw.com) is the best resource for up-to-date rules and regulations and other key information on closures and seasonal opportunities. Oregon anglers can download the free **MyODFW app,** which lets you tag salmon, steelhead, or sturgeon catches and display licenses and tags.

Fishing Licenses

In Oregon, anglers 13 and over are required to have a license, available online through the **Oregon Department of Fish and Wildlife** (myodfw.com; 1-day license $23, 2-day license $42, 3-day license $59.50) or at local retailers. A 7-day license ($93.50) is also available for nonresidents only.

Hunting Licenses

Plentiful hunting abounds around Oregon, especially in eastern and central Oregon; deer, elk, pronghorn, and waterfowl are among the most sought-after animals. Annual licenses run $34.50 for residents and $172 for non-residents, but tags for specific species run extra. The **Oregon Department of Fish and Wildlife** (myodfw.com) website offers a complete breakdown of rules, regulations, restrictions, and seasonal hunting information.

WATER SPORTS
Kayaking, Canoeing, and Stand-Up Paddling

Oregon is dotted with alpine lakes, peaceful rivers, and quiet streams for kayaking, canoeing, and stand-up paddling. If you're interested in getting on the water while in Oregon, you'll want to keep a few things in mind.

Adults are not required to wear personal floatation devices (PFDs or lifejackets)—but one PFD for each adult must be in the craft at all times, and we'd strongly encourage you to wear one whenever you're on the water; children 12 and younger are required to wear a

U.S. Coast Guard-approved life jacket whenever the boat is underway.

Additionally, all paddle craft 10 feet (3 m) and longer are required to carry an Oregon State Marine Board Waterway Access Permit ($7 for a seven-day pass, $19 for an annual pass, $32 for a two-year pass); these are available via the Oregon Department of Fish & Wildlife (ODFW) website (myodfw.com), the MyODFW mobile app, or at retailers throughout the state. If you take an organized tour or rent a paddle craft through an outfitter, this permit is included.

Paddlers must also carry an all-around white light (such as a flashlight) in dark and foggy conditions, and must carry a sound-producing device (such as a whistle) at all times. A whistle is typically included with all paddle craft rentals and on tours with outfitters.

Travel Tips

ALCOHOL

The minimum drinking age in Oregon, as it is in the rest of the United States, is 21. Liquor by the bottle must be purchased from state-sanctioned liquor stores, all of which are open Monday-Saturday; many choose to open on Sunday, as well. Liquor can be purchased for on-site consumption 7am-2:30am. Packaged beer, cider, and wine are available at grocery stores and bottle shops.

CANNABIS

Cannabis is legal in Oregon and you're well within your rights to partake, as long as you're at least 21 years of age and follow restrictions. Cannabis can only be purchased at licensed retail outlets. Legal amounts include up to 1 ounce (28 g) of useable marijuana (harvested flowers, leaves, or bud), 16 ounces (0.5 kg) of cannabinoids in solid form (such as edibles), 72 ounces (2 kg) of cannabinoids in liquid form, and either 5 grams of cannabinoid extracts or concentrates. Most cannabis stores do not accept debit or credit cards, so bring cash. It is illegal to use marijuana in public or to drive under the influence of marijuana, and doing so may lead to significant legal penalties. Most lodgings also prohibit smoking on their properties. Federal law supersedes state law, so cannabis use is not permissible on federally managed lands, and it's illegal to take cannabis across state lines.

ENTRY REQUIREMENTS

All visitors traveling from a foreign country must possess a valid passport in order to enter the United States—as well as a return or round-trip ticket already booked. Travelers from some countries must also have a valid visa before entering; the U.S. Department of State (state.gov) offers a full list of countries with visa requirements, travel advisories, and information about embassies and consulates in foreign countries.

Get the latest updates from the **U.S. Department of State's Bureau of Consular Affairs** (travel.state.gov), and learn about any possible restrictions or requirements related to Covid-19 from the **Centers for Disease Control and Prevention** (cdc.gov). It is recommended that all travelers get tested for Covid-19 three to five days after arrival.

ACCESSIBILITY FOR TRAVELERS WITH DISABILITIES

Oregon has taken strides in recent years to better serve people with disabilities. **Oregon State Parks** (800/551-6949; stateparks.oregon.gov), for instance, is currently undertaking a decades-long effort to remove physical barriers for visitors in wheelchairs by constructing wheelchair-accessible yurts and cabins, accessible kayak launches, and paved trails with gentle grades. Accessible sites may

also be available at campgrounds managed by the **U.S. Forest Service** (fs.usda.gov).

More than a dozen communities along the Oregon Coast—including Manzanita, Pacific City, and Lincoln City—offer **beach wheelchairs** and seasonal modi-mats that provide shoreline access for all; the tires are usually large enough to tackle dry sand, but those using the wheelchairs may need an occasional push. If interested in renting a wheelchair, inquire about availability with the visitor center or lodging where you will stay; local outfitters and rental companies may also be able to help. Try to request reservations at least one week in advance, especially during summer.

Admission is free to many federal lands throughout the state with an **America the Beautiful Access Pass** (nps.gov), available to those who have been medically determined to have a permanent disability. The lifetime pass is free, with a $10 processing fee and an application. In addition to free admission at more than 2,000 federal recreation sites throughout the United States, the pass also affords a 50 percent discount on some amenity fees for camping, boat launches, and other services.

TRAVELERS OF COLOR

Oregon is an extremely homogenous state; more than 75 percent of all Oregonians identify as white. Even so, communities of color, especially in and around Portland, boast more diverse populations. For its part, Portland has traditionally been seen (and rightfully so) as a very homogenous city; today, about 70 percent of Portlanders identify as white.

Portland-area and regional groups fighting for racial justice and equality include the NAACP Portland Branch (pdxnaacp.org), the Urban League of Portland (ulpdx.org), and Unite Oregon (uniteoregon.org). Oregon Black Pioneers (oregonblackpioneers.org) is another organization that works to preserve the history of Black Oregonians and share their stories through exhibits, events, and other forms of outreach.

A few regional groups aim to connect outdoor aficionados of color with nature and public lands—especially through events in the Portland area, on Mount Hood, and throughout the Columbia River Gorge. **Outdoor Afro** (outdoorafro.com) is a national organization dedicated to connecting Black outdoor aficionados with nature, while **Vive NW** (vivenw.org) aims to increase outdoor participation among Latino communities through guided events, volunteer opportunities, and more. And **Unlikely Hikers** (unlikelyhikers.org) is a Portland-based group that works to promote inclusion through group hikes, advocacy, and other events.

WOMEN TRAVELING ALONE

For better or worse, there's nothing "off the beaten path" about the destinations we've covered in this guide, and there is safety in numbers. Whether you're on a popular trail or at a winery's tasting room, chances are you'll find yourself in company. Women traveling alone might also want to join regional hiking groups on Facebook, of which there are dozens; women regularly use these groups (such as Hiking Oregon and Hiking in the Pacific Northwest) to find hiking buddies any time of year.

TRAVELING WITH CHILDREN

Oregon is an exceptionally kid-friendly state. Many attractions and museums offer discounts for children; rest areas are common along major highways; and ranger-led hikes, interpretive programs, and other educational opportunities are routinely offered each summer at parks across Oregon. Even most breweries and wineries are family friendly. Just keep in mind that most B&Bs and some upscale lodgings do not permit children under a certain age; we've indicated where such restrictions may apply in our accommodations listings, but it can't hurt to ask when making reservations.

LGBTQ TRAVELERS

In many ways, Oregon is a welcoming destination for LGBTQ travelers; the community of Silverton elected the nation's first transgender mayor in 2008, the state elected the nation's first openly LGBTQ governor in 2016, and Portland has long boasted a thriving queer community. Today, welcoming attitudes abound in the likes of Portland, Astoria, and other progressive communities. And while rural towns are typically more welcoming of LGBTQ travelers than in years past, visitors may occasionally feel unwelcome in these smaller communities.

Health and Safety

EMERGENCY SERVICES

In case of a medical, police, or fire-related emergency, dial 911 throughout Oregon.

Most communities have hospitals with 24-hour emergency rooms; if a situation doesn't require immediate medical attention, consider seeing whether your destination has an urgent-care clinic that's geared more toward common injuries and ailments. Emergency-room insurance bills can get expensive, even with health insurance, and wait times are typically far shorter.

CORONAVIRUS

At the time of writing in August 2023, Oregon had mostly stabilized from the effects of the coronavirus. Early in the pandemic, Oregon was widely lauded for keeping case counts low through mask mandates, vaccination requirements, and other measures to control the spread of Covid-19; more recently, the state has taken a hands-off approach and is today advocating for personal responsibility through voluntary masking when prudent, frequent testing, and updated vaccinations.

Now more than ever, Moon encourages readers to be courteous and ethical in their travel. Be respectful to residents and mindful of the evolving situation in your chosen destination when planning your trip. **Get vaccinated** if your health allows, and if possible, **test regularly** before, during, and after your trip to ensure you continue to test negative for Covid-19.

Resources

Oregon Health Authority (www.oregon. gov/oha/covid19) delivers regular updates on local case numbers, safety tips, travel advisories, and information on local health providers who can assist if you suspect you have Covid-19.

HEALTH HAZARDS
Heatstroke

The Pacific Northwest has a reputation for rain—after all, rain is why our waterfalls are so magical, and why our forests are so green—but in summer, and as you travel east of the Cascades, the region sees much more sun. Heatstroke symptoms can include headaches, dizziness, light-headedness, a lack of sweat, red or dry skin, cramps, nausea, and vomiting; it can be life-threatening if not treated quickly, so take proper precautions before venturing outside on warm days. Pack along plenty of sunblock (with an SPF of 30 or higher), bring more water than you think you'll need, don't overexert yourself, wear a hat and breathable fabrics (made with moisture-wicking material), and take breaks in the shade to cool off whenever possible. If planning outdoor activities and if your schedule allows, consider starting by 9am to avoid the harshest of the day's heat. If you suspect you're experiencing heatstroke, stop all activity, move to a cooler place, drink cold water or sports drinks, and rest; if symptoms don't improve within one hour, seek immediate medical attention.

Hypothermia

Hypothermia—which occurs when your body temperature falls below 95°F (35°C)—can happen any time of year, in almost any weather condition. It can occur by getting wet and not drying off after a rain shower on a chilly spring day, while taking a dip in a cold mountain lake, or when the fog rolls in at higher elevations on a sunny summer weekend. Symptoms include shivering; slurred speech; slow, shallow breathing; a weak pulse; drowsiness or low energy; confusion or memory loss; and loss of consciousness. Hypothermia can be especially dangerous because those afflicted don't generally know they have it; symptoms occur gradually, and that sense of confusion and memory loss has a debilitating impact on decision-making skills. To be safe, pack a hat or other protective covering that prevents body heat from escaping from your head, try not to overexert yourself in cold weather, wear layered clothing for the most efficient protection, and stay as dry as possible. Bring along a towel and change of clothes, get out of wet clothing as soon as possible, and take a warm shower at your hotel or campground as soon as possible. If you suspect you have or are with someone you suspect has hypothermia, seek medical attention immediately; until help arrives, try as possible to limit movement, move out of the cold, remove any wet clothing, and apply warm, dry compresses to the neck, chest wall, or groin.

Frostbite

In so many words, frostbite is an injury caused by freezing; it most commonly impacts the nose, ears, fingers, and toes—and causes a loss of feeling and color in the impacted appendages. It is usually caused by prolonged exposure to cold weather, mostly in winter. Common warning signs include numbness, redness, and pain on the impacted areas; if any signs of frostbite appear, get out of the cold (if possible) and take steps to protect the skin by wearing a hat, scarf, gloves, or other apparel items. If frostbite occurs, get to a warm place as soon as possible, try to avoid walking on frostbitten feet or toes, and immerse the impacted area in warm (but not hot) water; do not massage the frostbitten area, and avoid using a heating pad, heat lamp, radiator, or other external source of heating (all of which can cause burning). When possible, seek medical attention for frostbite.

Poison Oak

There's one plant you'll want to avoid at all costs: western poison oak. The nasty plant—most common in western Oregon—contains an oil that, when touched, can soak into the skin and cause painful rashes. It's easily identified by its three leaves, inspiring the mantra "Leaves of three, let it be." Its leaf color is variable, sometimes mostly green and then red in fall, and often has a glossy appearance. Even when bare of leaves in winter, its branches can transmit the oil. If you're hiking, consider long pants to minimize the risk of brushing up against the plant, which generally sits at about ground level. If you come in contact with poison oak, apply a wet compress or ice pack to the affected area, use an anti-itch cream, and wash your skin with soap and cool water as soon as possible. Resist the urge to scratch any blisters that may appear. Poison oak blisters and rashes generally disappear after a few weeks without any medical treatment.

Ticks

In spring and early summer, in particular, hikers all over the state should stay mindful that deer ticks may be present. These blood-sucking arachnids generally fall from trees or cling to brush, waiting to hitch a ride on passing hikers (or their dogs); once attached, they may bite and burrow into the skin—which is how they spread **Lyme disease.** Symptoms may begin as soon as three days after a tick bite and include a target-shaped rash (with a red ring around the initial bite), fever, chills, headache, fatigue, and achy muscles and joints. Oregon generally sees 40-50 human cases of Lyme disease each year, with most tick bites occurring in June and July. That said, tick bites can happen any time of year, so

wear long pants, close-toed shoes, and shin-high socks when you're hiking to avoid being bitten. Wearing DEET-based insect repellent can repel ticks as well. Hikers should always conduct a quick tick check back at the trail-head, scanning for the arachnid (which can be as small as a poppy seed), examining clothing, and checking between joints. Hikers should also take a shower soon afterward. If a tick attaches to your skin, use a pair of tweezers to grasp the bug and slowly pull it out; as soon as possible, wash the bite area and apply an antibiotic ointment.

Giardia

Tap water throughout Oregon is safe to drink, but water from streams, rivers, lakes, and creeks? Not so much. Untreated water may be infected with giardia, a parasite that's generally found in dirt, food, or water that's been contaminated by feces from infected animals or humans. Symptoms of the illness, which can last 1-2 weeks or longer, may include but aren't limited to stomach or abdominal cramps, diarrhea, nausea, vomiting, and dehydration. While giardia generally goes away on its own, consult a health professional to be safe. If you're hiking or camping, the safest way to treat water is to boil it for at least one minute prior to cooking, drinking, brushing your teeth, washing your hands, or cleaning dishes. Water filters and tablets are usually available at sporting goods stores as well.

Wildfires

Wildfires are an undeniable consideration when planning trips to Oregon in summer and early fall. In recent years, fires—whether originating in Oregon, California, or points north—have had impacts that range from occasionally hazy skies to wildly unhealthy air, highway closures around wildfires, and the cancelation of festivals and other large events. The peak of wildfire season is typically mid-July–mid-September; having backup plans or keeping your itinerary flexible is advised if planning a trip to Oregon during this timeframe. For the latest conditions, download the **OregonAir** or **AirNow** mobile apps, both available for free on iOS and Android devices.

Information and Services

COMMUNICATIONS AND MEDIA

The biggest newspaper in Oregon is **The Oregonian,** and its web-based counterpart is **OregonLive** (oregonlive.com); the news organization is based in Portland—but covers outdoor recreation, breaking news, and more across the state. Elsewhere around Portland, **Willamette Week** is an award-winning alt-weekly that covers breaking news, arts and culture, and regional recreation—while the **Portland Mercury** is an independent news site noted for breaking-news coverage and in-depth information on arts and culture events around town. And **Portland Monthly** covers citywide events, regional travel ideas, and the local arts scene through a quarterly magazine and oft-updated website.

Other large newspapers of note include **The Register-Guard,** a long-running newspaper based in Eugene, and Salem's **Statesman Journal;** in addition to breaking-news coverage from Oregon's state capital, the latter produces stellar stories and podcasts about outdoor recreation all over the state.

Another high-quality news source is **Oregon Public Broadcasting** (opb.org), which runs a news-focused radio station and produces television documentaries that explore the state's attractions and outdoor recreation, as well as programming that celebrates Oregon's arts and culture. You can listen to OPB's radio programming in the Portland area (91.5 FM) or anywhere in the state via the station's mobile app (iOS and Android, free).

Tax-Free Shopping in Oregon

Unlike most states, Oregon has no sales tax—so if the price tag on a Pendleton blanket reads $329, that's what you'll pay at the register.

That said, you will see small taxes (about 5 percent of the total bill) on prepared food items at restaurants in Ashland, Yachats, and Cannon Beach.

Telephones

Oregon has four area codes. **503** and **971** cover the northwest corner of Oregon—from the Portland area to the north coast and south to Salem—and **541** and **458** cover the rest of the state. You must dial the area code before the phone number—even if making a local call. Cell service is generally robust around popular communities—but can be inconsistent or nonexistent around mountainous and forested areas, as well as across wide swaths of the eastern half of the state.

MAPS AND TOURIST INFORMATION

Travel Oregon (traveloregon.com) is the state's official tourism marketing organization—and produces excellent content for enjoying all Oregon has to offer; resources include in-depth feature articles, idyllic itineraries, and printed travel guides—all written by knowledgeable writers with a deep affinity for Oregon. Travel Oregon also runs eight welcome centers around the state, with most near border communities; all are staffed by friendly professionals and stocked with brochures, maps, and other helpful resources. If you're flying, the organization's Portland International Airport Welcome Center offers several vacations' worth of pamphlets,

printed travel guides, maps, and other travel information.

If you're looking for maps, brochures, and other outdoor recreation offerings, you'll find plenty of each from the state's biggest land managers. **Oregon State Parks** (800/551-6949; stateparks.oregon.gov) offers brochures, maps, cultural information and more on its parks and day-use areas—of which there are more than 350. Similarly, the **U.S. Forest Service** (fs.usda.gov) provides information on the campgrounds, hiking trails, and day-use areas it manages across the state—along with helpful information on whether passes or permits are required, and how they can be purchased. And the **Bureau of Land Management** (503/808-6001; blm.gov) offers brochures, recreation suggestions, maps, and other resources for lands managed by the federal agency.

Trail Maps

The **U.S. Geological Survey** (usgs.gov) produces a variety of hiking and topographical maps for popular recreation destinations across the state—all available as folded paper maps (typically running $8-14), with some available as (free) digital downloads. Find these at **REI** stores and other outdoor retailers around the state.

Resources

Suggested Reading

Gulick, Bill. *Roadside History of Oregon.* Sevierville: Mountain Press, 1991. Get a feel for Oregon history with this guide, which looks at the past—natural, cultural, and otherwise—through the prism of highways and byways across the state.

Sawyer, Adam. *Unique Eats and Eateries of Portland, Oregon.* St. Louis: Reedy Press, 2018. Portland is known the world over for its pioneering culinary scene, and Adam Sawyer profiles dozens of eateries that made the scene what it is today.

Stark, Peter. *Astoria: Astor and Jefferson's Lost Pacific Empire.* New York: Ecco Press, 2014. This wildly entertaining book recounts how John Jacob Astor sought to establish a trading post on the Columbia River—and the founding of modern-day Astoria.

Steelquist, Robert. *The Northwest Coastal Explorer: Your Guide to the Places, Plants, and Animals of the Pacific Coast.* Portland: Timber Press, 2016. Learn all you could ever hope to know about the Pacific Northwest coast—its myriad ecosystems, the plants and animals that call the coast home, the geology that makes it such a striking region, and more.

Sullivan, William L. *Hiking Oregon's History.* Eugene: Navillus Press, 2014. William Sullivan covers Oregon's history—the good, the bad, the ugly—with more than 50 hikes throughout the Beaver State. Hiking profiles include total mileage, hand-drawn maps, directions, and other pertinent information.

Wastradowski, Matt. *Moon Oregon Hiking.* Berkeley: Moon Travel Guides, 2021. Get the skinny on 75 of the best hikes across the Beaver State—with full-color photos, trail maps, detailed directions, and suggestions for where to grab food and beer afterward.

Internet Resources

The Oregonian
oregonlive.com

The Portland-based newspaper covers breaking news, food and drink, and outdoor recreation throughout the state.

Willamette Week
wweek.com

The Portland-based alternative newspaper routinely covers travel, food and drink, and recreation opportunities in the city and nearby.

Oregon Public Broadcasting
opb.org

The Portland-based public broadcasting outlet runs several television stations and radio stations across the state—with a focus on breaking news, in-depth stories, newsy podcasts, and television documentaries.

Oregon Hikers Forum
oregonhikers.org

A service of the Trailkeepers of Oregon nonprofit, this website offers hike listings, trip reports, forums, maps, and other valuable services.

Oregon State Parks
stateparks.oregon.gov

The Oregon State Parks website includes brochures, maps, reservation information, and ideas for outdoor recreation.

U.S. Forest Service
fs.usda.gov/main/r6

Learn about hiking trails, campgrounds, day-use areas, and other outdoor recreation opportunities managed by the U.S. Forest Service.

Oregon Department of Fish & Wildlife
myodfw.com

Get updates and information on fishing, hunting, and wildlife-watching in Oregon—with helpful resources for which permits may be needed, where they're required, and where they're available.

Travel Oregon
traveloregon.com

Oregon's state tourism site shares stories, itineraries, and other planning tools for making the most of your time in the state.

Travel Portland
travelportland.com

Portland's official destination marketing organization shares recommendations, neighborhood breakdowns, an events calendar, and other resources.

Oregon Coast Visitors Association
visittheoregoncoast.com

Make the most of your time on the Oregon Coast with suggestions for where to eat, stay, play, and more.

TripCheck
tripcheck.com

The Oregon Department of Transportation's site provides information on road conditions, with traffic cameras, weather information, and updated alerts.

Together Anywhere
togetheranywhere.com

An Oregon-based team have developed several audio driving tours that cover much of the state—with engaging narration that touches on history and things to do.

Oregon Brewers Guild
oregoncraftbeer.org

Learn about Oregon's craft beer industry, get the skinny on upcoming events, and peruse maps of breweries throughout the state.

Oregon Wine Board
oregonwine.org

The Oregon Wine Board offers a deep dive into the state's wine industry—with breakdowns of grape-growing regions, a directory of tasting rooms, and helpful travel tips.

Index

INDEX

List of Maps

Photo Credits

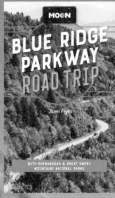

MOON

BLUE RIDGE PARKWAY ROAD TRIP

Jason Frye

WITH SHENANDOAH & GREAT SMOKY MOUNTAINS NATIONAL PARKS

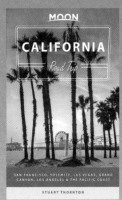

MOON

CALIFORNIA
Road Trip

SAN FRANCISCO, YOSEMITE, LAS VEGAS, GRAND CANYON, LOS ANGELES & THE PACIFIC COAST

STUART THORNTON

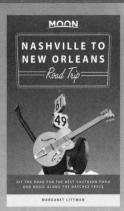

MOON

NASHVILLE TO NEW ORLEANS
Road Trip

HIT THE ROAD FOR THE BEST SOUTHERN FOOD AND MUSIC ALONG THE NATCHEZ TRACE

MARGARET LITTMAN

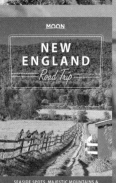

MOON

NEW ENGLAND
Road Trip

SEASIDE SPOTS, MAJESTIC MOUNTAINS & FALL FOLIAGE, COZY GETAWAYS

MILES HOWARD

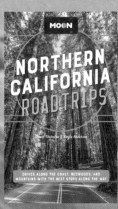

MOON

NORTHERN CALIFORNIA ROAD TRIPS

Stuart Thornton & Kayla Anderson

DRIVES ALONG THE COAST, REDWOODS, AND MOUNTAINS WITH THE BEST STOPS ALONG THE WAY

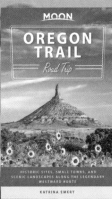

MOON

OREGON TRAIL
Road Trip

HISTORIC SITES, SMALL TOWNS, AND SCENIC LANDSCAPES ALONG THE LEGENDARY WESTWARD ROUTE

KATRINA EMERY

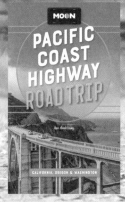

MOON

PACIFIC COAST HIGHWAY ROAD TRIP

Ian Anderson

CALIFORNIA, OREGON & WASHINGTON

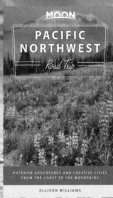

MOON

PACIFIC NORTHWEST
Road Trip

OUTDOOR ADVENTURES AND CREATIVE CITIES FROM THE COAST TO THE MOUNTAINS

ALLISON WILLIAMS

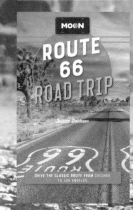

MOON

ROUTE 66 ROAD TRIP

Jessica Dunham

DRIVE THE CLASSIC ROUTE FROM CHICAGO TO LOS ANGELES

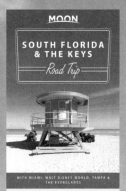

MOON

SOUTH FLORIDA
& THE KEYS
Road Trip

WITH MIAMI, WALT DISNEY WORLD, TAMPA &
THE EVERGLADES

JASON FERGUSON

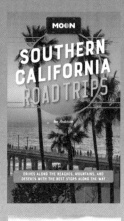

MOON

SOUTHERN
CALIFORNIA
ROAD TRIPS

DRIVES ALONG THE BEACHES, MOUNTAINS, AND
DESERTS WITH THE BEST STOPS ALONG THE WAY

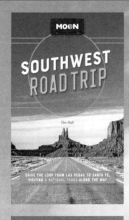

MOON

SOUTHWEST
ROAD TRIP

DRIVE THE LOOP FROM LAS VEGAS TO SANTA FE,
VISITING 8 NATIONAL PARKS ALONG THE WAY

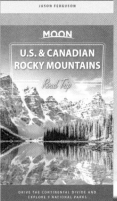

MOON

U.S. & CANADIAN
ROCKY MOUNTAINS
Road Trip

DRIVE THE CONTINENTAL DIVIDE AND
EXPLORE 9 NATIONAL PARKS

BECKY LOMAX

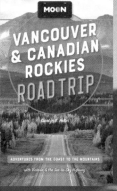

MOON

VANCOUVER
& CANADIAN
ROCKIES
ROAD TRIP

ADVENTURES FROM THE COAST TO THE MOUNTAINS

with Victoria & the Sea-to-Sky Highway

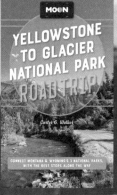

MOON

YELLOWSTONE
TO GLACIER
NATIONAL PARK
ROAD TRIP

CONNECT MONTANA & WYOMING'S 3 NATIONAL PARKS,
WITH THE BEST STOPS ALONG THE WAY

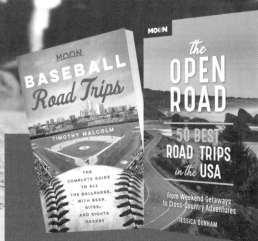

MOON

BASEBALL
Road Trips

TIMOTHY MALCOLM

THE
COMPLETE GUIDE
TO ALL
THE BALLPARKS,
WITH BEER,
BITES,
AND SIGHTS
NEARBY

the
OPEN
ROAD

50 BEST
ROAD TRIPS
in the USA

From Weekend Getaways
to Cross-Country Adventures

JESSICA DUNHAM

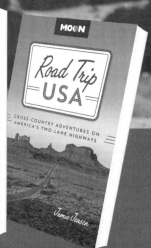

MOON

Road Trip
USA

CROSS-COUNTRY ADVENTURES ON
AMERICA'S TWO-LANE HIGHWAYS

Jamie Jensen

Get inspired for your next adventure

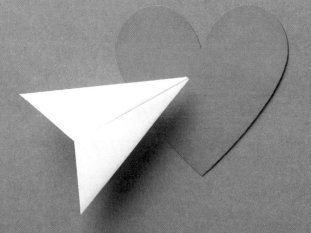

Follow @**moonguides** on Instagram or subscribe to our newsletter at **moon.com**

#TravelWithMoon

MAP SYMBOLS

≈≈≈≈ Expressway	○	City/Town	🛈	Information Center	▲ Park
══ Primary Road	◉	State Capital			⚷ Golf Course
══ Secondary Road	⊛	National Capital	🅿	Parking Area	✦ Unique Feature
─ · ─ Unpaved Road	✪	Highlight	⌖	Church	Waterfall
---------- Trail	★	Point of Interest	🍇	Winery/Vineyard	⬛ Camping
·········· Ferry	•	Accommodation	🆃	Trailhead	▲ Mountain
·-·-·-· Railroad	▼	Restaurant/Bar	🚇	Train Station	⛷ Ski Area
══ Pedestrian Walkway	■	Other Location	✈	Airport	Glacier
▥▥▥ Stairs			✕	Airfield	

CONVERSION TABLES

°C = (°F − 32) / 1.8
°F = (°C x 1.8) + 32
1 inch = 2.54 centimeters (cm)
1 foot = 0.304 meters (m)
1 yard = 0.914 meters
1 mile = 1.6093 kilometers (km)
1 km = 0.6214 miles
1 fathom = 1.8288 m
1 chain = 20.1168 m
1 furlong = 201.168 m
1 acre = 0.4047 hectares
1 sq km = 100 hectares
1 sq mile = 2.59 square km
1 ounce = 28.35 grams
1 pound = 0.4536 kilograms
1 short ton = 0.90718 metric ton
1 short ton = 2,000 pounds
1 long ton = 1.016 metric tons
1 long ton = 2,240 pounds
1 metric ton = 1,000 kilograms
1 quart = 0.94635 liters
1 US gallon = 3.7854 liters
1 Imperial gallon = 4.5459 liters
1 nautical mile = 1.852 km

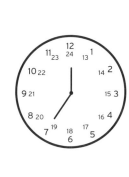

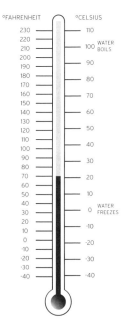

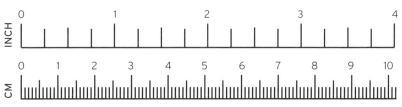

MOON COASTAL OREGON

Avalon Travel
Hachette Book Group
1700 Fourth Street
Berkeley, CA 94710, USA
www.moon.com

Editor: Vy Tran
Managing Editor: Hannah Brezack
Copy Editor: Matthew Hoover
Graphics and Production Coordinator: Suzanne Albertson
Cover Design: Toni Tajima
Interior Design: Avalon Travel
Map Editor: Kat Bennett
Cartographers: Erin Greb, Kat Bennett
Proofreader: Jessica Gould
Indexer: Greg Jewett

ISBN-13: 979-8-88647-046-8

Printing History
1st Edition — March 2024
5 4 3 2 1

Front cover photo: Sea stacks at sunset, Cannon Beach © James Hager / Alamy Stock Photo

Back cover photo: Sand Sculpture Canon Beach Oregon © Mickem | Dreamstime.com

Printed in Malaysia for Imago

All recommendations, including those for sights, activities, hotels, restaurants, and shops, are based on each author's individual judgment. We do not accept payment for inclusion in our travel guides, and our authors don't accept free goods or services in exchange for positive coverage.